Gender Violence
& HUMAN RIGHTS

SEEKING JUSTICE IN FIJI, PAPUA NEW GUINEA & VANUATU

Gender Violence
& HUMAN RIGHTS

SEEKING JUSTICE IN FIJI, PAPUA NEW GUINEA & VANUATU

Edited by Aletta Biersack, Margaret Jolly & Martha Macintyre

Australian
National
University

PRESS

ANU
PRESS

Published by ANU Press
The Australian National University
Acton ACT 2601, Australia
Email: anupress@anu.edu.au
This title is also available online at press.anu.edu.au

National Library of Australia Cataloguing-in-Publication entry

Title: Gender violence and human rights : seeking justice in Fiji,
                 Papua New Guinea and Vanuatu / editors :
                 Aletta Biersack, Margaret Jolly, Martha Macintyre.

ISBN: 9781760460709 (paperback) 9781760460716 (ebook)

Subjects: Sex discrimination against women--Fiji.
                 Sex discrimination against women--Papua New Guinea.
                 Sex discrimination against women--Vanuatu.
                 Women's rights--Fiji.
                 Women's rights--Papua New Guinea.
                 Women's rights--Vanuatu.

Other Creators/Contributors:
                 Biersack, Aletta, editor.
                 Jolly, Margaret 1949- editor.
                 Macintyre, Martha, editor.

Dewey Number: 305.420995

Cover design and layout by ANU Press.

The editors thank Mitiana Arbon for his help with the cover and Martha Macintyre for use of her photograph 'Woman in Kavieng market, wearing a T-shirt promoting human rights, Papua New Guinea', for the cover.

Contents

List of Maps and Figures

Acknowledgements

Gender Violence and Human Rights: Seeking Justice in Fiji, Papua New Guinea and Vanuatu began as the panel 'Gender Violence in Melanesia and Human Rights Discourse: Toward a Research Agenda' at the 2011 annual meeting of the American Anthropological Association (AAA) in Montreal, Canada. The panel was co-organised by Aletta Biersack, Martha Macintyre and Margaret Jolly. The editors thank the participants in that panel as well as the dedicated contributors to this volume, who have forborne a protracted process of publication. We also thank the two reviewers for their insightful comments and the Pacific Editorial Board at ANU Press for their approval and enthusiasm. Generous funding from the Australian Research Council, through Margaret Jolly's ARC Laureate Fellowship Project, Engendering Persons, Transforming Things: Christianities, Commodities and Individualism in Oceania (FL100100196), has been crucial to the production of the volume. We thank Kaye Dancey and her team at CartoGIS for the excellent maps. The editors are especially grateful to Carolyn Brewer for her superb editorial support in the preparation of this volume for publication. Margaret Jolly wishes to thank The Australian National University for long-term support of her research and of the very successful Gender Institute, where colleagues have created an empowering and mutually supportive environment. Finally, Aletta Biersack thanks the Department of Anthropology, University of Oregon, and the Center for the Study of Women in Society, University of Oregon, for travel funds enabling her to present her paper on the 2011 AAA panel and to conduct research in Papua New Guinea in 2015.

Abbreviations and Acronyms

AAA	American Anthropological Association
ACPACS	Australian Centre for Peace and Conflict Studies
ACWIN	Action Council of Women in Need
ADB	Asian Development Bank
ANU	The Australian National University
ART	antiretroviral therapy
AusAID	Australian Agency for International Development
CAVAW	Committee Against Violence Against Women
CBC	Catholic Bishops' Conference
CEDAW	Convention on the Elimination of All Forms of Discrimination against Women
CEDAW Committee	Committee on the Elimination of Discrimination against Women
CIMC	Consultative Implementation and Monitoring Committee
CLRC	Constitutional and Law Reform Commission (PNG)
CMC	Case Management Centre
CRC	Convention on the Rights of the Child
Criminal Code Act	Criminal Code (Sexual Offences and Crimes Against Children) Act
CSA	child sexual abuse
CSEC	commercial sexual exploitation of children
DFAT	Department of Foreign Affairs and Trade (Australia)
DJAG	Department of Justice and Attorney General
DVD	Domestic Violence Decree
DWA	Department of Women's Affairs (Vanuatu)

EVAW	Elimination of Violence Against Women
FLA	Family Law Act
FPA	Family Protection Act
FPO	Family Protection Order
FPU	Family Protection Unit
FSC	Family Support Centre
FSVAC	Family and Sexual Violence Action Committee
FSVU	Family and Sexual Violence Unit
FWCC	Fiji Women's Crisis Centre
FWRM	Fiji Women's Rights Movement
GNC	Gouvernement Nouvelle Calédonie
GoPNG	Government of Papua New Guinea
GBV	gender-based violence
HRW	Human Rights Watch
HWHRDM	Highlands Women's Human Rights Defenders Movement
IBBS	integrated bio-behavioural survey
IPO	Interim Protection Order
LRC	Law Reform Commission
MDGs	Millennium Development Goals
Ministry for Women	Ministry for Women, Children and Poverty Alleviation
MSC	Most Significant Change technique
MSF	Médecins Sans Frontières
NCC	National Council of Chiefs
NCWF	National Council of Women Fiji
NGO	non-governmental organisation
NSRRT	National Sex and Reproduction Research Team
ODW	Office for the Development of Women
OHCHR	Office of the High Commission for Human Rights
PC&SS	Pacific Counselling and Social Services
PERs	Public Emergency Regulations
PIAF	Pacific Islands AIDS Foundation
PNG	Papua New Guinea

PPDVP	Pacific Prevention of Domestic Violence Programme
RPNGC	Royal Papua New Guinea Constabulary
RRRT	Regional Rights and Resources Team
RTP	Regional Training Program
SCC	Sanma Counselling Centre
SDG	Sustainable Development Goals
SNAP	Sorcery National Action Plan
SOU	Sexual Offences Unit
SSGM	State, Society and Governance in Melanesia Program
TCC	Tafea Counselling Centre
ToCC	Torba Counselling Centre
UN	United Nations
UNGA	UN General Assembly
UNDP	United Nations Development Programme
UNFPA	United Nations Population Fund
UNICEF	United Nations Children's Fund
UN Women	United Nations Entity for Gender Equality and the Empowerment of Women
VAM	Violence Against Men
VAW	Violence Against Women
VCCT	Voluntary Confidential Counselling and Testing
VNCW	Vanuatu National Council of Women
VWC	Vanuatu Women's Centre
WHO	World Health Organization
WPA	Women's Plan of Action
YWCA	Young Women's Christian Association
ZTVFC	Zero Tolerance Violence Free Communities

Introduction: Gender Violence and Human Rights in the Western Pacific

Aletta Biersack and Martha Macintyre

University of Oregon and University of Melbourne

In October 2014, Malala Yousafzai, the Pakistani teenager who nearly died from a Taliban gunshot wound sustained two years prior, but who lived to address the UN on 12 July 2013, her 16th birthday, was named co-winner of the Nobel Peace Prize.[1] In her 2013 speech Malala defended every child's right to an education, but her focus more specifically was on the right of girls to an education as well as on women's rights, because, as she said, women 'are the ones who suffer the most'.[2] Even though Malala's cause is girls' education and the rights of females more generally, she is the most potent global symbol of another cause: the cause of ending violence against all females, young and old, in the name of human rights. Violence against females is not restricted to Pakistan, of course. It 'has epidemic proportions, and is present in every single country around the world',[3] occurring in developed, rich countries no less than in poorer developing countries.

---

1   'Pakistani activist Malala Yousafzai among winners of 2013 UN Human Rights Prize', 2013, *UN News Centre*, 5 December.

2   'Shot Pakistan schoolgirl Malala Yousafzai addresses UN', 2013, *BBC News Asia*, 12 July.

3   Lydia Alpizar, executive director, the global feminist group Association for Women's Rights in Development, quoted in Somini Sengupta, 2015, 'U.N. reveals "alarmingly high" levels of violence against women', *New York Times*, 9 March.

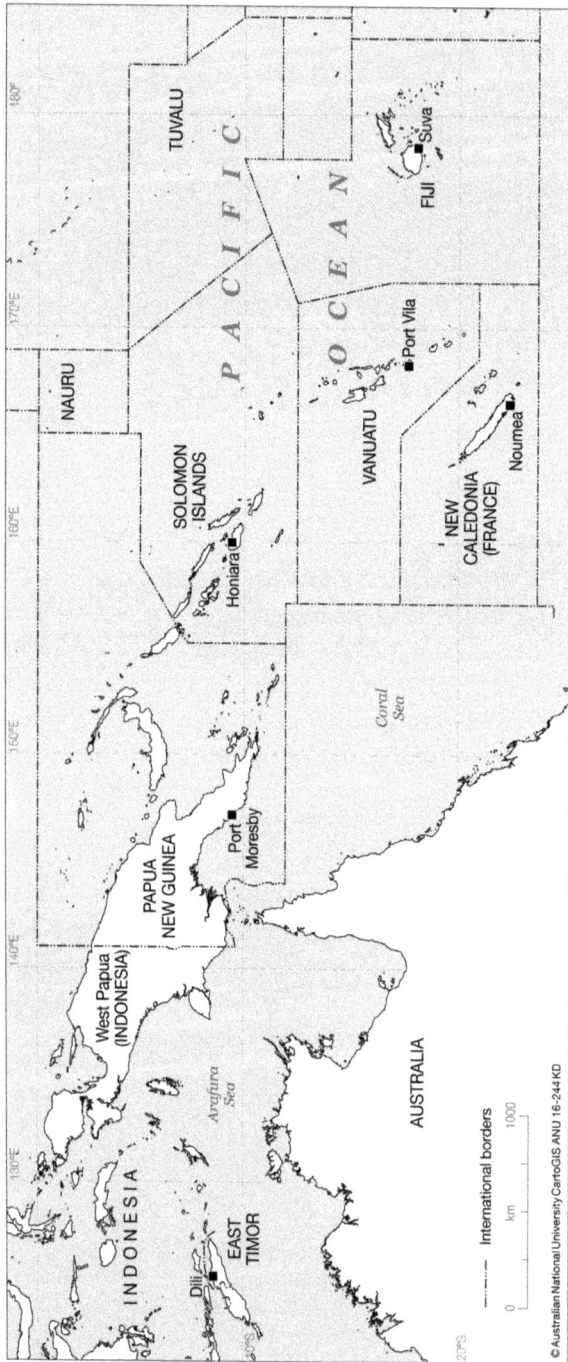

Map 1. Western Pacific showing Fiji, Vanuatu and Papua New Guinea

Source. © The Australian National University, CartoGIS ANU 16-244 KD

The western Pacific is no stranger to violence against females. A recent incident of gender violence there—not of rape but of sorcery accusation-related revenge murder[4]—attracted considerable international attention. Kepari Leniata, a young woman living with her husband, was accused of killing a six-year-old boy by occult means. In retaliation she was stripped, tortured, doused with petrol, and burned alive on a pile of tyres and trash at midday in Mt Hagen, the third largest city in Papua New Guinea. The police looked on, unable to control the murderous mob.[5] A photograph of a crowd arrayed around a fire known to be consuming Ms Leniata circulated on the internet and was printed in newspapers worldwide. The Prime Minister of Papua New Guinea, Peter O'Neill, was quick to denounce the 'despicable act'[6] and vowed to repeal the Sorcery Act of 1971, which criminalised sorcery, thus implying such acts were efficacious, and which recognised sorcery as a defence in murder cases of alleged sorcerers, to the same effect.[7] Within days of Ms Leniata's immolation, both the UN and Amnesty International urged immediate action to prevent further such killings and to bring the killers of Ms Leniata to justice.[8] The immolation of Ms Leniata galvanised public opinion under the banner of a 'Remembering Kepari Leniata Campaign', a campaign that has been pursued in the public spaces of Port Moresby, in global cities, and on Facebook.[9]

Gender Violence and Human Rights enquires into gender violence and the efficacy of human rights advocacy and related reformist strategies in three western Pacific countries: Fiji, Papua New Guinea and Vanuatu. The term 'gender violence' is inspired by Sally Engle Merry's *Human Rights and Gender Violence* and *Gender Violence:*

---

4   As many readers will know, sorcery refers to covert activity designed to damage its target by deploying a range of supernatural techniques. Anthropologists of Africa sharply distinguished sorcery from witchcraft in terms of whether the act was conscious and intentional (sorcery) or not (witchcraft). In this writing, we use the term *sorcery* to cover both forms of occult violence.
5   Meredith Bennett-Smith, 2013, 'Accused "witch" Kepari Leniata burned alive by mob in Papua New Guinea', *Huffington Post*, 7 February.
6   Ibid.
7   Matt Siegel, 2013, 'Papua New Guinea acts to repeal sorcery law after strife', *New York Times*, 29 May.
8   'UN urges Papua New Guinea to take action after woman burned alive for witchcraft', 2013, *UN News Centre*, 8 February.
9   See Biersack, 'Human rights work in Papua New Guinea, Fiji and Vanuatu', this volume.

A Cultural Perspective.[10] Merry defines gender violence as 'violence whose meaning depends on the gendered identities of the parties. It is an interpretation of violence through gender. For example, when a blow is understood as a man's right to discipline his wife, it is gender violence.'[11] Unlike another term sufficiently widespread that it is recognisable in acronymic form—'Violence Against Women' or 'VAW'—'gender violence', like 'gender-based violence', encompasses violence against children, the girl child in particular, as well as violence against males. As used here, the term is synonymous with 'gender-based violence', 'sexual violence' and 'family and sexual violence', a phrase that enjoys currency in Papua New Guinea. In the western Pacific women and girls are overwhelmingly the victims of gender violence, the perpetrators being overwhelmingly male. In this volume we focus on violence against females, including girls (females under 18 years).

Fiji, Papua New Guinea and Vanuatu are postcolonial nations operating in a global arena in which human rights doctrine is widely accepted and promoted. The three countries constitutionally guarantee gender equality and have ratified the key instrument for promoting women's rights globally: the Convention for the Elimination of All Forms of Discrimination against Women (CEDAW). They have also ratified the Convention on the Rights of the Child (CRC), a convention or treaty that is crucial to combatting gender violence in the western Pacific, where rape victims are often underage.

The global context for human rights advocacy is the 'international human rights regime',[12] a regime that articulates with 'transnational human rights networks' or 'transnational advocacy networks'[13] (Amnesty International, Human Rights Watch, etc.). The regime is philosophically undergirded by human rights ideology, which alleges

---

10   Sally Engle Merry, 2006, *Human Rights and Gender Violence: Translating International Law into Local Justice*, Chicago and London: University of Chicago Press; and Sally Engle Merry, 2009, *Gender Violence: A Cultural Perspective*, Chichester: Wiley-Blackwell.

11   Merry, *Gender Violence*, p. 3.

12   This term is adopted from Jack Donnelly, 1986, 'International human rights: A regime analysis', *International Organization* 40(3): 599–642. The contours of this regime are discussed in the next section and also in Jean Zorn, 'Translating and internalising international human rights law: The courts of Melanesia confront gendered violence', this volume.

13   Kathleen Keck and Margaret Sikkink, 1998, *Activists Beyond Borders: Advocacy Networks in International Politics*, Ithaca: Cornell University Press. See also Mary Kaldor, 2003, *Global Civil Society: An Answer to War*, Malden, MA: Polity Press.

universality and which views any doctrine that deviates from it as merely 'local' and aberrant. Thus, it sets itself against many of the world's cultural orders, which are viewed as obstacles in its path. How, if at all, does such a regime come to have an impact on gender violence in the western Pacific, which, despite protracted contact and a colonial history, remains significantly different culturally from Europe and America? To begin to answer that question requires examining the dynamics of human rights work or practice—efforts to transfer across national and cultural borders human rights ideology and the morality and behaviour it enjoins. Are such transfers contested and blocked, and, if so, by whom and for what reason? What conditions, ideological but also social, economic and political, are conducive to the reduction of gender violence and the promotion of gender equality?

Addressing such questions is timely, because the UN-anchored human rights movement has shifted from the Millennium Development Goals (MDGs) of 2000 as a framework for global rights-based initiatives to a 'post-2015 development agenda' rooted in the Sustainable Development Goals (SDGs) adopted by the UN General Assembly in September 2015 and in effect since 1 January 2016. Drawing on lessons learned from efforts to implement the MDGs,[14] the new framework envisions a 'world in which every woman and girl enjoys full gender equality and all legal, social and economic barriers to their empowerment have been removed'.[15] As social scientists who have done considerable place-based research in the western Pacific, it behooves us to take stock of the successes and failures of human rights work in the western Pacific as the new SDGs take hold. What specifically have been Fiji's, Papua New Guinea's and Vanuatu's strategies for fulfilling the third MDG of achieving gender equality and empowering women and have they been effective? Has human rights ideology travelled across national-cum-cultural borders or has such movement been impeded or redirected? Are the alternatives of flow and blockage comprehensive, or does admixture and commingling occur at the various threshold sites that human rights practices in the western Pacific create?

---

14   See Naomi M. McPherson (ed.), 2016, *Missing the Mark? Women and the Millennium Development Goals in Africa and Oceania*, Bradford, Ontario: Demeter Press.

15   United Nations, 2015, 'Transforming our world: The 2030 agenda for sustainable development', *Sustainable Development Knowledge Platform*, A/RES/70/1, item 8.

In tackling such questions, the writings of Sally Engle Merry and Mark Goodale, among others, provide invaluable guidance, and we will consult these in a section titled 'The global circulation of human rights ideology'. Several contributors question the adequacy of human rights–based approaches to gender violence, and we note the contradictions and weaknesses of the international human rights regime, including its inattention to the social, political and economic factors that militate against women securing their rights. Studying gender violence and human rights in the western Pacific opens up a fruitful space for ethnographic enquiry, a tool widely utilised in the social sciences to explore situated practices and their complexities in non-teleological ways, and we identify such a research agenda. Finally, we introduce the contributions to this collection, highlighting how they help us understand the dynamics of rights-based initiatives designed to reduce if not eliminate gender violence in the western Pacific.

The international context

The UN-centred international human rights regime

The international human rights regime is UN-centred and relies on 'conventions' or 'treaties' such as CEDAW (1979) and CRC (1989) as well as on 'state party' ratifiers of these to advance human rights causes.[16]

The Convention on the Elimination of All Forms of Discrimination against Women or CEDAW[17] is the key convention when it comes to women's rights. As a response to World War II, the international human rights regime sought to curb state atrocities. With CEDAW the definition of human rights violations was expanded to include violations beyond 'state violations of civil and political liberties'.[18] CEDAW builds upon the UN's 1948 Universal Declaration of Human

---

16   Donnelly, 'International human rights', p. 605. See also Zorn, 'Translating and internalising international human rights law'.
17   UN, 1979, Convention on the Elimination of All Forms of Discrimination against Women (CEDAW).
18   Charlotte Bunch, 1990, 'Women's rights as human rights: Toward a re-vision of human rights', *Human Rights Quarterly* 12(4): 486–98.

Rights: (Article 1) 'All human beings are born free and equal in dignity and rights'; and (Article 2) 'Everyone is entitled to all the rights and freedoms set forth in this Declaration, without distinction of any kind, such as race, colour, sex, language, religion, political or other opinion, national or social origin, property, birth or other status'.[19] By the same token, CEDAW opposes 'any distinction, exclusion or restriction made on the basis of sex which has the effect or purpose of impairing or nullifying the recognition, enjoyment or exercise by women, irrespective of their marital status, on a basis of equality of men and women, of human rights and fundamental freedoms in the political, economic, social, cultural, civil or any other field' (Article 1). Most states (but notably not the US) have ratified CEDAW. As ratifiers, these states are expected to 'modify the social and cultural patterns of conduct of men and women, with a view to achieving the elimination of prejudices and customary and all other practices which are based on the idea of the inferiority or the superiority of either of the sexes or on stereotyped roles for men and women' (Article 5a). Each ratifying state is obliged to report periodically to the CEDAW Committee: a committee of 'experts' convened at the UN in New York City to review such reports, pinpoint human rights violations and deficiencies, and make recommendations for further human rights work, thus placing ratifying states under close surveillance.

Gender violence was not originally considered a form of discrimination against women, but, as Jean Zorn reports in her contribution to this volume, in 1989 the CEDAW Committee declared it would treat gender violence as such. CEDAW is supplemented by the 1993 Declaration on the Elimination of Violence against Women,[20] the preamble of which asserts that 'violence against women constitutes a violation of the rights and fundamental freedoms of women and impairs or nullifies their enjoyment of those rights and freedoms'.[21] The Declaration enjoins states to 'condemn violence against women' and not to 'invoke any custom, tradition, or religious consideration to avoid their obligations with respect to its elimination' (Article 4). States should proceed 'without delay' in pursuing a policy of this elimination (Article 4).

---

19   UN, Declaration on the Elimination of Violence against Women, 1993, A/RES/48/104.
20   Ibid.
21   The Declaration on the Elimination of Violence against Women includes violence against children as an aspect of violence against women (Article 2a).

Like CEDAW, the Declaration 'has no binding force',[22] but it 'does have the moral force of world consensus'.[23] In 1994, the UN Commission on Human Rights created a 'special rapporteur' position devoted to violence against women with the intention of enlarging the scope of the UN's human rights mission to include the eradication of violence—not just 'discrimination'—against women. The Special Rapporteur on Violence against Women travels to gender violence hot spots, collects information on violence against women and makes recommendations to mitigate this violence.[24] Since 2006, this special rapporteur has filed her report with the UN Human Rights Council. In 1999, to promote gender violence awareness and public commitment to its eradication, the UN declared 25 November the International Day for the Elimination of Violence against Women and initiated the '16 Days of Activism against Gender Violence Campaign'. This annual campaign runs from 25 November to 10 December (International Human Rights Day) and is staged around the world to call attention to the unfinished task of eliminating violence against women.

Gender violence in the western Pacific affects girls and not just women, and for this reason the Convention on the Rights of the Child,[25] which was passed in 1989, is a necessary addition to the human rights arsenal for protecting females in the western Pacific. CRC makes 'the best interests of the child [defined as under 18 (Article 1)] a primary consideration' (Article 3.1), and requires state party ratifiers 'to ensure the child such protection and care as is necessary for his or her well-being, taking into account the rights and duties of his or her parents, legal guardians, or other individuals legally responsible for him or her, and, to this end, shall take all appropriate legislative and administrative measures' (Article 3.2). Article 34 enjoins state ratifiers of CRC to 'undertake to protect the child from all forms of sexual exploitation and abuse', while other articles focus on the nonsexual abuse of children.

---

22 Merry, *Human Rights and Gender Violence*, p. 23.
23 Ibid.
24 Ibid.
25 UN, Convention on the Rights of the Child, 1989.

Transnational forces

The creation of the UN in the wake of World War II constituted a response to 'the tragic failure of the sovereignty-based system of international relations' as exemplified in the atrocities of particular states and the failure of the international system at that time to curb them.[26] The impetus of the founding generation was thus anti-nationalist: to support human beings in their struggle against oppressive states. Indeed, the international human rights system upholds universal '*human,* rather than [parochial] national or political, principles'.[27] As Mark Goodale has pointed out, the international human rights regime is philosophically 'transnationalist or perhaps even "postnationalist"'.[28]

Little wonder that the international human rights regime operates today in league with 'transnational human rights networks' or 'transnational advocacy networks'[29] comprised of non-governmental entities dedicated to the global promotion of a human rights agenda and serving as watchdogs and whistle-blowers where human rights have been violated. Such networks are autonomous from state systems and inter-state systems such as the UN. 'The key distinction between "transnational" and "international" is the fact that "transnational" describes a set of connections, social relations, economic networks, and so on that transcend the boundaries of the nation-state.'[30] The actors within such networks operate without regard for political or cultural borders and independently of nationalist sentiment. In their quest to realise '*trans*national human rights [emphasis added]',[31] they operate according to logics that are 'starkly different'[32] from political and state logics: the logic of human rights per se. Such open-ended, non-state-based networks provide platforms for a variety of sympathetic

---

26   Mark Goodale, 2009, 'Introduction: Human rights and anthropology', in *Human Rights: An Anthropological Reader*, ed. M. Goodale, pp. 1–19, Malden, MA and Oxford: Wiley-Blackwell, p. 5. See also Mark Goodale, 2013, 'Human rights *after* the post–cold war', in *Human Rights at the Crossroads*, ed. Mark Goodale, pp. 1–28, New York: Oxford University Press, pp. 12–13.
27   Mark Goodale, 2009, *Surrendering to Utopia: An Anthropology of Human Rights*, Stanford: Stanford University Press, p. 98.
28   Ibid., p. 93.
29   Ibid., p. 92.
30   Ibid., p. 97.
31   Ibid., p. 96 and passim.
32   Ibid., p. 97. Goodale favours the term 'transnational human rights system' or 'regime' to Donnelly's term 'international human rights regime' to de-emphasise the role of states and to emphasise instead transnational network connections among people and groups.

agents, not only civil society organisations and 'transnational elites'[33] but activists of all stripes (including social scientists) to promote human rights.

The global circulation of human rights ideology

'Translation' and 'vernacularisation'

With this as background, we call upon Sally Engle Merry's terms 'translation' and 'vernacularization' to imagine how ideological transfer might happen and the pitfalls of the process.[34] Merry's groundbreaking research on the international human rights regime took her to the UN, where she observed the deliberations of the CEDAW Committee, the committee that reviews the periodic reports submitted to it by countries that have ratified CEDAW. She concluded that UN human rights workers thought of custom or culture as a barrier to change.[35] For them, culture belonged 'to the domain of the primitive and the backward, in contrast to the civilization of the colonizer',[36] who, unlike the colonised, could appreciate the moral force of human rights. Seen through this Orientalising lens,[37] the cultures of the Global South appeared as obstacles to women's human rights.[38]

If culture were indeed an obstacle in the path of the human rights movement, there would be little to no circulation of human rights doctrine beyond its historical heartland, Europe and North America.[39]

33 Merry, *Human Rights and Gender Violence*, p. 3.
34 Merry, *Human Rights and Gender Violence*. Also, Sally Engle Merry, 2006, 'Transnational human rights and local activism: Mapping the middle', in *Anthropology and Human Rights in a New Key*, ed. Mark Goodale, *American Anthropologist* 108(1): 38–51. See Peggy Levitt and Sally Engle Merry, 2009, 'Vernacularization on the ground: Local uses of global women's rights in Peru, China, India and the United States', *Global Networks* 9(4): 441–61. See also Margaret Jolly, '"When she cries oceans": Navigating gender violence in the western Pacific', this volume.
35 Merry, *Human Rights and Gender Violence*, pp. 4–5 and passim.
36 Sally Engle Merry, 2003, 'Human rights law and the demonization of culture (and anthropology along the way)', *PoLAR* 26(1): 55–76, p. 60.
37 Makau Wa Mutua, 2002, *Human Rights: A Political and Cultural Critique*, Philadelphia: University of Pennsylvania Press, pp. 10–38.
38 Merry, 'Human rights law and the demonization of culture', p. 60.
39 Lynn Hunt, 2007, *Inventing Human Rights: A History*, New York and London: W.W. Norton & Company.

Merry doubly challenges these assumptions. First, Orientalising views of the Global South are a holdover from the colonial era, when the coloniser but never the colonised was considered 'civilized',[40] views that were indefensible in their time and that merit no respect today. Second, culture is now envisioned as a 'fluid, contested, and changing set of values and practices'[41] rather than as ossified tradition. As such, culture is inherently exposed to two kinds of pressure for change: (1) from within, the pressure of dissent—or, at least, efforts to reach a new consensus, and (2) from without, the impacts of intercultural exchanges as these unfold in time. Merry's widely cited terms 'translation' and 'vernacularization' bear on externally inspired efforts at change.

Defining culture as open to, even the product of, hybridising intercultural processes sets the stage for Merry's further argument: human rights ideas and practices can be 'transplanted' by being 'translated into local terms and situated within local contexts of power and meaning', a possibility she poses on the very first page of her landmark book *Human Rights and Gender Violence*. Through translation, human rights are 'remade in the vernacular',[42] rendering them intelligible and palatable to those living outside a Euro-American cultural and historical milieu. In fact, vernacularisation is tantamount to the 'appropriation and local adoption of globally generated ideas and strategies [emphasis removed]',[43] a process in which 'transnational conceptions are made meaningful *within* [emphasis added]'.[44]

Merry acknowledges a spectrum of vernacularisations in this process, from replications to hybridisations.[45] Replications are truer to the source of the ideology and thus more acceptable to human rights workers in the Global North. Hybridisations, on the other hand, resonate more strongly with the mentality and mores of communities in the Global

---

40   Merry, 'Human rights law and the demonization of culture', p. 60.

41   Ibid., p. 67. See also Merry, *Human Rights and Gender Violence*, pp. 6–10; Ann-Belinda S. Preis, 2009, 'Human rights as cultural practice: An anthropological critique', in *Human Rights: An Anthropological Reader*, ed. Mark Goodale, pp. 332–55, Oxford: Wiley-Blackwell, p. 344. First published in 1996 in *Human Rights Quarterly* 18(2): 286–315.

42   Merry, *Human Rights and Gender Violence*, p. 219.

43   Levitt and Merry, 'Vernacularization on the ground', p. 441.

44   Daniel M. Goldstein, 2013, 'Whose vernacular? Translating human rights in local contexts', in *Human Rights at the Crossroads*, ed. Mark Goodale, pp. 111–21, New York: Oxford University Press, p. 112.

45   Merry, 'Transnational human rights and local activism', pp. 45–46, 48.

South and, for that reason, may be higher in impact but 'represent less of a challenge to the status quo'.[46] 'As women's human rights ideas connect with a locality, they take on some of the ideological and social attributes of the place, but retain some of their original formulation.'[47] The closer to the indigenous end of the spectrum the ideological outcome, the more problematic it becomes, because, according to Merry and her co-author, Peggy Levitt, to be 'legitimate as human rights',[48] 'rights ideas and practice' must 'reflect universal principles or standards'.[49] Complete indigenisation would belie the 'distinctive vision' of human rights[50] ('that all people have equal rights')[51] as well as its foundational values ('individualism, autonomy, choice, bodily integrity, and equality').[52] It follows that there are 'both legitimate and illegitimate forms of vernaculization'.[53] Human rights ideology is an orthodoxy. Thus, 'to translate human rights into the vernacular is not to change their fundamental meanings',[54] which remain grounded 'in global structures and understandings'.[55]

Agents of change

'Translation' and 'vernacularisation' do not happen in the august chambers of the UN, where committees such as the CEDAW Committee convene as a body of 'experts'. They are accomplished in part through collaborations and negotiations among agents who are at least partially place-based: people who 'have one foot in the transnational community and one foot at home',[56] and who are thus able to 'reach across the gulf'[57] between the two. These translators and vernacularisers do the crucial work of conveying 'ideas from one context to another, adapting and reframing them'[58] in ways that resonate with the receiving

---

46   Levitt and Merry, 'Vernacularization on the ground', p. 458.
47   Ibid., p. 446.
48   Ibid., p. 457.
49   Ibid.
50   Merry, 'Transnational human rights and local activism', p. 49.
51   Ibid.
52   Ibid.
53   Goodale, 'Human rights *after* the post–cold war', p. 16.
54   Merry, *Human Rights and Gender Violence*, p. 219.
55   Ibid.
56   Merry, 'Transnational human rights and local activism', p. 42.
57   Richard Eves, 2012, 'Resisting global AIDS knowledges: Born-again Christian narratives of the epidemic from Papua New Guinea', *Medical Anthropology* 31(1): 61–76, p. 72.
58   Levitt and Merry, 'Vernacularization on the ground', p. 449.

community.[59] They are 'people in between, conversant with both sides of the exchange but able to move across borders of ideas and approaches'.[60] Without these norm brokers the authoritarian efforts of the international human rights regime to impose the alien 'values of a secular global modernity'[61] upon others will fail. Legal and political initiatives, international and national, are, of course, important,[62] but 'if an enduring, effective, and legitimate transnational … human rights system is to be established, it will have to somehow be derived from these spaces of vernacularization [emphasis removed]'[63] through the efforts of intermediary translators and vernacularisers.

Who, then, are these intermediary translators and vernacularisers? Merry looks to cosmopolitans in the Global South, people who can bridge 'the gap between a cosmopolitan awareness of human rights and local sociocultural understandings'.[64] Postcolonial elites are more likely than others to be enticed by 'the glamour of the modern'[65] and to ally themselves with national and transnational advocates of gender equality. Such elites may have travelled internationally and been educated in or influenced by the Global North, and they may be fluent in English.[66] Those who are best positioned to effect the 'infiltration' of foreign ideologies include the judges who in their opinions uphold international law, if only to a degree, as Zorn shows in her contribution to this volume. Whoever they are, they are not strangers to human rights discourse and have embraced the ideology at least to a degree. Accordingly, they are drawn to and participate in the 'reformist space'[67] of human rights work.

This is as true of elite women as it is of elite men. As Margaret Jolly reminds us, 'women from the Global South have been centrally involved in talking about and promoting human rights for decades'.[68]

---

59   We use the words *translator* and *vernaculariser* interchangeably because Merry so uses them. In 'Transnational human rights and local activism', Merry writes of translators. In 'Vernacularization on the ground', she and her co-author Peggy Levitt use the word *vernaculariser*.

60   Levitt and Merry, 'Vernacularization on the ground', p. 449.

61   Merry, *Human Rights and Gender Violence*, p. 89.

62   See Zorn, 'Translating and internalising international human rights law', this volume.

63   Goodale, *Surrendering to Utopia*, p. 14.

64   Merry, 'Transnational human rights and local activism', p. 38.

65   Merry, *Human Rights and Gender Violence*, p. 102.

66   Ibid., pp. 100–101.

67   Ibid., p. 101.

68   Jolly, '"When She Cries Oceans"', this volume.

They have done so under decidedly transnational influences. The Fiji Women's Crisis Centre (FWCC), for example, which is crucial to human rights work in the western Pacific and beyond,[69] emerged in response to a 1983 report on rape (its frequency, communal attitudes towards rape, and the treatment of rape victims at the hands of Fijian law)[70] as 'a group of expatriate women' encouraged an organisational response to the report from local women.[71] A decade earlier, the Fiji YWCA had promoted family planning, among other transnationally inspired causes,[72] setting the stage for what was to become, through the FWCC and its sister organisation, the Fiji Women's Rights Movement, the most effective platform for women's rights advocacy in the western Pacific.

But the impetus for change could come from other quarters as well. Many Pacific Islanders are themselves troubled by the prevalence and manner of contemporary gender violence and consider it an abomination to be expunged, as the public outcry against the immolation of Kepari Leniata in Papua New Guinea showed.[73] For these Pacific Islanders, gender violence constitutes a *cultural* violation, the remedy for which is the reassertion of cultural principles and values that have lost their salience in the contemporary period. There are indeed Pacific Islanders who argue that gender violence, in its contemporary guise, is not customary. For example, in a study supported in part by the Government of the Republic of Vanuatu, Roselyn Tor and Anthea Teka acknowledge that Vanuatu males sometimes justify domestic violence in terms of the bridewealth payment they made in marrying, a payment seen as rendering wives chattels of their husband.[74] But in the past, according to these two ni-Vanuatu women, bridewealth was not bride*price* and the wife was never the husband's property, to do with as he wished. Bridewealth was instead a *social transaction*, one that was foundational to the

---

69   See Nicole George, 2012, *Situating Women: Gender Politics and Circumstance in Fiji*, Canberra: ANU E Press, pp. 80–82 and passim.

70   Ibid., p. 80.

71   Ibid., p. 81.

72   Ibid., pp. 39–74; see also Annelise Riles, 2000, 'The virtual sociality of rights: The case of "women's rights are human rights"', *Northwestern University School of Law, Public Law and Legal Theory Papers*, 40: 1–37, pp. 28–32.

73   For example, see the *Stop Sorcery Violence Papua New Guinea* website.

74   Roselyn Tor and Anthea Teka, 2004, *Gender, Kastom & Domestic Violence: A Research on the Historical Trend, Extent and Impact of Domestic Violence in Vanuatu*. Port Vila: Department of Women's Affairs, Republic of Vanuatu, pp. 29–30.

extension and solidification of relationships through marriage.[75] Yes, culture changes, but not always for the better. Globalisation involves circulations—of styles of sexuality and violence, for example—that may well undermine rather than advance the cause of women's rights and that, in any case, have an exogenous rather than an endogenous source.

Parties offended by contemporary gender violence may well organise to mitigate it in the name of treasured cultural principles. Such actors are intermediary in a sense Merry does not consider: poised between past and present, they judge the present in terms of their perceptions of a less gender-violent past, which, properly utilised, will steer their contemporaries towards reform. In this effort, they may collaborate with metropolitan human rights workers and those among the national elite, and they may serve as their allies, guiding vernacularisation towards a culturally legitimate endpoint.[76] Such a reassertion of dormant cultural standards is less likely among cosmopolitan elites, but village-based actors, especially older ones, may well recoil from contemporary levels and styles of gender violence they consider transgressive and enter a 'reformist space' that is to a degree of their own making and for their own purpose: to limit if not eradicate gender violence in the name of cultural revitalisation. This bottom-up thrust complements the largely 'top-down' thrust ('from the transnational to the local and the powerful to the less powerful')[77] of the international human rights regime.

The emergence of place-based reformers is symptomatic of the fact that villages in the contemporary western Pacific are 'divided and conflictual'[78] spaces. At the very least, one would expect conflict to erupt along gender lines,[79] but generational, ethnic, and emerging

---

75   Tor and Teka, *Gender, Kastom & Domestic Violence*, p. 29.

76   Shannon Speed, 2008, *Rights in Rebellion: Indigenous Struggle and Human Rights in Chiapas*, Stanford: Stanford University Press, quoted in Goodale, 'Introduction: Human rights and anthropology', p. 10.

77   Merry, 'Transnational human rights and local activism', pp. 48–49, quoted in Goldstein, 'Whose vernacular?' p. 113.

78   Goldstein, 'Whose vernacular?' p. 113.

79   See John P. Taylor, 2008, 'The social life of rights: "Gender antagonism", modernity and *raet* in Vanuatu', in *Changing Pacific Masculinities: The 'Problem' of Men*, ed. John P. Taylor, special issue of *The Australian Journal of Anthropology* 19(2): 165–78.

class differences might also be factors.[80] To the extent that place-based actors who represent specific local values become important in efforts to reduce gender violence, the dynamics of Merry's 'reformist space' become vastly more complicated: a matter of 'the interplay and mutual determination of "internal" and "external" factors and relationships [emphasis removed]'.[81] Through this interplay, human rights practice becomes 'an ongoing, socially constructed and negotiated process—not simply the execution of an already specified "plan of action" with expected "outcomes"'[82] but a process that is subject to more than one order of determination, global but also local.

Problems with the human rights approach

For the most part, the chapters in this volume make it clear that the footprint of the international human rights regime is weak in the western Pacific. An oft-repeated explanation for the failure of human rights advocacy in the western Pacific when it comes to gender violence is that women are considered inferior to men, to whom they are then subordinated, and some degree of domestic violence for disciplining purposes is widely accepted. But the international human rights regime is globally, not just regionally, weak, owing, in part, to internal contradictions. At best it is 'a relatively strong promotional regime, composed of widely accepted substantive norms', but with 'very limited international implementation ... There is no international enforcement.'[83] Here we consider some of the problems with the regime that weaken it, in the western Pacific but also beyond.

Universal or particular?

Considered in its entirety, the international human rights regime is inconsistent. On the one hand, the system aims to defeat any particularity that contravenes human rights principles, which are

---

80   See, for example, Deborah Gewertz and Frederick Errington, 1999, *Emerging Class in Papua New Guinea: The Telling of Difference*, Cambridge: Cambridge University Press.
81   Preis, 'Human rights as cultural practice', p. 350.
82   Norman Long, 1992, 'From paradigm lost to paradigm regained? The case for an actor-oriented sociology of development', in *Battlefields of Knowledge: The Interlocking of Theory and Practice in Social Research and Development*, ed. Norman Long and Ann Long, pp. 16–43, London and New York: Routledge, as quoted in Preis, 'Human rights as cultural practice', p. 350.
83   Donnelly, 'International human rights', pp. 613–14.

considered to be universal. On the other hand, cultural pluralism is explicitly defended. The UN Declaration on the Rights of Indigenous Peoples affirms that 'indigenous peoples are equal to all other peoples, while recognizing the right of all peoples to be different … and to be respected as such'.[84] Other international conventions take a similar stand, affirming the 'right to self-determination [International Covenant on Civil and Political Rights], the right to participate in [the] cultural life of the community [Universal Declaration of Human Rights] or to enjoy one's own culture [International Covenant on Civil and Political Rights]',[85] rights that are inconsistent with the presumption in rights ideology of a universal moral standard. As Merry has observed, there is a 'a fundamental tension within the structure of global reformism and human rights: the contradiction between the desire to maintain cultural diversity and at the same time to achieve progress in terms of equality, rights, and universality'.[86]

This contradiction brings into focus a nagging doubt. Are human rights really universal? According to Merry, human rights doctrine promotes 'ideas of individual autonomy, equality, choice, and secularism'[87] and as such is not only culturally particular but alien to moral philosophies that are equally culturally particular but 'less individualistic and more focused on communities and responsibilities'.[88] Indeed, western concepts of personhood highlight the individual 'at the expense of communities'.[89] This contrast between Western and western Pacific ideas about personhood and morality is a subtext in several chapters and is especially brought to the fore in Katherine Lepani's discussion of Trobriand sociality and notions of personhood in this volume. To the extent that Western and

---

84   UN, Declaration on the Rights of Indigenous Peoples, 2008, A/61/L.67 and Add.1.

85   Michael K. Addo, 2010, *The Legal Nature of International Human Rights*, Leiden and Boston: Martinus Nijhoff Publishers, pp. 57–58.

86   Sally Engle Merry, 2004, 'Tensions between global law and local social justice: CEDAW and the problem of rape in Fiji', paper delivered at the Justice Across Cultures Conference, Brandeis, March, p. 14.

87   Merry, *Human Rights and Gender Violence*, p. 4; see also Merry, 2004, 'Tensions between global law and local social justice', p. 101.

88   Merry, *Human Rights and Gender Violence*, p. 4.

89   Merry, 'Transnational human rights and local activism', p. 39.

western Pacific moralities and socialities are diametrically opposed (but see Margaret Jolly's comments in '"When she cries oceans"', this volume), human rights work becomes a form of 'moral imperialism'.[90]

Among those social scientists who have been committed to cultural relativism rather than universalism, the issue of whether human rights are cross-culturally valid and the related issue of cultural relativism continue to be battlefields of 'fierce, heated, and passionate debate',[91] although consensus still favours recognising the universality of human rights doctrine. Certainly, the matter has by no means been put to rest in the postcolonial world, commentators such as Makau Mutua arguing that the human rights movement 'is located within the historical continuum of Eurocentrism as civilizing mission',[92] to be understood, then, as a further chapter in the *longue durée* of western 'cultural dominance'[93] among the 'savages' lying outside its cultural sphere.[94] Why should postcolonial nations accede to the demands of ideologically foreign institutions that are identified with their colonial masters?

There has been at least one very dramatic instance of the reaffirmation of male privilege in the name of customary practices in the context of human rights advocacy in the western Pacific. John Taylor, one of the contributors to this volume, has elsewhere reported on a backlash to 'the insidious promotion of Western-style "women's rights"'[95] by women's organisations and other activists, who are accused of 'being harbingers of neo-colonialism and betrayers'[96] of local culture. The men who banded together under the banner of 'Violence Against Men' or VAM in Luganville, the second largest town in Vanuatu, rejected the promotion of women's rights as discrimination—in fact as violence—against men because this promotion disadvantaged

---

90   Goodale, *Surrendering to Utopia*, p. 108. Here Goodale cites Berta Esperanza Hernandez-Truyol (ed.), 2002, *Moral Imperialism: A Critical Anthology*, New York: New York University Press. See also Mary Ann Glendon, 2001, *A World Made New: Eleanor Roosevelt and the Universal Declaration of Human Rights*, New York: Random House, pp. 221–33; Makau Wa Mutua, 1996, 'The ideology of human rights', *Virginia Journal of International Law* 36: 589–657; and Mutua, *Human Rights*.
91   Preis, 'Human rights as cultural practice', p. 333.
92   Mutua, *Human Rights*, p. 15.
93   Ibid.
94   Ibid., p. 8.
95   Taylor, 'The social life of rights', p. 167.
96   Ibid.

men in divorce and rape cases as well as in custody battles. Over and against the ideological incursions of women's rights as facilitated by 'overseas funding sources and international allies',[97] this group upheld patriarchal practices believed to be not only customary (*kastom* in Bislama) but Christian.

Too authoritarian?

Getting beyond this critique of the human rights movement has proved difficult. Abdullahi Ahmed An-Na'im, a Sudanese scholar who is professor of law in Emory University's School of Law and who is well known for his writings on human rights in cross-cultural perspective, has observed that human rights advocacy has had a checkered history because human rights ideology simply lacks 'cross-cultural legitimacy [emphasis removed]'.[98] 'To dictate to a society is both unacceptable as a matter of principle and unlikely to succeed in practice.'[99] As a tonic, An-Na'im proposes 'cross-cultural dialogue' and the 'mutual influence' achieved through it.[100] In fact, reciprocal and mutual influence across the North–South global divide is 'continuously occurring in practice'.[101]

Merry's 'translation' and 'vernacularization' require 'cross-cultural dialogue', culminating in 'transplantation', but not the kind of cross-fertilisation that would result in modifications to human rights ideology itself. The aim in translation and vernacularisation is to transfer norms across cultural boundaries, not to transform those norms, the outcome of true cross-cultural fertilisation. Thus, from a human rights perspective, some translations and vernacularisations are legitimate while others are not. But norms can in fact change in the very process of diffusion. One could argue, with Mona Lena Krook and Jacqui True, that 'norms diffuse precisely because—rather than despite the fact

97 Ibid.
98 Abdullahi Ahmed An-Na'im, 2009, 'Toward a cross-cultural approach to defining international standards of human rights: The meaning of cruel, inhuman, or degrading treatment or punishment', in *Human Rights: An Anthropological Reader*, ed. Mark Goodale, pp. 68–85, Malden, MA: Wiley-Blackwell, p. 70. Originally published in Abdullahi Ahmed An-Na'im (ed.), 1992, *Human Rights in Cross-Cultural Perspectives*, Philadelphia: University of Pennsylvania Press, pp. 19–43.
99 An-Na'im, 2009, 'Toward a cross-cultural approach to defining international standards of human rights', p. 81.
100 Ibid.
101 Ibid.

that—they may encompass different meanings, fit in with a variety of contexts, and be subject to framing by diverse actors'.[102] To the extent they do, international norms become '"processes" ... works-in-progress, rather than finished products',[103] an 'evolving paradigm'[104] that is fashioned through 'flows between centers and peripheries'.[105] These claims second Charlotte Bunch's observation, made over two decades ago, that the 'concept of human rights, like all vibrant visions, is not static or the property of any one group; rather, its meaning expands as people reconceive of their needs and hopes in relation to it'.[106] Human rights ideology must then be reimagined not as a '"final" answer',[107] an axiomatic, and thus universal, normativity, but, like all culture, whether Northern or Southern, as amenable to change.

If these arguments are correct, then the effectiveness of the human rights movement ultimately depends upon its openness to genuine intercultural exchange. Yet there are no structures or processes within the international human rights system to facilitate the dialogue that could lead to 'significant agreement'[108] on moral standards in an effort to avoid the cultural imperialism to which human rights doctrine is otherwise prone. Without An-Na'im's 'greater consensus on international standards',[109] the international human rights regime remains an authoritarian system dictating a compliance it is unlikely to achieve.

---

102 Mona Lena Krook and Jacqui True, 2012, 'Rethinking the life cycles of international norms: The United Nations and the global promotion of gender equality', *European Journal of International Relations* 18(1): 103–27, p. 105.
103 Ibid., p. 104.
104 Preis, 'Human rights as cultural practice', p. 347. Preis is here quoting Virginia A. Leary, 1992, 'Postliberal strands in western human rights theory: Personalist-communitarian perspectives', in *Human Rights in Cross-Cultural Perspectives: A Quest for Consensus*, ed. Abdullahi Ahmed An-Na'im, pp. 105–32, Philadelphia: University of Pennsylvania Press, pp. 105, 128.
105 Preis, 'Human rights as cultural practice', p. 348.
106 Bunch, 'Women's rights as human rights', p. 487.
107 Mutua, 'The ideology of human rights', p. 653; Mutua, *Human Rights*, p. 2. See also Glendon, *A World Made New*, p. 231.
108 An-Na'im, 'Toward a cross-cultural approach to defining international standards of human rights', p. 82.
109 Ibid.

The state as enforcer of international law

State ratifiers of conventions such as CEDAW and CRC are held responsible for 'due diligence' in protecting women and girls and promoting their rights. They do so largely by passing laws that enforce these conventions. Yet the three countries this volume concerns have neither the police force nor the judicial resources to enforce the laws that would protect women and promote their rights. Also, given that some degree of gender violence is widely tolerated in many if not most western Pacific societies, many citizens find these laws unsympathetic. In fact, many of these laws have been passed only after years of heated debate, inside and outside national parliaments, as Aletta Biersack's contribution to this volume indicates. The VAM movement of Luganville, Vanuatu, is but one manifestation of the debates within western Pacific civil societies. There are also incompatibilities in procedures, values and moralities between Northern principles, which emphasise punishment and deterrence, and Southern community-based remedies, which are designed to secure reconciliation and the rehabilitation of relational networks.[110] This in a nutshell is the conflict between, on the one hand, Fijian *bulubulu* practices—involving the tendering of an apology and valuables to the victim's group by the offender and his or her group to restore the relationship or relationships the offence has placed at risk, as Lynda Newland describes in her contribution—and, on the other hand, Western-style resolutions, which punish the offender in the name of justice for the individual victim. Such 'friction'[111] between the core values of Northern and Southern societies means that the postcolonial states of the Global South sometimes lack the political will to enforce vigorously the treaties they have ratified, especially given the resistance of their respective citizenries.

There is also the thorny issue of state sovereignty and its relation to the colonial past. Worldwide, UN efforts to compel ratifying states to comply with the terms of the conventions they have ratified have been met with 'widespread, vociferous, and usually effective claims

---

110 Sinclair Dinnen, 2003, 'Restorative justice in the Pacific Islands: An introduction', in *A Kind of Mending: Restorative Justice in the Pacific Islands*, ed. Sinclair Dinnen with Anita Jowitt and Tess Newton Cain, pp. 1–34, Canberra: ANU Press, pp. 12–22.

111 Anna Lowenhaupt Tsing, 2004, *Friction: An Ethnography of Global Connection*, Princeton: Princeton University Press.

of national'[112] and also cultural sovereignty. Great Britain, France and Australia, advocates one and all for human rights, colonised the western Pacific and continued to do so deep into the 20th century. Fiji gained its independence from Great Britain in 1970; Papua New Guinea, at one time colonised by Germany and Great Britain, ultimately received its independence from Australia in 1975; and Vanuatu became independent from Great Britain and France in 1980. The international human rights regime links rich, 'first world' former colonial powers, and now major aid donors, to their poor, postcolonial 'third world' others, the recipients of that aid. Pacific Islanders understand very well the politics of the gift. As relatively new nation-states, Fiji, Papua New Guinea and Vanuatu could easily resent the fact that promoting women's rights is a condition on their receiving aid, in effect making a mockery of independence.

Beyond human rights practice

For all her promotion of cultural solutions (translation, vernacularisation, ideological transplantation), Merry has faulted UN advocates for 'a general tendency to culturalize problems',[113] ignoring causes that often involve armed conflict and displacement as well as poverty; problems that are occasioned by 'the havoc wreaked by expansive capitalism and global conflicts'.[114] Following this lead, we should look beyond male attitudes and the cultures that inculcate them towards the political and economic circumstances under which men become violent towards women and girls. The causes of gender violence would then lie less in the ideological sphere and more in social institutions, political perturbations at all levels, and the dislocations and pathologies engendered by globalisation, including market integration and its local impacts. Adopting the term 'structural violence' that Paul Farmer has made famous,[115] Merry points towards supra-community, even supra-national, large-scale processes and the damage they cause: 'the violence of poverty, hunger, social exclusion,

112 Donnelly, 'International human rights', p. 609.
113 Merry, 'Human rights law and the demonization of culture', p. 63.
114 Ibid., p. 64.
115 See, for example, Paul Farmer, 2004, 'An anthropology of structural violence', *Current Anthropology* 45(3): 305–25.

and humiliation'[116] and, again, 'injuries and assaults that are produced by collective actions and institutions'.[117] The term 'includes [but is not restricted to] the violence following conquest and dislocation suffered by indigenous peoples ... and the violent consequences of poverty and the inability to support oneself'.[118]

Along these lines, it is important to remember that the changes associated with globalisation in the Pacific have been so rapid that most western Pacific societies suffer from a generation gap that has stripped older men of the authority they once had in mentoring and censuring younger men. This loss of social control has coincided with the growing influence of Western media and the ideas about Western gender and sexual relations formed through the consumption of TV, film and magazines and including pornography, as well as with the increasing availability of intoxicants (beer, home brew and marijuana), which are widely recognised as playing a role in gender violence in the region. Moreover, the countries of the western Pacific are now monetised but employment is low, and many men find themselves at the bottom of novel social and economic hierarchies and are humiliated as a result.[119] In the event, the contemporary level and style of gender violence would stem not from ideology and mindset but from trauma occasioned by rapid social, political and economic upheavals, which have handicapped many males in the new arenas of competition for status that have opened up. By the same token, as Nicole George argues in her important contribution to this collection, recent economic and political convulsions in Fiji have made men feel emasculated and impotent, and so (quoting an interview with Shamima Ali, the head of the Fiji Women's Crisis Centre) they 'take it out on the most vulnerable' members of society: women and children.

Richard Eves offers another explanation of violence against women: gender violence is a strategy for preserving male dominance. Quoting the UN Division for the Advancement of Women, Eves notes that violence against women is 'a "policing mechanism"

---

116 Merry, *Gender Violence*, p. 2.
117 Ibid., p. 182.
118 Ibid.
119 Frederick Errington and Deborah Gewertz, 2005, 'On humiliation and class in contemporary Papua New Guinea', in *The Making of Global and Local Modernities in Melanesia: Humiliation, Transformation and the Nature of Cultural Change*, ed. Joel Robbins and Holly Wardlow, pp. 163–70, Burlington, VT: Ashgate.

to "keep women ... in their place"' and subordinated to their husbands, 'to assert "who makes the decisions" in a relationship or "who holds the power"'.[120] The implication here is that we should examine 'the structural relationships of power, domination and privilege between men and women in society'[121] and dismantle those arrangements and institutions that disadvantage women, simultaneously empowering men.

The obvious target here is bridewealth. Whatever its role in social exchange in the past, it has always also been a means for indebting, and thus subordinating, wives to husbands.[122] Many contemporary males take this a step further, interpreting bridewealth as bride*price*: the warrant for exercising proprietary rights over their wives. Absent national bans on bridewealth, changes in marriage practices will only be effected through community-level deliberations as to whether bridewealth should persist and, if so, under what understanding of it. Does it connect groups in amicable exchanges, elevating women as indispensable links in community-centred networks, or does it strip wives of their rights, further empowering their husband-creditors? Important related questions, ones that are inspired by the chapter by George, are: What are the circumstances, if any, under which a woman can avoid bridewealth-based marriage without damaging her reputation?[123] Can a woman shun marriage and still be economically viable, and, if so, at what cost to her reputation? Do economically independent women risk being attacked by envious husbands?

For all the promise of this approach, remedying social, political and economic inequalities is probably insufficient to combat the ingrained male sexism—and its corollary: a sense of female inferiority—

---

120 UN Division for the Advancement of Women, 2004, *The Role of Men and Boys in Achieving Gender Equality*, [Final] Report of the Expert Group Meeting, Brasilia, Brazil, 21–24 October 2003, EGM/MEN-BOYS-GE/2003/REPORT, 12 January, p. 31, item 82, as quoted in Richard Eves, 2010, 'Masculinity matters: Men, gender-based violence and the AIDS epidemic in Papua New Guinea', in *Civic Insecurity: Law, Order and HIV in Papua New Guinea,* ed. Vicki Luker and Sinclair Dinnen, pp. 47–79, Studies in State and Society in the Pacific, no. 6, State, Society and Governance in Melanesia Program, p. 49.
121 Bunch, 'Women's rights as human rights', p. 491.
122 See Holly Wardlow, 2006, *Wayward Women: Sexuality and Agency in a New Guinea Society*, Berkeley: University of California Press.
123 See Martha Macintyre, 2011, 'Money changes everything: Papua New Guinean women in a modern economy', in *Managing Modernity in the Western Pacific*, ed. Mary Patterson and Martha Macintyre, pp. 90–120, St Lucia: University of Queensland Press.

encountered in the western Pacific.[124] In addition to giving females the education, skills and opportunities they need to compete in the monetised economies of the contemporary western Pacific and achieve leadership positions—'capacitating' them, as George describes—human rights advocacy is also needed to counter male sexism and embolden female agents.

Towards an ethnography of human rights work in the western Pacific

Merry's notion of vernacularisation paves the way for what promises to be a fruitful area of ethnographic enquiry: the ethnography of 'the practice of human rights', as Goodale has dubbed it,[125] an ethnography, if you will, of vernacularisation and transplantation, but with all of the groping, wobbliness, and transformative potential of the process duly noted and from the critical perspectives on the human rights regime itself presented here.[126] Ethnography is a methodology that is widely utilised in the social sciences. Its strength lies in its focus on actual practices (rather than ideals), the semantics and politics of communications and interactions, and open-ended processes. Building on the materials in this collection, an ethnography of human rights practice or human rights work would have a range of targets. Let us suggest several fertile avenues of enquiry.

Philip Gibbs's contribution to this collection reminds us that Christian churches have become core civil society institutions that advocate for a reduction in gender violence in the western Pacific, and, in the course of doing so, play 'a role in interpreting human rights discourse in a vernacular idiom'. His contribution follows closely the thinking of men enrolled in a 'Men's Matters' rights-based program (albeit from

124 Ashlee Betteridge and Kamalini Lokuge, 2014, 'Combatting the family and sexual violence epidemic in Papua New Guinea: A submission to the inquiry of the Human Rights Subcommittee of the Foreign Affairs, Defence and Trade Joint Standing Committee into the human rights issues confronting women and girls in the Indian Ocean–Asia Pacific region', Development Policy Centre, The Australian National University, May, pp. 8–9.
125 Mark Goodale, 2007, 'Introduction: Locating rights, envisioning law between the global and the local', in *The Practice of Human Rights: Tracking Law Between the Global and the Local*, ed. Mark Goodale and Sally Engle Merry, pp. 1–38, Cambridge: Cambridge University Press, pp. 24–27.
126 Mark Goodale, 2006, 'Toward a critical anthropology of human rights', *Current Anthropology* 47(3): 485–511.

a Christian perspective) who as participants confront and critique their own gender violence and affirm the ideals of manhood of the past. What lasting impact do such faith-based programs have? Do they provide a foundation for human rights discourse that is alternative to the 'modern' and secular foundations scholars such as Merry emphasise? How are Christianity- and human rights–based moralities the same and/or different?

Secular institutions dedicated to the amelioration of women's and children's situations arguably have had an even higher impact. In addition to women's associations, many institutions—local, provincial, national and regional—that are designed to protect women and their rights have emerged in recent decades, and their successes and/or failures, and the support and/or pushback they provoke, would be worthy targets for an ethnography of human rights work. Of particular interest are male advocates, now trained in all three countries this volume concerns to defend women's and children's rights and to oppose gender violence. The contexts in which they operate, the strategies and arguments they use, and the reactions they draw would provide crucial information on efforts to translate and vernacularise human rights discourse as well as on any oppositional politics these efforts might incite. Women's associations are often the vanguard in promoting women's rights in the western Pacific, and their histories, strategies and campaigns, and strengths and limitations, given the climate of opinion in which they operate and the resources they have at their disposal, would provide invaluable insight into the dynamics of human rights practice in the region. In this regard, George's study of women's associations in Fiji, *Situating Women: Gender Politics and Circumstance in Fiji*,[127] serves as an exemplary model.

George's contribution to this volume makes a strong case for the need to investigate the social, political and economic conditions of men's and women's lives, as these impinge upon gender violence. In 'Sorcery talk, gender violence, and the law in Vanuatu', John Taylor and Natalie Araújo feature such conditions in the 'modernity as rupture' backstory they provide in their examination of contemporary Vanuatu sorcery narratives and the violence against females they portray. Sorcery accusation-related violence is rapidly gaining recognition as a virulent

127 George, *Situating Women*.

form of violence against women in some parts of the western Pacific, and any rights-based attempt to defeat it will merit close ethnographic attention in the future.

Several contributions touch on the gender violence–mitigating laws passed by the parliaments of the western Pacific and the judicial and police institutions that strive to implement them. Much of this legislation was passed only after a protracted period of resistance and debate, and implementing these laws is more often than not extremely difficult. How does a female and/or her kin decide whether to take matters of rape or domestic violence to the police, a move that would activate the state justice system, with its laws and penal institutions, or, alternatively, to the village courts, which operate largely independently of that system and which promote reconciliation between an offender and the victim's family rather than the punishment of perpetrators in the name of justice for the victim? Or does a victim maintain her silence and, if so, why? Does the victim even have a say in the matter? Who decides and why? Some of these questions are addressed in Lynda Newland's informative discussion of village-based justice in Fiji. Jean Zorn's contribution to this volume shows us how to take such questions further in the event the victim reports an offence to the police and a state court rather than to a village court. Does the state court judge make a rights-based decision, and if so, on what grounds? Do villagers, the victim and the perpetrator accept this decision? What are the repercussions of the decision?

For reasons already given, in human rights work the state is assumed to be 'not only the central actor, but also the indispensable and pivotal actor around which all other entities revolve'.[128] A state may dodge its obligations to international treaties by dragging its feet in reporting to watchdog committees such as the CEDAW Committee and the CRC Committee or by failing to pass rights-based legislation. But western Pacific states cannot resist indefinitely without jeopardising their claim to foreign aid and risking embarrassment on a global stage. In parallel with the kind of ethnographic research Merry conducted at the UN, researchers might sit in on relevant parliamentary debates, interview ministers, prime ministers and other governmental leaders,

---

128 Philip Alston, 2005, 'The not-a-cat syndrome: Can the international human rights regime accommodate non-state actors?' in *Non-state Actors and Human Rights*, pp. 3–36, New York: Oxford University Press, p. 3.

and supplement these observations and interviews with a review of national newspapers and policy papers for indications of debates about rights-based agendas and government officials' (as well as citizens') attitudes towards them. By the same token, state-led campaigns and initiatives designed to reduce gender violence and/or promote women's rights—as described, for example, in Lepani's and Biersack's contributions to this volume—should be studied for their impacts. Do they modify behaviour, elicit support, or spur antagonism?

This research agenda implicitly addresses the dynamics of local–global interfaces, with a view towards observing how ordinary citizens and representatives of the international human rights regime and the state interact. What is the fit or lack of fit between international ('universal') human rights norms and local, national and regional norms? What are the cultural investments and intolerances of the international human rights system? Is it open to genuine cross-cultural engagement, one that modifies rights talk? If yes, what are the modifications and how do they occur? If no, is 'translation' open to more than one interpretation and what are the differences among interpretations and interpreters?

As we have suggested, to focus on ideological transfer (Merry's 'translation') is merely a partial approach to gender violence and human rights. One must enquire as well into the social, political and economic conditions of the lives of western Pacific men and women, asking how these exacerbate or alleviate gender violence and hamper or aid translation. Ethnographic work will expose relevant social, political and economic factors that can be explored further for a more complete picture of women's situation, its possible futures, and the conditions under which these might be achieved.

Additionally, this ethnographic work must be historically informed. As already indicated, the western Pacific has undergone rapid change since colonialism, and the causes and modalities of contemporary gender violence must be understood in terms of that change. Taylor and Araújo's discussion of sorcery in Vanuatu makes the point. Pre-colonial sorcery was a power Vanuatu chiefs monopolised to assure law and order in the face of violations of *kastom* or customary practices. They write that, with the 'breakdown of *kastom* structures of governance during the colonial period', sorcery became 'unbound … from chiefly structures' and in the present-day may be used by 'young and sometimes disempowered men' to assert their masculine power over females in acts of sexual assault. There is little in this volume that does not at least implicitly acknowledge the importance of the history of the region in understanding gender violence: its historical arc and its contemporary manifestations. That the topics of gender violence and human rights can now be productively linked is itself a consequence of the history of a globalising western Pacific.

Chapter summaries

In this section, we look more closely at individual contributions with an eye towards elucidating their specific contributions to the study of gender violence and human rights in the western Pacific.

The translatability of concepts of human rights into culturally acceptable terms, making them consonant with Melanesian ideologies of justice—a central tenet of Merry's argument—is challenged by both Lynda Newland and Nicole George, social scientists who study Fiji. Whereas George locates the failure in translation within the broad framework of 'law and order' state policies, Newland's article focuses on the ways that traditional systems of conflict resolution, atonement and reparation perpetuate discrimination against women. Her article draws on ethnographic research in *iTaukei* (indigenous Fijian) villages and engages with arguments Merry makes against the CEDAW Committee's suggestion that a particular ritual, *bulubulu*, be abandoned as a means of compensating and atoning for violence against women.[129] In particular, Newland examines the views of men who perceive the maintenance of relationships between communities as a higher priority than justice for women. She demonstrates that the principles that inform *bulubulu* rest on strong beliefs about gender hierarchy, which privilege male authority over women and children, based on values and principles derived from Christianity and tradition. Newland, like George, observes that gender violence appears to be escalating in Fiji and that the current gap between rhetorical commitments to the crisis made by government and NGOs has not resulted in a decline in incidence. The provision of refuge and counselling services is confined to towns. Responses in the village setting are aimed at reconciliation of the couple and the promotion

---

129 Merry, *Human Rights and Gender Violence*, pp. 113–33.

of communal harmony rather than justice for victims. Like many others who have undertaken research on the subject, she maintains that campaigns against violence must incorporate and challenge men if they are to effect change.[130]

If Newland concentrates on the values that flourish and the various ways that gender-based violence is justified and normalised, George emphasises the structural factors that marginalise women, reinforcing male dominance and providing a context for violence to occur. She argues there that the emphasis on translation in the writings of Merry and others occludes 'the factors that obstruct women's economic and political participation'[131] and thus the exercise of their rights. In this argument, she is guided by the 'capabilities' approach first enunciated by Amartya Sen and subsequently taken up in Martha Nussbaum's *Women and Human Development*.[132] For Sen, human rights, though granted, cannot be realised unless a person can 'achieve valuable combinations of human functionings: what a person is able to do or be'.[133] For example, a person may be granted the right to vote but will only be able to exercise that right if s/he can, by virtue of the functions s/he is able to perform, actually vote. A 'capabilities' approach emphasises the pragmatics of human rights practice rather than the morality of human rights precepts. Embracing the 'capabilities' framework for understanding female vulnerability and exclusion, George stresses 'structural factors, political and economic, that diminish women's ability to realise'[134] or secure their rights, however intelligible or perfectly translated the rights talk may be. Specifically, Fiji's successive coups, the imposition of authoritarian, militarist rule, and national economic and political interests and policies have adversely affected Fijian women's capacities to participate equally in political and economic arenas.

---

130 See especially Richard Eves, 2006, *Exploring the Role of Men and Masculinities in Papua New Guinea in the 21st Century*, Caritas Australia.
131 George, '"Lost in translation"', this volume.
132 See, for example, Amartya Sen, 1999, *Development as Freedom*, Oxford: Oxford University Press; see also Martha Nussbaum, 2000, *Women and Human Development: The Capabilities Approach*, Cambridge: Cambridge University Press.
133 Amartya Sen, 2004, 'Elements of a theory of human rights', *Philosophy and Public Affairs* 32(4): 315–56, p. 332.
134 George, '"Lost in translation"'.

Philip Gibbs, like Newland, provides invaluable information about male perceptions. Men not only believe themselves to have an obligation and perhaps a right to punish women who are thought to be delinquent in some way, but view state laws and secular notions of human rights as alien impositions. In particular, against the precepts of corporeal integrity and female autonomy implicit in human rights discourse, males reject the view that rape is necessarily a criminal act. In the workshop described by Gibbs, husbands indicated that a wife's refusal to have sex was the most common reason for violence and held fast to the idea that a man's right to sexual access was paramount (especially if bridewealth had been paid). In Papua New Guinea, the passing of the 2002 Criminal Code Act criminalising rape within marriage in PNG[135] has apparently had little effect on men's attitudes or behaviour. Similarly, in rural Fiji, as Newland reports, male village leaders regard a woman's marriage to her rapist as an appropriate alternative to criminal proceedings insofar as it mends the breach in social relations that might otherwise have ensued because the woman's parents receive the bridewealth prestation they consider necessary if the man is to have sexual access to their daughter. There is an emerging regional and international consensus that significant reductions in the violence against females will only occur if the males of a society embrace the cause, and Gibbs provides an ethnography of a faith-based initiative ('Men's Matters') to confront men with their transgressions against women and encourage them to accept past notions of what a 'real' and thus non-violent man is.[136]

In the course of doing so, Gibbs reminds us of the importance of the work of PNG churches in promoting women's rights and ending gender violence, albeit from a Biblical rather than a secular humanist perspective. 'Men's Matters' was established by the Catholic Diocese in Papua New Guinea's Western Province in response to men's requests and as part of the Caritas International project, which is aimed at promoting human rights and Christian understandings of tolerance, social justice and gender equity and which commissioned Eves's

---

135 See Biersack, 'Human rights work in Papua New Guinea, Fiji and Vanuatu', this volume.
136 On the importance of male advocacy in promoting women's rights, see Gary Barker, Christine Ricardo and Marcos Nascimento, 2007, *Engaging Men and Boys in Changing Gender-Based Inequity in Health: Evidence from Programme Interventions*, WHO: Geneva; Eves, *Exploring the Role of Men and Masculinities in Papua New Guinea in the 21st Century*; Eves, 'Masculinity matters'; and Eves, 'Resisting global AIDS knowledges'. See also Caroline Sweetman (ed.), 2001, *Men's Involvement in Gender and Development Policy and Practice: Beyond Rhetoric*, London: Oxfam.

2006 report, *Exploring the Role of Men and Masculinities in Papua New Guinea in the 21st Century*. This raises the question of cultural mutability in two ways. First, it implicitly reveals the historical changes that have occurred across Papua New Guinea, as Christianity has been embraced in successive waves of missionary endeavour, to the point where the nation itself is defined as Christian. Second, it suggests that the contradictions between traditional or customary sanctions and introduced legal systems might best be resolved by appealing to (already indigenised) Christian precepts that are consonant with human rights ideology and gender equity. The workshops initially explored men's ideas about masculinity and appropriate social conduct, but in discussing the problems the men faced, marital conflict and violence against women emerged as critical topics. The workshops encouraged men to express and scrutinise their use of violence in a range of situations, especially those where they hit a wife for being disobedient or for in some way affronting male self-esteem or status.[137] Thus confronted with their own gender violence in a religious context that affirmed Christian morality, the men committed to reforming their behaviour.

The variations in incidence and acceptance of violence against women across the region tend to be obscured in national statistical studies and estimates. Katherine Lepani's chapter draws attention to the culturally specific responses to violence in Trobriand society, where gender-based violence is comparatively rare. Her case study also reveals some of the problems inherent in notions of cultural translation that depend on points of similarity or analogy (as does much of the appeal to Christian doctrine of equality in God's sight). For Trobrianders, the identification with place as the basis of rights and protection incorporates ideas of personhood that do not fit easily into liberal discourses emphasising individual integrity and abstract conceptions of personal legal status.[138] While we have emphasised the ways that human rights discourses have been introduced through engagement with CEDAW and related initiatives, Lepani reminds us that in Papua New Guinea, international and national campaigns related to HIV and

---

137 See also Laura Zimmer-Tamakoshi, 2001, '"Wild pigs and dog men": Rape and domestic violence as women's issues in Papua New Guinea', in *Gender in Cross-Cultural Perspective*, third edition, ed. Caroline B. Brettell and Carolyn F. Sargent, pp. 565–80, Upper Saddle, New Jersey: Prentice-Hall.

138 Cf. Marilyn Strathern, 1999, *Property, Substance, and Effect: Anthropological Essays on Persons and Things*, London: Athlone Press.

AIDS were a major vehicle through which the public first encountered arguments for human rights. Moreover, the human rights discourse surrounding the HIV and AIDS campaigns, with their emphasis on female vulnerability, especially given sexual violence, ensured that human rights arguments were regularly perceived as foreign ideologies about the status of women.

The privileging of male authority and male agency in determining which offences should be punished or deemed criminal emerges as a theme throughout this volume. John Taylor and Natalie Araújo take up this topic with respect to Vanuatu, exploring male rights to inflict violence on women and the complicated relationship between hierarchical, customary authority invested in Vanuatu chiefs and the authority of the state. They observe that sorcery narratives in Vanuatu are often structured in such a way that by turns challenges and upholds hegemonic relations of power. In particular, in this context, sorcery (in Bislama, *nakaemas*) is understood to be typically controlled by men (although not exclusively so), and while both men and women are potential victims of health- or fortune-related sorcery attacks, women also live in fear of sex-related sorcery attacks. In this respect, and in contrast to the idealised past in which sorcery represented a legitimate mechanism of juridical authority tied to chiefly power, examination of sorcery-related narratives shows contemporary *nakaemas* to represent a largely negative social force, one that works to uphold patriarchy and contributes to the generalised subjugation and surveillance of women, including by naturalising sexual violence as a form of social justice.

Jean Zorn explores the fraught relationship between customary practices, cultural norms and state law across the region through an examination of the ways that CEDAW has been embraced in legal codes, endorsed by Melanesian governments, and used as a reference point in court cases and judgements. She challenges Merry's faith in processes of vernacularisation of CEDAW within Melanesian communities, but mainly on the grounds that, as the state adopts the convention as part of its laws, parliaments and courts are the primary translators of international norms. Merry acknowledges this as she presents the success of CEDAW in the Pacific in terms of the numerous national governments that have introduced laws relating to gender discrimination and violence against women. Zorn's article is broadly comparative, examining the ways that CEDAW has been invoked in courts in Fiji, Papua New Guinea, the Solomon Islands and Vanuatu in a variety of contexts where gender discrimination was a factor. She reveals that the decisions taken in these cases show how international law can be incorporated into domestic law and argues that the changes in law thus constituted inevitably have social consequences. The process she envisages will not in itself prevent wife beating, but as a gradual form of 'infiltration' will effect changes in the ways that women and men make decisions and resort to law.

Like Zorn, Aletta Biersack is interested in the role the state and state actors play in transferring human rights ideology across national and cultural boundaries. The development of legislation, policies, law enforcement capacity, and facilities such as safe houses and family support centres and networks of such facilities are the key strategies state ratifiers of CEDAW and CRC employ to honour their obligation to promote women's and children's rights and to regulate gender violence. Biersack traces the historical trajectory of governmental and civil society initiatives in Papua New Guinea, Fiji and Vanuatu, observing for each country the strides made but also the impediments to actualisation. In each country, legislation has been passed and governmental responsibility for implementing policies has been assumed. Foreign aid donors such as Australia and various NGOs support strategies aimed at eliminating gender discrimination. Yet laws work only if they are enforced, and policies require implementation to have an effect. In all three cases, enforcement and implementation thus far have been disappointing, with Papua New Guinea trailing Fiji and arguably Vanuatu in the strength and effectiveness of its response to gender violence. Since UN conventions are enforced through the 'due diligence' of states, this speaks to the relative ineffectualness of advocacy, prevention and law enforcement at all levels and both reflects and helps constitute the congenital weaknesses of the international human rights regime per se.

Conclusion

In the western Pacific, the international human rights regime—self-contradictory and reliant upon the actions and initiatives of postcolonial states that were liberated from various Euro-American colonial yokes mere decades ago—has had an unmistakable but regrettably still modest impact. Gender ideology there continues to support gender inequality, violence against women and girls being the most egregious manifestation of it. Also disturbing is the way in which modalities of gender violence now proliferate. Taylor and Araújo's chapter provides concrete evidence of this for Vanuatu. In Papua New Guinea, revenge for alleged sorcery attacks inspires diabolically innovative forms of gender violence, as the public immolation of Kepari Leniata graphically showed. Yet there have been victories for human rights in the last several decades, and the capacity for rights-based activism and transformation in the western Pacific has steadily increased, which several chapters concretely illustrate.

As a group, the contributors to this book are committed to understanding better the causes of, and remedies for, gender violence in the western Pacific. We proudly offer this volume as an exercise in engaged social science. But the volume also affords much to think about for the theoretically inclined. Two decades ago Arjun Appadurai wrote that 'the central problem of today's global interactions is the tension between cultural homogenization and cultural heterogenization'.[139] In the area of human rights, this is clearly still the case. Since the 1980s, the international human rights system, operating in tandem with national, regional and international entities, has waged a campaign to mitigate gender violence in the western Pacific. This campaign joins ex-colonial Northern and postcolonial Southern nations within a world of marked political and economic inequality, the history of which is rooted in colonialism and market penetration. As 'first world' meets 'third world' within the various sites of human rights advocacy and in the context of a history of uneven development, the dynamics of these global connections are the dynamics of globalisation per se. About these dynamics the chapters in this volume have a great deal to say.

---

139 Arjun Appadurai, 1996, *Modernity at Large: Cultural Dimensions of Globalization*, Minneapolis: University of Minnesota Press, p. 32.

Figure 1. Human rights activists request that Paiyam (or Porgera) Hospital be transferred to the state to lower the cost of health care for women and children in Porgera, Enga Province, PNG[140]

Source. Photographed by Aletta Biersack, Porgera, 12 June 2015

Figure 2. Porgera women throughout the valley convene by village to participate in this demonstration

Source. Photographed by Aletta Biersack, Porgera, 12 June 2015

---

140 Human rights activists requested the transfer to the state of Porgera (or Paiyam or Paiam) Hospital, which had been closed for a month due to insolvency. It was hoped that such a transfer would reopen the hospital and render it solvent and affordable to local clientele. The context for this sign was an event that took place on the old Porgera airstrip on 12 June 2015. The event was attended by throngs of women from the Porgera and Paiela valleys (Enga Province, PNG) and was unique in its attention to women's and children's medical care issues, which, as the sign indicates, were promoted in the name of human rights. In the postcolonial era, the old Porgera airstrip is the ultimate venue for discussing public affairs, and the keynote speaker at the event was the Member for Parliament Nixon Mangape. This and the venue itself signified the elevation in importance of women's issues and rights.

Acknowledgements

Gender Violence and Human Rights: Seeking Justice in Fiji, Papua New Guinea and Vanuatu began as the panel 'Gender Violence in Melanesia and Human Rights Discourse: Toward a Research Agenda' at the 2011 annual meeting of the American Anthropological Association in Montreal, Canada. The panel was co-organised by Aletta Biersack, Martha Macintyre and Margaret Jolly. Aletta Biersack would like to thank the Department of Anthropology, University of Oregon, for travel funds and the Center for the Study of Women in Society, University of Oregon, for a Travel Award to present a paper on this panel. The editors wish to thank Carolyn Brewer for her superb editorial support in the preparation of this volume for publication.

References

Addo, Michael K. 2010. *The Legal Nature of International Human Rights*. Leiden and Boston: Martinus Nijhoff Publishers.

Alston, Philip. 2005. 'The not-a-cat syndrome: Can the international human rights regime accommodate non-state actors?' In *Non-state Actors and Human Rights*, ed. Philip Alston, pp. 3–36. New York: Oxford University Press. Online: www.ivr.uzh.ch/institut smitglieder/kaufmann/archives/hs11/humanrights/03%20-%20 Not%20a%20Cat%20Syndrome.pdf (accessed 1 January 2016).

Alston, Philip (ed.). 2005. *Non-state Actors and Human Rights*. New York: Oxford University Press.

An-Na'im, Abdullahi Ahmed. 1992. 'Toward a cross-cultural approach to defining international standards of human rights: The meaning of cruel, inhuman, or degrading treatment or punishment'. In *Human Rights in Cross-Cultural Perspectives: A Quest for Consensus*, ed. Abdullahi Ahmed An Na'im, pp. 19–43. Philadelphia: University of Pennsylvania Press.

———. 2009. 'Toward a cross-cultural approach to defining international standards of human rights: The meaning of cruel, inhuman, or degrading treatment or punishment'. In *Human Rights: An Anthropological Reader*, ed. Mark Goodale, pp. 68–85. Malden, MA: Wiley-Blackwell.

Appadurai, Arjun. 1996. *Modernity at Large: Cultural Dimensions of Globalization*. Minneapolis: University of Minnesota Press.

Barker, Gary, Christine Ricardo and Marcos Nascimento. 2007. *Engaging Men and Boys in Changing Gender-Based Inequity in Health: Evidence from Programme Interventions*. World Health Organization: Geneva.

Bennett-Smith, Meredith. 2013. 'Accused "witch" Kepari Leniata burned alive by mob in Papua New Guinea'. *Huffington Post*, 7 February. Online: www.huffingtonpost.com/2013/02/07/kepari-leniata-young-mother-burned-alive-mob-sorcery-papua-new-guinea_n_2638431.html (accessed 29 December 2015).

Betteridge, Ashlee and Kamalini Lokuge. 2014. 'Combatting the family and sexual violence epidemic in Papua New Guinea: A submission to the inquiry of the Human Rights Subcommittee of the Foreign Affairs, Defence and Trade Joint Standing Committee into the human rights issues confronting women and girls in the Indian Ocean–Asia Pacific region'. Development Policy Centre, The Australian National University, May, pp. 8–9. Online: devpolicy.org/publications/submissions/Submission%20to%20Women%20and%20Girls%20Inquiry%20FINAL.pdf (accessed 1 January 2016).

Bunch, Charlotte. 1990. 'Women's rights as human rights: Toward a re-vision of human rights'. *Human Rights Quarterly* 12(4): 486–98. Online: www.jstor.org/stable/762496?seq=1#page_scan_tab_contents (accessed 7 November 2015).

Dinnen, Sinclair. 2003. 'Restorative justice in the Pacific Islands: An introduction'. In *A Kind of Mending: Restorative Justice in the Pacific Islands*, ed. Sinclair Dinnen with Anita Jowitt and Tess Newton Cain, pp. 1–34. Canberra: ANU Press. Online: press.anu.edu.au/titles/a-kind-of-mending/pdf-download/ (accessed 1 January 2016).

Dinnen, Sinclair with Anita Jowitt and Tess Newton Cain (eds). 2003. *A Kind of Mending: Restorative Justice in the Pacific Islands.* Online: press.anu.edu.au/titles/a-kind-of-mending/pdf-download/ (accessed 1 January 2016).

Donnelly, Jack. 1986. 'International human rights: A regime analysis'. *International Organization* 40(3): 599–642.

Errington, Frederick and Deborah Gewertz. 2005. 'On humiliation and class in contemporary Papua New Guinea'. In *The Making of Global and Local Modernities in Melanesia: Humiliation, Transformation and the Nature of Cultural Change*, ed. Joel Robbins and Holly Wardlow, pp. 163–70. Burlington, VT: Ashgate.

Eves, Richard. 2006. *Exploring the Role of Men and Masculinities in Papua New Guinea in the 21st Century: How to Address Violence in Ways that Generate Empowerment for Both Men and Women.* Online: xyonline.net/sites/default/files/Eves,%20Exploring%20 role%20of%20men%20PNG.pdf (accessed 16 November 2016).

——. 2010. 'Masculinity matters: Men, gender-based violence and the AIDS epidemic in Papua New Guinea'. In *Civic Insecurity: Law, Order and HIV in Papua New Guinea,* ed. Vicki Luker and Sinclair Dinnen, pp. 47–79. Studies in State and Society in the Pacific, no. 6. State, Society and Governance in Melanesia Program. Canberra: ANU E Press. Online: press.anu.edu.au/publications/ series/state-society-and-governance-melanesia/civic-insecurity (accessed 4 December 2014).

——. 2012. 'Resisting global AIDS knowledges: Born-again Christian narratives of the epidemic from Papua New Guinea'. *Medical Anthropology* 31(1): 61–76.

Farmer, Paul. 2004. 'An anthropology of structural violence'. *Current Anthropology* 45(3): 305–25.

George, Nicole. 2012. *Situating Women: Gender Politics and Circumstance in Fiji.* Canberra: ANU Press. Online: press.anu.edu. au/publications/situating-women (accessed 30 December 2015).

Gewertz, Deborah and Frederick Errington. 1999. *Emerging Class in Papua New Guinea: The Telling of Difference.* Cambridge: Cambridge University Press.

Glendon, Mary Ann. 2001. *A World Made New: Eleanor Roosevelt and the Universal Declaration of Human Rights*. New York: Random House.

Goldstein, Daniel M. 2013. 'Whose vernacular? Translating human rights in local contexts'. In *Human Rights at the Crossroads*, ed. Mark Goodale, pp. 111–21. New York: Oxford University Press.

Goodale, Mark. 2006. 'Toward a critical anthropology of human rights'. *Current Anthropology* 47(3): 485–511.

——. 2007. 'Introduction: Locating rights, envisioning law between the global and the local'. In *The Practice of Human Rights: Tracking Law Between the Global and the Local*, ed. Mark Goodale and Sally Engle Merry, pp. 1–38. Cambridge: Cambridge University Press.

——. 2009. 'Introduction: Human rights and anthropology'. In *Human Rights: An Anthropological Reader*, ed. Mark Goodale, pp. 1–19. Malden, MA and Oxford: Wiley-Blackwell.

——. 2009. *Surrendering to Utopia: An Anthropology of Human Rights*. Stanford: Stanford University Press.

——. 2013. 'Human rights *after* the post-cold war'. In *Human Rights at the Crossroads*, ed. Mark Goodale, pp. 1–28. New York: Oxford University Press.

Goodale, Mark (ed). 2006. *Anthropology and Human Rights in a New Key. American Anthropologist* 108(1): 1–83.

—— (ed.). 2009. *Human Rights: An Anthropological Reader*. Malden, MA and Oxford: Wiley-Blackwell.

—— (ed.). 2013. *Human Rights at the Crossroads*. New York: Oxford University Press.

Goodale, Mark and Sally Engle Merry (eds). 2007. *The Practice of Human Rights: Tracking Law Between the Global and the Local*. Cambridge: Cambridge University Press.

Hernandez-Truyol, Berta Esperanza (ed.). 2002. *Moral Imperialism: A Critical Anthology*. New York: New York University Press.

Hunt, Lynn. 2007. *Inventing Human Rights: A History*. New York and London: W.W. Norton & Company.

Kaldor, Mary. 2003. *Global Civil Society: An Answer to War*. Malden, MA: Polity Press.

Keck, Kathleen and Margaret Sikkink. 1998. *Activists Beyond Borders: Advocacy Networks in International Politics*. Ithaca: Cornell University Press.

Krook, Mona Lena and Jacqui True. 2012. 'Rethinking the life cycles of international norms: The United Nations and the global promotion of gender equality'. *European Journal of International Relations* 18(1): 103–27.

Leary, Virginia A. 1992. 'Postliberal strands in western human rights theory: Personalist-communitarian perspectives'. In *Human Rights in Cross-Cultural Perspectives: A Quest for Consensus*, ed. Abdullahi Ahmed An-Na'im, pp. 105–32. Philadelphia: University of Pennsylvania Press.

Levitt, Peggy and Sally Engle Merry. 2009. 'Vernacularization on the ground: Local uses of global women's rights in Peru, China, India and the United States'. *Global Networks* 9(4): 441–61.

Long, Norman. 1992. 'From paradigm lost to paradigm regained? The case for an actor-oriented sociology of development'. In *Battlefields of Knowledge: The Interlocking of Theory and Practice in Social Research and Development,* ed. Norman Long and Ann Long, pp. 16–43. London and New York: Routledge.

Long, Norman and Ann Long (eds). 1992. *Battlefields of Knowledge: The Interlocking of Theory and Practice in Social Research and Development*. London and New York: Routledge.

Macintyre, Martha. 2011. 'Money changes everything: Papua New Guinean women in a modern economy'. In *Managing Modernity in the Western Pacific,* ed. Mary Patterson and Martha Macintyre, pp. 90–120. St Lucia: University of Queensland Press.

McPherson, Naomi M. (ed.). 2016. *Missing the Mark? Women and the Millennium Development Goals in Africa and Oceania*. Bradford, Ontario: Demeter Press.

Médecins Sans Frontières (MSF). 2016. 'Return to abuser: Gaps in services and a failure to protect survivors of family and sexual violence in Papua New Guinea'. Online: www.msf.org.au/sites/default/files/attachments/msf-pngreport-def-lrsingle.pdf (accessed 16 November 2016).

Merry, Sally Engle. 2003. 'Human rights law and the demonization of culture (and anthropology along the way)'. *PoLAR* 26(1): 55–76.

———. 2004. 'Tensions between global law and local social justice: CEDAW and the problem of rape in Fiji'. Paper delivered at the Justice Across Cultures Conference, Brandeis, March. Online: www. brandeis.edu/ethics/pdfs/internationaljustice/otheractivities/JAC_Merry.pdf (accessed 31 December 2015).

———. 2006. 'Transnational human rights and local activism: Mapping the middle'. In *Anthropology and Human Rights in a New Key*, ed. Mark Goodale. *American Anthropologist* 108(1): 38–51.

———. 2006. *Human Rights and Gender Violence: Translating International Law into Local Justice*. Chicago and London: University of Chicago Press.

———. 2009. *Gender Violence: A Cultural Perspective*. Chichester: Wiley-Blackwell.

Mutua, Makau Wa. 1996. 'The ideology of human rights'. *Virginia Journal of International Law* 36: 589–657. Online: www.google.com/#q=The+Ideology+of+Human+Rights+%2B+Makau+Wa+Mutua (accessed 11 June 2016).

———. 2002. *Human Rights: A Political and Cultural Critique*. Philadelphia: University of Pennsylvania Press.

Nussbaum, Martha. 2000. *Women and Human Development: The Capabilities Approach*. Cambridge: Cambridge University Press.

'Pakistani activist Malala Yousafzai among winners of 2013 UN Human Rights Prize'. 2013. *UN News Centre*, 5 December. Online: www.un.org/apps/news/story.asp?NewsID=46668#.Uua9M_bTlNY (accessed 30 January 2016).

Patterson, Mary and Martha Macintyre (eds). 2011. *Managing Modernity in the Western Pacific*. St Lucia: University of Queensland Press.

Preis, Ann-Belinda S. 2009. 'Human rights as cultural practice: An anthropological critique'. In *Human Rights: An Anthropological Reader,* ed. Mark Goodale, pp. 332–55. Oxford: Wiley-Blackwell. First published in 1996, *Human Rights Quarterly* 18(2): 286–315.

Riles, Annelise. 2000. 'The virtual sociality of rights: The case of "women's rights are human rights"'. *Northwestern University School of Law, Public Law and Legal Theory Papers*, 40: 1–37. Online: law. bepress.com/nwwps-plltp/art40 (accessed 21 March 2016).

Robbins, Joel and Holly Wardlow (eds). 2005. *The Making of Global and Local Modernities in Melanesia: Humiliation, Transformation and the Nature of Cultural Change*. Burlington, VT: Ashgate.

Sen, Amartya. 1999. *Development as Freedom*. Oxford: Oxford University Press.

———. 2004. 'Elements of a theory of human rights'. *Philosophy and Public Affairs* 32(4): 315–56. Online: www.mit.edu/~shaslang/ mprg/asenETHR.pdf (accessed 31 January 2016).

Sengupta, Somini. 2015. 'U.N. reveals "alarmingly high" levels of violence against women'. *New York Times*, 9 March. Online: www. nytimes.com/2015/03/10/world/un-finds-alarmingly-high-levels-of-violence-against-women.html (accessed 29 December 2015).

'Shot Pakistan schoolgirl Malala Yousafzai addresses UN'. 2013. *BBC News Asia*. 12 July. Online: www.bbc.co.uk/news/world-asia-23282662 (accessed 30 January 2016).

Siegel, Matt. 2013. 'Papua New Guinea acts to repeal sorcery law after strife'. *New York Times*, 29 May. Online: www.nytimes. com/2013/05/30/world/asia/papua-new-guinea-moves-to-repeal-sorcery-act.html (accessed 29 December 2015).

Speed, Shannon. 2008. *Rights in Rebellion: Indigenous Struggle and Human Rights in Chiapas*. Stanford: Stanford University Press.

Stop Sorcery Violence Papua New Guinea website. Online: www. stopsorceryviolence.org (accessed 30 December 2015).

Strathern, Marilyn. 1999. *Property, Substance, and Effect: Anthropological Essays on Persons and Things*. London: Athlone Press.

Sweetman, Caroline (ed.). 2001. *Men's Involvement in Gender and Development Policy and Practice: Beyond Rhetoric*. London: Oxfam. Online: policy-practice.oxfam.org.uk/publications/mens-involvement-in-gender-and-development-policy-and-practice-beyond-rhetoric-121177 (accessed 1 January 2016).

Taylor, John P. 2008. 'The social life of rights: "Gender antagonism", modernity and *raet* in Vanuatu'. In *Changing Pacific Masculinities: The 'Problem' of Men*, ed. John P. Taylor. Special issue of *The Australian Journal of Anthropology* 19(2): 165–78.

Tor, Roselyn and Anthea Teka. 2004. *Gender, Kastom & Domestic Violence: A Research on the Historical Trend, Extent and Impact of Domestic Violence in Vanuatu*. Port Vila: Department of Women's Affairs, Republic of Vanuatu.

Tsing, Anna Lowenhaupt. 2004. *Friction: An Ethnography of Global Connection*. Princeton: Princeton University Press.

'UN urges Papua New Guinea to take action after woman burned alive for witchcraft'. 2013. *UN News Centre*, 8 February. Online: www.un.org/apps/news/story.asp?NewsID=44096#.VJOFp8BAeA (accessed 29 December 2015).

Wardlow, Holly. 2006. *Wayward Women: Sexuality and Agency in a New Guinea Society*. Berkeley: University of California Press.

Zimmer-Tamakoshi, Laura. 2001 [1997]. '"Wild pigs and dog men": Rape and domestic violence as "women's issues" in Papua New Guinea'. In *Gender in Cross-Cultural Perspective*, third edition, ed. Caroline B. Brettel and Carolyn F. Sargent, pp. 565–80. Englewood Cliffs, NJ: Prentice-Hall.

United Nations Documents

Convention on the Elimination of All Forms of Discrimination against Women (CEDAW). 1979. Online: www.un.org/womenwatch/daw/cedaw/cedaw.htm (accessed 30 December 2015).

Convention on the Rights of the Child (CRC). 1989. Online: www.ohchr.org/en/professionalinterest/pages/crc.aspx (accessed 12 June 2016).

Declaration on the Elimination of Violence against Women. 1993. A/RES/48/104. Online: www.un.org/documents/ga/res/48/a48r104.htm (accessed 30 December 2015).

Declaration on the Rights of Indigenous Peoples. 2008. March. A/61/L.67 and Add.1. Online: www.un.org/esa/socdev/unpfii/documents/DRIPS_en.pdf (accessed 31 January 2016).

Division for the Advancement of Women. 2004. *The Role of Men and Boys in Achieving Gender Equality*. Final Report of the Expert Group Meeting, Brasilia, Brazil, 21–24 October 2003. New York: UNDAW.

International Covenant on Civil and Political Rights. 1966. Online: www.ohchr.org/en/professionalinterest/pages/ccpr.aspx (accessed 8 May 2016).

Office of the High Commissioner. 1989. Convention on the Rights of the Child, G.A Res. 44/25. Online: www.ohchr.org/en/professionalinterest/pages/crc.aspx (accessed 18 April 2016).

Transforming our world: The 2030 agenda for sustainable development. 2015. *Sustainable Development Knowledge Platform*. A/RES/70/1, item 8. Online: sustainabledevelopment.un.org/post2015/transformingourworld (accessed 7 February 2016).

United Nations Entity for Gender Equality and the Empowerment of Women. 2000–2009. 1979. Convention on the Elimination of All Forms of Discrimination against Women (CEDAW). Online: www.un.org/womenwatch/daw/cedaw/cedaw.htm (accessed 30 December 2015).

Universal Declaration of Human Rights, G.A. Res. 271A(III), U.N. GAOR, 3d Sess., U.N. Doc. A/810 (1948). Online: www.un.org/en/universal-declaration-human-rights/ (accessed 18 April 2016).

1

Villages, Violence and Atonement in Fiji

Lynda Newland

University of the South Pacific, University of Western Australia and University of St Andrews

Over the last 10 years or so, Violence Against Women (VAW) and gender violence more generally have been conceptualised as major obstacles to development insofar as they increase healthcare costs and reduce productivity.[1] The types of violence these terms most commonly refer to are domestic violence between spouses and other intimate partners, rape, sexual assault and child sexual abuse in which men are overwhelmingly the perpetrators and women and girls are overwhelmingly the victims and/or survivors.

---

[1] While the term 'gender-based violence' (GBV) may be used to broaden understandings of violence to include women's violence against men, it is not always used this way. For instance, a recommendation made to the CEDAW committee defines GBV as 'violence that is directed against a woman because she is a woman or that affects women disproportionately'. See Sally Engle Merry, 2006, *Human Rights and Gender Violence: Translating International Law into Local Justice*, Chicago and London: University of Chicago Press, pp. 76–77.

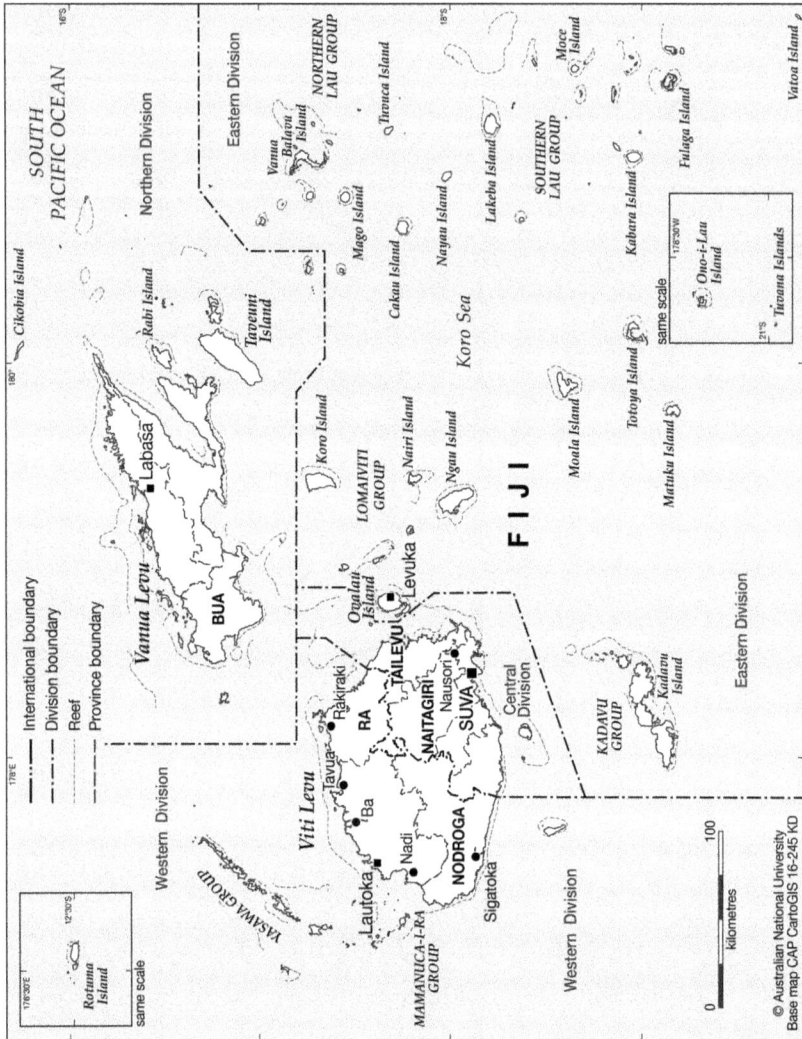

Map 2. Fiji
Source. © The Australian National University. Base Map. CartoGIS ANU 16-245 KD

In the Pacific, and in Melanesia in particular, VAW is considered severe and pervasive. A survey undertaken by the Fiji Women's Crisis Centre (FWCC) in 1999 found that 66 per cent of the 1,575 women surveyed had been physically abused by partners,[2] which suggests that roughly two-thirds of the women in Fiji can expect violence in the domestic sphere at some time during their lives. In cases of rape and child sexual abuse, statistics indicate that 70 per cent of rape victims knew their perpetrators, and in 'cases of sexual abuse against children, 94 per cent of perpetrators were known to the victim. Of these, fathers, stepfathers and grandfathers made up around 32 per cent of the perpetrators.'[3] Although responses from government, non-governmental organisations (NGOs), and churches have been immensely important in enabling girls and women to find help escaping violent relationships or coping with violent situations, my research shows that in Fiji the building of refuges and safe houses in urban centres has limited effectiveness. Often women and girls do not know about this accommodation and, even when they do, it often does not—and cannot—meet the needs of the victim, or of the community.

At the international level, cultural practices such as female circumcision, child marriage and the *iTaukei*[4] practice of atonement (*bulubulu*)[5] are viewed as oppressive to women to the extent that governments have come under pressure to outlaw such practices. With regard to

---

2   Australian Aid (AusAID) Office of Development Effectiveness, 2008, *Violence Against Women in Melanesia and East Timor: Building on Global and Promising Approaches*, Canberra: Commonwealth of Australia, pp. 9, 151; cf. Nicole George, '"Lost in translation": Gender violence, human rights and women's capabilities in Fiji', this volume.

3   United Nations Population Fund (UNFPA) Pacific Sub Regional Office, 2008, *An Assessment on the State of Violence Against Women in Fiji*. Suva: UNFPA, p. 18.

4   *ITaukei* is the most recent term used to denote the indigenous people of Fiji, once known as Fijians. On 30 June 2010, the Cabinet approved the Fijian Affairs [Amendment] Decree, which shifted the meaning of the word 'Fijian' from a race to a nationality. Since the Decree, the people once known as Fijians have been renamed as *iTaukei* or 'land owners'. See Ministry of *iTaukei* Affairs, 2010, '*ITaukei* now replaces Fijian and indigenous Fijian', Internal Circular (signed by Meli Bainimarama, Permanent Secretary for *iTaukei* Affairs), 16 July. In this paper, I follow the more recent usage for consistency, except when I use quotes from interviews conducted in 2009, the year before the Decree, where I have retained the old usage of the word 'Fijian', which refers to the indigenous people only. For an analysis of this shift, see Lynda Newland, 2013, 'Imagining nationhood: Narratives of belonging and the question of a Christian state in Fiji', in *State, Society and Religion in the Asia-Pacific Region*, ed. Sven Schottman and Monika Winarnita, pp. 1–15, Special issue of *Global Change, Peace and Security*.

5   *Bulubulu* is the Bauan or standard Fijian. In other regions, it may be known by the word *soro* (the term used by George, this volume).

the *bulubulu*, the committee formed to enforce the Convention on the Elimination of All Forms of Discrimination against Women (CEDAW) has called for the elimination of the ritual. By contrast, Sally Engle Merry argues that the *bulubulu* has been adapted in such a way that it now supports the victim,[6] and suggests that the performance of the ritual 'is increasingly rare even in the villages'.[7] However, my own research suggests that the *bulubulu* remains deeply problematic in this context because its objectives are fundamentally different from those intended in human rights discourse and because for the most part it continues to prioritise male relationships rather than justice for the victim.

Fiji has two major and very distinct communities, the *iTaukei* and the Indo-Fijian community, together with a small minority formed from Chinese, Koreans, Australians and others.[8] In most parts of Fiji, the two main communities have retained very separate identities: living in different areas, holding different religious beliefs, marrying endogamously, and regarding each other as distinct. Although violence against women is prevalent in both communities, results from fieldwork suggest that it often occurs in ethnically distinct ways.[9] While this article is based on research in both communities, I limit my discussion here to the *iTaukei* (who practise the *bulubulu*).

---

6   Sally Engle Merry, 2004, 'Tensions between global law and local social justice: CEDAW and the problem of rape in Fiji', paper given at the Justice Across Cultures Conference, Waltham, MA: Brandeis University, March, p. 9.

7   Merry, *Human Rights and Gender Violence*, p. 121.

8   According to the 2007 Census, *iTaukei* number 475,739 or 57 per cent of the total population, and Indo-Fijians number 313,798 or 37 per cent. The remaining 6 per cent is comprised of a mixture of ethnicities, including Korean, Chinese, and a loose category that, until recently, was officially cast as 'European'. See Fiji Islands Bureau of Statistics 2007, Population by Race, Gender, Marital Status and Province of Enumeration, Fiji. The term 'Indo-Fijian' is an ethnic category to describe the descendants of Indian indentured labourers and free settlers and tends to be used by academics at the University of the South Pacific seeking to promote multiracialism. Outside the university, the term 'Indian' is still popular, although, by rights, Indo-Fijians can call themselves 'Fijians' under the most recent legislation. See Ministry of *iTaukei* Affairs, '*ITaukei* now replaces Fijian and indigenous Fijian'.

9   For instance, stereotypes depict *iTaukei* men as using their fists and Indian men as using knives. Often violence does seem to proceed in this way—but not always. While I focus on *iTaukei* here, more research needs to be done on high-profile cases of Indian men from Fiji murdering their wives and children, often as migrants in neighbouring countries like Australia and New Zealand, but also in Fiji. In the Indian community, violence against wives and girls is also said to come from mothers-in-law. This issue is clearly not covered in prevailing approaches to VAW in the region and needs more detailed study.

I conducted research on women's crisis accommodation[10] for a consultancy in 2009.[11] In the course of this project, I trained three local female research assistants: a Rotuman in administration and an *iTaukei* and an Indo-Fijian as interviewers. Over a period of about three months, we interviewed a wide range of people working on VAW, including police, referral agencies, caretakers of crisis accommodation, and some of the women who used their services in Suva, Tavua and Rakiraki. We travelled into *iTaukei* villages and Indo-Fijian settlements in both urban and rural areas of Viti Levu, Vanua Levu and Kadavu, holding focus groups or *talanoa* sessions (discussions around the kava bowl) with both men and women. In all, we spoke to around 244 people, approximately 141 of whom were *iTaukei*. The results of our research suggest that much of the violence in *iTaukei* villages continues to go unreported, whether it occurs in the villages and settlements of urban or rural areas across the Fijian archipelago.

As just over half the *iTaukei* population lives in the rural sector—264,235 as opposed to 211,504 in urban areas[12]—this kind of research is not an easy undertaking. Travelling between and within islands and into the interior of the main islands is expensive and involves organisation. Before entering a village, visitors must acquire permission either through someone related to that village or through government channels. On arrival, the visitor must have an appropriate representative to present the *yaqona* (kava or Piper methysticum) and conduct a *sevusevu* ceremony to introduce the researcher and the project to the chief and the village, which is often followed by a protracted session of *yaqona* drinking. Such protocol prevents informal or unscheduled visits and requires more planning than most researchers have the time and resources to do. Yet without it, researchers will not have access to more than half of the *iTaukei* population.

---

10   I use the term 'crisis accommodation' to gloss shelters and refuges. The idea of a shelter or refuge is not widely understood in Fiji. Crisis accommodation was the term that came closest and was more readily understood, although people sometimes assumed we were referring to the places that people living in low-lying areas moved to during flood warnings.

11   I conducted this consultancy while working at the University of the South Pacific. In all, I lived and worked in Fiji for a total of nine years and therefore was interpreting my findings in relation to long-term experience in Fiji.

12   Fiji Islands Bureau of Statistics, 2007 Census of Population. Further, *iTaukei* men outnumber *iTaukei* women in every province except Rewa and Naitasiri. See Fiji Islands Bureau of Statistics, 2007 Census of Population.

In this chapter, I focus on three main areas of VAW: domestic violence (particularly husbands' violence against wives), rape and child sexual abuse (which often includes rape—or 'defilement' in police terminology). After describing the contemporary institutional network that supports victims of VAW, I analyse under-reporting in relation to village values such as *vakaturaga* and village-based responses such as the *bulubulu*, through which perpetrators atone for their actions. In evaluating men's views of spousal violence, local conceptions of community in *iTaukei* communities in Fiji, and the effectiveness of urban responses, some of the contributing factors to this violence become apparent. These include men's expected status in the household and the community, practices around *yaqona* consumption, family obligations and feuds, and the introduction of easily accessible pornography. I note that, in most areas of Fiji, *iTaukei* values motivate a focus on maintaining village harmony between men, not on reparations for the victim.

At the international level, the CEDAW Committee, which reviews all reports filed by countries that have ratified CEDAW, has condemned the practice of the *bulubulu* as deleterious to the rights of women. Merry critiques the CEDAW Committee's views, arguing that they have not understood the breadth of contexts the *bulubulu* is used in, and that they have assumed that culture does not change. She further argues that the *bulubulu* has been adapted in the victim's favour,[13] a point I strongly question on the basis of my own research. First, however, I review the institutions currently responding to VAW.

Response to gender violence: The Fiji context

In Fiji, there are already a number of organisations that work with victims of gender violence. The most well-known and best funded is the Fiji Women's Crisis Centre (FWCC), which is focused on supporting women and girls surviving gender violence through counselling, and which also engages in research, advocacy, community education and the development of a regional network of gender violence activists.

---

13   Merry, 'Tensions between global law and local social justice'; Merry, *Human Rights and Gender Violence*.

Another NGO, the Pacific Counselling and Social Services (PC&SS), also offers counselling services. Government agencies involved with helping victims of violence and sexual abuse are the Women's Department; the Social Welfare Department; St Giles Mental Hospital, run by the Ministry of Health; and the police, who have set up the Sexual Offences Unit. In addition, while most churches in Fiji are very conservative about women's roles in the family, their leaders are often the first people to whom women turn for advice.

Religious organisations are important in this field because they manage almost all the existing crisis accommodation. All but two in Fiji are Christian. The Salvation Army runs two girls' homes and the Family Care Homes in Suva, Lautoka and Labasa for women and children who have survived violence or poverty or who have been evicted from their homes. The Methodist Church and the Anglican Church run orphanages in Suva, and the Assemblies of God manages a home for orphans in Nadi, all of which sometimes house children who have faced sexual abuse. A Christian organisation called Homes of Hope is set up to accommodate sexually exploited women and their young children. Another Christian organisation, The Good Neighbour International, has rooms for girls who arrive in Suva from rural areas looking for work. Housing destitute men and women, the HART Homes were built by an NGO on behalf of the World Council of Churches. The Society of Saint Vincent de Paul runs a home that takes in mentally ill, crippled, blind and destitute men and women who have nowhere else to go. The Ark of Hope is a faith-based home for street kids, the homeless, and anyone else who walks into the compound needing shelter. There are also two non-Christian shelters: Darul Iqamah, which is a home run by the Muslim Women's League for poverty-stricken women and children, and Clopcott Home, which was originally set up by the Social Welfare Department but which was later transferred to a voluntary committee. Last, although not technically a home, St Giles, a psychiatric hospital in Suva, takes in abused women and girls who have been abandoned on its doorstep.[14]

---

14   In 2009, the Anglican Church was planning to open the House of Sera, a counselling centre, with the possibility of expanding it to a halfway house. The FWCC was also exploring the possibility of opening a secular and feminist refuge. Lastly, since the project, there has been a discussion about opening a safe house in Kadavu. Another option of last resort is to billet the child or woman out to a family. Sometimes, young perpetrators must also be billeted for their own safety.

Until just over a decade ago, almost all the programs were focused on counselling female victims and very little was done by way of prevention. In 2002, the FWCC began to run a male advocacy program in Vanua Levu, encouraging men to become positive role models in their communities. At the request of village elders in Ba, Tavua and Rakiraki, male advocacy programs have since been implemented on the main island of Viti Levu.[15] Another initiative has been set up by the Department of Women, which launched its pilot program for establishing Zero Tolerance Violence Free communities in 2008.[16] However, the funding for this project is minimal, which means that not as much has been achieved in these communities as was hoped.

In 1995, the police set up the Sexual Offences Unit (SOU) with branches in the Suva area and in Labasa specifically charged with managing sexual assault more effectively. In regard to the law, a 'no drop' policy, in which police became duty-bound to prosecute reported domestic violence cases, was put in place in 1998. Eleven years later, in November 2009, the military government implemented the Domestic Violence Decree, giving the police and courts extensive powers to prevent perpetrators from continuing to assault their victims.[17] Despite these initiatives and responses aimed at alleviating VAW, male violence against women and girls remains a part of everyday life in much of Fiji.

Maintaining the peace through atonement: *Vakaturaga* and the *bulubulu*

ITaukei villages are, in many ways, strongly bounded entities, which in most parts of Fiji maintain hierarchies based on submission to the chief. Asesela Ravuvu, for instance, notes that the 'most important and commonly used term for ideal behaviour is *vakaturaga*', a word literally meaning 'in the way of the chief' but which also refers

---

15   Margaret Wise, 2010, 'Men learn to respect women', *Fiji Times Online*, 27 May.
16   CEDAW, Committee on the Elimination of Discrimination against Women, 2008, Consideration of reports submitted by States parties under article 18 of the Convention on the Elimination of All Forms of Discrimination against Women. Combined second, third and fourth periodic reports of States parties, Fiji. CEDAW/C/FJI/2-4.
17   'Family violence to become a criminal offence', 2009, *Fiji Times Online*, 4 August.

to behaviour that 'befits the presence of a chief'.[18] 'An individual who is labeled *vakaturaga* in his behaviour knows his place in the society and complies unquestioningly with his various traditionally defined obligations and responsibilities.'[19] Although leaders are also expected to behave towards others in this way, the values of *vakaturaga* sustain a male hierarchy in which subordinate men (and women) are expected to obey the chiefs, who are considered to represent God's order. It is a hierarchy in which, as a former President of the Methodist Church of Fiji put it, 'The word "spoken" (authority) and the word "heard" (land, people) essentially belong together'.[20] Women are among those expected to listen silently rather than speak because women are not usually considered to be representatives at any level, a view that is supported in the teachings of a majority of the Christian churches in Fiji.[21]

The values of *vakaturaga* are embedded within broader ideas about *matanitu* (the chiefly system), *lotu* (Christianity, usually Methodism) and *vanua*, which is usually glossed as 'community' or 'land and people', but which also connotes the connection between the living and the ancestors and, through that, connection with one another.[22] Maintaining these values requires a strong sense of communalism, often represented by conformity, reciprocity and obligation. If they are breached, it may be deemed necessary to perform a *bulubulu*, a term that means the burial of a wrong through a collective apology and atonement. Usually, the offender brings an offering to the family or village that has been offended as compensation and to improve relationships between offending and offended groups, whether families or villages. For important matters between villages, *bulubulu* offerings will include *tabua* (a whale's tooth, which holds significant cultural and economic value). For less important matters, gifts of kerosene and cigarettes may be enough to heal the breach.

---

18   Asesela D. Ravuvu, 1983, *Vaka iTaukei: The Fijian Way of Life*, Suva: Institute of Pacific Studies, University of the South Pacific, p. 103.

19   Ibid.; cf. Karen Brison, 2001, 'Crafting socio-centric selves in religious discourse in rural Fiji', *Ethos* 29(4): 453–74, p. 454.

20   I.S. Tuwere, 2002, *Vanua: Towards a Fijian Theology of Place*, Suva: Institute of Pacific Studies, University of the South Pacific, and College of St John the Evangelist, p. 73.

21   Lynda Newland, 2006, 'Fiji', in *Globalisation and the Re-Shaping of Christianity in the Pacific Islands*, ed. Manfred Ernst, pp. 317–89. Suva: The Pacific Theological College.

22   Winston Halapua, 2003, *Tradition, Lotu and Militarism in Fiji*, Lautoka: Fiji Institute of Applied Studies.

Christianity and colonialism have radically changed the shape of marriage and family forms and augmented husbands' control over wives. Missionaries transformed *iTaukei* social arrangements. Polygyny gave way to monogamy, men's houses gave way to nuclear family households, and a focus on brother–sister ties shifted to a focus on conjugal bonds.[23] In the early colonial period of the 1880s, the newly formed *Bose Vakaturaga* (Council of Chiefs) made decisions that eroded women's position in decision-making, curbed their freedom to drink *yaqona* and expropriated their rights to land. Because women of the time were freely wandering and refusing to marry, their movement was restricted to their villages unless they could show good reason to move beyond the village.[24] In villages today the husband's control over the wife as head of the household is socially sanctioned by both the village hierarchy and the church. Marriages tend to be virilocal, further limiting the support a woman might garner from her kin to gain influence in her marriage. Although expectations about gender roles are changing as villagers are exposed to other ideas during their visits to urban centres, in many places such changes have been strongly resisted.

When it comes to cases of domestic violence, people are reluctant to interfere in actual fights because this can cause wider problems within the community. Ideally intervention is only done by close relatives. After the argument has finished, the man's parents may advise the couple about how to deal with the problem. If the matter is serious and the dispute is prolonged, it may be referred to the police but police action is often limited for a variety of reasons. For example, police in Kadavu say that it can be difficult for them to intervene because they are required first to receive permission from the *turaga ni koro* (village head) to enter the village concerned, and then to participate in the *sevusevu* ritual described earlier. However, such conditions are not enforced across Fiji. For example, police in Vanua Levu are not expected to follow protocol when they are charging offenders.

Whether the perpetrator of physical violence is a husband or father, the victim is frequently blamed by both men and women for not having given the perpetrator enough respect. A male respondent from

---

23   Asesela D. Ravuvu, 1987, *The Fijian Ethos*, Suva: Institute of Pacific Studies, University of the South Pacific.
24   Robert Nicole, 2006, *Disturbing History: Resistance in Early Colonial Fiji, 1874–1914*, Honolulu: University of Hawai'i Press.

a village in western Viti Levu said that if the violence got worse and the woman died, that was just the way it was; men should always have the dominant place in the household. Ra informants said that they were told in church that women have to listen to men because men are the heads of the household: 'Man represents God in the family.' Near Suva, informants explained that women are beaten when they have overstepped 'their female boundaries' or gender role expectations.

In Methodist villages, domestic violence between husband and wife is often viewed as a problem for the church, to be addressed by the *talatala* or lay preachers. It is considered discourteous to be direct about this kind of problem, and the *talatala* will in all likelihood not talk about the domestic violence directly but preach instead about the religious aspect of marriage and the values underlying *iTaukei* protocol, such as the respect a wife needs to have for her husband. *Talatala* tend to concentrate on reconciling the couple and are very unlikely to involve the police.

Another option is to go to the *turaga ni koro* or village head. *Talanoa* (focus group) participants in Kadavu described how problems are usually taken to the *turaga ni koro* and *talatala* together, who counsel the couple together. The *talatala* tends to talk about the spiritual aspect of marriage, and the *turaga ni koro* tends to talk about the laws of the village. As the island of Kadavu is at some distance from the urban communities in Viti Levu, the laws affirmed there are not necessarily those of the Constitution (which, at any rate, was abrogated in 2009, re-written in 2012, and revised again by the military government in 2013) but those considered to belong to the traditions that support the ideal of *vakaturaga* and that place a premium on local harmony and on upholding the village's reputation.

It is only if the *talatala* and the *turaga ni koro* cannot solve the problem that the police are contacted. In Viti Levu, a *turaga ni koro* explained that he aims to keep the family intact by holding weekly meetings, but he goes to the police if it becomes too difficult (although none of the villagers interviewed had actually witnessed this occurring). In some instances, the victim goes directly to the police, but, rather than laying charges, the police may advise the victim to return to the *turaga ni koro* to solve the problem with him instead, contravening the 'no drop' policy in favour of prioritising local relationships with men who are acknowledged as having legitimate and direct authority in the community. One village head claimed that this has been effective in solving disputes and in bringing peace and harmony to the village. Another said that the best prevention against violence was to tell the couple that they would end up in prison alone. If a girl is raped, this same village chief told my assistants that he talks to the boy and his parents, which generally results in the couple being married. A third told us:

> One time a girl who got married into this village came running to me because her husband had punched her up. I hid her to keep her safe and waited for the husband's anger to cool down. When he came to his senses, I went to him and told him how he had badly frightened his wife. At the same time, I kindly asked him why he did this. Finally, I gave him some fatherly advice and told him that what he did was wrong.

These responses show that, while the *turaga ni koro* might be considered to be in an ideal position to mediate, the overarching principles for many village heads are not about notions of justice with regard to individual acts of violence or even about protection of the victim but about village harmony. How a village head manages this is up to his (and it is almost always 'his') discretion; and the quality of the mediation is dependent on his personal traits and biases and his relationships with each party and with the village as a whole. However, with some good management skills, *turaga ni koro* can reduce conflict across the village. For example, because over-consumption of *yaqona* is often considered a cause of domestic arguments,[25] curfews and bans on *yaqona* drinking can be enacted at village meetings. In one Kadavu village, the curfew is imposed from 10 p.m. on every night, although its success remains unclear.

Instead of reporting violence to the police, many *iTaukei* women and girls resort to accepted tactics. A wife facing repeated and/or severe domestic violence is expected to find sanctuary at a brother's, father's or other close relative's house. The husband will then be compelled

---

25   After drinking a large amount of *yaqona*, the drinker experiences a relaxing, even sedating effect and, while allegedly thinking more lucidly, may experience an inability to speak and to walk. Like alcohol, *yaqona* in small quantities is said to heighten sex-drive, but in great quantities nullifies the ability to perform. Although the drink is considered calming while being consumed, the after-effects include heightened sensitivity to light and sound and bad temper. Another aspect of *yaqona* consumption that creates domestic conflict is the time spent consuming it, as men can spend long hours on most evenings drinking with other men.

to make amends to the woman's family by taking an offering such as kerosene or a whale's tooth. A man in a *talanoa* session in Kadavu described the process in the following way:

> Over here, women know what to do, where to go. They usually run off to their brothers and then wait for the *bulubulu* and get back together again [jokes about coming and going] but at times we just call and ask them to come back. If a woman runs off to her parents, we take kerosene to ask her to come back. Her mother at this time usually tells us to love one another. Parents say to the husband, 'Take her [laughter], accept the *bulubulu*', and say to the girl, 'it was your decision to marry him'.

Although the woman's return to her brother's household or to her natal household gives her family an opportunity to intervene and mediate, the pressure is often on the father or brother to accept the husband's and husband's family's attempt to atone, especially if the offering is a *tabua* or whale's tooth. However, when asked what men would do if a daughter arrived with a bruised face as a result of domestic violence, some men insisted that they would not accept the *bulubulu* offering, either because husbands frequently turn up with very little or because accepting it could lead to problems later. If it is accepted, the wife must return to the husband, and she often appears to do this willingly. An oft-cited reason was that women must go back for the children's sake, and in some areas they are faced with having to leave the children with their father if they do not return to him. In some villages, the wife is not asked whether or not she is ready to reconcile but is expected to accept the *bulubulu* offering because the husband arrives with his *vanua* (community) and the recipient *vanua* feels obliged to maintain the relationship between the villages.[26]

---

26   It is likely that many of these cases never go through the court system. Customarily, women are considered to be responsible for relationships, whether affinal or consanguineal, and therefore are vulnerable to being blamed for their failure. Children are expected to stay with their father and/or his parents in order to enable them to claim their land and village rights. When such cases do reach court, if the husband divorces the wife because of her adultery, he is likely to be awarded custody of children; but in other circumstances women may have a better chance of retaining custody. See P. Imrana Jalal, 2001, 'Ethnic and cultural issues in determining family disputes in Pacific Island courts', Paper given at the 17th LAWASIA Biennial Conference, Christchurch: New Zealand Family Law Section Conference, September.

In effect, as Pauline McKenzie Aucoin argues, 'the rituals assuage tension without actually challenging or eliminating its sociological source'.[27]

In addition to the widely varying responses of *turaga ni koro*, there are still very strong sanctions against women or girls reporting rape and abuse, as it can exacerbate an already difficult situation within the family and bring shame to both the girl and her family. Victims of rape are frequently assumed to have enticed the rapist, and victims of violence and especially sexual violence are vulnerable to being blamed and resented for bringing shame upon their family. The conventional view is that a girl's future is ruined within the social group, but she is able to rebuild her life by moving to Suva or overseas and is likely to leave any children with her parents. Gang rape can indicate an ongoing feud between families; and incidents involving the rape of very young girls were explained in terms of past conflicts both within families and within communities, as episodes in family or community feuds.[28]

In some villages, the victim is expected to report the rape; but, in others, it is the father's role, which limits the likelihood of the matter going beyond the family because of the expectation that fathers exemplify the values of *vakaturaga* and maintain village order. Some respondents discussed an awareness of the media, noting that if the father was implicated, the women would approach the police and the Department of Social Welfare and then call the immediate families together in case the media becomes involved. As in many societies, the wider kin group's honour is affected by rape and child sexual abuse, especially if it is reported in the national media.

In another instance that occurred 16 years ago in a settlement near Suva, a girl was raped by her cousin; but when her mother took her for medical treatment, her father went to the police and told them to dismiss the case because the boy was his sister's son. This left the mother completely shattered. The fact that the boy was a cousin did not sanction the violence in any way, but it did make it very delicate

---

27   Pauline McKenzie Aucoin, 1990, 'Domestic violence and social relations of conflict in Fiji', *Pacific Studies* 13(3): 23–42, p. 37.

28   Family feuding is a delicate area that should be better investigated. A high-profile case concerning the rape of a young girl in primary school toilets in Suva a few years ago was briefly alleged by the media to be one such case. Unfortunately, this mention was so brief that I have not been able to find the source of this allegation.

because he was a close relative. However, the mother's mental state affected the community in such a way that it could not be ignored. The villagers asked if they could revive the case and bring the boy to justice, so that the girl's mother could get better. The male's offence continued to severely affect close family relationships, and he was eventually charged and imprisoned because of it.

In relation to child sexual abuse, a community in Ra, northern Viti Levu, went so far as to say that tradition was the line that stood between them and the law because when a *bulubulu* was held it was felt there was no longer any need to report the incident to the police. For example, one boy impregnated his 16-year-old cousin, but the girl's family did not feel they were able to report it after his family performed the *bulubulu*. The participants from the settlement near Suva responded in a similar fashion when a physically disabled young girl was raped by a close relative and had two children by him. There was not much reaction from the community or family because the traditional atonement ceremonies had been performed and the gifts (*tabua, yaqona* and kerosene drums) had been presented to the girl's family.

Here, the tension between trying to maintain harmony within the family through the *bulubulu* ceremony and the women's views regarding the sexual exploitation of a young girl is explicit. Women see the value of harmony between men and their clans but do not necessarily accept that this should replace justice through the court system. The *iTaukei* women with whom we talked expressed the view that the *bulubulu* does not solve the problem but prevents them from accessing the services of the law. The fact that many women desire this to change is borne out by the fact that in places like Kadavu women are turning up in ever higher numbers at police stations, despite significant pressure to resolve matters at the village level.

If the crime is reported, negative repercussions can continue for the girl after the perpetrator has been charged, because the rape becomes public knowledge. We were told that in a village in Vanua Levu, 'a 14-year-old was gang raped by adult men in a Fijian community, some of them married with children. The family suffered. The girl was left sitting alone, even in church; no one talked to her.' The parents sought assistance from the Department of Social Welfare to get her a room at a shelter but were refused because the perpetrators were not family members.[29] Eventually, she was accommodated in a hostel.

However, depending on the outlook of the village, a lone rapist or paedophile is not necessarily going to get off lightly. Participants from one village in Kadavu said that they took perpetrators to the police to protect them from the relatives of the victim. In this case, gender violence could well lead to further rifts between families and violence between men. On the other hand, perpetrators are known to develop tricks of their own. In one instance, an old man had been charged with molestation but every time the court case was called, he became seriously ill.

In this way, in much of Fiji, the *bulubulu* continues to be used for incidents of domestic violence and also for rape and child sexual abuse. The ritual is not intended to offer justice or to protect the victim but to maintain village harmony by containing feuding, and it tends to do this at the expense of the victim. In the discussions about the *bulubulu* that my research assistants and I had with men and women in villages across Fiji, it was clear that women had little influence over the *bulubulu* because there was no space in which their views had credence. Yet, while the importance of male harmony is evident to women, many do not accept its consequences in matters of gender violence.

However, while the villages are, by and large, very conservative in the way they manage gender violence, many of the sessions in the communities we visited would finish with men and women asking for advice on what to do when confronted with the scenarios we raised with them, where they could get help, and what kinds of programs were available. Our discussions were often the first occasions on which they had discussed these issues, and it was clear that they were interested in learning about alternatives that could further enhance relationships between men and women within the village.

---

29   Children are directed to homes through the Department of Social Welfare. They are not removed from their families unless they are considered to be at risk directly from family members. It is testament to the rigidity of institutional requirements that no place could be found for this girl because she was at risk not from her family but from the wider village.

Notions of community and gender hierarchy

Yaqona ceremonies are classically staged around the *tanoa* or kava bowl within the village hall, around which men sit according to their importance. Unless they have an important title of their own, the women of the village are usually seated at the rear of the hall, behind the men. The sequence in which men speak and *yaqona* is offered reflects the accepted public hierarchy, which constantly shifts according to contestations between and among men. For these reasons, men can be very competitive about issues of rank.[30] I have experienced the display of hierarchy many times in *yaqona* ceremonies, observing the attentiveness of men in arranging guests to receive *yaqona*, according to their perceived importance. In some villages everybody may eventually drink, but in others *yaqona* drinking is limited to men.

Notions of the husband's dominance over the wife as being part of the natural order of things are widespread in Fiji, but villages in the southeastern seaboard of Viti Levu—particularly from Bau northward to Tailevu, inland toward Naitasiri and westward towards Nadroga—are known to be very conservative about gender issues. Women in these areas are usually included in the formal line of guests and receive *yaqona* only if they are from chiefly families or if they have educational and institutional affiliations, but they will be served only a small cup of *yaqona* and may not be served at all. The rules regarding drinking order are more relaxed in other areas of Fiji, but the same principle of male-centredness applies.[31] Women do have important roles in many communities, ones that are often conceptualised in terms of being keepers of kinship pathways, remembering and keeping active the web of relationships they were born and married into through the

---

30   Karen Brison reports that in Rakiraki women also compete over rank, arguing over whether the status of their natal village or their husband's status is to be acknowledged. Karen Brison, 2001, 'Constructing identity through ceremonial language in Fiji', *Ethnology* 40(4): 309–27.
31   For example, Christina Toren, 1994, 'All things go in pairs or the sharks will bite: The antithetical nature of Fijian chieftainship', *Oceania* 64(3): 197–216, for Gau; Brison, 'Constructing identity through ceremonial language in Fiji', for Rakiraki; and Ravuvu, *The Fijian Ethos*, for the Wainimala Valley. S.G. Aporosa emphasises the relationship between *yaqona* drinking and masculinity for young male teachers. S.G. Aporosa, 'Yaqona and education in Fiji: A clash of cultures?' MA thesis, Palmerston North: Massey University, 2006.

exchange of women's valuables such as mats.[32] However, in everyday social hierarchies, in which formal village decision-making takes place, women take a back seat to men.

Another aspect of gender conservatism found in villages is expressed through clothing. Dressing inappropriately for village life is said to be one of the causes of gender violence. In almost all villages, everyone is obliged to follow a dress code. No commoner is permitted to wear a hat and sunglasses as this is perceived to be acting as if above the chief. The dress code is especially strict for women, who are expected to wear a *sulu* (a sarong covering the legs) and to cover their shoulders, especially in the meeting hall. In some areas, village heads may insist that women obey a 'traditional' dress code, which requires wearing a *sulu-jaba* (a long skirt and short-sleeved top, usually in bright floral designs and with varying degrees of trim) and a hairstyle called the *buiniga* (*iTaukei* equivalent of an 'Afro'). Girls are not allowed to wear pants in the village because they blur very clear gender distinctions. This gender hierarchy is also expressed spatially in both the village hall and private homes. Women are expected to sit on the side that is, figuratively speaking, 'below' the male side.[33]

In her study of a Ba village in western Viti Levu, Aucoin records that a husband has authority over his wife (although opposite-sexed cross-cousins tend to treat each other as equals).[34] Christina Toren, in her study of village life in Gau, takes these claims a step further, noting that cross-cousins, once married, cease to be equal:

> It is axiomatic that a wife is subordinate to her husband, so when cross-cousins marry (by definition one always marries a cross-cousin) their equal relation becomes a hierarchical one. This shift is evident in betrothal and marriage ceremonies and further established, at least in part, by the young man's periodic violence towards his wife. Not *all* young married men beat their wives, but violence does seem to characterise the early years of marriage and is attributed by both women and men to male sexual jealousy.[35]

---

32 Jacqueline Ryle, 2010, *My God, My Land: Interwoven Paths of Christianity and Tradition in Fiji*, Farnham: Ashgate.

33 Cf. Christina Toren, 1995, 'Cosmogonic aspects of desire and compassion in Fiji', in *Cosmos and Society in Oceania*, ed. Daniel de Coppet and André Itéanu, pp. 57–82, Oxford and Herndon: Berg, p. 59.

34 Aucoin, 'Domestic violence and social relations of conflict in Fiji'.

35 Toren, 'Cosmogonic aspects of desire and compassion in Fiji', p. 58.

Cross-cousin marriage is not practised in areas such as northern Vanua Levu,[36] but husbandly authority is the ideal as elsewhere in Fiji.

Many female respondents in our *talanoa* or focus-group sessions recognised that issues of hierarchy, power and control in the household underlie much of the violence against both wives and daughters or step-daughters. They noted that men tend to assume they can make decisions without consulting their wives, and tend to see women who are the main income-earners as challenging their status. One respondent expressed it this way: 'In Fijian custom, men have to be superior. Women who earn more will always tell their husbands what to do. Women should obey their husbands.' According to *talanoa* participants, domestic violence occurs when women do not listen to their husbands or do what the husbands want. For instance, if the wife converts to another church, this is likely to cause tension because it flouts the husband's authority as well as that of the chief's—given that conversion may involve a renunciation of major village practices.[37] On their part, women do convert to incoming churches, sometimes as a way of asserting themselves in the household, particularly with regard to *yaqona* consumption.[38]

As previously mentioned, extended sessions of *yaqona* drinking often lead to marital disputes. From both this and previous research conducted in *iTaukei* communities, from listening to student responses in class discussions, and from witnessing neighbours' fights while living in Suva, a few very common scenarios in which domestic violence occurs in relation to *yaqona* consumption are worth mentioning:

> **Scenario 1:** Arriving home late from a *yaqona* session, the husband finds his wife has fallen asleep. There is no dinner ready. He becomes enraged.

> **Scenario 2:** The wife wakes early in the morning to discover her husband still asleep. She is worried about the state of the gardens and whether there is enough to eat in the house. She wakes him, and they fight.

36 Personal communication, Akanisi Tarabe, 30 October 2012.
37 Conversion to Pentecostal churches usually entails giving up *yaqona* drinking, because it is seen as idolatry, linking the chief with the ancestors. However, the symbolism of *yaqona* consumption is also enmeshed with concepts of *vanua* (land and community) and chiefly power, both temporal and cosmological. To refuse to drink an offering of *yaqona* is to insult the chief and the community. For more detail, see Lynda Newland, 2004, 'Turning the spirits into witchcraft: Pentecostalism in Fijian villages', *Oceania* 75(1): 1–18.
38 Newland, 'Turning the spirits into witchcraft'.

> **Scenario 3:** A male student from Vanua Levu pointed out that it can
> be reversed: the wife might drink too much *yaqona*. The man arrives
> home to a dirty house, which also causes conflict.

Although the third scenario reflects a situation where the gender
expectations in drinking *yaqona* are reversed, the husband exerts
his authority as head of the house in all of these cases. Because the
husband is asserting his culturally sanctioned authority, a certain
level of domestic violence is deemed acceptable, just as a father is
considered to have the authority to discipline his children.

As discussed earlier, the wife may escape her husband's violence
by moving to her father's or brother's house (which is likely to be
in another village) until the husband comes to conduct the *bulubulu*.
This strategy brings domestic conflicts into the open, but the pressure
is clearly on the woman's family to accept the husband's gesture
without necessarily addressing the root causes of the conflict. Aimed
at restoring harmony and preventing further feuding between
male members of the community, the ritual does not seek justice or
reparation for the victim. Further, although women may be invited to
discuss their problems at village meetings, the presence of the chief
and the *talatala* (lay preacher) mark the gathering as formal and male-
centred territory. In these gatherings, women's views are secondary
to those of men, making it very difficult for women to speak about
domestic violence because, as listeners, they are not credited with any
authoritative place from which to speak. Women's informal access to
chiefs is more dependent upon the circumstances, including their own
village position relative to their husband's and the chief's openness
to such approaches.

In one village, a group of relatively well-educated women took some
time to open up and speak about the violence they had witnessed
in other families and the tensions they experienced on a daily basis
in their own relationships. Their experiences indicated that *yaqona*
caused many conflicts and that, when the men were home, they
'growled' at their families and ordered them around. One woman
noted, 'Only the mouth and stick will be talking'. Yet they also
acknowledged that women participate in the perpetuation of violence
in families by beating their children: 'You pass on what has been done
to you—women to girls also.' A woman spoke of how her mother-in-
law had beaten her husband and his sister when they were young and

how the sister had once fainted from '10 sticks'. In turn, her husband was now beating their children. Associating this kind of violence with sickness and early death, the woman asked, 'With all those bruises, where does the dead blood go?'[39]

When we held focus groups with women, whether in Kadavu or Vanua Levu, they confessed they had never discussed these topics, even among themselves. Yet, despite their lack of access to advice and support, women in Vanua Levu insisted that the *bulubulu* should not be allowed to substitute for justice, especially in cases of molestation. Moreover, once the concept of crisis accommodation, safe houses, shelters, and refuges was explained to them, most *iTaukei* women viewed the idea of building one of these in the locality as a positive step because it offered both the possibility of a place of safety and healing and a signal to men that violence would not be tolerated. This, they hoped, would change men's perspective on their treatment of women.

Child sexual abuse

The question of child sexual abuse was still more daunting to approach and, in our fleeting visits to the communities, we could not address this directly. However, at least three different contexts of child sexual abuse were reported to us: teenage experimentation, involving male sexual abuse of younger sisters; sexual abuse between an adult male and a young girl (often a daughter or step-daughter), which perpetrators tended to justify in terms of being in a romantic relationship with the victim; and sexual abuse between an adult male and a young girl (a step-daughter or girl of the extended family), justified in terms of the perpetrator's resentment at having to feed children from his wife's former husband or husbands or the children of other close relatives.[40]

---

39 This comment appears to be referring to the idea that dead blood accumulates as a result of bruising, which was at the base of 19th-century notions of bloodletting and which was probably introduced by missionaries and early colonists. Personal communication, Martha Macintyre, August 2012.
40 Unfortunately, some of this information was gathered from workers in the field who did not always differentiate *iTaukei* from Indo-Fijian responses. Likewise, in mixed groups, most responses were recorded anonymously, and therefore it is not always possible to cleanly separate out *iTaukei* data from Indian data. Clearly, long-term research on the differences between the two communities needs to be conducted.

All of these instances suggest the idea that men are considered not only the heads of households but the owners of the bodies within it. This has been vividly portrayed in another recent study:

> We learned of a Fijian girl who had been sexually abused by her uncle. Her uncle and aunt were acting as her caregivers while her parents were living in the village. There were other female family members living in the house at the time. When it was discovered that this girl had been sexually abused by her uncle, the other female members also admitted that they had been sexually abused by their uncle as well. Upon questioning the uncle, he said that he sexually abused the girls because he was fed up with looking after his relatives' children. He had abused his nieces in the hope that it would deter his relatives from sending their children to live with him and his family.[41]

Here, sexual abuse is intended to be a form of communication of anger directed at other adults. As one caretaker noted, 'There are a lot of people who have had several marriages in a row and children in each marriage. Both Fijians and Indo-Fijians might have two or three marriages. The women say openly that they don't want to bring up the man's other children. Men won't say it openly. Instead, they abuse them.'

Another factor that appears to be exacerbating child sexual abuse is the increasing availability of pornography through DVDs downloaded from the internet and sold for FJ$1 as well as imagery uploaded onto mobile telephones. Observing an increasing trend of sexual abuse occurring between relatives, a policewoman told us: 'We had a case where a 14-year-old boy was the perpetrator. I asked him why he committed the offence, and he said, "I was watching blue movies at my uncle's house and became aroused." Four boys raped a girl. During our investigation I checked their mobile phones and saw graphic images of nude women.' Media seem to have added to an already potent mix of values and ideas about gender relations, especially as pornography is not simply about sex but is also about power relations between men and women, where women are, on the whole, devalued as sexualised objects subject for the male gaze and grasp. Thus, pornography gives impetus to the notion that men have a right of access to women's and girls' bodies for their own sexual satisfaction, even if taken violently.

---

41   Regional Rights Resource Team, 2006, *Child Sexual Abuse and Commercial Sexual Exploitation of Children in the Pacific: A Regional Report*, Suva, p. 83.

Combined with frustration, boredom and peer pressure, pornography sends the message that sex is one of the ways boys can continue to express their dominance over girls.

The limits of urban responses to gender violence

Throughout our study, it was clear that the idea of a women's refuge or shelter was a new concept to many and a very alien one, particularly in *iTaukei* villages. A representative of the Department of Women in Suva echoed this, when she said, 'The truth is that a lot of people are ignorant and don't know about it. I can't emphasise that enough!' While most people we asked responded to the terms 'refuge' and 'shelter' with incomprehension, they thought of crisis accommodation as accommodation for flood victims, the poor and orphans. Many suggested that women and girls needed to reconcile with their families, using the extended family, the police, religious help and counselling, and Social Welfare Department. They were unaware of the work of the FWCC and crisis accommodation in helping women and girls escape violence. Even in Suva, women's religious organisations that were predominantly *iTaukei* did not necessarily know about the existence of such accommodation.

Of those who knew about it, the most crucial issue was access. Since nearly all the accommodation is located in the Suva/Nausori region, many knew that they would have to relocate in order to use it, which would entail cutting themselves off from their families, communities and workplaces. For women and girls living, working and/or attending school outside Suva, accepting referral to accommodation in Suva is difficult because of the distance they have to commute. The situation is only more difficult for those living outside regional centres like Labasa in Vanua Levu. According to the Social Welfare officer in Bua, girls are only sent to Labasa if there is a risk of abuse at home. Returning home after a court case can create unbearable tensions in a small community. Yet, family members find it too expensive to travel to Labasa and therefore are inhibited from visiting girls who have been referred there. Once in Labasa, there is only one formal home, and the only alternative is to send women and girls to Suva, which also comes at high cost. In one example recounted by a counsellor, a 13-year-old was sexually assaulted and impregnated by the uncle's father's brother:

> She was taken to the Salvation Army for a few days and then sent to Suva crisis accommodation, where she gave birth. She had to give birth alone in Suva while her mother was here because her mother could not afford to [join her in Suva for the birth]. A girl needs her mother when she is giving birth.

As one Social Welfare officer in Labasa put it, 'Putting children in Suva is *not* strengthening family well-being'.

Despite the distances, the demand for crisis accommodation services is high, and chances are that facilities are full. While a vast amount of aid is spent on gender violence, very little of it finds its way to crisis accommodation. The accommodation cannot cater to special needs, and the caretakers who manage the accommodation are often not trained social workers and face burnout. A respondent from the Assemblies of God in Suva summed up the situation by saying, '[The caretakers at the accommodation] have the heart to take them in but are facing many constraints, like finances, lack of space, and resources'. These factors often lead referral organisations to intensify their efforts to locate immediate or extended family members or friends who can accommodate the victim. More often than not, the referral agencies will use crisis accommodation as a last resort, when all other options have been exhausted.

While the preference for community-based resolutions stems from practicalities (Suva may be a long way away, there may be a waiting period to get accepted into crisis accommodation, etc.), it also reflects community family ideals stipulating that, in the case of domestic violence, husband and wife should be reconciled, but, if this is impossible, a wife should return to her natal family. Thus, respondents noted that, although crisis accommodation was important for the safety of women and girls, it might also encourage marriage breakups or the victim becoming a wanton. For instance, a representative from the Methodist Church's Women's Department in Suva claimed, 'I think there is [both] a good [side] and a bad side to crisis accommodation. It helps resolve the problem, but sometimes some victims are just to blame. They want to be on their own and will still give way to worldly lust', suggesting that accommodation facilitates women to become prostitutes. Likewise, an informant in Tavua said, 'Women over 18 years may be put in a home or refuge, but at that age, they can be tempted to go astray and do things that are against the principles of refuges'. For these respondents, the order in the villages enforces morality and sexual constraint, the very basis of communal sociality.[42]

As children facing problems are expected to live with the grandparents or aunts, the view that crisis accommodation was a dumping ground for unwanted children and especially handicapped children, street kids and single parents was relatively widespread. As one informant saw it, 'Most of the people are villagers and they come from close-knit communities. They might think that the victim's family has neglected her if she is placed in a refuge.'

If women and girls are seen as morally wayward when they stay in crisis accommodation institutions, they are doubly stigmatised if they end up being patients in St Giles Hospital, because mental illness is strongly stigmatised (although a number of campaigns in the last several years are beginning to change this). The Superintendent at St Giles, Dr Shishram Narayan, explained that women run away from home and walk into the hospital or are dropped off, some without any mental illness but with nowhere else to go. 'We stabilise them and have to send them home. They have lots of relapses. Some would like to come out of that environment but there is no place to go. It's a big problem.' Sometimes *iTaukei* women arrive with bruises and black eyes or with their hair ripped out in an exorcism.[43] They are given medication so they become docile and their families are given advice, and then they are released. Others are elderly women who have become difficult to care for at home. Dr Narayan continued, 'It's mostly women, married women. It used to be the Indian community. Now, it's the Fijian community as well.'

---

42 This may also reflect the desperate straits that some women find themselves in, if they are accepted in long-term accommodation.

43 More research is needed on exorcisms in both *iTaukei* and Indian communities.

The normalisation of violence and the question of representation

While international aid is being channelled into particular urban organisations with some success, the focus on male behaviour, and the inclusion of men in the process of combatting gender violence in the villages, has been too recent to show any major change in community attitudes toward gender violence. Although there is no doubt that boys and men are almost always the perpetrators of gender violence, these forms of violence exist in a wider field of violence that includes male-to-male violence, female-to-female violence, and female-to-male violence. For instance, until recently, punishment of children has been heavy-handed, with stories such as: a child hospitalised with *sasak* broom spines in her skin and eventually dying,[44] teachers admonishing a teenage girl for not showing enough respect to the father who was severely beating her, teachers beating students (and when this has been made illegal, a concerted call to the Constitution Commission in 2012 to bring back corporal punishment), and males describing how they were hung up in sacks as a form of discipline when they were children. A psychology student at the University of the South Pacific wrote her master's thesis on her experience as a nurse dealing with men who were too ashamed to admit they had been abused by women.[45] Given that these kinds of violence seem to have been uncommented upon until recently, this wider field clearly needs to be addressed.[46]

With regards to violence against women, *iTaukei* women and girls do have the option of going to a relative's house and waiting for the *bulubulu*. Yet, because women and girls have little say in the outcome, international women's rights groups such as the CEDAW Committee have called for its elimination. Merry critiques this position, noting its role in preventing male conflict from escalating. She argues that the *bulubulu* should not be used in rape cases, but neither should the practice be eliminated because the structure of the ritual has wider

---

44   In this case, the perpetrator had not been identified but because a *sasak* broom is closely associated with women's domesticity, the perpetrator was assumed to be a female relative.
45   Akisi Kasami, 2010, 'Spouse abuse by women: The hidden side of domestic violence in Fiji'. MA thesis. Suva: University of the South Pacific.
46   Periodically there are projects addressing different aspects of these behaviours. For instance, there was an advertising campaign running on television raising awareness of bullying in 2012.

cultural applications than its responses to rape.[47] However, from a couple of limited examples, Merry then infers that communities are changing and the practice of the *bulubulu* 'has begun to shift from a practice that focuses on preventing vengeance between clans to one that supports a victim and holds the offender accountable'[48] and that the ritual is 'adapting to a more gender equal, urban society'.[49]

It is clear that the gift-giving and male oratory at the base of the *bulubulu* recurs throughout *iTaukei* ritual, but Merry has greatly overstated the case for the *bulubulu* being redesigned to support the victim. In my research, many respondents—mostly men—showed resistance to changing attitudes towards gender violence because it would undermine concepts of gender hierarchy: specifically the idea that men are household heads who have authority over their families (although sometimes the same men would consider our questions seriously later in the discussion). Village communities (in which more than half of *iTaukei* still live) continue to be strong, relatively bounded and, in many areas, very patriarchal. As shown in this research, the *bulubulu* is not, as Merry describes it, 'increasingly rare even in villages'.[50] Nor is it a local arrangement that 'can promote human rights and social justice'[51] because it is directed to fundamentally different ends—namely, negotiating relationships between men as heads of clans and households. Moreover, it is clear that the victim continues to have very little say over the outcome.

As Merry intimates, the judgements of the CEDAW Committee are likely to appear neocolonial to many *iTaukei*—and particularly those in conservative areas—but it is also clear from women's responses to

---

47   Merry, 'Tensions between global law and local social justice'; Merry, *Human Rights and Gender Violence*.
48   Merry, 'Tensions between global law and local social justice', p. 9.
49   Merry, *Human Rights and Gender Violence*, p. 130. In her book *Human Rights and Gender Violence*, there is an odd disjunction in Merry's argument. On the one hand, she argues that the use of the *bulubulu* for rape cases appeared at the time when a chauvinistic ethno-nationalism was at its strongest, in the 1987 coups. On the other, she argues that the CEDAW Committee uses the word 'culture' in such a way that they do not acknowledge cultural change, and proposes that the *bulubulu* has adapted in such a way that it reflects a more gender-equal society. See Merry, *Human Rights and Gender Violence*, pp. 125–30. Yet, a significant gap remains in her explanation about how and when the *bulubulu* changed from being a tool of ethno-nationalism to a ritual that supports women. At this point, Merry underestimates the broad support among the *iTaukei* for values that are often attributed only to the most vocal ethno-nationalists. See Newland, 'Imagining nationhood'.
50   Merry, *Human Rights and Gender Violence*, p. 121.
51   Ibid., p. 104.

our questions that many women would like to see other options emerge that would support them in regard to the gender violence occurring in villages. At the same time, because men play a central role in leading villages and church groups and therefore in managing conflict, they must be included in discussions and processes that might lead to change. Without them, it is unclear how deep structural change could possibly occur.

As elsewhere in the world, conservative church leaders are often in opposition to women's rights groups, arguing that they are against God and against culture; but some church leaders are more moderate, having experienced the violence in villages or watched their female kin experience it and thus understand the need for change. In our study, some women went so far as to use their religion to confront gender violence. For example, women in a settlement near Suva noted:

> Because of this culture, women are abused and men have their way in the family. Because of the cultural structure, men have the right to beat up women. Through religion, these women have found the courage and strength to overcome their violent situation. People should be encouraged to spend time with the family to break the cultural values that cause this problem.

Statements like this show very clearly the need to involve the churches.

Despite the fact that Christianity is a very strong part of *iTaukei* life, many organisations devoted to mitigating gender violence and its effects have been reluctant to become involved with the churches. Yet nearly all of the crisis accommodation is funded by them. Existing crisis accommodation faces enormous challenges as they are run on shoestring budgets, have no facilities at all for the disabled, and only two have the expertise to care for those in psychological trauma. Moreover, in almost all the villages we visited, women and girls did not know that crisis accommodation was available. While a number of urban-based support services now exist, our study shows that women and girls in the villages were not receiving any information about them. In the words of one gender violence activist:

> Stakeholders are working separately instead of together … there is a need for more training brought to the village level. In the past, there was a tendency to bring representatives [out of the villages] to a program [in the urban areas]. The representatives were women

who, when they got back to their community, found they didn't have the weight to make much difference. If the program is conducted at the village level, you can affect the whole village.

Toward the end of our *talanoa* sessions, both male and female participants were asking for anger-management programs to be brought to their villages. Women responded particularly passionately:

> There should be anger management courses conducted in the village. They should start from Bua because mothers and children died in their own houses there. Have one in Bua, Macuata, Cakaudrove, Savusavu, Nabouwalu, and Labasa. The women want this kind of workshop because domestic violence is happening in their village and surrounding community. They also want to target newly married couples in the village so that problems that cause domestic violence can be resolved at the beginning. Some of the women need to be trained and work in a committee to help resolve these issues.

Such programs are unlikely to resolve tensions resulting from the structure of *iTaukei* village life, but the fact that both women and men were asking about them suggests that some men are open to enabling change, and village chiefs can be primary motivators. Indeed, some *turaga ni koro* in our study asked to be trained in marriage counselling, feeling that it would make them better leaders when faced with tensions in the villages. A respondent from the Department of Women in Labasa noted similar responses coming from chiefs of villages participating in the Zero Tolerance Violence Free Community campaign:

> When we first started with the Zero Tolerance initiatives, there was resistance from men. As we kept pushing, men began to agree that violence is not acceptable. Men are coming forward for training. In one instance, a woman was killed. Two months later, the *turaga ni koro* requested training. The challenge now is to get people to embrace it and internalise it and act on it.

Since this research was completed, chiefs such as Roko Tui Aca Mataitini from Cakaudrove in Vanua Levu have been very vocal about their support of the Zero Tolerance initiative, banning violence against women and children and accepting women's participation in discussions in their villages.[52] More recently, the Methodist Church

---

52 Serafina Silaitoga, 2011, 'No violence', *Fiji Times Online*, 1 December.

of Fiji, which is well-known for its conservative ideas about the family, has posted an article on their blog affirming their commitment to addressing abuse and violence, particularly towards children.[53] While gender violence remains endemic in Fiji, there is evidently cause for hope.

Acknowledgements

This research was undertaken while I was working at the University of the South Pacific in Fiji. Thank you to my three assistants, Makereta Mu'a, Maraia Likuvono and Sunita Sunder, who were pivotal to its success. A *vinaka vakalevu sara* must also go to all those who participated in this study, who did their best to respond to our questions on what were often taboo subjects. Thanks to the staff in the School of Social Sciences at the University of Adelaide, who gave me feedback on an earlier version of this chapter and to the editors who helped me shape the direction of my argument. Thank you also to the University of Western Australia for an Honorary Fellowship.

References

Aporosa, S.G. 2006. 'Yaqona and education in Fiji: A clash of cultures?' MA thesis, Palmerston North: Massey University.

Aucoin, Pauline McKenzie. 1990. 'Domestic violence and social relations of conflict in Fiji'. *Pacific Studies* 13(3): 23–42.

Australian Aid (AusAID) Office of Development Effectiveness. 2008. *Violence Against Women in Melanesia and East Timor: Building on Global and Regional Promising Approaches*. Report prepared by the Office of Development Effectiveness. Online: aid. dfat.gov.au/Publications/Pages/4140_9790_4186_8749_8769.aspx (site discontinued).

Brison, Karen. 2001. 'Constructing identity through ceremonial language in Fiji'. *Ethnology* 40(4): 309–27.

---

53   Methodist Church in Fiji, 2015, 'Methodist Church is committed to addressing abuse and violence in the family', 6 February.

———. 2001. 'Crafting socio-centric selves in religious discourse in rural Fiji'. *Ethos* 29(4): 453–74.

CEDAW. 2008. Committee on the Elimination of Discrimination against Women. Consideration of reports submitted by States parties under article 18 of the Convention on the Elimination of All Forms of Discrimination against Women. Combined second, third and fourth periodic reports of States parties, Fiji. CEDAW/C/FJI/2-4. Online: www.bayefsky.com//reports/fiji_cedaw_c_fiji_2_4_2008.pdf (accessed 20 November 2014).

'Family violence to become a criminal offence'. 2009. *Fiji Times Online*, 4 August. Online: www.fijitimes.com/story.aspx?id=126736 (site discontinued).

Fiji Islands Bureau of Statistics. *2007 Census of Population, Fiji*. Online: www.statsfiji.gov.fj/index.php/2007-census-of-population (accessed 28 November 2014).

Halapua, Winston. 2003. *Tradition, Lotu and Militarism in Fiji*. Lautoka: Fiji Institute of Applied Studies.

Jalal, P. Imrana. 2001. 'Ethnic and cultural issues in determining family disputes in Pacific Island courts'. Paper given at the 17th LAWASIA Biennial Conference, Christchurch: New Zealand Family Law Section Conference, September.

Kasami, Akisi. 2010. 'Spouse abuse by women: The hidden side of domestic violence in Fiji'. MA thesis. Suva: University of the South Pacific.

Merry, Sally Engle. 2004. 'Tensions between global law and local social justice: CEDAW and the problem of rape in Fiji'. Paper delivered at the Justice Across Cultures Conference, Brandeis, March. Online: www.brandeis.edu/ethics/pdfs/internationaljustice/otheractivities/JAC_Merry.pdf (accessed 29 October 2014).

———. 2006. *Human Rights and Gender Violence: Translating International Law into Local Justice*. Chicago: Chicago University Press.

Methodist Church in Fiji. 2015. 'Methodist Church is committed to addressing abuse and violence in the family', 6 February. Online: methodistfiji.blogspot.co.uk/search?updated-max=2015-02-11T17:23:00%2B12:00&max-results=7 (accessed 26 January 2016).

Ministry of *iTaukei* Affairs. 2010. '*ITaukei* now replaces Fijian and indigenous Fijian'. Internal Circular (signed by Meli Bainimarama, Permanent Secretary for *iTaukei* Affairs), 16 July.

Newland, Lynda. 2004. 'Turning the spirits into witchcraft: Pentecostalism in Fijian villages'. *Oceania* 75(1): 1–18.

———. 2006. 'Fiji'. In *Globalisation and the Re-Shaping of Christianity in the Pacific Islands*, ed. Manfred Ernst, pp. 317–89. Suva: The Pacific Theological College.

———. 2013. 'Imagining nationhood: Narratives of belonging and the question of a Christian state in Fiji'. In *State, Society and Religion in the Asia-Pacific Region*, ed. Sven Schottman and Monika Winarnita, pp. 1–15. Special issue of *Global Change, Peace and Security*. Online: dx.doi.org/10.1080/14781158.2013.784247 (accessed 30 October 2014).

Nicole, Robert. 2006. *Disturbing History: Resistance in Early Colonial Fiji, 1874–1914*. Honolulu: University of Hawai'i Press.

Ravuvu, Asesela D. 1983. *Vaka iTaukei: The Fijian Way of Life*. Suva: Institute of Pacific Studies, University of the South Pacific.

———. 1987. *The Fijian Ethos*. Suva: Institute of Pacific Studies, University of the South Pacific.

Regional Rights Resource Team. 2006. *Child Sexual Abuse and Commercial Sexual Exploitation of Children in the Pacific: A Regional Report*. Suva: UNICEF.

Ryle, Jacqueline. 2010. *My God, My Land: Interwoven Paths of Christianity and Tradition in Fiji*. Farnham: Ashgate.

Silaitoga, Serafina. 2011. 'No violence'. *Fiji Times Online*, 1 December. Online: www.fijitimes.com/story.aspx?id=187276 (site discontinued).

Toren, Christina. 1994. 'All things go in pairs or the sharks will bite: The antithetical nature of Fijian chieftainship'. *Oceania* 64(3): 197–216.

———. 1995. 'Cosmogonic aspects of desire and compassion in Fiji'. In *Cosmos and Society in Oceania*, ed. Daniel de Coppet and André Itéanu, pp. 57–82. Oxford and Herndon: Berg.

Tuwere, I.S. 2002. *Vanua: Towards a Fijian Theology of Place*. Suva: Institute of Pacific Studies, University of the South Pacific, and College of St John the Evangelist.

United Nations Population Fund (UNFPA) Pacific Sub Regional Office. 2008. *An Assessment on the State of Violence Against Women in Fiji*. Suva: UNFPA.

Wise, Margaret. 2010. 'Men learn to respect women'. *Fiji Times Online*, 27 May. Online: www.fijitimes.com/story.aspx?id=147297 (site discontinued).

2

'Lost in Translation': Gender Violence, Human Rights and Women's Capabilities in Fiji

Nicole George

University of Queensland

Gender advocates working to eliminate gender violence in Fiji navigate a difficult path. They regularly decry the pernicious presence of this violence as a violation of women's internationally recognised right to physical security. Yet they do so in an environment constrained by state authoritarianism, militarism, and communal division.[1] This requires them to adopt a cautious political stand. Processes of 'human rights translation' have taken on a profound importance in these circumstances. Much of this work is framed by the idea that Fiji's women are the twin victims of violence *and* a culture that ordains this violence. Activists confront the allegation that there is an incompatibility between local cultural affiliations and rights-based

---

1   This chapter was substantially written prior to the 2014 elections which saw Fiji return to democratic rule, although it has been updated to take account of current events. It is important to recognise that continuities in the gendered exercise of political power persist in Fiji even in the wake of the 2014 election. This event did not produce a dramatic shift in Fiji's political leadership or upset the more general tendency towards authoritarian government in this context. Most of the most influential leaders of the post-coup military government were returned to power and, consequently, current government policy on gender is largely a continuation of the programs developed by the military government since 2006. The analysis presented here remains highly pertinent to the post-2014 context.

universals in Pacific societies through acts of rights 'translation'.[2] These challenge homogenised and static representations of culture, and instead open the way for women's place in culture to be understood in more open, contested and rights-accommodating terms.[3]

These rights translation strategies evince an important political creativity that is much celebrated in the region. They have also resulted in some success at the level of state policy and law making. But these political gains have not been matched by any practical abatement in levels of gender violence according to available statistics (see next section for current figures).[4] This suggests that human rights translation strategies, on their own, may not be enough to apprehend the pervasive gender violence that persists in this context. In this chapter, I examine the limitations of the human rights approach to gender advocacy with the aim of exposing what gets 'lost' or obscured by this political strategy. More particularly, I show that while extensive efforts put into the translation of human rights tend to emphasise cultural 'fit', this strategy detracts attention from the structural factors, political and economic, that diminish women's ability to realise their human right to physical security.

I defend this view by referring to the capabilities framework advocated by Amartya Sen[5] and Martha Nussbaum[6] and later works examining how this framework is pertinent to the issue of violence against women. Building on ideas that emphasise the relationship between women's functioning, their capabilities, and their ability to 'secure' human rights in practical terms,[7] I examine the impact of increasing levels of militarisation and authoritarianism in Fiji and post-coup trajectories of economic development to show how questions about women's political and economic standing are vital to debates

---

2   Sally Engle Merry, 2006, 'Transnational human rights and local activism: Mapping the middle', *American Anthropologist* 108(1): 38–51, p. 39.
3   Ibid.; Sally Engle Merry, 2009, *Gender Violence: A Cultural Perspective*, West Sussex: Wiley-Blackwell.
4   UN Women (Pacific), 2011, *Ending Violence against Women and Girls: Evidence, Data and Knowledge in Pacific Island Countries*, Suva: UN Women, p. 15; Christine Salomon, 2000, 'Les femmes Kanakes face aux violence sexuelles: le tournant judiciaire des années 1990', *Journale des anthropologues* 82–83: 1–12.
5   Amartya Sen, 1999, *Development as Freedom*, Oxford: Oxford University Press.
6   Martha Nussbaum, 2000, *Women and Human Development: The Capabilities Approach*, Cambridge: Cambridge University Press.
7   Ibid., p. 98.

about gender violence. My discussion shows that in Fiji women have a reduced functional capability to exert political or economic control over their environment and that this, in turn, prevents them from securing their right to lives free of violence. My overall contention is that, while human rights advocacy translation is attentive to women's cultural standing, there is less of a focus placed on the factors that obstruct women's economic and political participation. Because these factors compound women's vulnerability to violence and impede the realisation of human rights, we require an analytical framework and political strategies that address both these dimensions of disempowerment simultaneously.

Admittedly, raising the subject of women's marginalisation in economic or political terms may take Fiji's gender advocates into an even more volatile political territory than they currently occupy. Nonetheless, linking the anti-violence agenda with efforts to promote women's economic and political empowerment presents a set of novel advocacy possibilities that are only beginning to be explored in Pacific contexts.[8] These may provide important support for the human rights-focused strategies that are already a well-rehearsed part of efforts to combat gender violence in Fiji.[9]

The analysis that follows examines the terrain of gender violence and gender advocacy as it occurs in post-Independence Fiji. I show this arena to be one which has been shaped by repeated episodes of political upheaval; two military-led coups occurring in 1987, the civilian insurgency that overturned a democratic government and ushered in a period of nationalist political authoritarianism in 2000, and the later 2006 coup, again perpetrated by Fiji's military, which remains in political control of the country to this day. My analysis will

---

8   Martha Macintyre's recent use of a 'capabilities' framework to examine women's agency in Papua New Guinea has prompted me to consider how this same approach is applicable to the human rights–gender violence scenario in Fiji. In this chapter, I build upon Macintyre's examination of women's economic capabilities in PNG to also examine how political capabilities are pertinent to the task of securing rights. I contend that in Fiji women's political and economic capabilities are restricted by episodes of political instability and authoritarianism, a scenario that prevents them from securing lives free of violence. See Martha Macintyre, 2012, 'Gender violence in Melanesia and the problem of Millennium Development Goal No. 3', in *Engendering Violence in Papua New Guinea*, ed. Margaret Jolly, Christine Stewart and Carolyn Brewer, pp. 239–66, Canberra: ANU E Press.

9   See Aletta Biersack, 'Human rights work in Papua New Guinea, Fiji and Vanuatu', this volume.

demonstrate the gendered economic and political contingencies that have accrued from these events and explain how these contingencies undermine Indian and Indigenous women's capacities to secure their right to lives free from violence.

This chapter proceeds in three parts. The first examines the advocacy terrain as it currently exists in Fiji and the strategies used by women's organisations to advance the idea of women's human rights as a crucial plank of anti-violence campaigning. In this context, Pacific Islands culture is commonly understood as a barrier toward the realisation of women's rights, an obstruction to be navigated via processes of cultural translation, or 'vernacularization',[10] which 'localise' the international rights discourse so that it becomes more acceptable in Pacific Islands contexts. The twinning of rights and culture is deemed profoundly important if women's organisations are going to win the support of their political leaders as well as local communities for anti-violence work. However, it can also be argued that this cultural translation work has become harnessed to narrower 'law and order'– focused policy objectives that privilege the state as the agent central to improving the lives of women. This approach aims to reform existing juridical practices to make them more attentive and responsive to the violent crimes perpetrated against women. In Fiji, these strategies have achieved some traction at the institutional level. However, the fact that violence persists undiminished also indicates that this approach has failed to come to terms with the broader structural factors that make women vulnerable to violence and limit their capacities to resist this violence. To develop this line of argument, I advance the capabilities framework, as developed by Sen and further refined by Nussbaum, as a means by which to understand how the broader marginalisation of women in political and economic domains increases women's exposure to gendered forms of violence.

The second and third sections of this chapter explore this proposition in more detail. Section two examines the political domain and the extent to which Fiji's apparent 'coup culture' has been disempowering for women. Here it is argued that rates of gender violence reflect a pervasive militarism and authoritarianism that has taken hold nationally, and a widely held view within the community that manifest grievances,

---

10   Merry, 'Transnational human rights and local activism', p. 39.

in both national politics and everyday life, can be legitimately and efficiently resolved by forceful means. While the history of coups in Fiji has made women vulnerable to direct violence committed by the state, it has also contributed to an increased lawlessness and rising levels of gender violence within Fiji's communities.[11] At the same time, repeated episodes of military rule have denied women an active role in post-coup governance and any opportunity of mobilising state resources in ways that might address this gender violence effectively. Under the current military regime, the state has applied a typically 'absolutist' line to the ongoing problem of gender violence, developing what it terms a 'zero tolerance' approach to the phenomenon. However, these efforts are undermined by the regime's lamentable human rights record toward women and its record of authoritarianism and intimidation, which diminishes women's political capabilities in more general terms.

The third section of this chapter considers women's economic marginalisation in Fiji and how this compounds their exposure to gender violence. Fiji women have seen their economic standing erode as post-coup regimes follow international prescriptions of economic reform in order to garner the support of international financial institutions (IMF and World Bank) as well as foreign investors wary of the country's track record of political instability.[12] State policies of trade liberalisation, rationalised public expenditure in the areas of health, welfare and education, and labour deregulation to encourage foreign direct investment have not been kind to Fiji's vulnerable classes and have hit women particularly hard. Women's organisations have sought to expose the economic dimensions of gender violence by calculating how this phenomenon contributes to the loss of productive women's labour and its cost to the state as public policing and health services respond to victims of violence. By contrast, this advocacy has not concentrated in the same way on the global and local factors that intersect to compound women's economic vulnerability, entrapping them in violent relationships with few possibilities to exercise autonomy or to resist violent treatment. Rajagopal Balakrishnan's work

11   Margaret Mishra, 2012, 'A history of Fijian women's activism (1900–2010)', *Journal of Women's History* 24(2): 115–43; Shamima Ali, 2009, interview with Jemima Garret for *Pacific Beat*, ABC Radio Australia, Suva broadcast, 24 February 2009; Winston Halapua, 2003, *Tradition, Lotu and Militarism in Fiji*, Lautoka: Fiji Institute of Applied Studies.
12   Claire Slatter, 1997, 'Banking on the growth model: The World Bank and market policies in the Pacific', in *Sustainable Development or Malignant Growth? Perspectives of Pacific Island Women*, ed. Atu' Emberson-Bain, pp. 17–36, Suva: Marama Publications.

on international law from the 'bottom-up' has shown that the human rights agenda offers little scope for addressing the violence of the contemporary neoliberal development trajectory.[13] This may explain why women's human rights advocates campaigning against gender violence in Fiji have tended to avoid investigating the relationships between global political economy, women's declining economic standing, and their resulting vulnerability to violence.

I conclude this piece with a reflection on the importance of understanding gender violence as a complex social phenomenon that can be intensified when prevailing sociopolitical and economic norms work to undermine *both* women's standing *and* their functional capacity to challenge violent and discriminatory treatment. Increasingly we have seen gender advocacy evolve in global and local terms in ways that cloister debate on the challenges women face, whether that be their exposure to violence, their standing within decision-making realms, or their economic marginalisation. As this discussion aims to demonstrate, now is the time to examine the gains that might be made if closer attention were paid to the way these challenges intersect.

Gender violence and women's human rights: Strategies and results

Gender violence is said to be present within Fijian communities at extreme levels. Although the collection of meaningful statistics on this type of issue is difficult, and fraught with ethical contention,[14] United Nations (UN) Women has compiled figures that suggest that 66 per cent of Fiji's women have been exposed to family or intimate partner violence at some point in their lives, with roughly half this number experiencing violence on a regular basis.[15] Other sources also suggest that 40 women out of every 100,000 inhabitants are victims of rape in Fiji.[16] Conventional explanations as to why this violence persists, and is seemingly tolerated, point to the prevailing

---

13   Rajagopal Balakrishnan, 2003, *International Law from Below: Development, Social Movements and Third World Resistance*, Cambridge: Cambridge University Press.
14   Macintyre, 'Gender violence in Melanesia and the problem of Millennium Development Goal No. 3'.
15   UN Women (Pacific), *Ending Violence against Women and Girls*, p. 15.
16   Salomon, 'Les femmes Kanakes face aux violence sexuelles'.

sociocultural terrain. It has been argued that the strong stigma attached to crimes of sexualised and physical violence experienced by women prevent victims of these crimes from coming forward to police to report their attacks. Within the Indian community, the high value placed on notions of *izzat* (honour) and *sharm* (shame) means that victims of sexual and physical violence face pressure from clan members or relatives not to report attacks to state authorities to avoid bringing disrepute upon the family. Women tend also to fear that reporting these incidents will make them targets of even more serious violent reprisals from their aggressors.[17]

Within ethno-Fijian communities, women victims of violence face similar pressures.[18] As Lynda Newland has expertly demonstrated in Chapter 1 of this volume, rather than reporting such incidents to state authorities, women are frequently encouraged to see ceremonies of ritual apology (*i soro*) as the more appropriate avenue for redress.[19] However, activists in Fiji also complain that the customary penalties applied to those found guilty of gender violence carry a much lighter social and economic significance in contemporary society than was evident in precolonial times and place a much reduced burden on offenders.[20] Despite this alleged lenience, these processes have been defended by indigenous nationalists as part of their broader efforts to assert an exclusive cultural identity and to uphold indigenous juridical traditions.[21] As Newland's chapter in this volume has also shown, these customary practices of atonement retain considerable weight when family heads and village authorities decide on 'appropriate' courses of action to regulate problems of gender violence occurring in their communities.[22]

Religious leaders are often deemed similarly culpable of encouraging a high tolerance of gendered violence by urging women to endure this phenomenon rather than resist it. Women taking complaints of

---

17   Shireen Lateef, 1990, 'Rule by the Danda: Domestic violence among Indo-Fijians', *Pacific Studies* 13(3): 43–62, p. 45.

18   Pauline McKenzie Aucoin, 1990, 'Domestic violence and social relations of conflict in Fiji', *Pacific Studies* 13(3): 23–41.

19   Lynda Newland, 'Villages, violence and atonement', this volume; Viviane Cretton, 2005, 'Traditional Fijian apology as a political strategy', *Oceania* 75(4): 403–17.

20   Cretton, 'Traditional Fijian apology as a political strategy', p. 410.

21   Ibid.; Sally Engle Merry, 2006, *Human Rights and Gender Violence: Translating International Law into Local Justice*, Chicago: University of Chicago Press, pp. 116–17.

22   Newland, 'Villages, violence and atonement'.

family violence to Christian church leaders are likely to be counselled that it is a 'sin' to divorce or separate and advised to return home.[23] These factors combine to make gender violence a pervasive, if often unacknowledged, problem within Fiji's communities. Fiji Women's Crisis Centre (FWCC) figures suggest that 74 per cent of women do not report cases of family violence to police.[24] Similarly, only an estimated 5 to 10 per cent of rape victims bring their case to police attention.[25]

Women's organisations in Fiji have played an important role in combatting the seeming normalisation of gender violence. The chapters by Aletta Biersack and Lynda Newland in this volume rightly note the important role played by the Fiji Women's Crisis Centre in spearheading local programs to address this issue in Fiji and the broader Pacific Islands region.[26] These have included partnerships forged with anti-violence organisations in other Melanesian states and territories. This organisation was formed in response to a disturbing report authored by the Action Council for Women in Need, or ACWIN, in the early 1980s that found that while women in Fiji were exposed to high rates of sexualised violence, they were additionally penalised by a poor provision of support services and state inattention to such 'domestic' crimes.[27] Women keen to change this state of affairs made up the early membership of the group. In the intervening years the FWCC has become synonymous with efforts to prevent gender violence in the region. Its campaigns, designed to raise public awareness of violence against women, change social behaviour, and elicit government support for policy reforms to better police this phenomenon, broke new ground for women's organisations in Fiji and the region as a whole. This work introduced a sensitive topic into the public domain and challenged robust sociocultural protocols that had previously ensured that the subject of violence against women remained taboo, firmly located within the private sphere, unacknowledged and hidden.

---

23   Fiji Coalition of Women's NGOs for the CEDAW Shadow Report, 2009, *Shadow NGO Report on Fiji's Second, Third and Fourth Combined Periodic Report to the Committee on the Elimination of Discrimination against Women*, p. 27.

24   UN Women (Pacific), *Ending Violence against Women and Girls: Evidence, Data and Knowledge in Pacific Island Countries*, p. 31.

25   Mensah Adinkrah, 1995, *Crime, Deviance and Delinquency in Fiji*, Suva: Fiji Council of Social Services, pp. 75–79.

26   Aletta Biersack, 'Human rights work in Papua New Guinea, Fiji and Vanuatu'; Newland, 'Villages, violence and atonement', this volume.

27   Action Council of Women in Need (ACWIN), 1983, *Rape in Fiji: A Preliminary Report Prepared by the Action Centre for Women in Need (ACWIN)*, Suva: ACWIN.

Like many other anti-violence organisations operating around the globe, the FWCC has placed an increasing emphasis upon the centrality of women's human rights to its advocacy efforts. This focus on human rights reflected international trends emerging in the mid-1990s challenging the alleged 'human rights myopia' at work in international law. The claim was that conventional interpretations of human rights law were firmly focused on rights violations occurring in the public domain but simultaneously blind to the physical, sexual and psychological violence inflicted upon women in the private domain and beyond the purview of legal jurisdiction.[28] For many feminist observers, the international campaign spearheaded by women's human rights advocate Charlotte Bunch was an innovative intervention in international policymaking. This campaign won institutional acceptance within the United Nations of the idea that women were indeed 'human' and that their vulnerability to particular types of physical and sexualised aggressions constituted a violation of their human rights.[29] From this perspective the 'human rights' gender advocacy turn was viewed as a deft political 'reframing' of a universal, if hidden menace, that states were now obligated to confront.[30]

When the focus was shifted from the global to the local, however, the extent to which human rights frameworks could be interpreted as a gain for women became more contested. This has become increasingly apparent in the work of feminist scholars seeking to understand the

---

28   Ursula O'Hare, 1990, 'Realizing human rights for women', *Human Rights Quarterly* 21(2): 364–402; Jacqui True, 2010, 'The political economy of violence against women: A feminist international relations perspective', *The Australian Feminist Law Journal* 32(June): 39–59.

29   Arvonne Fraser, 1999, 'The origins and development of women's human rights', *Human Rights Quarterly* 21(4): 853–906; see also Jutta Joachim, 1999, 'Shaping the human rights agenda: The case of violence against women', in *Gender Politics in Global Governance*, ed. Mary K. Meyer and Elisabeth Prügl, pp. 142–60, Lanham, MD: Rowman and Littlefield; Jutta Joachim, 2003, 'Framing issues, seizing opportunities: The UN, NGOs and women's rights', *International Studies Quarterly* 47(2): 247–74; Karen Brown Thompson, 2002, 'Women's rights are human rights', in *Restructuring World Politics: Transnational Social Movements, Networks and Norms*, ed. Sanjeev Khagram, James V. Riker and Kathryn Sikkink, pp. 96–122, Minneapolis: University of Minnesota Press; Niamh Reilly, 2009, *Women's Human Rights: Seeking Gender Justice in a Globalizing Age*, London: Polity Press.

30   Kathleen Keck and Margaret Sikkink, 1998, *Activists Beyond Borders*, Ithaca: Cornell University Press.

sociocultural issues at stake when the universalist discourse of rights is applied to the often sensitive question of women's physical security in localised contexts.[31]

Many feminist scholars working in this area tend to explain non-Western women's exposure to violence as a problem of culture. Cultural practices and values are said to expose women to serious levels of violence. These are often described in ways that powerfully suggest a vast gulf between liberal notions of rights and non-Western value systems.[32] Other observers of the relationship between culture and women's human rights in locations beyond the West argue that the gulf is bridgeable.[33] They contend that the construction of a conceptual distance between non-Western cultural values and liberal rights discourses relies on a 'demonization' of culture[34] which is equated, unproblematically, with 'tradition' and understood to be frozen in time. From this perspective culture looks very much like a historical relic that impedes women's progress[35] and places them directly in the pathway of violence.[36]

As the introduction to this volume has already made clear, critical responses to this framing of culture as a wholesale problem for women have exposed the racist undertone to these arguments.[37] They challenge the 'Othering' of non-Western women as the sole victims of 'culturally ordained violence' and expose the extent to which women in the west are also the targets of violent, sexist and gender discriminatory

---

31   Merry, *Gender Violence*; Merry, 'Transnational human rights and local activism'; Jane K. Cowan, 2006, 'Culture and rights after *Culture and Rights*', *American Anthropologist* 108(1): 9–24; Brooke Ackerly, 2001, 'Women's human rights activists as cross-cultural theorists', *International Feminist Journal of Politics* 3(3): 311–46.
32   Sylvie Bovarnick, 2007, 'Universal human rights and non-Western normative systems: A comparative analysis of violence against women in Mexico and Pakistan', *Review of International Studies* 33(1): 59–75; Janet Afari, 2004, 'The human rights of Middle Eastern and Muslim women: A project for the 21st century', *Human Rights Quarterly* 26: 106–25; Susan Moller Okin, 1999, *Is Multiculturalism Bad for Women?* Princeton: Princeton University Press; Gayle Binion, 1995, 'Human rights: A feminist perspective', *Human Rights Quarterly* 17: 509–26.
33   Ackerly, 'Women's human rights activists as cross-cultural theorists'.
34   Sally Engle Merry, 2003, 'Human rights law and the demonization of culture (and anthropology along the way)', *Political and Legal Anthropology Review* 26(1): 55–77, p. 55.
35   Ibid.
36   Bovarnick, 'Universal human rights and non-Western normative systems', p. 73; Binion, 'Human rights: A feminist perspective'.
37   Aletta Biersack and Martha Macintyre, 'Introduction: Gender violence and human rights in the western Pacific', this volume.

cultural practices.[38] Equally, these depictions of culture ignore the fluidity of cultural interpretation and practice and the extent to which contestation around questions of 'cultural authenticity' offer women advocates the possibility of 'translating' human rights norms in ways that reinforce their local resonances. Contesting the notion that women in non-Western settings are the twin victims of violence *and* culture, this focus on rights vernacularisation challenges homogenised and static representations of culture[39] and instead opens the way for these things to be understood in more open, contested and rights accommodating terms.[40]

This perspective on culture has been important for those gender advocates in Fiji who aim to create awareness of gender violence as a problem and increase state attention to the issue. Although FWCC coordinator Shamima Ali has often decried contemporary cultural excesses that naturalise patriarchal authority in Fiji and legitimate the treatment of women, in her words, as 'doormats',[41] her organisation works hard to contest these perspectives. Ali argues that it is important to work with authority figures from all of Fiji's religions to demonstrate how the ideas she promotes about women's rights are reinforced within religious teachings. According to Ali, 'very often women are told to forgive and forget' when they discuss issues of family violence with their religious leaders.[42] They are also often ostracised from their religious communities if they choose to make

38   Margaret Jolly, 2012, 'Introduction – Engendering violence in Papua New Guinea: Persons, power and perilous transformations', in *Engendering Violence in Papua New Guinea*, ed. Margaret Jolly, Christine Stewart and Carolyn Brewer, pp. 1–45. Canberra: ANU E Press, p. 29; Merry, *Human Rights and Gender Violence*, pp. 10–16. For example, while Australian commentators are quick to point out the patriarchal cultural traditions they allege to be detrimental to progress on gender issues in the Pacific region and beyond, they fail often to consider the deep misogyny within Australian 'culture' that allows extreme levels of violence to persist in this setting and which has also authorised strongly gendered public criticisms targeted at Australia's first female Prime Minister, Julia Gillard, without protest or restraint. Virginia Hausegger, 2010, 'Feminism is failing in the war against women', *The Drum*, ABC, 28 October; Anne Summers, 2012, 'Conspiracy of silence lets persecution of PM fester', *The Age*, 1 September; 'Domestic violence: Our biggest law and order issue', *The Age*, 4 March 2012. Online: www.theage.com.au/opinion/editorial/domestic-violence-our-biggest-lawandorder-issue-20120303-1u9tg.html (accessed 4 September 2012).
39   Cowan, 'Culture and rights after *Culture and Rights*', p. 9.
40   Merry, 'Transnational human rights and local activism'; Merry, *Gender Violence: A Cultural Perspective*.
41   Shamima Ali cited in Nicole George, 2012, *Situating Women: Gender Politics and Circumstance in Fiji*, Canberra: ANU E Press, p. 101.
42   Shamima Ali cited in Fiji Women's Crisis Centre (FWCC), 2012, 'Taking the message to the people', press release posted to *Pacific Women's Information Network ListServe*, 21 November.

public their violent treatment in the home public.[43] To counter these trends, her organisation has made many efforts to include sympathetic church representatives in their anti-violence campaigns or media events. Indeed, in November 2012 the FWCC held a workshop in Nadi which was designed to educate religious leaders about how they too can contribute to the advocacy effort to reduce the incidence of gender violence in the country. This meeting had an ecumenical focus and engaged 'pastors, priests, pundits and imams' from all of Fiji's major religious institutions.[44] As well as recognising the need for a more sympathetic response to women who are victims of gender violence, all 25 participants were encouraged 'to examine their own religious interpretations and see how key messages can be used in the prevention of violence against women' within religious teachings.[45]

Ilisapeci Meo,[46] a Fijian feminist theologian and coordinator of WEAVERS, a women's advocacy group that is part of the South Pacific Association of Theological Schools,[47] has also discussed the importance of this type of work. Meo cites the New Testament parable of the persistent widow and the unjust judge (Luke 18: 1–8) as a Biblical example that authorises women not only to 'speak out for their rights',[48] but to do so persistently. For Meo, the persistent widow's repeated demands for justice, made both to the judge and her community, are courageous. She encourages Christian women in the Pacific to emulate the woman in the parable and challenge conventional church expectations about women's subordinate place within church hierarchies without fear that claims for rights or justice, or lives free of violence, conflict with spiritual values.[49]

---

43   Ibid.
44   FWCC, 'Taking the message to the people'.
45   Ibid.
46   Ilisapeci Meo, 2003, 'Asserting women's dignity in a patriarchal world', in *Weavings: Women Doing Theology in Oceania*, ed. Lydia Johnson and Joan Alleluia Filemoni-Taefaeono, pp. 150–60, Suva: Institute of Pacific Studies.
47   Helen Hill, 2010, 'Women and religious diversity', in *Religious Diversity in South East Asia and the Pacific*, ed. Gary D. Bouma, Douglas Pratt and Rod Ling, pp. 247–54, London: Springer.
48   Meo, 2003, 'Asserting women's dignity in a patriarchal world', p. 155.
49   This theological definition of women's right to resist mistreatment resonates with similar examples mentioned in Newland's contribution to this volume. For reflections on women's place in church hierarchy, see Eta Varani-Norton, 2005, 'The church versus women's push for change: The case of Fiji', *Fijian Studies* 3(2): 223–47, p. 240.

In a similar vein, gender activists have made strong efforts to demonstrate the local cultural resonances of rights-based campaigns to resist gender violence. This has been particularly important in Fiji, given the ethno-nationalist rhetoric that has been invoked by coup leaders to legitimate their claims to national political power and that emphasises indigenous cultural integrity. Nationalist political leaders have often voiced strong criticism of women's groups such as the FWCC or the Fiji Women's Rights Movement (FWRM), whose defense of women's rights is said to threaten the cultural centrality of 'family'[50] or violate Fijian norms of 'quiet diplomacy'.[51]

To counter these allegations, gender advocates, both Ethno- and Indo-Fijian, frequently preface their efforts to challenge pervasive levels of violence by making the claim that they speak as 'women and mothers'. These references provide an important cultural legitimation for debate on an issue many would prefer to avoid. They also demonstrate the conflict that exists between cultural discourses of revered motherhood and simultaneous tolerance of pervasive forms of violence in the family setting.[52]

A recent example of the importance of this type of argument for Fiji's indigenous population appeared in a *Fiji Times* article authored by the Executive Director of 'Partners in Community Development, Fiji', Alisi Daurewa. In this article Daurewa discussed how it was possible to reconcile the idea of women's human rights as a supposed '*palagi* [foreign] and superior concept' with the 'traditional' realm of Fijian indigenous culture.[53] Daurewa argued that the respectful treatment of women was not antithetical to indigenous culture in Fiji but central to the rightful negotiation of gender relationships. She discussed the *i tatau*, a customary practice that involved husbands making a formal vow on prestation of a *tabua* or whale's tooth to their wife's family to care for and protect their daughter. Failure to uphold this vow made the husband answerable to his in-laws, and in the past had been severely punished, according to Daurewa.

50   Jacqueline Leckie, 2002, 'The complexities of women's agency in Fiji', in *Gender Politics in the Asia-Pacific Region*, ed. Brenda S.A. Yeoh, Peggy Teo and Shirlena Huang, pp. 156–79, New York: Routledge.

51   George, *Situating Women*, p. 139.

52   Nicole George, 2010, '"Just like your mother": The politics of feminism and maternity in the Pacific Islands', *The Australian Feminist Law Journal* 32(June): 77–96.

53   Alisi Daurewa, 2009, 'The power of Fiji's women', *Fiji Times*, 5 May.

Daurewa's commentary on the reverence for women in Fijian culture also examined funeral ceremonies and the various traditions performed by sons that honoured their mothers and upheld their maternal lineage. Daurewa claimed this practice recognised women as 'links in a lengthy chain' of ancestry that brought families together and 'strengthened blood ties'.[54] She concluded her commentary with the observation that this cultural respect for women could provide a localised basis for making sense of the 'international treaties we agree to' but that are often perceived in the village setting as being 'disrespectful' to local culture. Daurewa concluded that rethinking claims about women's rights in these terms could potentially create a situation where 'we would not be still beating our mothers, wives, sisters and daughters, we would still not be sexually abusing them' and could expose the hypocrisy of a situation where 'we would continue to think nothing of these acts as we ready ourselves, gigantic Bible in hand, to attend another Sunday service or mass'.[55]

This culturing of the women's human rights debate is pursued to achieve twin aims. The first is to challenge the widespread tolerance of gender violence that is said to persist at extreme levels across the country. The second is to win policy-makers' support on this issue so that they will mobilise state resources in a way that might make the reduction of gendered violence a government policy priority. Advocacy directed towards the state demands reformed judicial and police responses to gender violence. These campaigns, led by the FWCC and FWRM in particular, have sought to increase awareness of the need for a more 'victim-focused' juridical response when women, who have experienced violence, report these crimes to state authorities. They emphasise the importance of more sensitive and effective policing responses to these crimes when they are reported,[56] a reduced evidentiary burden placed on victims of rape in the court room, the need for harsher sentencing regimes for crimes of sexual and physical violence perpetrated against women, and the importance

---

54   Ibid.
55   Ibid.
56   George, *Situating Women*, p. 145.

of reclassifying a range of offenses as sexualised crimes of violence.[57] While these strategies have increased the public profile of the advocacy organisations involved, state response to this campaigning has been mixed.

In 2003, Fiji's parliament passed a new Family Law Act, which aimed to provide women with easier access to divorce as well as guaranteed access to maintenance. This was the culmination of a 15-year process that had frequently been stalled by Fiji's coups. When the new Act was created, it was hailed as a development that would empower women, making it easier for them to escape violent domestic relationships through no-fault divorce provisions and providing them with enforced spousal maintenance should they be raising children as single parents.[58] The FWCC has also pushed heavily for the creation of a new Domestic Violence Bill with heavier sentencing provisions for a range of reclassified gender violence crimes. The Fiji Law Reform Commission has been involved in this project.[59]

The military regime which assumed power in 2006 later introduced a Domestic Violence Decree in 2009, which was designed to improve policing and judicial responses to cases of gender violence.[60] This decree may have also been designed to appease the many critical pro-democracy voices within women's groups such as FWRM and FWCC who were strongly opposed to the 2006 military takeover.

There is no doubt that the human rights advocacy framework has opened up lobbying possibilities for women advocates in Fiji. The fact that even Fiji's authoritarian military government seems keen to appear progressive on the issue of gender violence is, at one level at least, testimony to the broader impact of this agenda and its effectiveness in helping to promote gender sensitive reform in state policy.

---

57   They achieved minor successes in 1995 when the Fiji police force adopted a 'no-drop' policy toward gender violence, obligating them to take cases of violence through the legal process even if complainants wished to withdraw them. In response to advocacy on this question, the police also established Sexual Offences Units in the Southern and Northern Divisions. The hope was that these units would respond more sympathetically to the needs of victims and that this in turn would encourage increased reporting of sexual assaults. See Biersack, 'Human rights work in Papua New Guinea, Fiji and Vanuatu', this volume.

58   UN Women (Pacific), *Ending Violence against Women and Girls*, p. 31.

59   Asian Development Bank, 2006, *Country Gender Assessment: Republic of the Fiji Islands*, Manila: Asian Development Bank, p. 51.

60   Republic of Fiji, 2009, 'Domestic Violence Decree 2009', in *Republic of Fiji Islands Government Gazette* 10(67) (14 August).

Certainly, cultural and religious 'translation' work has been crucial to advocacy efforts that aim to localise the universal discourse of rights for both Fiji's indigenous and Indian populations. This is particularly important given that efforts to promote women's human rights occur within a highly politicised environment, in which communal divisions have hardened as a result of Fiji's periodic political upheavals and in which ethno-nationalists have made the protection of indigenous culture and political privilege a key site of struggle. At the same time, the human rights framework has also allowed gender advocates in Fiji to remind the state that the types of violence that women are subjected to in the private domain are not beyond its jurisdiction. In this regard, the women's movement in Fiji has logged considerable success in promoting more gender equitable family law and improved policing and judicial policy with respect to crimes of gender violence.

However, even though important successes have been achieved on the juridical front in the last 20 years, there is little evidence to suggest that any of this activity has in fact reduced the incidence of gender violence in Fiji. More worrying, perhaps, is the finding from other Pacific Island contexts that invocations of women's human rights tend often to provoke a masculine backlash, which may in fact increase women's exposure to violence. In Vanuatu, John Taylor has described how men have responded to debate on women's rights by proposing the formation of men's rights groups such as the Violence Against Men group that formed on Espiritu Santo in the 2000s in response to proposed reforms to marriage laws.[61] In Papua New Guinea, Macintyre contends that women emulating human rights values in their daily lives as a means to resist discriminatory treatment may be exposed to increased violence in repayment of their challenges to masculine privilege.[62] It might be going too far to suggest that the human rights approach is doing more harm than good in the Pacific Islands, but clearly the impact of this type of advocacy has not secured, on its own, the physical safety of women that many human rights advocates anticipated with enthusiasm in the 1990s.

---

61   John P. Taylor, 2008, 'The social life of rights: "Gender antagonism", modernity and *Raet* in Vanuatu', *The Australian Journal of Anthropology* 19(2): 165–78.
62   Macintyre, 'Gender violence in Melanesia and the problem of Millennium Development Goal No. 3', pp. 201–202.

Securing human rights: Examining the links between gender violence and capabilities

In the following pages I consider why this might be the case by examining how prevailing political circumstances limit women's capacity to realise their right to physical security. To sustain this perspective on women's vulnerability to violence in Fiji, I draw on the capabilities approach advocated by human development thinkers such as Amartya Sen and Martha Nussbaum, as well as on the many who have later followed in their footsteps.[63] Building on important insights from this literature, I contend that beyond proclaiming women's right to live their lives free of violence, we need also to examine women's capabilities to 'secure' that right.[64] In my view, this consideration has been lost or obscured in the human rights debate on gender violence that has taken place in Fiji, which has been focused more centrally on affirming women's cultural standing and by implication the resonance between culture and a liberal/universalist discourse on rights. This project is then harnessed to campaigns that aim to improve judicial and policing responses to gender violence. While these strategies have played some part in helping to localise acceptance of the women's human rights discourse, important political and economic constraints obstruct how far women can progress their human rights ambitions. My overriding contention, therefore, is that the broader factors that undermine women's standing in economic and political realms in Fiji directly impact on women's capability to promote the human rights framework in a way that will allow them to resist violence in their daily lives.

Nussbaum, in her book *Women and Human Development*, explains how women's functional capability to exert some control over their environment, in political and economic terms, has a more general relevance for women's 'life quality [emphasis removed]'[65] or for what

---

63   Ingrid Robeyns, 2003, 'Sen's capability approach and gender inequality: Selecting relevant capabilities', *Feminist Economics* 9(2–3): 61–92; Fabienne Peter, 2003, 'Gender and the foundations of social choice: The role of situated agency', *Feminist Economics* 9(2–3): 13–32; Vergerd Iversen, 2003, 'Intra-household inequality: A challenge for the capability approach', *Feminist Economics* 9(2–3): 93–115; Patricia McGrath Morris, 2002, 'The capabilities perspective: A framework for social justice', *Families in Society* 83(4): 365–73.
64   Nussbaum, *Women and Human Development*, p. 98.
65   Ibid., p. 6.

women are 'actually able to do and be'.[66] Nussbaum defines political capabilities in this sense as women 'being able to participate effectively in political choices that govern one's life; having the right of political participation, protections of free speech and association'.[67] She defines economic capabilities as 'having the right to hold property (both land and movable goods) not just formally but in terms of real opportunity, and as having the right to seek employment on an equal basis with others'.[68]

Adopting a capabilities approach to examine the relationship between gender violence and human rights in Fiji requires us to develop an 'evaluative space' that facilitates exploration of the relationship between (a) women's political and economic functioning— 'what people actually do'—(b) the gendered inequities that shape their political and economic capabilities—'what people are capable of doing'[69]—(c) the implications this has for claiming women's bodily integrity as an 'important freedom'.[70] In the following section of this chapter I apply these insights to a discussion of women's broader political and economic standing in Fiji with a view to identifying the factors preventing women in this setting from securing their human right to bodily integrity, even as advocacy on this issue retains its critical, human rights–oriented inflection. My argument here is that gender violence prevention efforts have been overly preoccupied with the task of promoting women's human rights and have failed to give adequate attention to the question that is perhaps more difficult: How do women secure these rights in their daily lives?

---

66   Ibid., p. 5.
67   Ibid., p. 80.
68   Ibid.
69   We are reminded that individuals and groups may have capabilities that they do not fully exercise. For example, women may not take up the opportunity to work in the formal economic sector but rather focus on reproductive and caring responsibilities even if they have the capability to do so.
70   As Loretta Pyles notes, bodily integrity is an important freedom as defined by Nussbaum, but at the same time, it is also a means to achieve other stipulated freedoms such as 'control over the material environment'. Deprivation of bodily integrity can have severe implications for women's capability to realise economic goals or objectives. See Loretta Pyles, 2012, 'The capabilities approach and violence against women: Implications for social development', in *Companion Reader on Violence Against Women*, ed. Claire M. Renzetti, Jeffrey L. Edleson and Raquel Kennedy Bergen, pp. 25–36, Thousand Oaks, CA: Sage, p. 36. As Pyles notes, bodily integrity is an important freedom as defined by Nussbaum, but at the same time, it is also a means to achieve other stipulated freedoms such as 'control over the material environment' (p. 36).

Gender and institutional politics in Fiji

Commentators on women's standing in institutional politics in the Pacific Islands have regularly argued that Fiji has achieved noteworthy success when it comes to representation of women in elected parliaments. Prior to the coups of 2000 and 2006, Fiji's parliamentary statistics seemed to indicate a regionally unique acceptance of female representatives, with women making up 11 per cent of the national legislature in 1999 as compared with the regional average of roughly 3 per cent.[71] However, this optimistic picture masks the highly gendered nature of authoritarian political rule as it has been practised in Fiji since the first coup occurred in 1987 and, more particularly, during Fiji's second period of military rule, which began in 2006. During this second period of military government, women's political standing has been significantly diminished in a number of ways outlined below. While this scenario has practical implications for how far women are able to rally state attention to the gender violence issue, it can also be argued that authoritarian rule in Fiji has directly increased women's vulnerability to violence in everyday terms.

To begin with, it is clear that military rule in Fiji has seen the dismissal of national- or local-level deliberative forums that might allow women to have a critical political voice. In 2009, Shamima Ali of the FWCC was particularly critical of the military's seizure of government and its absolutist exercise of authority, which has involved 'government by decree' accompanied by an extensive system of news media censorship preventing critical voices from being heard. Ali called attention in particular to the dissolution of the national parliament and, later, local councils; all developments which, according to Ali, prevented women from accessing public forums where 'they could speak out.'[72]

Activists' efforts to protest the restrictive nature in which constitutional deliberations were occurring in Fiji ahead of planned elections in 2014 are also indicative of how far women's political capabilities have been restricted under the current military regime. Three women's

---

71   UNIFEM (Pacific), 1999, *Women and Political Empowerment: A Resource Manual for the Pacific*, Suva: UNIFEM; UNIFEM, 1999, *Pacific Women: Getting into Politics: Fiji as a Best Practice Case Study*, Suva: UNIFEM; Meredith Burgmann, 2011, 'Time for women to represent the Pacific', *Sydney Morning Herald*, 16 September.
72   Ali, interview with Garret.

organisations—fem'Link, FWCC and FWRM—were behind efforts to publish a joint advertisement in Fiji's daily newspapers criticising the 2012 constitution-making process. This advertisement protested against the immunity provisions proposed for coup perpetrators within the document and was critical of the restricted access to the supposedly 'public' constitutional forums that were held around the country at this time.[73]

Fiji's newspapers, however, refused to publish these criticisms. The harsh military treatment of critical reporters and newspaper editors in the period of military rule involved detention, as well as deportation of foreign journalists and news editors. This history of punitive retaliation dissuaded media publishers from putting their employees at risk of government wrath. Although government officials began to articulate a more moderate line in later years, and encouraged Fiji's media to abandon its cautious self-censorship practice,[74] this episode demonstrates how a general level of fear and distrust of military authority within the media has further restricted women's political capabilities and their ability to critique a project defended by the regime as 'building a new way for Fiji'.[75]

At the same time, military authority has functioned in ways that have made women the direct targets of state-perpetrated violence. Since 2006, attacks on the political standing of women have become commonplace, seemingly designed to reduce women's political visibility and clamp down on their capacity to promote dissent. The following incidents are noteworthy examples of this type of practice.

1. In late December 2006, women's rights campaigner Virisila Buadromo was allegedly taken from her home by military representatives with a group of other outspoken coup-critics and subjected to physical assault and intimidation, culminating in

---

73   FWCC, 2012, 'Taking the message to the people', press release posted to *Pacific Women's Information Network ListServe*, 21 November.
74   Sharon Smith-Johns, 2012, 'Fiji journalists urged to stop censoring themselves', ABC Radio Australia, 10 September.
75   FWCC, 2012, 'Women's rights groups question freedom of expression', press release posted to *Pacific Women's Information Network ListServe*, 29 August.

a forced march through the rainy streets of Suva.[76] She and fellow women's rights campaigner Shamima Ali were later deprived of the right to travel internationally.

2. In 2007, Kuini Lutua, head of the Fiji Nursing Association (FNA), was the public face of a strike action that saw the majority of Fiji's 1,700 nurses walk off the job. During the strike, Lutua was repeatedly targeted by threatening phone calls and was once confronted by an intruder to her home, who made a verbal threat on her life. She was in no doubt that these various acts of intimidation were authored by members of the military regime.[77] Undaunted, Lutua led a protest action in front of the government buildings in Suva on 3 August 2007, in full knowledge that she and her fellow protesting nurses faced certain arrest. Recounting how the decision to protest was discussed in the FNA offices in the lead-up, Lutua stated: 'There were lots of tears that day. But we had to stand up to them—as mothers, as women of Fiji—we had to tell them they were wrong.'[78] Lutua and her fellow nurse-protestors were indeed arrested by police but were later released without charge.

3. In June 2011, state security shut down a planning meeting staged by the Fiji Women's Rights Movement (FRWM) at the Pearl Resort in Pacific Harbour, some 70 kilometres outside Suva. Local police alleged this meeting contravened the regime's Public Emergency Regulations (PERs). The FWRM coordinator, Virisila Buadromo, again found herself detained by state authorities for some hours without charge. While this meeting was eventually disbanded, FWRM argued that this heavy-handed approach was specifically designed to frustrate women's human rights activists. They noted that a similar planning meeting, held by a group known as Pacific Disability Forum, in a neighbouring room at the resort, was allowed to proceed unimpeded.

4. In November 2011, Ro Teimumu Kepa, a high-ranking woman holding the chiefly title Roko Tui Dreketi, and a well-known advocate for indigenous nationalist principles, spoke at the Rewa Provincial Council meeting. She used this opportunity to denounce

---

76 Nicole George, 2009, 'Women's organizing in Fiji: Shifting terrains of transnational engagement', in *Gender and Global Politics in the Asia-Pacific*, ed. Katrina Lee Koo and Bina D'Costa, 175–93, New York: Palgrave-Macmillan.

77 Kuini Lutua, personal communication with author, September 2009.

78 Ibid.

the 2006 military coup. The regime had threatened to withdraw FJ$3 million in funding to the Rewa Provincial Council if it did not take a more politically acquiescent line. During her speech Ro Teimumu Kepa revealed that she had been the victim of state intimidation: some months previously she alleged that 16 military and police officers had presented themselves at her home and threatened her with arrest because of her outspoken opposition to the regime.

In sum, these incidents demonstrate that the experience of post-coup military government limited the political capabilities that women activists could draw upon to promote women's rights to physical security, and actively contributed to the contravention and undermining of those rights. This has been done through acts of detention, intimidation and harassment designed to degrade, shame and instill fear in women it deems dangerous.

But activist women are not the only ones to feel the detrimental impacts of these practices. It can also be argued that militarised political authority in Fiji has been exercised since 2006 in ways that institutionalise and normalise gendered forms of violence in a more indirect but no less serious fashion. As the lines that define military and civilian aspects of social and cultural life become more comprehensively blurred in Fiji,[79] violent expressions of masculine authority have become normalised with devastating effects. Cynthia Cockburn has noted in other contexts that the impact of increased militarism in any society is almost never positive for women who contend with a situation in which norms of violence seep beyond the military context from the 'barracks' to 'the bars, the streets, to the bedroom'.[80] Such observations indicate the ways in which gendered 'relations of power' operating through state institutions can structure gender relations beyond the institution and encourage a normalisation of gender violence.[81]

---

79   Teresia Teaiwa, 2008, 'Globalizing and gendered forces: The contemporary militarization of Pacific/Oceania', in *Gender and Globalization in Asia and the Pacific*, ed. Kathy E. Ferguson and Monique Mironescu, pp. 318–32, Honolulu: University of Hawai'i Press; Halapua, *Tradition, Lotu and Militarism in Fiji*.
80   Cynthia Cockburn, 2011, 'Don't talk to me about war, my life's a battlefield', *50.50 Open Democracy*, 25 November.
81   R.W. Connell, 2002, *Gender*, Cambridge: Polity Connell, p. 59.

Since 2006, Fiji's gender activists have described this as a 'continuum of violence' that extends from the military barracks to the lives of families.[82] Military leader Frank Bainimarama defended the right of Fiji's military to act on its political grievances by contrasting his commitment to good governance with the alleged corrupt governance of his predecessors. At the same time he warned of 'serious consequences' for potential dissenters.[83] Since that time, the military leadership in Fiji has repeatedly defended its political legitimacy by pointing to the efficiency of military force in dealing with division, or dissent. Gender activists allege that these lessons have been absorbed with a disturbing success within the community and contributed to a post-coup spike in gender violence rates occurring at the community level. In her commentary on the relationship between violence occurring at the national level and violence occurring within families, Shamima Ali has argued that militarism in Fiji contributes to generalised feelings of social powerlessness and disenfranchisement among men, who then choose to punish the women in their lives. A veteran observer of such events, Ali claims this to be a strong pattern replicated after each coup in Fiji, whereby men are prompted to 'take it out on the most vulnerable' when they feel their 'manhood has been taken away'.[84]

Perhaps in response to these allegations, and as other chapters in this volume have also noted, the military regime has developed new programs aiming to improve the state response to gender violence. The 2009 Domestic Violence Decree, which aimed to reclassify a range of offenses occurring in the 'family situation' as criminal acts, is one example of this shift.[85] Another is the Zero Tolerance Violence Free Community Campaign, which aims to encourage a rejection of gendered forms of violence at the village level.[86] While government representatives have hailed the campaign as a success, others have offered a more guarded assessment, questioning the state's capacity

---

82 *fem'Link*, 2009, cited in George, *Situating Women*, p. 193.
83 George, *Situating Women*, p. 186.
84 Ali, interview with Garret. Pickup has noted how 'cultures of violence' can take hold in the wake of conflict or political crisis, and that persistent levels of violence in societies afflicted by conflict can be attributed to the responses that are developed during the crisis period and that allow individuals to cope. Francine Pickup, 2001, *Ending Violence against Women: A Challenge for Development and Humanitarian Work*, Oxfam: Bournemouth.
85 Brenda Ragi, 2009, '"Overwhelming and extremely positive response to domestic violence decree" says Attorney General', press release, Attorney-General's Chambers (Fiji), 14 September.
86 Anshoo Chandra, 2012, 'Economic drivers', *Fiji Times*, 9 June.

to oversee and manage these programs effectively.[87] Interestingly, none of these initiatives is publicly underwritten by the regime's commitment to women's human rights or discussions about the relevance of this international principle for women's physical security. This stands in stark contrast to the way women's organisations have approached the issue but is hardly surprising given that the military government has, since 2006, acted in ways that directly contravene human rights principles but also enjoyed tacit support from institutions charged with investigating such practices, such as the Human Rights Commission.[88]

Fiji's 2014 return to democracy may have given some cause for optimism, but transformative results are yet to be seen. Elections held in September 2014 were conducted under a new, and tightly restricted national constitution. This ensured many of the figures that had assumed power undemocratically in December 2006 were returned to power, including former military commander and coup leader Voreqe (Frank) Bainimarama, who was elected as Prime Minister with 'landslide' support. Eight women won seats in the new parliament, with five women candidates elected to represent Bainimarama's Fiji First party. All of these women were allocated ministerial responsibilities. However, as I have demonstrated elsewhere, this return to democracy has not guaranteed a less punitive state response to critical political debate. Neither has the numerical representation of women in government guaranteed a more liberal institutional approach to policymaking on gender.[89] While these female government representatives have touted the positive impacts of their efforts to promote reforms such as the Domestic Violence Decrees and Zero Tolerance Violence Free Community initiatives put in place by the military government in the period between 2009 and 2013 they have also described women's inappropriate dress (wearing shorts) and

87   Ragi, '"Overwhelming and extremely positive response to domestic violence decree" says Attorney General'.

88   Brij V. Lal, 2009, 'One hand clapping: Reflections on the first anniversary of Fiji's 2006 coup', in *The 2006 Military Takeover in Fiji: A Coup to End All Coups*, ed. Stewart Firth, Jon Frankael and Brij V. Lal, pp. 425–48, Canberra: ANU E Press.

89   Nicole George, 2014, 'Business as usual in post-election Suva?' *East Asia Forum*, 22 October. Online: www.eastasiaforum.org/2014/10/22/business-as-usual-in-post-election-suva/ (accessed 8 July 2015).

behaviour (drinking with boys) as 'inviting' trouble.[90] Likewise, they have failed to adequately address the gap between these new state legal provisions and programs promising gender-sensitive reform and the everyday practice of state policing responses to gender crimes (particularly cases of violence against women) which continues to be shaped by conservative religious and cultural protocols stipulating the importance of conjugal order.[91]

Against this backdrop, the absolutist 'zero tolerance' approach to the issue of gender violence might be seen as a further iteration of the Fiji government's authoritarian response to a problematic phenomenon. Its failure to engage with civil society activists who have developed local and regional expertise on this issue is indicative of the more general pattern of military authority in Fiji, which, even under the guise of constitutional democracy, exhibits a grave distrust of women, and particularly those who voice regime criticism—seeking to marginalise these from the political process altogether.[92] The fact that the military regime continues this strategy even while it seeks to address the issue of gender violence seems both extreme and counter-productive to the government's stated ambitions to develop a 'progressive' response to this issue.[93] For the purposes of this discussion, however, it demonstrates the extent to which broader political structures can constrain women's political agency. As I have shown, Fiji's women are living currently under a system of nominal democratic rule, but the authoritarian military presence remains highly influential. This severely constrains their general political capabilities. This scenario has made women vulnerable to state-sanctioned forms of violence as well as heightened levels of everyday violence in the community. Neither of these trends is conducive to

90   Pacific.Scoop, 2014, 'Fiji women's right groups calls for Minister to resign over rape comments', *Pacific Scoop*, 16 May 2014. Online: pacific.scoop.co.nz/2014/05/fiji-womens-rights-groups-call-for-minister-to-resign-over-rape-comments/ (accessed 8 July 2015).
91   FWCC, 2013, *Somebody's Life, Everybody's Business! National Research on Women's Health and Life Experiences in Fiji (2010/2011): A survey exploring the prevalence, incidence and attitudes to intimate partner violence in Fiji*, Suva: FWCC.
92   Indeed, this privileging of masculine authority continues to be a hallmark of the new gender violence initiatives enacted by the military government. Biersack's assessment of this program in this volume indicates that the community stakeholders that are nominated to assist police work on gender violence at the village level, according to the 'Zero Tolerance' program, are nearly always men. See Biersack, 'Human rights work in Papua New Guinea, Fiji and Vanuatu', this volume.
93   Sayed-Khaiyum, cited in Ragi, '"Overwhelming and extremely positive response to domestic violence decree" says Attorney General'.

expanding women's capabilities in Fiji. And together they seriously undermine women's ability to secure their human right to lives free of violence.

Women's economic standing

An understanding of women's economic capabilities is also highly important when seeking to assess if and how Fiji's women can secure their right to violence-free lives. Such a task again invites critical appraisals of Fiji's ongoing experimentation with authoritarian political rule. In general terms there has been concern expressed about the 'feminisation of poverty' in the last decades in Fiji, with a range of studies finding that a 'disproportionate number of poor households in Fiji—almost one in every seven', is headed by a woman[94] and that women are more likely to experience poverty than men.[95]

Indications of a rising female labour-force participation rate over the past three decades, from 23 per cent in 1986 to 39 per cent in 2005, may seem to contradict these concerns. However, further examination shows that women's employment tends to be 'ghettoised' in a few subsistence or low-waged sectors. These include subsistence agriculture and fisheries industries (45 per cent), manufacturing (12 per cent), tourism and hospitality (12 per cent), and community and social services sectors (17 per cent).[96] Subsistence sector work is defined in Fiji as 'growing vegetables, root crops, gathering wild fruits and herbs, raising poultry and other livestock and catching fish, prawns, shellfish and other seafood'.[97] This work is not paid as waged labour. Most produce is used to feed families, and surpluses earn only small amounts of cash through local market sales.[98] Women's presence in the community and social service sectors reflects their overrepresentation in feminised professions such as teaching, nursing

---

94   United Nations Development Program (UNDP), 1996, *Fiji Poverty Report*, Suva: UNDP and Fiji Government, p. 54.
95   Jenny Bryant, 1993, *Urban Poverty and the Environment in the South Pacific*, Sydney: University of New England Press; Priya Chattier, 2007, 'The capability approach: Mainstreaming gender into poverty discourses in Fiji', *Fijian Studies: A Journal of Contemporary Fiji* 5(2): 329–59.
96   Dharma Chandra and Vasemaca Lewai, 2005, *Women and Men of Fiji Islands: Gender Statistics and Trends*, Suva: University of the South Pacific and Fiji Islands Bureau of Statistics, p. 93.
97   Ibid.
98   Ibid.

and other forms of care work. Much of this work is done within a public sector that has experienced substantial falls in funding in recent years and declining wage values in real terms.[99]

Women's increasing participation in Fiji's manufacturing sector has been solely explained by the growth in garment manufacturing, an industry created and largely sustained by government tax incentives. This industry was developed as part of a broader program of economic restructuring designed to halt rapid economic downturn after the 1987 coup. Fiji's women have provided a source of 'low-skilled', low-waged labour for this industry and have contributed to the growth of an export industry that, by 2003, rivalled Fiji's sugar industry at FJ$252 million per annum, employing nearly 14,000 on its production lines.[100] At the same time, however, women employed in this industry endured difficult conditions, intense disciplinary supervision, and little more than subsistence wages of FJ$45–50 a week.[101] Many women garment workers lived in squatter settlements, and for those raising families as single parents the threat of 'slipping into poverty' has been constant.[102]

In addition to women's disadvantaged earning capability, strongly gendered norms can operate within the family in Fiji in ways that compound women's poor economic standing.[103] Priya Chattier's study of Indo-Fijian farming communities shows that when household resources are scarce, women are often likely to attend to the needs of other household members—husbands, sons and children—before their own. This means they may eat less to ensure 'hard-working' men have more access to food and children do not go hungry. They also tend to ignore their own health problems to ensure that there are adequate household resources to attend to the ailments of spouses and children.[104] Within Indo-Fijian families, norms of property inheritance also favour sons over daughters, so that women tend to be 'dependent on males for access to land' and other forms of inherited wealth.[105]

---

99   Fiji's nurses, for example, earn the rough equivalent of AU$300 a month in the domestic setting, but in Australia or New Zealand might be averaging about AU$1,100 per month.
100   Chandra and Lewai, *Women and Men of Fiji Islands*, p. 93.
101   Christy Harrington, 2004, '"Marriage" to capital: The fallback positions of Fiji's women garment workers', *Development in Practice* 14(4): 495–507, p. 504; George, *Situating Women*, p. 176.
102   Chandra and Lewai, *Women and Men of Fiji Islands*, p. 95.
103   Chattier, 'The capability approach'.
104   Ibid., pp. 344–47.
105   Ibid., p. 349.

These economic challenges have been compounded by Fiji's history of coups, events which Satish Chand estimates have pushed Fiji's economic development back three years in real terms.[106] The economic standing of Fiji's women has been undermined both as a result of coup-related job losses caused by international economic boycotts and withdrawal of international investment in local industry such as garment manufacturing.[107] For example, in the wake of the 2000 coup, the sustainability of Fiji's garment industry seemed in serious doubt as international embargos and investor fears resulted in factory closures and job losses.[108]

Coups have caused similar downturns in the tourism sector in Fiji, with regional governments such as Australia and New Zealand releasing critical travel advisories and potential holiday tourists choosing other destinations in which to spend their tourist dollars when political stability is in jeopardy. The practical consequences of continued political instability for those employed in the tourism sector has been devastating as tourism workers deal with reduced working hours or indefinite lay-offs.[109]

Women's economic standing has also been undermined by post-coup regimes' efforts to restructure their economies in ways that meet the expectations of international financial institutions and the conditions placed on receipt of international aid. A stringent program of economic restructuring was put in place soon after the Rabuka-led coup of 1987 and continued into the early 1990s. This included currency devaluations, the imposition of a value-added tax, and a significant reduction in public expenditure supporting state welfare, health and education programs. While real wages and incomes declined in this period, government military spending doubled. These same remedies were emulated by later post-coup regimes to avoid economic collapse; again the currency was devalued, taxes were increased, and state spending was severely cut.[110] It follows that women's already marginal economic functioning has been further undermined by Fiji's apparent

106 Satish Chand, 2007, 'Swim or sink: The predicament of the Fiji economy', *Pacific Economic Bulletin* 22(2): 1–21.
107 Anas Khan and Riad Khan, 2007, 'Political and economic instability, and poverty in Fiji', *Fijian Studies: A Journal of Contemporary Fiji* 5(2): 315–27.
108 George, *Situating Women*, p. 149.
109 Khan and Khan, 'Political and economic instability, and poverty in Fiji', p. 321.
110 Khan and Khan, 'Political and economic instability, and poverty in Fiji'; Chand, 'Swim or sink'.

coup cycle and the increased financial pressure that all citizens have experienced in the wake of these events. The resulting financial pressures have impacts on many aspects of social life. In 2001 it was found that increasing economic pressures following the 2000 coup had intensified a range of 'social problems' such as domestic violence, child abuse, suicide and drug and alcohol abuse, as people of all ages reported feeling 'fearful, frustrated, angry and powerless'.[111]

Within the literature on violence against women there is a strong interest in understanding the links between poverty and vulnerability to violence. I contend that it is important to understand these links when we examine how women might secure their right to live violence-free lives in Fiji. While it would be a mistake to argue a straight causal link between poverty and gender violence, there are good reasons to suppose that economic vulnerability is highly relevant to understanding both women's exposure to violence and their ability to resist violence in their daily lives.

When resources are scarce, conflicts over money within the household or domestic setting can expose women to violence. This is particularly so in cultural contexts where women are charged with managing household budgets while men take on the role of primary wage earners. Paula Wilcox has shown the strategies that women effect to ensure that male wages are managed in ways that allow family obligations to be met. She also shows how these strategies can be the cause of family violence as men contest this attempt to control how their earnings are used.[112]

Women's exposure to violence in turn compounds their economic vulnerability, disrupting women's 'patterns of employment' or making it harder for women to engage in continued income-generating activities.[113] This disruption may occur because of physical injury,

---

111 Mercia Carling and Colleen Peacock-Taylor, 2001, *Study of the Impacts of the Political Crisis on Children and Families in Fiji*, Suva: Save the Children Fund/UNICEF, p. 9.

112 Paula Wilcox, 2006, *Surviving Domestic Violence: Gender Poverty and Agency*, Houndmills: Palgrave Macmillan, pp. 117–19. Although Martha Macintyre also notes that in PNG women who earn more than men can also be perceived as 'threatening and legitimate targets for violence'. Macintyre, 'Gender violence in Melanesia and the problem of Millennium Development Goal No. 3', p. 247.

113 Wilcox, *Surviving Domestic Violence*, p. 111.

mental stress, or from masculine attempts to 'isolate' women from work opportunities and deny them access to financial resources that might facilitate their autonomy.[114]

There is also strong evidence to suggest that women's capacities to resist violence are limited by their marginal economic standing. Susan Pickup contends that women often find themselves in relationships that make them economically dependent upon men, and this limits their capacity to leave those relationships if they become violent. A lack of financial autonomy in these situations may encourage women to endure regular violence rather than contemplate the difficult possibility of building a life with dependents but without male economic support.[115]

At the same time, poverty can handicap female victims in their efforts to utilise juridical mechanisms put in place to help them. Complaints against experiences of family violence or rape are frequently treated more seriously when they are made by women from wealthy backgrounds than when they are made by women living in poverty.[116] Wealthier women may also have greater capability to access other formal institutions that might alleviate their situation, such as health services, counselling services, and legal advisers.[117] Poorer women on the other hand may avoid contacting these institutions because of the costs they fear they will incur.[118]

---

114 Pyles, 'The capabilities approach and violence against women', p. 35; Vasala K.B. Kumari, 2008, 'Violence and microcredit: A snapshot of Kerala, India', in *Violence and Gender in the Globalized World: The Intimate and the Extimate*, ed. Sanja Bahun-Radunović, V.G. Julie Rajan, pp. 43–55, Aldershot: Ashgate, p. 47; Syed Masud Ahmed, 2005, 'Intimate partner violence against women: Experiences from a woman-focused development program in Matlab, Bangladesh', *Journal of Health, Population and Nutrition* 23(1): 95–101, p. 99.
115 Pickup, *Ending Violence against Women*, p. 26.
116 Ibid., p. 27.
117 Pickup also notes, however, that an 'ideology of privacy in the home' may also restrict women's abilities to resist gender violence, making it difficult for them to expose violent treatment to family members, friends, or professional colleagues. This is attributed to a sense of shame and a desire to protect 'reputation'. See Pickup, *Ending Violence against Women*, p. 27.
118 Pickup contends that this situation is compounded in many ways by government policy-making, which tends to silo the 'women's issues' portfolio from other relevant policy areas, such as health, education, and law. Pickup, *Ending Violence against Women*, p. 26.

These types of concerns are highly relevant to experiences of gender violence in the Pacific Islands.[119] As I have shown in Fiji, many women, indigenous and Indian, live in conditions of financial dependency or increasing vulnerability. Their reduced economic functioning equates to a reduced economic capability to seek out ways of avoiding or resisting the violence that many live with on a daily basis. In my discussions with local researchers examining the predicament of female garment workers in Fiji in 2002, for example, I learned that women earning average industry wages and living in increasingly crowded squatter settlements on the perimeters of Suva were in such a precarious financial situation that even if their long working hours allowed it, the payment of an extra bus-fare into central Suva to discuss their situation with legal representatives or state welfare authorities represented a prohibitively costly financial investment with no guarantee of return.[120]

Such considerations illustrate the problem with focusing on juridical remedies to reduce women's vulnerability to violence, which underestimate the practical financial barriers that restrict women's access to juridical institutions. Recent evidence assessing the effectiveness of Fiji's Family Law Act (2005) indicated that 'many women are unaware' of its provisions and how it might assist them in 'obtaining protection orders', for example.[121] This lack of awareness is undoubtedly most pronounced among Fiji's growing numbers of poor women. Those promoting the proposed legislative changes in the early 2000s were enthusiastic about how they would act as a tool of poverty alleviation for women caught in violent relationships with diminished economic autonomy.[122] Yet there are obvious limitations to this highly juridicalised approach to securing women's human rights. It can be argued that in this context the legalist approach offers a uniform solution to the phenomenon of gender violence and/or family violence that obscures more difficult and complex questions about women's diminishing economic capability, which limits their autonomy within households. Deliberation on this question has, to date, been relatively muted in women's advocacy circles.

119 Macintyre, 'Gender violence in Melanesia and the problem of Millennium Development Goal No. 3'; Michelle Bachelet, 2012, interview with Fran Kelly, for *Pacific Beat*, ABC Radio Australia, 24 August.
120 See Harrington, '"Marriage" to capital', p. 498.
121 UN Women (Pacific), *Ending Violence against Women and Girls*, p. 31.
122 Cited in George, *Situating Women*, p. 157.

Conclusion

In June 2007, Shamima Ali, coordinator of the Fiji Women's Crisis Centre, addressed the 10th Triennial Conference of Pacific Women, held in Nouméa, on the relevance of feminism. Here she argued that 'feminism was about women's human rights'. Reaction to her claims was mixed. Replaying concerns about the term (feminism) that have been raised in regional contexts for many decades,[123] many in the audience of conference delegates found her references to feminism troubling and alleged it was inappropriate to the Pacific Islands context. Remarkably, none questioned the applicability of the 'rights' discourse she also invoked. The previous pages have shown that there are good reasons why, in Fiji, we might be sceptical of the assumption that human rights, on their own, can 'do the work of feminism'. Nonetheless, this episode is illustrative of an important current trend in the debate on the status of women in Fiji, and indeed across the Pacific Islands, whereby the language of rights is more acceptable than the language of feminism.

In the last two decades, the human rights discourse has become ubiquitous, the predominant framework for advocacy which contests gender discriminatory treatment in general and pervasive levels of gender violence in particular. Acts of rights translation have helped break down some of the resistance to the universalising aspects of human rights. As I have shown, women activists in Fiji have worked creatively to incorporate religious and cultural references as part of the efforts to convince their audiences that the concepts they discuss are not foreign but resonate with existing value systems and Pacific ways of thinking. In Fiji these strategies have been an important aspect of community advocacy. They have also assisted activist efforts to win support from the state for proposed legal and policy changes that might enable better policing of gender violence.

---

123 Vanessa Griffen, 1987, *Women, Development and Empowerment: A Pacific Feminist Perspective. Report of a Pacific Women's Workshop, Naboutini, Fiji, 23–26 March 1987*, Kuala Lumpur: Asian and Pacific Development Centre; Leckie, 'The complexities of women's agency in Fiji'; Margaret Jolly, 2005, 'Beyond the horizon? Nationalisms, feminisms and globalization in the Pacific', *Ethnohistory* 52: 138–66.

Yet important questions remain about how far this framework enables women to secure a pathway to lives free of violence in practical terms. These are most clearly brought into focus when consideration is given to the factors that undermine women's economic and political functioning in contemporary Fiji. As I have shown, repeated instances of post-coup authoritarian rule did great damage to women's political standing in Fiji, limiting their capability to promote a right to lives free from violence. Fiji's coups have encouraged an increasing lawlessness along with widespread political and social alienation. Many contend this exposes women to heightened levels of physical insecurity. At the same time, the coups and the political regimes they engender function to expose 'dissenting' women to the risk of state-perpetrated violence and intimidation. In a political context where the state itself has been accused of widespread human rights violations, the promotion of a rights-based framework for addressing gender violence appears to have limited political traction. Indeed, in important instances it has placed women activists directly in the path of state-sanctioned violence. While there is a disturbing irony to this scenario, there is also an important lesson to be taken away from these events. They demonstrate that women are only able to fully secure their right to lives free from violence when they have the political capability to do so. Fiji's history of political instability and authoritarianism has profoundly undermined that capability in the last four decades.

At the same time, women's diminished economic standing also limits how far they are able to resist their exposure to violence. As I have shown, women in Fiji may have increased their rate of labour-force participation in the past four decades, but they remain predominantly ghettoised in low-income, low-status, feminised professions. Their already low incomes have been further diminished by Fiji's coups. Each set of post-coup leaders is faced with the same difficulty: how to reduce public sector spending, halt foreign investment outflow, and meet the conditions attached to foreign aid and economic assistance. The economic remedies they choose invariably reduce income-earning opportunities for women workers in a dramatic fashion. This in turn has profound implications for those who are exposed to violence. Diminished economic circumstances may disincline women victims of violence from accessing health, counselling or legal services for fear that they will incur debts they cannot repay. Moreover, a lack of financial autonomy and a fear of destitution may also disincline women from leaving violent partners.

Together these scenarios remind us, once again, that beyond proclaiming women's right to lives free from violence, we need also to be attentive to women's economic and political functioning and their capacities to secure these rights. Recent efforts to document the changing attitudes towards gender violence amongst Kanak women in New Caledonia provide further evidence to support this claim. In New Caledonia, women have gained an elevated level of political representation thanks to electoral parity laws that were adopted in 2001. However, beyond a simple statistical increase in women's representation, these laws have also enabled women political representatives to mobilise state resources to fund a series of agencies specifically devoted to women's well-being known collectively as 'la secteur de la condition féminine'.[124]

The existence of these agencies, operating at both the national and provincial levels, and the explicit attention they pay to the issue of violence against women, is unique to the region and contrasts starkly with how questions on the status of women are addressed by the state in Fiji. In New Caledonia, the public profile of these agencies has increasingly encouraged Kanak women to resist their exposure to violence and renegotiate gender relations in ways which challenge male conjugal authority.[125] Further, these developments have encouraged Kanak women victims of violence to challenge the perceived leniency of custom court rulings on the crimes perpetrated against them and to pursue cases of gender violence through the criminal justice system.[126] The success of the parity provisions has also emboldened Kanak women to challenge the male-only makeup of New Caledonia's customary senate[127] and to demand a fuller role in economic production.[128] This impetus for gender reform across the social, political and economic domain contrasts starkly with women's relative political invisibility in Fiji and the seemingly static nature of national deliberations on gender disadvantage that occur as a result.

---

124 *Guide educative sur les droits des femmes et sur l'égalité entre les sexes*, 2009, Nouméa: Gouvernement Nouvelle Calédonie, p. 20.
125 Christine Salomon and Christine Hamelin, 2010, 'Vers un changement des norms de genre', in *La Nouvelle Calédonie: Vers un destin commun*, ed. Elsa Faugère and Isabelle Merle, pp. 203–24, Paris: Karthala.
126 Christine Salomon, 2003, 'Quand les filles ne se taisent plus: un aspect du changement postcolonial en Nouvelle Calédonie', *Terrain: Revue d'ethnologie de l'Europe* 40: 1–17, p. 3.
127 Salomon and Hamelin, 'Vers un changement des norms de genre', p. 216.
128 Déwé Gorodé, 2009, 'Preface', in *Guide educative sur les droits des femmes et sur l'égalité entre les sexes*, Nouméa: Gouvernement Nouvelle Calédonie, p. 6.

In this chapter I have discussed the complex array of factors preventing women in Fiji from exerting the level of control over their political and economic environment that might allow them to secure their rights. While much of the debate on gender violence and women's human rights has been predominantly focused on the relationship between the universalist nature of human rights claims and their local cultural fit, this addresses only one aspect of the broader challenge that faces women activists in Fiji and the broader Pacific region. Questions around women's diminished political and economic standing are also highly relevant to experiences of gender violence in Fiji and require the same kind of attention. For the moment, however, these challenges are confronted in a highly cloistered fashion. In the debate on gender violence and human rights, women's capabilities appear to be all but 'lost' from view.

Acknowledgements

My thanks to Aletta Biersack, Martha Macintyre, Margaret Jolly and Katherine Gelber as well as University of Queensland colleagues attending the POLSIS seminar series who have all read, heard, and offered helpful advice on various iterations of this chapter as it has evolved.

References

Ackerly, Brooke. 2001. 'Women's human rights activists as cross-cultural theorists'. *International Feminist Journal of Politics* 3(3): 311–46.

Action Council of Women in Need (ACWIN). 1983. *Rape in Fiji: A Preliminary Report Prepared by the Action Centre for Women in Need (ACWIN)*. Suva: ACWIN.

Adinkrah, Mensah. 1995. *Crime, Deviance and Delinquency in Fiji*. Suva: Fiji Council of Social Services.

Afari, Janet. 2004. 'The human rights of Middle Eastern and Muslim women: A project for the 21st century'. *Human Rights Quarterly* 26: 106–25.

Ahmed, Syed Masud. 2005. 'Intimate partner violence against women: Experiences from a woman-focused development program in Matlab, Bangladesh'. *Journal of Health, Population and Nutrition* 23(1): 95–101.

Ali, Shamima. 2009. Interview with Jemima Garret for *Pacific Beat*, ABC Radio Australia, Suva broadcast, 24 February.

——. 2014. 'Violence free community initiative needs more work'. *Fiji One*. Online: fijione.tv/violence-free-community-initiative-needs-more-work (accessed 19 June 2014).

Asian Development Bank. 2006. *Country Gender Assessment: Republic of the Fiji Islands*. Manila: Asian Development Bank.

Bachelet, Michelle. 2012. Interview with Fran Kelly, for *Pacific Beat*, ABC Radio Australia, 24 August. Online: www.radioaustralia.net.au/international/radio/program/pacific-beat/a-top-un-womens-rights-advocate-heads-for-pacific-islands-forum/1005468 (accessed 11 December 2014).

Bahun-Radunovik, Sanja and V.G. Julie Rajan (eds). 2008. *Violence and Gender in the Globalized World: The Intimate and the Extimate*. Aldershot: Ashgate Publishing.

Balakrishnan, Rajagopal. 2003. *International Law from Below: Development, Social Movements and Third World Resistance*. Cambridge: Cambridge University Press.

Bhagwan Rolls. 2009. Interview with Jemima Garret for *Pacific Beat*, ABC Radio Australia, Suva Broadcast, 24 February.

Binion, Gayle. 1995. 'Human rights: A feminist perspective'. *Human Rights Quarterly* 17: 509–26.

Bouma, Gary D., Douglas Pratt and Rod Ling (eds). 2010. *Religious Diversity in South East Asia and the Pacific*. London: Springer.

Bovarnick, Sylvie. 2007. 'Universal human rights and non-Western normative systems: A comparative analysis of violence against women in Mexico and Pakistan'. *Review of International Studies* 33(1): 59–75.

Brown Thompson, Karen. 2002. 'Women's rights are human rights'. In *Restructuring World Politics: Transnational Social Movements, Networks and Norms*, ed. Sanjeev Khagram, James V. Riker and Kathryn Sikkink, pp. 96–122. Minneapolis: University of Minnesota Press.

Bryant, Jenny. 1993. *Urban Poverty and the Environment in the South Pacific*. Sydney: University of New England Press.

Burgmann, Meredith. 2011. 'Time for women to represent the Pacific'. *Sydney Morning Herald*, 15 September. Online: www.smh.com.au/ federal-politics/political-opinion/time-for-women-to-represent-the-pacific-20110914-1k9lq.html (accessed 12 December 2014).

Callick, Rowan. 2012. 'At last PM rides high on the poles'. *The Australian*, 30 August.

Carling, Mercia and Colleen Peacock-Taylor. 2001. *Study of the Impacts of the Political Crisis on Children and Families in Fiji*. Suva: Save the Children Fund/UNICEF.

Chand, Satish. 2007. 'Swim or sink: The predicament of the Fiji economy'. *Pacific Economic Bulletin* 22(2): 1–21.

Chandra, Anshoo. 2012. 'Economic drivers'. *Fiji Times*, 9 June. Online: fijitimes.com/story.aspx?id=203452 (site discontinued).

Chandra, Dharma and Vasemaca Lewai. 2005. *Women and Men of Fiji Islands: Gender Statistics and Trends*. Suva: University of the South Pacific and Fiji Islands Bureau of Statistics.

Chattier, Priya. 2007. 'The capability approach: Mainstreaming gender into poverty discourses in Fiji'. *Fijian Studies: A Journal of Contemporary Fiji* 5(2): 329–59.

Cockburn, Cynthia. 2011. 'Don't talk to me about war, my life's a battlefield'. *50.50 Open Democracy*, 25 November. Online: www.opendemocracy.net/5050/cynthia-cockburn/%E2%80%9Cdon%E2%80%99t-talk-to-me-about-war-my-life%E2%80%99s-battlefield%E2%80%9D (accessed 21 August 2012).

Connell, R.W. 2002. *Gender*. Cambridge: Polity.

Cowan, Jane K. 2006. 'Culture and rights after *Culture and Rights'*. *American Anthropologist* 108(1): 9–24.

Cretton, Viviane. 2005. 'Traditional Fijian apology as a political strategy'. *Oceania* 75(4): 403–17.

Daurewa, Alisi. 2009. 'Power of women'. *Fiji Times*, 5 May. Online: www.fijitimes.com/story.aspx?ref=archive&id=120437 (site discontinued).

Emberson-Bain, Atu' (ed.). 1997. *Sustainable Development or Malignant Growth? Perspectives of Pacific Island Women*. Suva: Marama Publications.

Faugère, Elsa and Isabelle Merle (eds). 2010. *La Nouvelle Calédonie: Vers un destin commun*. Paris: Karthala.

Ferguson, Kathy E. and Monique Mironescu (eds). 2008. *Gender and Globalization in Asia and the Pacific*. Honolulu: University of Hawai'i Press.

Fiji Coalition of Women's NGOs for the CEDAW Shadow Report. 2009. *Shadow NGO Report on Fiji's Second, Third and Fourth Combined Periodic Report to the Committee on the Elimination of Discrimination against Women*. Online: lib.ohchr.org/HRBodies/ UPR/Documents/Session7/FJ/FWRM_UPR_FJI_S07_2010_Fiji_ WomensRightsMovement_annex1.pdf (accessed 24 August 2012).

Fiji Women's Crisis Centre (FWCC). 2012. 'Women's rights groups question freedom of expression'. Press release posted to Pacific Women's Information Network ListServe, 29 August.

——. 2012. 'Taking the message to the people'. Press release posted to Pacific Women's Information Network ListServe, 21 November.

——. 2013. *Somebody's Life, Everybody's Business! National Research on Women's Health and Life Experiences in Fiji (2010/2011): A survey exploring the prevalence, incidence and attitudes to intimate partner violence in Fiji*. Suva: FWCC. Online: fijiwomen.com/wp-content/uploads/2014/11/1.pdf (accessed 28 November 2015).

Fijilive. 2009. 'Fiji Presidential decree limits human rights commission'. Online: archives.pireport.org/archive/2009/may/05-20-01.htm (accessed 27 August 2012).

Fraser, Arvonne. 1999. 'The origins and development of women's human rights'. *Human Rights Quarterly* 21(4): 853–906.

George, Nicole. 2009. 'Women's organizing in Fiji: Shifting terrains of transnational engagement'. In *Gender and Global Politics in the Asia-Pacific,* ed. Katrina Lee Koo and Bina D'Costa, pp. 175–93. New York: Palgrave-Macmillan.

——. 2010. '"Just like your mother": The politics of feminism and maternity in the Pacific Islands'. *The Australian Feminist Law Journal* 32(June): 77–96.

——. 2012. *Situating Women: Gender Politics and Circumstance in Fiji.* Canberra: ANU E Press. Online: press.anu.edu.au/publications/ situating-women (accessed 28 October 2014).

——. 2014. 'Business as usual in post-election Suva'. *East Asia Forum,* 22 October. Online: www.eastasiaforum.org/2014/10/22/business-as-usual-in-post-election-suva (accessed 28 November 2014).

Gorodé, Déwé. 2009. 'Preface'. In *Guide educative sur les droits des femmes et sur l'égalité entre les sexes.* Nouméa: Gouvernement Nouvelle Calédonie.

Gouvernement Nouvelle Calédonie. 2009. *Guide educative sur les droits des femmes et sur l'égalité entre les sexes.* Nouméa: Gouvernement Nouvelle Calédonie.

Griffen, Vanessa. 1987. *Women, Development and Empowerment: A Pacific Feminist Perspective. Report of a Pacific Women's Workshop, Naboutini, Fiji, 23–26 March 1987.* Kuala Lumpur: Asian and Pacific Development Centre.

Halapua, Winston. 2003. *Tradition, Lotu and Militarism in Fiji.* Lautoka: Fiji Institute of Applied Studies.

Harrington, Christy. 2004. '"Marriage" to capital: The fallback positions of Fiji's women garment workers'. *Development in Practice* 14(4): 495–507.

Hausegger, Virginia. 2010. 'Feminism is failing in the war against women'. *The Drum,* ABC, 28 October. Online: www.abc.net. au/news/2010-09-28/feminism-is-failing-in-the-war-against-women/2277406 (accessed 12 September 2014).

Hill, Helen. 2010. 'Women and religious diversity'. In *Religious Diversity in South East Asia and the Pacific*, ed. Gary D. Bouma, Douglas Pratt and Rod Ling, pp. 247–54. London: Springer.

Iversen, Vergerd. 2003. 'Intra-household inequality: A challenge for the capability approach'. *Feminist Economics* 9(2–3): 93–115.

Joachim, Jutta. 1999. 'Shaping the human rights agenda: The case of violence against women'. In *Gender Politics in Global Governance*, ed. Mary K. Meyer and Elisabeth Prügl, pp. 142–60. Lanham, MD: Rowman and Littlefield.

——. 2003. 'Framing issues, seizing opportunities: The UN, NGOs and women's rights'. *International Studies Quarterly* 47(2): 247–74.

Johnson, Lydia and Joan Alleluia Filemoni-Taefaeono (eds). 2003. '*Weavings: Women Doing Theology in Oceania*. Suva: Institute of Pacific Studies.

Jolly, Margaret. 2005. 'Beyond the horizon? Nationalisms, feminisms and globalization in the Pacific'. *Ethnohistory* 52: 138–66.

——. 2012. 'Introduction—Engendering violence in Papua New Guinea: Persons, power and perilous transformations'. In *Engendering Violence in Papua New Guinea*, ed. Margaret Jolly, Christine Stewart and Carolyn Brewer, pp. 1–45. Canberra: ANU E Press. Online: press.anu.edu.au/publications/engendering-violence-papua-new-guinea (accessed 28 October 2014).

Keck, Kathleen and Margaret Sikkink. 1998. *Activists Beyond Borders*. Ithaca: Cornell University Press.

Kepa, Ro Teimumu. 2011. *Address by the Gone Marama Bale Na Roko Tui Dreketi: A Clarification of Rewa's Perspective Regarding the Illegal Overthrow of the Fiji Government*. Delivered at the Bose Ni Yasana 'O Rewa Burenivudi, Lamanikoro, Rewa, 16 November 2011. Electronic version posted to PACWIN ListServe, 18 November 2011.

Khagram, Sanjeev, James V. Riker and Kathryn Sikkink (eds). 2002. *Restructuring World Politics: Transnational Social Movements, Networks and Norms*. Minneapolis: University of Minnesota Press.

Khan, Anas and Riad Khan. 2007. 'Political and economic instability, and poverty in Fiji'. *Fijian Studies: A Journal of Contemporary Fiji* 5(2): 315–27.

Koo, Katrina Lee and Bina D'Costa (eds). 2009. *Gender and Global Politics in the Asia-Pacific*. New York: Palgrave-Macmillan.

Kumari, Vasala, K.B. 2008. 'Violence and microcredit: A snapshot of Kerala, India'. In *Violence and Gender in the Globalized World: The Intimate and the Extimate*, ed. Sanja Bahun-Radunović and V.G. Julie Rajan, pp. 43–55. Aldershot: Ashgate Publishing.

Lal, Brij V. 2009. 'One hand clapping: Reflections on the first anniversary of Fiji's 2006 Coup'. In *The 2006 Military Takeover in Fiji: A Coup to End All Coups*, ed. Stewart Firth, Jon Frankael and Brij V. Lal, pp. 425–48. Canberra: ANU E Press. Online: press.anu.edu.au/publications/2006-military-takeover-fiji (accessed 13 March 2016).

Lateef, Shireen. 1990. 'Rule by the Danda: Domestic violence among Indo-Fijians'. *Pacific Studies* 13(3): 43–62.

Leckie, Jacqueline. 2002. 'The complexities of women's agency in Fiji'. In *Gender Politics in the Asia-Pacific Region*, ed. Brenda S.A. Yeoh, Peggy Teo and Shirlena Huang, pp. 156–79. New York: Routledge.

Macintyre, Martha. 2012. 'Gender violence in Melanesia and the problem of Millennium Development Goal No. 3'. In *Engendering Violence in Papua New Guinea*, ed. Margaret Jolly, Christine Stewart and Carolyn Brewer, pp. 239–66. Canberra: ANU E Press. Online: press.anu.edu.au/publications/engendering-violence-papua-new-guinea (accessed 28 October 2014).

McKenzie Aucoin, Pauline. 1990. 'Domestic violence and social relations of conflict in Fiji'. *Pacific Studies* 13(3): 23–41.

Meo, Ilisapeci. 2003. 'Asserting women's dignity in a patriarchal world'. In *Weavings: Women Doing Theology in Oceania*, ed. Lydia Johnson and Joan Alleluia Filemoni-Taefaeono, pp. 150–60. Suva: Institute of Pacific Studies.

Merry, Sally Engle. 2003. 'Human rights law and the demonization of culture (and anthropology along the way)'. *Political and Legal Anthropology Review* 26(1): 55–77.

——. 2006. 'Transnational human rights and local activism: Mapping the middle'. *American Anthropologist* 108(1): 38–51.

——. 2006. *Human Rights and Gender Violence: Translating International Law into Local Justice*. Chicago: University of Chicago Press.

——. 2009. *Gender Violence: A Cultural Perspective*. West Sussex: Wiley-Blackwell.

Meyer, Mary K. and Elisabeth Prügl (eds). 1999. *Gender Politics in Global Governance*. Lanham, MD: Rowman and Littlefield.

Mishra, Margaret. 2012. 'A history of Fijian women's activism (1900–2010)'. *Journal of Women's History* 24(2): 115–43.

Morris, Patricia McGrath. 2002. 'The capabilities perspective: A framework for social justice'. *Families in Society* 83(4): 365–73.

'New measures to combat domestic violence in Fiji'. 2009. *Australia Plus*, 8 September 2009. Online: australiaplus.com/international/2009-09-08/new-measures-to-combat-domestic-violence-in-fiji/147772 (site discontinued).

Nussbaum, Martha. 2000. *Women and Human Development: The Capabilities Approach*. Cambridge: Cambridge University Press.

O'Hare, Ursula. 1990. 'Realizing human rights for women'. *Human Rights Quarterly* 21(2): 364–402.

Okin, Susan Moller. 1999. *Is Multiculturalism Bad for Women?* Princeton: Princeton University Press.

Pacific.Scoop. 2014. 'Fiji women's right groups calls for Minister to resign over rape comments'. *Pacific Scoop*, 16 May 2014. Online: pacific.scoop.co.nz/2014/05/fiji-womens-rights-groups-call-for-minister-to-resign-over-rape-comments/ (accessed 8 July 2015).

Peter, Fabienne. 2003. 'Gender and the foundations of social choice: The role of situated agency'. *Feminist Economics* 9(2/3): 13–32.

Pickup, Francine. 2001. *Ending Violence against Women: A Challenge for Development and Humanitarian Work*. Oxfam: Bournemouth.

Pyles, Loretta. 2012. 'The capabilities approach and violence against women: Implications for social development'. In *Companion Reader on Violence Against Women*, ed. Claire M. Renzetti, Jeffrey L. Edleson and Raquel Kennedy Bergen, pp. 25–36. Thousand Oaks, CA: Sage.

Radio New Zealand International. 2009. 'New Fiji decree augments court powers in domestic violence cases', 13 August. Online: www.rnzi.com/pages/news.php?op=read&id=48431 (accessed 15 September 2013).

Ragi, Brenda. 2009. '"Overwhelming and extremely positive response to domestic violence decree" says Attorney General'. Press release, Attorney-General's Chambers (Fiji), 14 September. Online: sgdatabase. unwomen.org/uploads/Fiji%20-%20Domestic%20Violence%20 Decree%20PR%20%282009%29.pdf (site discontinued).

Reilly, Niamh. 2009. *Women's Human Rights: Seeking Gender Justice in a Globalizing Age*. London: Polity.

Renzetti, Claire M., Jeffrey L. Edleson and Raquel Kennedy Bergen (eds). 2012. *Companion Reader on Violence Against Women*. Thousand Oaks, CA: Sage.

Republic of Fiji. 2009. 'Domestic Violence Decree 2009'. In *Republic of Fiji Islands Government Gazette* 10(67) (14 August). Online: www.judiciary.gov.fj/images/dvro/Domestic%20Violence%20 Decree%202009.pdf (accessed 21 November 2014).

Robeyns, Ingrid. 2003. 'Sen's capability approach and gender inequality: Selecting relevant capabilities'. *Feminist Economics* 9(2–3): 61–92.

Salomon, Christine. 2000. 'Les femmes Kanakes face aux violence sexuelles: le tournant judiciaire des années 1990'. *Journale des anthropologues* 82/83: 1–12.

———. 2003. 'Quand les filles ne se taisent plus: un aspect du changement postcolonial en Nouvelle Calédonie'. *Terrain: Revue d'ethnologie de l'Europe* 40: 1–17.

Salomon, Christine and Christine Hamelin. 2010. 'Vers un changement des norms de genre'. In *La Nouvelle Calédonie: Vers un destin commun*, ed. Elsa Faugère and Isabelle Merle, pp. 203–24. Paris: Karthala.

Sen, Amartya. 1999. *Development as Freedom*. Oxford: Oxford University Press.

Slatter, Claire. 1997. 'Banking on the growth model: The World Bank and market policies in the Pacific'. In *Sustainable Development or Malignant Growth? Perspectives of Pacific Island Women*, ed. Atu' Emberson-Bain, pp. 17–36. Suva: Marama Publications.

Smith-Johns, Sharon. 2012. 'Fiji journalists urged to stop censoring themselves'. *Pacific Beat*, ABC Radio Australia, 10 September. Online: www.radioaustralia.net.au/international/radio/program/ pacific-beat/fiji-journalists-urged-to-stop-censoring-themselves /1013552 (accessed 12 September 2012).

Summers, Anne. 2012. 'Conspiracy of silence lets persecution of PM fester'. *The Age*, 1 September. Online: www.theage.com.au/opinion/ politics/conspiracy-of-silence-lets-persecution-of-pm-fester- 20120831-255tt.html#ixzz25JrcQW1o (accessed 4 September 2012).

Taylor, John P. 2008. 'The social life of rights: "Gender antagonism", modernity and *Raet* in Vanuatu'. *The Australian Journal of Anthropology* 19(2): 165–78.

Teaiwa, Teresia. 2008. 'Globalizing and gendered forces: The contemporary militarization of Pacific/Oceania'. In *Gender and Globalization in Asia and the Pacific*, ed. Kathy E. Ferguson and Monique Mironescu, pp. 318–32. Honolulu: University of Hawai'i Press.

True, Jacqui. 2010. 'The political economy of violence against women: A feminist international relations perspective'. *The Australian Feminist Law Journal* 32(June): 39–59.

UN Women (Pacific). 2011. *Ending Violence against Women and Girls: Evidence, Data and Knowledge in Pacific Island Countries*. Suva: UN Women.

UNDP (United Nations Development Program). 1996. *Fiji Poverty Report*. Suva: UNDP and Fiji Government.

UNIFEM (Pacific). 1999. *Women and Political Empowerment: A Resource Manual for the Pacific*. Suva: UNIFEM.

UNIFEM. 1999. *Pacific Women: Getting into Politics: Fiji as a Best Practice Case Study*. Suva: UNIFEM.

Varani-Norton, Eta. 2005. 'The church versus women's push for change: The case of Fiji'. *Fijian Studies* 3(2): 223–47.

Wilcox, Paula. 2006. *Surviving Domestic Violence: Gender, Poverty and Agency*. Houndmills: Palgrave Macmillan.

Yeoh, Brenda S.A., Peggy Teo and Shirlena Huang (eds). 2002. *Gender Politics in the Asia-Pacific Region*. New York: Routledge.

3

Men's Matters: Changing Masculine Identities in Papua New Guinea

Philip Gibbs

Divine Word University, Madang

Visiting Fellow, School of Culture, History and Language,
The Australian National University

Human rights discourse has increasingly been called upon to provide a foundation for greater equality between men and women. This is particularly the case when confronted by the issue of men and violence in the current context of Papua New Guinea (PNG). Human rights as an ideal inspires most aid agencies, and church-based agencies such as Caritas promote human rights ideals, but also draw inspiration from Scriptural and theological traditions. In PNG, given that most people profess Christianity, a church-based agency may play an important role in interpreting rights language and values into cultural frameworks meaningful to people in a given local context. This article tells of the strategies used and issues encountered by church workers meeting about masculinities (or what have been called 'Men's Matters') over a number of years with a group of men from the Western Province in PNG. This case study of the Men's Matters program provides insights from men's perspective on the task of negotiating concepts of human rights in PNG.

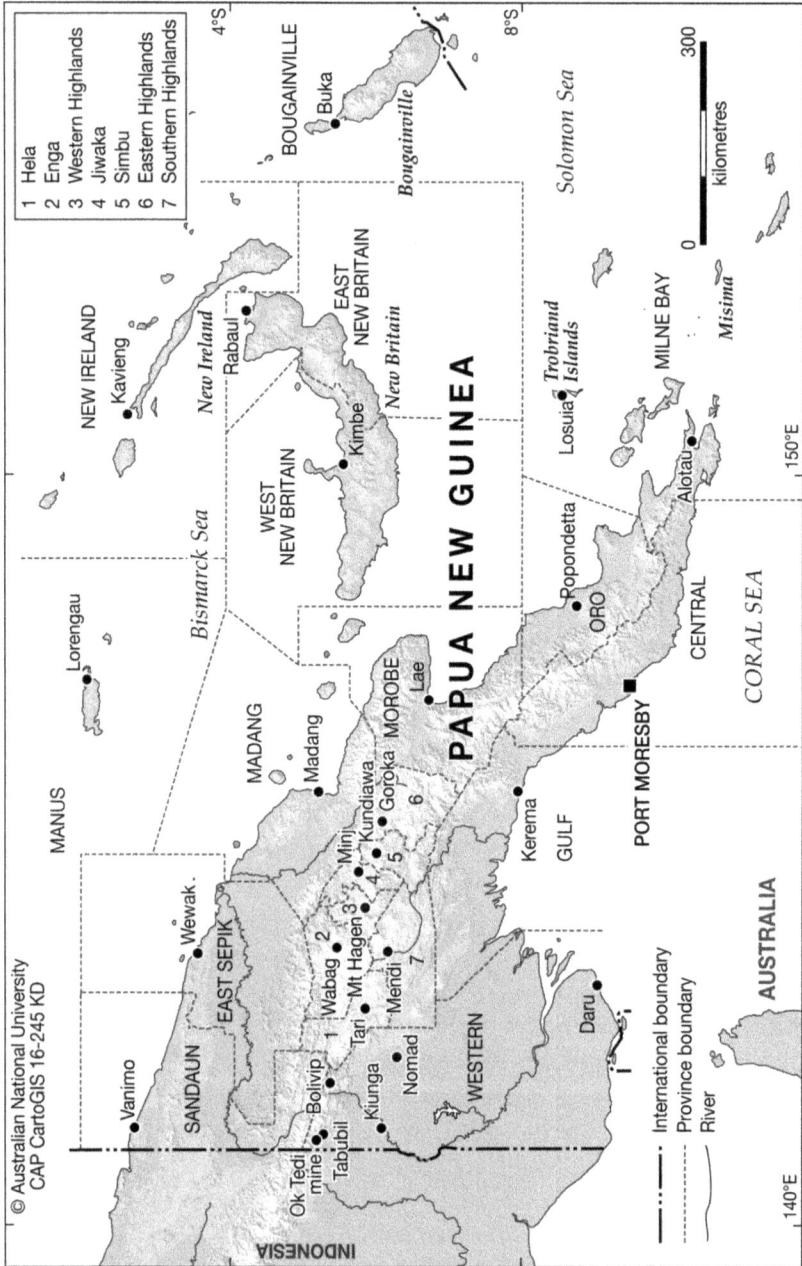

Map 3. Papua New Guinea

Source. © The Australian National University. CartoGIS ANU 16-245 KD

The program with men in the Western Province began in 2006 and continues to the present day. There were two principal initial motivating factors. First, men in the Catholic Diocese of Daru-Kiunga noted how women met in women's groups, which seemed to recognise women and to benefit women and girls in terms of projects and support. The men expressed the desire to have their own groups. Bishop Gilles Côté agreed to their request, but aware of the limitations of attempts to set up 'papa groups' in other places, he wanted to have a Men's Movement that would not reinforce traditional concepts of male authority over women but that would support men in facing the modern world, including healthy mutual relationships with their wives and with their families.

The second motivating factor was the Caritas Australia report by Richard Eves exploring the role of men and masculinities in PNG.[1] Eves noted how in parts of PNG many men see their manhood as dependent on their control over women and that they use violence to achieve this. Could violence be addressed in a way that generates empowerment for both men and women? Eves recommended working with men and boys but that men's groups be completely reconceptualised and restructured to better foster gender equity.[2] Eves visited Kiunga in the Western Province and was told how violence was becoming less acceptable and that there had been some success in reducing it.[3] He notes, though, that there was some misreading of the issue and that gender equity was still conceptualised within a model of opposition and dominance: entailing the equal right to tell one's partner what to do.

The initial workshop for Men's Matters in Kiunga (13–17 November 2006) brought together 39 men from all 12 parishes of the Diocese— extending from Daru in the south to Bolivip in the Star Mountains to the north. Men from the eastern parish of Nomad walked five days to come to Kiunga. It was a diverse group ranging in age from the mid-20s to the 60s and with formal education from nil to tertiary level.

---

1   Richard Eves, 2006, *Exploring the Role of Men and Masculinities in Papua New Guinea in the 21st Century: How to Address Violence in Ways that Generate Empowerment for Both Men and Women*, Report for Caritas Australia.

2   Ibid., p. 63.

3   Ibid., p. 23.

They were invited to come to reflect on their identity and roles as men and on the many issues that men face today in a society that is rapidly changing from the impact of copper mining and logging in the area, among other impacts. Though violence was not mentioned specifically at first, it was a significant underlying theme on the part of the organisers. Nor was rights-based language and values a topic for explicit discussion at first. Rather, the facilitators (the Bishop as recognised leader, I was advisor and Mr Joe Kirinam was the men's coordinator for the diocese) decided to start where 'men were at' and to work from there. Themes for the first four days in 2006 were: boyhood, becoming a man, men and women, men facing the future. The principal outcomes sought were those of reflecting together to identify how men understand their roles as men and to develop a strategic plan that would assist men in the diocese to free themselves from whatever was preventing them from living out their roles 'in a life-giving way'.

The workshops involved presentations, free discussion and dramatic presentations. Typically facilitators provided a brief introduction to a theme, then participants would meet in groups to share their own experiences and later report back to the full assembly—verbally, in writing, graphically or in the form of drama. Group reporting often raised questions and issues that could be discussed by the larger group. Other than themes, such as those mentioned above, there was no detailed pre-established program. Facilitators took detailed notes of the discussion and feedback and met each evening with a steering committee to discern how best to proceed the next day. At the end of the third year, there was an afternoon using the 'Most Significant Change' (MSC) technique for evaluation.[4] All the men participated in this exercise. With their permission, the stories were recorded and many of the quotations in this article are from those stories.

---

4   Rick Davies and Jess Dart, 2005, *The 'Most Significant Change' (MSC) Technique: A Guide to its Use.*

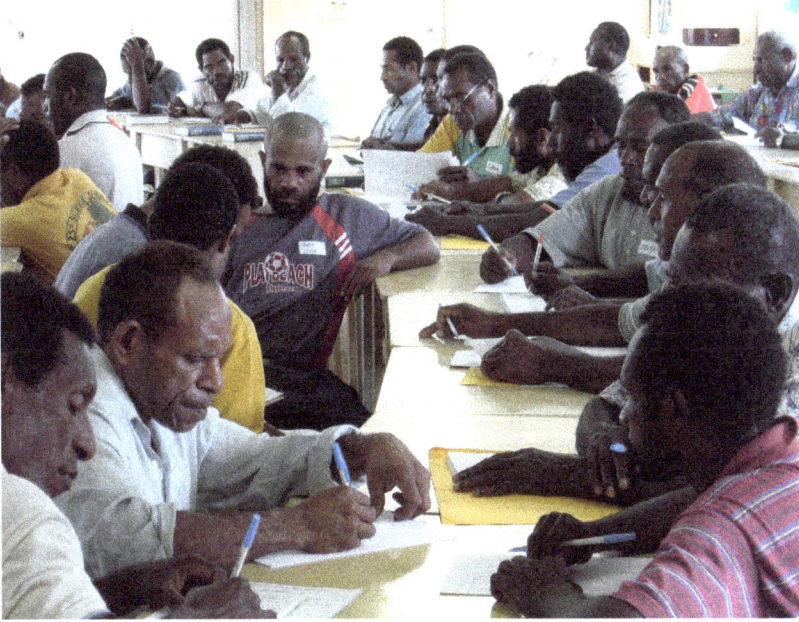

Figure 3. Men's Matters meeting at Kiunga
Source. Photographed by Philip Gibbs, June 2008

An important insight from the initial meeting was that frequently gender roles and identities involve inequality and power imbalance between men and women, and that this imbalance is associated with gender violence. So, the second workshop in Kiunga in July 2007 focused specifically on violence in its many forms. This disclosed a number of issues touching on men's emotional life, so the third gathering for a week in June 2008 focused on the 'inner life' of men. As part of the meeting, the men engaged creatively with the images of chief, warrior, wise man and lover. The fourth workshop in June 2009 followed the theme 'Men building hope for the future'. Concentrating on three issues—the environmental and social effects of the huge Ok Tedi mine, the spread of HIV and AIDS, and sorcery or *sanguma*—they decided to work to counter the negative effects of such concerns and to establish a Men's Movement launched publicly at the 50th Jubilee celebrations of the diocese that same year.

The participants clearly recognised the need for such a program, as evidenced by their commitment over time. Gatherings for the Men's Movement continued for three years at the parish level until a meeting in Kiunga in October 2012 with the core group team of 12 men from six parishes. At that meeting we evaluated developments to date and made recommendations for the future. The principal topics considered at that meeting were the framework used for understanding relations between men and women and the ways that human rights are part of men's ongoing awareness program about the roles and responsibilities of men in the communities.

In this chapter I illustrate how issues associated with masculinity, violence and human rights were interpreted by the men and how the gatherings promoted awareness, with understandings developed over time as they have worked to form a Men's Movement in the Diocese of Daru-Kiunga.[5] Specifically I will discuss how we have discovered three significant points that influence the framework by which men relate to women, namely roles and duties that are not exclusive to men, equality within the discourse on difference, and the move from a hierarchical to an egalitarian model of control within a community context.

Becoming a 'man'

Details of men's initiation traditions differ throughout the Western Province.[6] However, now, due to influences including Western education, Christian churches, modern media and wage labour, formal initiation is no longer practised. Those who had experienced formal initiation mentioned a sense of belonging, security and responsibility they felt as a consequence of going through the rites and ceremonies. In former times boys were separated from their mothers and sisters and advised that inappropriate contact with women would weaken them and prevent their growth. They would learn from sayings about discipline in relationships. For example, 'When you see a nice flower growing in someone else's garden, don't pick it' (meaning, no adultery). Today young men and women attend school together,

---

5   The Diocese of Daru-Kiunga received financial support from Caritas Australia toward funding for the Men's Matters workshops.
6   F.E. Williams, 1936, *Papuans of the Transfly*, Oxford: Oxford University Press; Fredrik Barth, 1987, *Rituals and Knowledge among the Baktaman in New Guinea*, New Haven: Yale University Press; Bruce M. Knauft, 1999, *From Primitive to Postcolonial in Melanesia and Anthropology*, Ann Arbor: University of Michigan Press; Tony Crook, 1999, 'Growing knowledge in Bolivip, Papua New Guinea', *Oceania* 69(4): 225–42.

join the same youth groups, and meet together on social occasions, raising the question of how young men negotiate their gender identity nowadays.

In cultural groups we discussed the initiation rites that most of our more mature participants had experienced and then considered values associated with them and how we could somehow apply those values in today's world. For example, the boys would go for long periods into the forest. That was to learn the value of independence. 'We don't expect boys to go and spend months in the forest today. So how can they learn the value of independence?' In another example, the boys would be hit by nettles in order to teach them discipline and the ability to endure pain. 'Without such practices how can we teach them values such as discipline and the ability to endure pain?' The latter example raises questions about attitudes to intentionally inflicting pain and whether such practices are helpful at all. Traditional or not, we need to consider what values are helpful, particularly in terms of developing gender identity suited to healthy and harmonious relationships today.

The men settled on three roles defining their identity as men: provider, protector and leader. It was said that a real man provides food and shelter for his family and community. He protects his family and community, his land and his pride. He makes wise decisions that guide his family and community 'lest they be adrift on the ocean with no rudder to steer'. Such roles fit easily with traditional understandings such as the hunter providing meat, the protector in warfare, and the leader in a village.

However, as the workshops progressed, men came to realise that, though culture and cultural traditions came from their 'ancestors', their ancestors were people, so that people can change cultural practices. As one man put it, culture 'is not like a stone'. It can change with human decisions, so they had to make informed and wise decisions about what is helpful and to be retained today and what is not helpful and is to be discarded. For example, they agreed that knowledge and practices associated with sorcery to harm or kill others should to be set aside today.

So, what should fathers or uncles seek to pass on to the next generation? Fathers settled on values associated with the roles of provider, protector and leader. They noted that there are too many 'boys walking around in men's bodies'. These are irresponsible men who abuse alcohol and drugs and seem not to know boundaries to their behaviour. There are many men seeking an identity in wealth, power and many wives. The group questioned whether these are healthy qualities for a 'real man' today. 'Masculine' qualities such as responsibility, assertiveness and strength should be found first of all in the roles of provider, protector and leader.

Further insight came when we tried to assign 'women's' roles corresponding to 'men's' roles of provider, protector and leader. Terms such as nurturer, care giver, etc., seemed not to fit and some of the men pointed out how women can be providers, protectors and leaders also. They gave examples:

> My wife provides just as much if not more of the food for our family. She also provides in other ways; for example, she teaches our baby to call me papa. (of female providers)

> When I got drunk and was in court, my wife defended and protected me. She told them how I am really a good man and that it is just when I drink beer that I do wrong things. She even offered to pay for the damage I had caused. (of female protectors)

> My wife and I observed how our son was coming home late. One time he came very late and my wife told me, 'Don't open the door', and she called out to our son, 'Go and sleep with your friends elsewhere, you're not coming into the house at this time of night'. I think she was right. It was a way of teaching our son discipline and that there are boundaries. (of female leaders)

So, over time, the men discovered that the qualities of provider, protector and leader are not simply masculine qualities within a dualistic concept of male and female. They are qualities the genders share but learn to express in different ways. There is no single way of being a man. A man might be a biological father, but he can learn to be a social father also—actually caring for children, something not typically looked upon as a male role. The men agreed that the challenge today is to find the support and assistance required, particularly by people who provide examples of healthy qualities and values. This is needed to counter peer pressure that might shame a man who departs from stereotyped male roles. It is easier said than done because with rapid social and cultural change there are few men and women who have trodden the same path as those who are negotiating their gender identity today. This process might be considered as the initial step toward 'vernacularization',[7] whereby new, or introduced, ideas about sociocultural change and the incorporation of alternative values are rendered acceptable.

Why violence?

Violence, particularly gender-based violence or gender violence, has been noted in many reports, including the Law Reform Commission,[8] Susan Toft and Susanne Bonnell,[9] Christine Bradley,[10] Margaret Jolly, Christine Stewart and Carolyn Brewer's edited collection,[11] and the UN Special Rapporteur on Violence against Women.[12] The topic received wide coverage in 2011 over the case of Joy Wartovo, who is the victim of numerous assaults by her policeman husband.[13] There is an active Facebook site with daily accounts of gender-based violence in PNG.[14]

Why such violence? I began by supporting the opinion of Richard Eves when he says that violence is seen as a normal and justified way of resolving conflict or expressing anger and that 'many men see their manhood as dependent on their control over women and they use violence to achieve this'.[15] The men in Kiunga did not disagree with this view, but their examples reveal a more personal understanding of the complexity of the issues involved.

---

7   Sally Engle Merry, 2006, *Human Rights and Gender Violence: Translating International Law into Local Justice*, Chicago and London: University of Chicago Press, p. 219.
8   Law Reform Commission, 1987, *Interim Report*, Port Moresby: Papua New Guinea Law Reform Commission.
9   Susan Toft and Susanne Bonnell (eds), 1985, *Marriage and Domestic Violence in Rural Papua New Guinea*, Occasional Paper no. 18, Port Moresby: Law Reform Commission.
10   Christine Bradley, 2001, *Family and Sexual Violence in PNG: An Integrated Long-Term Strategy*, Report to the Family Violence Action Committee of the Consultative Implementation and Monitoring Council, Discussion Paper no. 84, Port Moresby: Institute of National Affairs.
11   Margaret Jolly, Christine Stewart and Carolyn Brewer (eds), 2012, *Engendering Violence in Papua New Guinea*, Canberra: ANU E Press.
12   Office of the High Commission for Human Rights, 2012, 'Special rapporteur on violence against women finalises country mission to Papua New Guinea', *United Nations Human Rights*, Port Moresby, 26 March.
13   Rait man, 2011, 'Police bombarded with emails over Joy Wartovo case', *ActNow: For a Better Papua New Guinea*.
14   *Unite to End Family Violence: Papua New Guineans Against Domestic Violence*.
15   Eves, *Exploring the Role of Men and Masculinities in Papua New Guinea in the 21st Century*, p. 14.

The men noted that there are different forms of violence and that while a man might use physical violence, women might resort to provocative verbal violence. A woman who says the names of former boyfriends who are 'better' than her husband, for example, or who tells him to 'go and eat his mother's vagina' risks receiving a violent response. Men also may resort to verbal and emotional violence. Examples of verbal and emotional violence used by the men include statements such as: 'Go and sell yourself if you want money.' 'I paid bride price, so you have to do what I say.' 'I must have married the wrong rib.'

The men noted how arguments arise over money, discipline of children, the frequency and demands of relatives, and one partner returning home late, provoking mistrust and jealousy and accusations of bringing sickness into the family. The men noticed how domestic life could have added strains in a town setting, with social clubs and the availability of alcohol. They seemed particularly offended when wives in town drank alcohol. They said that taking control, even in violent ways, makes a man feel good, particularly if the wife has been *bikhet* (assertive, obstinate). He feels that he has taught her a lesson. 'But then afterward I feel sorry for her.' This is particularly so if she needs hospital treatment and he has to pay hospital fees.

In one session we showed a drawing of a man beating his wife in front of three young children and asked the men in groups to imagine the story behind the picture (Figure 4). Several groups thought that the man was returning home to find his wife had not prepared food in time. One group noted that a girl child in the picture is crying and thought that the man was beating his wife because she had hit the girl. Another group thought that the woman appeared pregnant and that the man was her husband and was beating her because he thought she had been unfaithful and was pregnant to another man. One group said that the man was her husband and that he is angry with his wife because she refused to have sex with him (referred to as a 'bedroom problem'). With three young children in the picture, they assumed that the couple was not following family planning and that the wife was avoiding sex because she did not want to become pregnant.

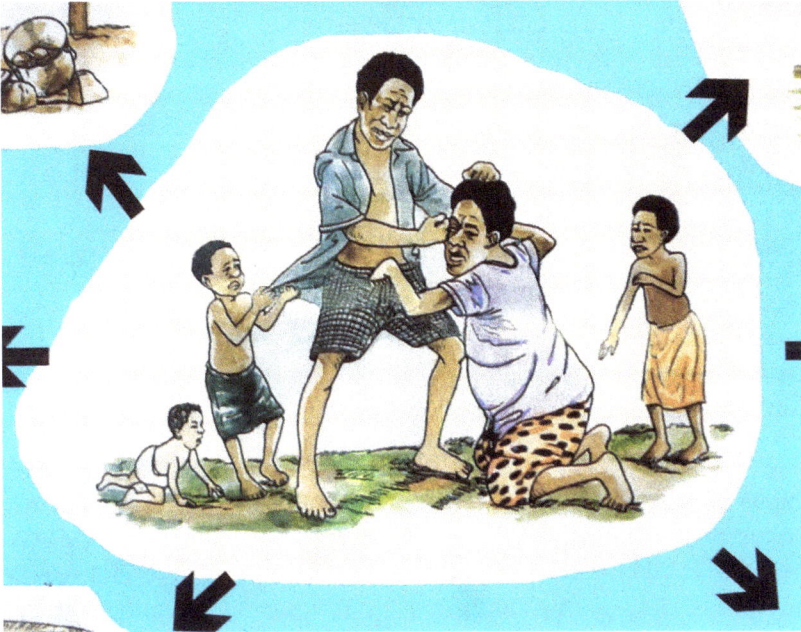

Figure 4. Poster on domestic violence, displayed in Mt Hagen
Hospital, PNG
Source. Department of Health poster, 18 September 2012

The men agreed that there might be many excuses offered, but that the principal reason for violence between partners is one partner (usually the woman) declining sex. *'Las wik yu gat sikmun na nau yu gat gen!'* (Last week you gave the excuse that you had your period and now you say you have it again!). As these responses indicate, men concentrated on *female* behaviour that implicitly justified their violence. Their use of violence as a form of punishment for affront or non-compliance with their desires was seldom questioned, even though some felt remorse because of its effects. A number of the men noted that family planning is an issue, but even more fundamental is the issue of trust and communication between the partners. 'It is not a matter of control. We have to understand and respect our partner as a human being and learn to manage our emotions and desires.'

Violence in its cultural context

Cases of gender violence are not just random individual acts of misconduct but are deeply rooted in structural relationships.[16] These structural relationships include kinship relations, marriage relationships, religious belief and practice, the socioeconomic setting and many more. Customary rights are integrated in these structures. We are in a situation today where customary rights may be questioned in the context of massive social changes. These changes include the commoditisation of the economy, the introduction of new legal and biomedical regimes, and the influence of Christianity.[17] Such changes can mean greater antagonism between men and women, fuelled by novel, modern tensions.[18]

Papua New Guinea ratified the Convention on the Elimination of All Forms of Discrimination against Women (CEDAW) in 1995. CEDAW helps reveal the breadth of the structural relationships of violence in any one society with indicators such as education, health, political representation, legislation and many more. In 2008, PNG sent a delegation to the UN to report for the first time on compliance with the convention. The delegation reported compliance with 28 of 113 indicators, partial compliance with 32 more indicators, and no compliance with the remaining 53 indicators.[19] The review committee was highly critical of the PNG situation. In its concluding comments the committee noted 'its deep concern at the persistence of violence against women including sexual violence at the domestic and community levels ... such violence appears to be socially legitimized and accompanied by a culture of silence and impunity'.[20] There is little to indicate that the situation has improved since then.

---

16   Ibid., p. 10.
17   Margaret Jolly, 2012, 'Introduction—Engendering violence in Papua New Guinea: Persons, power and perilous transformations', in *Engendering Violence in Papua New Guinea*, ed. Margaret Jolly, Christine Stewart and Carolyn Brewer, pp. 1–45, Canberra: ANU E Press, p. 31.
18   Ibid., p. 9.
19   UNIFEM and UNDP, 2007, *Translating CEDAW into Law: CEDAW Legislative Compliance in Nine Pacific Island Countries*.
20   Committee on the Elimination of Discrimination against Women, 'Concluding observations of the Committee on the Elimination of Discrimination against Women, Papua New Guinea', Forty-sixth session. 12–30 July 2010, para. 29.

The men's group in Kiunga tested out opinions through discussion on several assumptions that some local men seem to make. One such assumption is that 'men are naturally aggressive, so they cannot help hitting their wives when they get angry with them'. The men as a group disagreed with this assumption, noting that it was more that men cannot control their emotions. Men need to channel their energy into less hurtful practices. An opinion was offered that by hitting women some men cover up their own inadequacies. We viewed the film *Stap Isi* (Take it Easy) produced in 1989 by Christine Bradley for the PNG Law Reform Commission.[21] The film is about two men, both of whom are in the habit of hitting their wives, and how they changed through the intervention of a teacher, a judge and a pastor, among others. The film depicts how men can learn to deal with their emotions, and on the many occasions I have screened the film, I have noted that men viewing the film appreciate that message.

Peer pressure is a significant cultural issue. Men noted how if a man helps his wife, other men would offer smart comments to make him feel ashamed—'*Em harim tok bilong meri tumas*' (He listens too much to his wife). '*Em kago boi bilong yu ah?*' ('Is he your [the wife's] labourer/servant?'). 'If I am on a bush track I don't mind helping my wife carry the load or helping to carry our child, but once we get to the public market, I don't like to carry the child. I wouldn't want men to see and talk behind my back.'

In such a context legal and judicial measures focusing on men and women will not solve the problem. In fact stress on legal rights of men and women can miss the point that gender operates in a broadly gendered field of discourse and is much more complex, fluid and relational than just male and female sexed bodies.[22]

---

21   Christine Bradley, 1989, *Stap Isi* (film), Port Moresby: PNG Law Reform Commission.
22   John P. Taylor, 2008, 'The social life of rights: "Gender antagonism", modernity and *raet* in Vanuatu', in *Changing Pacific Masculinities*, ed. John P. Taylor, special issue of the *Australian Journal of Anthropology* 19(2): 165–78, p. 171.

Inner states and energies

Attitudes and behaviour are influenced by external forces. However, persons are also influenced by the very personal context of inner states and personal tensions. We talked about the physical and psychological signs of anger, and different ways to manage anger by acting, not reacting. 'I need to find where the tension is lodged in my body and to find ways to get rid of that tension. Drinking only drives it deeper, and eventually it will come out in unhealthy ways.'

During our gatherings we spoke about aspects of a man's inner life, and there was time for prayer and personal reflection. Discussion focused on power and various energies. Power can be 'power over', 'power with/for', and 'power within'. Abuse involves misuse of power—usually as 'power over'. 'Being a man is indeed about power, but—power for good and power for others. I think power itself is not evil since the Holy Spirit is the source of power, but bashing a woman is power out of control.'

We talked about sexuality as a power within us that attracts us toward the other sex. However, too often men are like 'roosters', making noise to attract the hens and chase away the other roosters. Roosters compete with each other. We also talked about violence—physical, sexual, emotional, social, psychological. The men considered rape as a form of sexual violence in which men act like dogs. (Some were incredulous when we raised the topic of marital rape, since it challenges their understanding of male sexual rights.)

We also engaged creatively with the images of chief, warrior, wise man and lover. The images come from the work of Richard Rohr in the USA (2005).[23] After some explanation, the men interpreted these images and applied them to their own life situations. When do we exercise the energies of these types? To summarise the kinds of observations made:

---

23   Richard Rohr with Joseph Martos, 2005, *From Wild Man to Wise Man: Reflections on Male Spirituality*, Cincinnati: St Anthony Messenger Press. Richard Rohr, an American priest, writes on male spirituality. He is founder of the international movement, 'Men As Learners & Elders' (MAL.E.s).

Chief

When everything seems to be going wrong—people are fighting and arguing—the chief comes and suddenly everything seems to be right. That person has chiefly energy. The world is safe and reasonable. The chief is the symbol of power used well. A man who builds fear and beats his wife is the opposite of a chief. A person with true chiefly energy uses authority to serve others and encourages others to use their creative energies. As one person put it:

> The person with the best chiefly energy that I have met is my wife. She encouraged me to take on responsibilities to serve others and not only to serve myself. I learned from her how important it is to greet people in the right manner and care for those in need. Because of her I am now a leader in the family, the church, and the community.

Warrior

The warrior in all cultures is a person of courage, persistence, stamina and devotion to a cause. Warrior energy allows us to protect property, life, the truth and the good. Without boundaries or submission to the chief warrior, energy can lead to violence. Somebody explained:

> I have been organising sports with the youth. It is difficult work. You think the game is going OK and then others come in and cause trouble. They have no boundaries and simply run around looking for entertainment. I don't go in there to beat them physically, but I do go in to challenge them.

Wise man

People need wise persons in their lives so that they walk together on the right road and live happy lives. Wisdom energy allows one to correct and challenge what is wrong. Fake wise persons believe too much in themselves, thinking that they are wise and can go on their own. As someone observed:

> It used to be that before a man and woman would get together, the parents would meet with them and give advice: things like carrying firewood, not fighting, sharing work, and so on. So often now young people get together without that wise advice.

Lover

Lover energy allows us to see what is beautiful, true and good in life. It goes wrong (the dark lover) when the lover seeks things selfishly, looks for artificial good feelings (using drugs, etc.). Often the dark lover is a wounded lover who has tasted love but who cannot find it and so looks for it in superficial shortcut ways. One of the participants gave a personal testimony that illustrates the transition from a dark lover to a man more in tune with what we called lover energy:

> Having attended two men's seminars in 2006 and 2007, I literally made great improvements and changes in my life. At the end of 2006 my wife deserted me and went back to her home. Her main reasons behind her desertion are genuine, being that I've been strongly married to my job and had little time for the family, always getting drunk and bashing her for unknown reasons, and being a womaniser. After absorbing the fruit of the two seminars, I came to realise my true identity as a man. I decided not to repeat the same mistakes. I said to myself, if someone out there can change, I can too. So that's what I literally did. While back in the village, my wife wrote numerous letters to her friends to put an eye on me and advise her if I had another wife, whether I'm still drinking, womanising, and socialising with friends. After she had positive reports from her friends, she then wrote a love letter to me, apologising for her desertion, asking for my forgiveness and if I could accept her returning. Without delay I phoned her and told her to pick up her ticket at the airlines office, which she did. From there on we have lived happily. Our place is now a good place to work and live. I'm not doing it for my sake but for everyone in the community because we live in one community.

As advisor I was wary of introducing the images of chief, warrior, wise man and lover, lest we slip into a form of pop psychology. But the men really did like it, and entered into long conversations using the images. It was a decidedly 'modern' way of getting in touch with their inner lives in a way they were not used to doing, but they were intrigued interpreting these universal images in local narratives.

Men and Christianity

The group gathered together by the Bishop is not a random sample of men in Western Province. They identify as Catholic leaders, and presumably their Christian faith has some influence on their attitudes and their behaviour.[24] Meetings began and ended with prayer and ample time was given for personal meditative reflection.

We should note with Eves that Christianity is not monolithic and that different churches have different interpretations.[25] Nor is there a uniform approach within a particular church. For example, a majority of Catholic priests would not fully agree with the advice on virtuous patience given by the late Father Ernst Golly that a woman should rely just on prayer and faith in God to change her violent partner.[26] However, the Catholic Church has not had good press in recent times, and Bishop Côté admitted in a presentation during the fourth workshop, 'Our church tends to be a patriarchal church—which does not recognize the feminine. The church is struggling with this and in our Diocese we are trying to promote community and team work where men and woman participate together.'

The church relies on Biblical and other traditions to educate members about the origins of men and women and appropriate behaviour. There are two accounts of creation in Genesis. The first is where Yahweh creates man and woman together: 'So God created humankind in his image, in the image of God he created them, male and female he created them' (Genesis 1: 27–28, NRSV). This is the origin of the *Imago Dei* concept of human dignity stemming from human beings being made in the 'image of God'. The second creation account in

---

24   The majority (96 per cent) of citizens in PNG identify as Christian. See National Statistical Office, 2003, *Papua New Guinea 2000 Census National Report*, Port Moresby: National Statistical Office, p. 25.

25   Richard Eves, 2012, 'Christianity, masculinity and gender violence in Papua New Guinea', SSGM Discussion Paper 2012/2, Canberra: The Australian National University, p. 4. The men in this case study view moral action based on Christian virtue as part of the process of change that has already gained currency, unlike the dramatic disjunction between old and new recorded by Robbins during a period of ritual revival among the Urapmin of Sandaun Province. See Joel Robbins, 2004, *Becoming Sinners: Christianity and Moral Torment in a Papua New Guinea Society*, Berkeley: University of California Press.

26   Anna-Karina Hermkens, 2012, 'Becoming Mary: Marian devotion as a solution to gender-based violence in urban PNG', in *Engendering Violence in Papua New Guinea*, ed. Margaret Jolly, Christine Stewart and Carolyn Brewer, pp. 137–62. Canberra: ANU E Press.

the second chapter of Genesis includes the well-known passage of woman being formed from Adam's rib. The story continues with God presenting Eve as *ishshah* (Hebrew woman) to Adam, and that is why 'a man leaves his father and his mother and clings to his wife and they become one flesh' (Genesis 2: 21–24). The men in the group generally interpreted the story meaning that the woman was formed from a man's side (close to his heart) in order for her to face life at his side. Such an image may be interpreted in terms of either complementarity or equality between women and men. The complementarity of male and female is usually understood to mean that men and women have different social roles, which easily leads to a claim that women should be excluded from some of these roles.

Other scripture passages were noted during the meetings: for example, the passage in which Saul, threatened by David, threw a sword at him (1 Samuel 18: 11). David could have retaliated but didn't and spared Saul. The book of Sirak gives advice to parents, 'He who educates his son will make his enemy jealous … His son is like him' (Sirak 30: 1–4). The Pauline corpus is somewhat controversial in terms of instruction on relations between men and women; however, the passage that we heard from the men referred to there no longer being male or female, 'for all of you are one in Christ Jesus' (Galatians 3: 28). The scriptures contain many passages related to management of anger: for example, 'Do not be quickly provoked in your spirit, for anger resides in the lap of fools' (Ecclesiastes 7: 9) and 'Be angry but do not sin; do not let the sun go down on your anger' (Ephesians 4: 26). Such passages support a message of equality and peace, which also finds expression in the Catechism of the Catholic Church.[27]

The message from these passages comes together well in an evaluation from St John's parish, Matkomnai:[28]

> We are all created differently and gifted with different gifts and talents. Physically we are different. We have different attitudes and characters, and we belong to a different family, clan and tribe. But we are coming from the same Father, God in Heaven. As children of God we have the same dignity. We are created in his own image.

---

27 Catholic Bishops' Conference, 2009, *Bai Olgeta Manmeri i Pulap Tru Long Laip Bilong Krais*, Katekismo bilong ol Katolik Manmeri bilong Papua Niugini na Solomon Ailan, Goroka: Catholic Bishops' Conference of PNG and SI, n. 944.

28 Eves, 'Christianity, masculinity and gender violence in Papua New Guinea', p. 5.

God created human beings making them to be like him (Genesis 1: 27), we have the same Holy Spirit. We are all one in Christ so that we are EQUAL. We are no longer Jews or Greeks or slaves or free persons or even men or women, but we are all the same, we are Christians: We are one in Christ Jesus (Galatians 3: 28).[29]

As Eves points out, this passage illustrates a way of framing the discourse on equality within a discourse on difference. The men in the Men's Matters workshops were more likely to view humanity and human relations from a Biblical perspective than from a perspective based on secular understandings of human rights.[30] They, like the women Martha Macintyre discusses, based ideas of humanity, justice and virtue in their understanding of all human beings as God's creation. Thus, the process of vernacularisation is one that men managed through their embrace of Christianity rather than through the secular humanism that underpins understandings of human rights in countries such as Australia or the United States.

Rights—natural, customary and universal

When discussing rights, the men concluded that everyone has rights by virtue of being a human being made in the image of God. The *Imago Dei* concept provided the ultimate justification for engagement in human rights. Examples cited were right to life, right to eat, right to shelter, etc. However, rights are closely associated with human dignity, and I noticed that the quality of life, what one eats, and the type of shelter seemed seldom to be considered. Human rights discourse in Catholic theological circles in recent times has increasingly been associated with a preferential option for the poor; beginning with actual victims, rather than generalised terms such as 'human beings'.[31] The men in Kiunga admitted that customary rights generally favour men, and initially they felt little need to apologise for that. So from a gender perspective, even though the Biblical text refers to both

---

29   St John Parish, 2005, 'Evaluation', unpublished report, Catholic Church, St John Parish, Matkomnai: Diocese of Daru-Kiunga, p. 3.

30   See also Martha Macintyre, 2000, '"Hear us, women of Papua New Guinea": Melanesian women and human rights', in *Human Rights and Gender Politics: Perspectives in the Asia Pacific Region*, ed. Anne-Marie Hilsdon, Martha Macintyre, Vera Mackie and Maila Stivens, pp. 141–71, London and New York: Routledge, p. 163.

31   Ethna Regan, 2010, *Theology and the Boundary Discourse of Human Rights*, Washington DC: Georgetown University Press, pp. 151, 161.

men and women being made in the image of God, there is ample room for a more just interpretation if lower status is attributed to one representation of that image. We also discussed land rights, which in the primarily virilocal custom of the Western Province applies more to men than to women.

When did they first hear that 'wife-bashing' is a crime? Most had heard during the past 10 years, either on the radio, TV, or through newspapers. Several heard about it during instruction prior to church weddings. One heard about it from the nurses at the hospital and another in notices in church on Mother's Day. It was new to them. As one said, 'My father had four wives, and I used to see my father hitting them, and I thought it was normal'. Most took what I would term a pragmatic as opposed to a legal approach to wife-bashing, aware that if they caused serious injury they might be faced with hospital bills, and besides, women have brothers who could come and threaten a man if he hit their sister too hard and too often.

The national law against 'wife-bashing' is referred to as *ok an ye lo* or *ok an amop* in the Yongom language around Kiunga. The expressions are best glossed as 'what is forbidden by the whiteman' or 'whiteman law'. So customary law is compared with modern law as old versus new (from the 'whites'), and local people try to find a *modus vivendi* with the two. A village court magistrate provided an example. If a married man had sex with a young unmarried girl, following customary law he would convict the man of having sex with the young girl without having paid bride price and so would require him to pay compensation to the girl's family for having 'ruined' her, since future suitors would consider her 'second-hand' and not be prepared to pay a full bride price. But he would also follow 'modern' or 'whiteman' law and convict her for having had sex with a married man without the consent of his wife. This view of the offense shows clearly that in this region bride price entailed rights of male sexual access. The fact that sanctions against wife-beating are seen as alien—introduced by the 'whiteman'—even though most participants had only become aware of the laws in the past decade (25 years after independence from colonial rule), suggests, too, that men perceive the state and its laws as foreign impositions.

It is in this context that the question of the legitimate use of violence is crucial. We asked whether there were occasions when violence of a husband against his wife is justified. Most agreed that there must be such occasions. After some deliberation they cited two examples: if a woman would be too slow in cleaning the excreta of their child and it was in public in front of other people, or if his wife would steal from another person's garden and be found out. In both cases the 'wrong' was not the tardiness of cleaning the child or of stealing but the shame that the man would feel in front of other people. Such public shame would justify a strong and possibly violent censure. In appealing to these breaches of 'wifely duty' as instances where violence is legitimate, they are not only making statements about the importance for men of maintaining public 'face' in their marriage, but also about the marriage relationship itself. The wife's moral or social failings reflect not on her but on her husband's inadequate management of his household, including her.

Public shame helps illustrate how customary law and modern law function from different premises. The universalist values of human rights and modern law are based on an understanding of the autonomous self with a capacity to make choices and with a responsibility for the consequences of those choices. Customary rights fit with a notion of the person within a community and social conceptions of justice. Following customary law a man will try to regain his damaged masculine identity by publicly reasserting his authority.

Examples were given where women have been justified in insisting on their rights: for example, a woman demanding that she had the right to give her vote to the candidate of her choice and not that of her husband in the national elections. We also heard about cases where women have reported their husband's violent behaviour to village court officials and to the police and had their husband arrested, fined, put in jail, given a restraining order or put on a good behaviour bond. The general feeling of the men was that such a response does not address root causes and risks making the situation worse. Such actions are appropriate only as a last resort if one wants to break up a relationship. It seemed to them that the threat of legal enforcement of rights might best work as a deterrent rather than as a way of solving a problem or ensuring more harmonious relationships.

The men reported that a universal rights concept is difficult to apply in PNG. They preferred to discuss duties rather than rights. Admittedly rights and duties are closely related. Rights imply a person's claims on society, and duties indicate the claim of society on a person. However, this distinction can also support attitudes that regard the woman as a 'jural minor' and a man's claim on the person of his wife. In discussing the duties of men and women, duties were generally seen within a framework of male control. In time (years), some of the men have begun to view duties from a more egalitarian perspective. Women, but also men, have duties as providers, protectors and leaders.

Duty from a Christian perspective is seen as service, as appears in the *Singaut bilong Papa* (Voice of Fathers) newsletter of 29 November 2010: 'As men we need to be at the service of others, starting with our wives, our children, our family members, our community members and our co-workers. To serve is not a duty. We serve because we are followers of Christ. Service is always given out of love.'[32] The men I worked with express such sentiments, using terms such as *poroman* or *poro* to refer to one's partner in life. This equality was agreed to as a good idea, but it only gradually dawned on them what it really means in practice: for example, sharing money equally, respecting the other in decision-making, or never shaming the other in public. One man gave a simple but significant example: 'My wife and I both like the tail part of the chicken. So we take turns. When we eat chicken, I will offer her that part and she might say, "No, it's your turn"'.

Challenging social values and cultural norms

Cultural norms in a society with patriarchal values tend to situate relations between men and women in a framework of opposition and of dominance and submission. Particularly in the public sphere the man is ultimately in control, though he might delegate responsibility to women. As noted above, for the male leaders in the Diocese of Daru-Kiunga, Christian values raise questions about such dominance and advise a more egalitarian, monogamous understanding of married life.

---

32 *Singaut bilong Papa*, 2010 Newsletter—November, Men's Movement, Kiunga: Diocese of Daru-Kiunga.

Modernisation and social change have also brought transformations redefining the household. But it is not a simple matter to change in just one or two generations from the homosocial life of the men's house to the domestic family dwelling, where a man is expected to live with his wife and children in the same quarters. Men are gradually accepting more participation in the family and responsibility in the household, but still in most cases the decision-making process in the household could best be called 'patriarchy in the last instance', where the man makes the final decision when an accord cannot be reached.[33]

In a workshop with the men in Kiunga, the patriarchal system was depicted with the man 'above' and the woman 'below' (see model A in Figure 5). At best the patriarchal system is a convenient arrangement that, when accepted, leads to a relatively peaceful domestic scene. At worst it can lead to violent confrontation with the man demanding control 'because he has paid for it' (through bride price).

An alternative arrangement places the man and woman on equal terms (see model B in Figure 5), a modern idea that requires considerable change to put into practice in a PNG setting. The men in Kiunga were intrigued by the illustrations and recognised the side-by-side latter arrangement as being more in accord with Christian values and also with what they are hearing from those promoting equality in the name of human rights. But some were resistant and wondered whether the ideal is realistic. They want to see the community brought into the equation. Thus, individuals would have rights (and duties) not just as autonomous individuals but also as persons within a family and/or community. They point out how the community provides boundaries to hierarchical authority, allowing the community to censure any person who oversteps the accepted boundaries. Likewise, they see rights as guaranteeing fundamental freedoms within the community context. Rights put into practice will be evident in peace, harmony, and welfare in the family and the community.

---

33   Eves, 'Christianity, masculinity and gender violence in Papua New Guinea', p. 9.

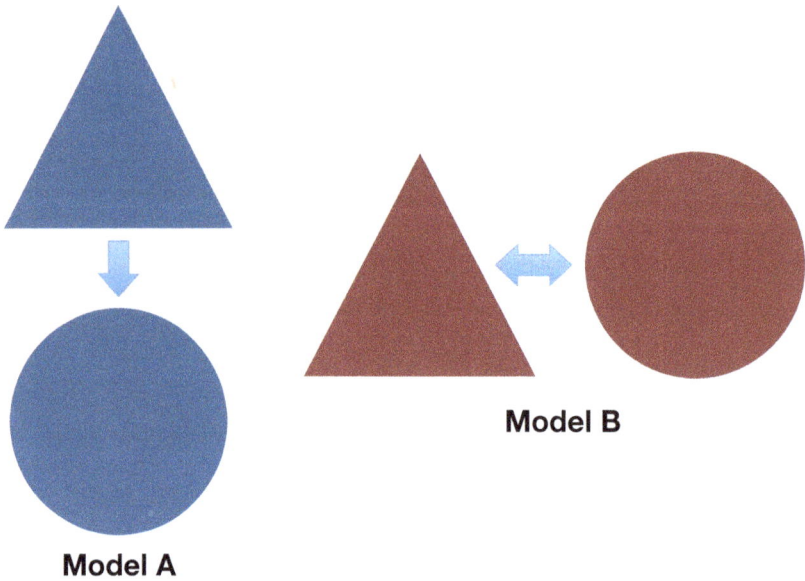

Model B

Model A

Figure 5. Hierarchical and egalitarian models of relationship
Source. Model developed by Philip Gibbs

Helpful strategies for change will include decision-making together (particularly in the area of family planning) and sharing responsibilities and duties. Some couples appear to be well on the way toward the egalitarian ideal. As one man explained, 'When we got married we agreed to stick together in good and bad times. Then the new law came in, but it didn't make much difference because we were already used to forgive and forget. If we relied on the law we would be spoiling ourselves. The new law is for those who don't want to continue their marriage.'

The Men's Movement is trying to gradually bring about a change from a hierarchical control-based framework to a more egalitarian one based on care and respect. The strategy does not apply to families in isolation but to families in the context of Basic Christian Communities in both the rural and urban settings.[34] The strategy must apply on at least three levels: awareness, skills training and organisational change.

---

34   Within the Catholic Church a 'parish' will include a number of Basic Christian Communities. The parish is usually a large assembly that meets on Sundays. Basic Christian Communities comprise people motivated by faith who meet and cooperate together in a way that provides a more communal experience of faith.

For awareness the men continue to hold workshops at the parish level and publish a biannual newsletter *Singaut bilong Papa* that typically includes words of encouragement from the Bishop and testimonies from men who have made a change. The following is an excerpt from the newsletter: 'We came to realize that we are not reptiles hiding in the bushes and harming people but human beings created as men to be fathers to provide, protect and lead our family, fostering peace and harmony in our families and communities.'[35]

Skills training with the Men's Matters group has been limited to exercises during annual diocesan workshops and one-off week-long meetings in parishes. With planning and trained personnel, these could well broaden the focus from provider, protector and leader so that participants could benefit from skills training in areas such as effective communication, sex education, marriage enrichment, dealing with alcohol and drugs, being a father, anger management and skills to prevent violence. Organisational change is part of a relatively effective Diocesan Pastoral Plan with active Basic Christian Communities and the establishment and continuation of the Men's Movement integrated with the Diocesan Plan.[36]

The challenge remains to participate in changing and developing social values and cultural norms suited to the situations of increasingly rapid change (in both rural and urban settings). As someone wrote in the newsletter, 'Many modern influences are happening: mining, logging, politics, oil search, and many others which are challenging the lives of many of us. Easily men who get jobs misuse their money on drugs, alcohol, sex and other social entertainment. The meaning of a true PNG man with its identity is disappearing fast.'[37]

35   *Singaut bilong Papa*, 2011 Newsletter—August, Men's Movement, Kiunga: Diocese of Daru-Kiunga, p. 6.
36   The Daru-Kiunga Diocese puts great emphasis on Basic Christian Communities, developing pastoral policies and strategies following the 'Movement for a Better World'.
37   *Singaut bilong Papa*, 2010 Newsletter—November, pp. 4–5.

Layering rights and kinship obligations

Sally Engle Merry raises the possibility of a layering of frameworks whereby a rights framework does not displace other frameworks but adds a new dimension to the way individuals think about problems.[38] Layering allows people to think about issues in different ways and to have distinctive ways of framing a problem and acting on it.[39] Thus, it is not a matter of replacing one framework with another, but of adding a new dimension or way of understanding the situation.

I have noted three significant points that affect frameworks by which men relate to women. First, men have come to realise that women are also providers, protectors and leaders—roles that previously they had claimed only for themselves as men. Just as roles and duties are not exclusive, neither are rights. Second, we have seen how with the assistance of Christian scripture, one can frame a discourse on equality within the discourse on difference. Though different, we are 'one in Christ'. Third, I have noted how men and women are dealing with two quite dissimilar models of control: hierarchical and egalitarian. I suggest that Merry's idea of layering might help resolve the existence of frameworks that at first appear to be mutually exclusive. Layers would include the community as the basic layer along with a new dimension associated with rights and duties, thus layering a rights framework over kinship and conjugal obligations.

For example, consider the case of a man returning home after some months away working in the mining town of Tabubil, associated with the Ok Tedi copper mine. From a rights perspective, his wife has a right to ask for money to support the family. If there is any likelihood that he was involved in extramarital liaisons while away, she has a right to ask him to be tested for STIs and HIV, and he has a right to ask the same of her. From a hierarchical perspective of control and superiority, such questions might easily lead to a violent reaction. However, if inserted in the context of a functioning Christian community, there would be values and safeguards to prevent such violence, based not on a modern liberal philosophy but more on human solidarity and the common good within the community.

---

38 Merry, *Human Rights and Gender Violence*, p. 179.
39 Ibid., p. 194.

Conclusions

Eves includes empowerment for both men and women in the title of his Caritas Australia publication on exploring the role of men and masculinities.[40] Martha Macintyre is not so confident, noting how '"empowering women" often means wrestling power from men so that women might represent their own interests'.[41] From the experience of working with men in small groups, I recognise Macintyre's concern. Men prefer peace and harmony and are normally not actively looking for clashes on the domestic front. However, men are also reluctant to relinquish their 'right' to punish those who would disrupt their own idea of the nature of that harmony. Cultural norms generally give men a superior social status, and a man is acutely sensitive to denial of that status, whether at home in a domestic situation or, even more so, in public. The language of rights challenges male superiority with the ideal of the inherent equality and dignity of all persons. This provides an entry into a larger discourse on justice, and seeking justice can involve conflict.

The group of men from throughout the Western Province that met in Kiunga over a number of years and continues as a Men's Movement is extraordinary in that they are leaders, most in monogamous marriages, and practising Christians. As such, they are men of relatively high status, bringing with them attitudes and ideas that have been constitutive of their identity as men in PNG. They are also idealistic, seeking ways to live out their faith in their family lives and their communities. They do not typify 'troubled masculinities'[42] and for the most part are not wanting to shore up patriarchal authority, but they are men who want to have time for their wives and children and to be attentive to their needs. As one explained:

> I used to be a rough man and this aspect is still quite strong in me. As we go through the seminar I see more and more the importance of being a true man, and controlling my temper is one way to become

---

40   Eves, *Exploring the Role of Men and Masculinities in Papua New Guinea in the 21st Century*.
41   Martha Macintyre, 2012, 'Gender violence in Melanesia and the problem of Millennium Development Goal No. 3', in *Engendering Violence in Papua New Guinea*, ed. Margaret Jolly, Christine Stewart and Carolyn Brewer, pp. 239–66, Canberra: ANU E Press, p. 247.
42   Laura Zimmer-Tamakoshi, 2012, 'Troubled masculinities and gender violence in Melanesia', in *Engendering Violence in Papua New Guinea*, ed. Margaret Jolly, Christine Stewart and Carolyn Brewer, pp. 73–106, Canberra: ANU E Press.

a true man. I want to be a true lover and a good father able to take care of my wife and children. I don't want to scare the children with my rough attitude, because I want them to come close to me. If they see me angry often, they will also grow into persons who are angry. The children won't listen to me if they don't love me.

These men live in villages and towns affected by one of the most profitable yet destructive mines in PNG (OK Tedi). The mine and other industries such as logging have produced social change that their grandparents and even parents could hardly have imagined. These men also have to negotiate their way in relationships with women and reimagine the roles and duties that contribute to their masculine identity.

Their masculinity has not died with Christian commitment, but it has been challenged by the concept of human dignity based on the *Imago Dei* and the consequent equality of all persons. This has led to a journey of self-discovery in an effort to reconcile their duties as husbands and fathers with the ideal of equality between men and women. Human rights discourse also requires observance of equal rights of women and men and the elimination of discrimination and violence against women. Human rights are an essential part of the vocabulary of international agencies, including Church agencies such as Caritas, but (interpreting what they have said) these men in the community context still prefer to layer a rights framework over kinship and community obligations.

The many quotations in this article illustrate the efforts made by this group of men to reframe the new ideals into their system of changing cultural meanings and how religious belief plays a role in interpreting human rights discourse in a vernacular idiom. The project has focused on men on the premise that men and boys are not only part of the 'problem' but they are also an important part of the solution. We might even go further and observe the ways that these changes are forming part of a cultural narrative shared by both women and men. It will be most interesting to learn what will happen with this Men's Movement in future years and also to hear the comments of their mothers, sisters, wives and daughters on what has been said and achieved.

Acknowledgements

I wish to acknowledge the invaluable contribution of Bishop Gilles Côté and the men from the Men's Movement in the diocese of Daru-Kiunga. Their courage and honesty have been an inspiration for me. I also wish to recognise the support of Caritas Australia and to thank the many people who commented on earlier drafts of this paper.

References

Barth, Fredrik. 1987. *Rituals and Knowledge among the Baktaman in New Guinea*. New Haven: Yale University Press.

Bradley, Christine. 1989. *Stap Isi* (film). Port Moresby: PNG Law Reform Commission.

——. 2001. *Family and Sexual Violence in PNG: An Integrated Long-Term Strategy*. Report to the Family Violence Action Committee of the Consultative Implementation and Monitoring Council. Discussion Paper No. 84. Port Moresby: Institute of National Affairs.

Catholic Bishops' Conference. 2009. *Bai Olgeta Manmeri i Pulap Tru Long Laip Bilong Krais*. Katekismo bilong ol Katolik Manmeri bilong Papua Niugini na Solomon Ailan. Goroka: Catholic Bishops' Conference of PNG and SI.

Committee on the Elimination of Discrimination against Women (CEDAW). 2010. 'Concluding observations of the Committee on the Elimination of Discrimination against Women, Papua New Guinea', Forty-sixth session. 12–30 July 2010.

Crook, Tony. 1999. 'Growing knowledge in Bolivip, Papua New Guinea'. *Oceania* 69(4): 225–42.

Davies, Rick and Jess Dart. 2005. *The 'Most Significant Change' (MSC) Technique: A Guide to its Use*. Online: www.mande.co.uk/docs/MSCGuide.pdf (accessed 27 October 2012).

Eves, Richard. 2006. *Exploring the Role of Men and Masculinities in Papua New Guinea in the 21st Century: How to Address Violence in Ways that Generate Empowerment for Both Men and Women.* Online: xyonline.net/sites/default/files/Eves,%20Exploring%20 role%20of%20men%20PNG.pdf (accessed 16 November 2016).

———. 2012. 'Christianity, masculinity and gender violence in Papua New Guinea'. SSGM Discussion Paper 2012/2. Canberra: The Australian National University. Online: digitalcollections.anu. edu.au/handle/1885/9856 (accessed 2 November 2014).

Hermkens, Anna-Karina. 2012. 'Becoming Mary: Marian devotion as a solution to gender-based violence in urban PNG'. In *Engendering Violence in Papua New Guinea*, ed. Margaret Jolly, Christine Stewart with Carolyn Brewer, pp. 137–62. Canberra: ANU E Press. Online: press.anu.edu.au?p=182671 (accessed 28 October 2014).

Jolly, Margaret. 2012. 'Introduction—engendering violence in Papua New Guinea: Persons, power and perilous transformations'. In *Engendering Violence in Papua New Guinea*, ed. Margaret Jolly, Christine Stewart and Carolyn Brewer, pp. 1–45. Canberra: ANU E Press. Online: press.anu.edu.au/publications/engendering-violence-papua-new-guinea (accessed 28 October 2014).

Knauft, Bruce M. 1999. *From Primitive to Postcolonial in Melanesia and Anthropology*. Ann Arbor: University of Michigan Press.

Law Reform Commission. 1987. *Interim Report*. Port Moresby: Papua New Guinea Law Reform Commission.

Macintyre Martha. 2000. '"Hear us, women of Papua New Guinea": Melanesian women and human rights'. In *Human Rights and Gender Politics: Perspectives in the Asia Pacific Region*, ed. Anne-Marie Hilsdon, Martha Macintyre, Vera Mackie and Maila Stivens, pp. 141–71. London and New York: Routledge.

———. 2012. 'Gender violence in Melanesia and the problem of Millennium Development Goal No. 3'. In *Engendering Violence in Papua New Guinea*, ed. Margaret Jolly, Christine Stewart and Carolyn Brewer, pp. 239–66. Canberra: ANU E Press. Online: press. anu.edu.au/publications/engendering-violence-papua-new-guinea (accessed 28 October 2014).

Merry, Sally Engle. 2006. *Human Rights and Gender Violence: Translating International Law into Local Justice*. Chicago and London: University of Chicago Press.

National Statistical Office. 2003. *Papua New Guinea 2000 Census National Report*. Port Moresby: Port Moresby, National Statistical Office.

Office of the High Commission for Human Rights. 2012. 'Special rapporteur on violence against women finalises country mission to Papua New Guinea'. *United Nations Human Rights*. Port Moresby, 26 March. Online: www.ohchr.org/EN/NewsEvents/Pages/Display News.aspx?NewsID=13374&LangID=E (accessed 17 October 2012).

Rait man. 2011. 'Police bombarded with emails over Joy Wartovo case'. *ActNow: For a Better Papua New Guinea*. Online: actnowpng.org/content/police-bombarded-emails-over-joy-wartovo-case (accessed 18 October 2012).

Regan, Ethna. 2010. *Theology and the Boundary Discourse of Human Rights*. Washington DC: Georgetown University Press.

Robbins, Joel. 2004. *Becoming Sinners: Christianity and Moral Torment in a Papua New Guinea Society*. Berkeley: University of California Press.

Rohr, Richard with Joseph Martos. 2005. *From Wild Man to Wise Man: Reflections on Male Spirituality*. Cincinnati: St Anthony Messenger Press.

Singaut bilong Papa. 2010 Newsletter—November, Men's Movement. Kiunga: Diocese of Daru-Kiunga.

Singaut bilong Papa. 2011 Newsletter—August, Men's Movement. Kiunga: Diocese of Daru-Kiunga.

St John Parish. 2005. 'Evaluation'. Unpublished report, Catholic Church, St John Parish. Matkomnai: Diocese of Daru-Kiunga.

Taylor, John P. 2008. 'The social life of rights: "Gender antagonism", modernity and *raet* in Vanuatu'. In *Changing Pacific Masculinities*, ed. John P. Taylor. Special issue of the *Australian Journal of Anthropology* 19(2): 165–78.

Toft, Susan and Susanne Bonnell (eds). 1985. *Marriage and Domestic Violence in Rural Papua New Guinea*. Occasional Paper no. 18. Port Moresby: Law Reform Commission.

Unite to End Family Violence: Papua New Guineans Against Domestic Violence. Online: www.facebook.com/groups/nodomesticviolencepng/ (accessed 29 October 2014).

UNIFEM and UNDP. 2007. *Translating CEDAW into Law: CEDAW Legislative Compliance in Nine Pacific Island Countries.*

Williams, F.E. 1936. *Papuans of the Transfly*. Oxford: Oxford University Press.

Zimmer-Tamakoshi, Laura. 2012. 'Troubled masculinities and gender violence in Melanesia'. In *Engendering Violence in Papua New Guinea*, ed. Margaret Jolly, Christine Stewart and Carolyn Brewer, pp. 73–106. Canberra: ANU E Press. Online: press.anu.edu.au/publications/engendering-violence-papua-new-guinea (accessed 29 October 2014).

4

Proclivity and Prevalence: Accounting for the Dynamics of Sexual Violence in the Response to HIV in Papua New Guinea

Katherine Lepani
The Australian National University

The unexpected turns of daily life encountered during ethnographic research offer unique entry points for closer consideration of how social issues are conceptually and morally framed. This chapter begins by recounting one such moment that occurred during my research on culture, sexuality and HIV in the Trobriand Islands.[1] In retrospect, the event offers a local narrative about how people perceive rights in contemporary Papua New Guinea and, in particular, how strong identification with place provides a moral basis for ensuring protection against violence. My intention is to illustrate how the variables of risk and vulnerability associated with sexual violence and HIV are enmeshed in daily life but often in ways that do not assume prominence, or even become visible, in people's relational and moral responses, or in official interventions. Similarly, the principles of human rights promoted through global discourse and policy frameworks do not

---

1   Katherine Lepani, 2012, *Islands of Love, Islands of Risk: Culture and HIV in the Trobriands*, Nashville: Vanderbilt University Press.

necessarily make tangible connections to people's lived experience, or to the circumstances of their deaths. The ethnographic focus on the Trobriands serves to illustrate the diverse textures of gender relations and gender violence in Papua New Guinea.

On a late Saturday afternoon in December 2003, after a day of interviews and group discussions, two of my research collaborators and I were relaxing on the veranda of a village aid post in the Trobriand Islands, a group of coral atolls in the Milne Bay Province of Papua New Guinea. As we sat talking with several local women who were hosting our visit, the shortwave radio housed inside the small clinic building suddenly started crackling. The frequency signal cut sharply into our casual conversation, a tone of urgency clearly detected in the static. The community health worker received the message, transmitted in English from the provincial health office in Alotau, the capital of Milne Bay. The remote voice of the health official relayed news of a Trobriand woman's death in the provincial hospital; news that had not yet reached her relatives in the village despite her body having been in the morgue for a week. Such news of death away from home typically travels quickly to the islands through informal channels, but in this case word found its way to the Trobriands only belatedly by official notice via the aid post radio. The health official was anxious to arrange the release of the body to the deceased's immediate relatives in the village since no one in Alotau had come forward to claim the body. Apparently, no member of the woman's clan in the urban migrant community was prepared to *toli tomota*, or take responsibility for looking after the deceased and organising *libu*, the mourning rituals. The official instructed the community health worker to tell the woman's relatives that a decision was required as soon as possible to determine if the burial should take place in town or if arrangements would be made to transport the body back to the village. The health worker acknowledged the order, signed off, and quickly left the aid post to go and notify the ward counsellor and break the news to next of kin.

The women on the veranda responded to the unsettling news with shock, disbelief and sorrow; two of them abruptly took leave from the group and followed the health worker into the village. After a few minutes of murmurs and silent tears, vocal expressions of inevitability and resignation washed over the grief. As I listened to the remaining women discuss the situation, it became apparent that the reluctance of the Trobriand community in Alotau to take responsibility for the deceased related to the circumstances of the woman's demise and the social exigencies of her domestic situation. As we spoke of the death and the dilemma it presented to the community, a moral narrative was woven around the life of the woman, a young mother of two in her early 30s. Various explanations were given for her death and various evaluations were made of her unfortunate fate. The rendering of the narrative revealed how cultural boundaries are imagined, evoking a strong sense of Trobriand identity and the importance of relational networks in defining one's connection and belonging to place.

The first explanation offered was that the woman died of complications arising from chronic gynecological problems. This was asserted by a nurse whose authority in naming the medical facts of illness and death was widely respected in the Trobriands. She elaborated on her forensic claim with a multiple diagnosis—the woman had cervical cancer, pelvic inflammatory disease, a long history of sexually transmitted infections. *Aiseki?* (Who knows?) was the conjecture; maybe the woman had succumbed to the deadly AIDS virus. This possibility entered into the conversation almost as a matter of fact, but with the ever present proviso—'Who knows?' Such speculations about HIV are often 'in the back of the mind'[2] when contemplating the causes of death, particularly the deaths of young and middle-age people who suffered prolonged or debilitating illness after travelling or residing outside of the islands.[3] This commonplace conjecture, not unique to the Trobriands, reveals how HIV has been absorbed into people's perceptions and evaluations of illness and death, and although the association with HIV might precipitate gossip and moral judgements, it does not necessarily result in exclusion, overt stigma, or violence, at least not in the Trobriands.[4] I did not want to stir the speculation further but I did ask the nurse how she knew about the woman's medical history; she replied matter-of-factly that she became aware of the woman's malady through her professional work, that health workers and clinical staff sometimes share case information during workshops and meetings. What was known for certain, the nurse

2   Staff consultation, Losuia District Health Centre, 16 June 2003.
3   Lepani, *Islands of Love, Islands of Risk*, pp. 31–32.
4   Cf. Nicole Haley, 2010, 'Witchcraft, torture and HIV', in *Civic Insecurity: Law, Order and HIV in Papua New Guinea*, ed. Vicki Luker and Sinclair Dinnen, pp. 219–35, State, Society and Governance in Melanesia Program, Studies in State and Society in the Pacific, No. 6. Canberra: ANU E Press.

emphasised, was that the woman often suffered physical abuse at the hands of her husband, a man from the Highlands of Papua New Guinea whom she had met in Alotau.

Another woman confirmed that on a number of occasions the deceased was admitted to Alotau hospital for medical treatment of assault injuries inflicted by her husband. She said she knew this because she had spent several months in Alotau a year earlier, awaiting the birth of her fourth child, where she stayed with a relative who lived in staff housing on the hospital grounds. She said they had talked about the deceased's situation, how the woman was in a violent marital relationship and often ended up in the emergency ward with injuries. She then told how the woman attempted to escape the violence by leaving her husband and taking her two children to Misima Island in Milne Bay, which at the time was the site of a large open pit gold mining project. It seems that the deceased's livelihood in the bustling mining town became dependent on sex work; it was explained that the woman had no choice but to 'take what she can get' and 'walk around looking for money'.

Apparently the woman did not remain for long in Misima but returned to her husband in Alotau when he threatened to take her to court over custody of the children, a prospect that would expose her situation to male judges, likely to be unsympathetic and rule in favour of the father's rights. At this point in the narrative someone added that the husband worked as a security guard in Alotau, an observation that prompted a derisive reaction among the group of women. The job of 'security' in urban centres is often recast by popular estimation as the generic catch-all for unskilled itinerate labourers, a position with which many Trobriand men are reluctant to associate. I was momentarily reminded of the circumstances of a young man from another village, a husband and father of a small baby who had been absent for over eight months, having gone to Alotau to purchase cloth material for his wife's contribution to her deceased mother's *sagali*, or mortuary feast. Word had travelled back to his village in the Trobriands that he was working as 'security' in a Chinese trade store. When people shared this news they scoffed in speculation, implying that he was just hanging out, not gainfully employed. The evaluation was definitive: Why be a security guard in Alotau when he could be gardening yams at home in the village?

Piecing together the details of the deceased's circumstances, and contemplating the plight of being married to a violent man, evinced a solemn expression of empathy among the women on the veranda. *Kapisila* (sorry), how could she live with him? Poor one, how did she cope? Empathy then spilled into a torrent of rhetorical questions and evaluations about her judgment, voiced by the women in conversation. Why did she choose him for a husband? What did she expect anyway, marrying someone from the Highlands? She should have known better, that he would be abusive; it's the Highlands' way with women. And why did she put up with it? Why didn't she just come home? For that matter, why did she leave the village in the first place? *Mokwita* (True)! What did she expect, going to Alotau for no reason!

Someone then mentioned that the woman had not been home to the village for almost 10 years. Her children were born in Alotau and the woman had never brought them back home to the village to be with their relatives on their matrilineal land. A further indictment was voiced—not only had the woman failed to maintain ties with her kinfolk at home, she did not have active ties with other Trobrianders residing in Alotau. Someone suggested that the act of marrying out and living away for so long had made her forget who she was. Someone else offered that perhaps it was shame that kept her away, shame for being in a violent relationship, shame for the uncertain fate of marrying an outsider. Why did she go to Alotau in the first place, if for no reason? I asked. For a spin, of course, was the answer; for youthful adventure. To see for herself what town life was like and maybe look for work, not knowing she would end up staying, not knowing she would not find passage back home, that the return boat fare would not be forthcoming from relatives; not knowing that her fate would be estrangement from her place of belonging.

Local narratives, global discourses

Conversational story-telling, such as that recounted here, is not only an important way for people to re-enact lived experience but is intimately reflective of shared values and the larger social structures and processes that shape life pathways. While this particular narrative unfolded in response to the unexpected news of death, and as such was more contemplative than explicitly performative (especially in the sense that it was not directed toward a receptive audience, apart from the questioning researcher), the reflective space created by the women's conversation revealed the everyday performance of social identities and cultural values.[5] I acknowledge that the event also confronted me with the ethical challenges of ethnographic research, when participant observation becomes subsumed by unsettling social events as they occur. How such events are then retold through ethnographic analysis represents another layer of interpretation and representation.[6]

I suggest that this local narrative from the Trobriands offers an important entry point for thinking about the place of violence in daily life, particularly in marriage and intimate relationships, and its significance as a defining feature of social and sexual practice. The narrative also exposes the social structuring of violence—how mobility, labour migration, and income opportunities, or the lack thereof, configure the circumstances and consequences of violence. It further reveals how the institutional systems of health and law are also implicated in the structuring of violence—and the production of moral subjects—even as they are designed to provide protective interventions.

By extension, the narrative offers productive links for considering the place of violence in relation to sexual health and the HIV epidemic, how violence shapes the gendered dimensions of HIV risk and vulnerability, and how it is accounted for as an epidemiological variable. The narrative, situated thus, provokes consideration about how the global discourse on human rights represents gender violence and HIV in a conjoined relationship, and sets the agenda for mobilising HIV prevention, treatment and care strategies. Globally, gender violence and HIV are recognised as 'twin epidemics',[7] inextricably linked by the social structures and processes that perpetuate gender and sexual inequalities.[8] The causal pathways between the physiology

---

5   Kate Winskell et al., 2013, 'Making sense of HIV in Southeastern Nigeria', *Medical Anthropology Quarterly* 27(2): 193–214, p. 196.
6   For a discussion of the ethics of ethnographic co-presence in times of social disruption and distress, see Shelley Mallett, 2003, *Conceiving Cultures: Reproducing People and Places on Nuakata, Papua New Guinea*, Ann Arbor, Michigan: University of Michigan Press, pp. 222–23.
7   Global Coalition on Women and AIDS, 2005, 'Concerted action required to address the twin epidemics of violence against women and AIDS', Press statement, 25 November, Geneva: UNAIDS.
8   Kristin L. Dunkle and Michele R. Decker, 2013, 'Gender-based violence and HIV: Reviewing the evidence for links and causal pathways in the general population and high-risk groups',

of sexual trauma, HIV transmission and pathogenesis, and host immunology are not well documented or understood medically, yet there is substantial and consistent evidence indicating 'a significant and reciprocal relationship between sexual violence and HIV transmission risk' in terms of the contextual factors that contribute to vulnerability.[9] The coupling of gender violence and HIV also contributes to and reinforces the destructive effects of fear and stigma, which persistently define the epidemic in Papua New Guinea and affect the experience of living with HIV for many people, especially women who bear the burden of blame for transmitting the virus.[10]

Since the mid-1990s, the national program for responding to HIV in Papua New Guinea has followed global best practice by taking a human rights approach, milestones of which include the drafting and passage of protective legislation for upholding the rights of individuals infected and affected by the virus, and the HIV/AIDS Management and Prevention Act 2003. The National HIV program has paved the way for integrating human rights principles into development policies and programs more broadly.[11] Moreover, the response to HIV in Papua New Guinea has been the main policy arena for addressing gender violence as a human rights issue. Yet the standard models for HIV interventions, including strategies for addressing gender violence in the context of the epidemic, tend to isolate the individual person, and the rights of the individual, from the social contexts of lived experience.[12] The conjoining of gender violence

American Journal of Reproductive Immunology 69(1): 20–26.

9   Jennifer F. Klot, Judith D. Auerbach and Miranda R. Berry, 2013, 'Sexual violence and HIV transmission: Summary proceedings of a scientific research planning meeting', *American Journal of Reproductive Immunology* 69(1): 5–19, p. 5; see also World Health Organization, 2012, *Violence Against Women: Intimate Partner and Sexual Violence Against Women*, WHO Fact Sheet No. 239, November.

10   Lawrence Hammar, 2010, *Sin, Sex and Stigma: A Pacific Response to HIV and AIDS*, Anthropology Matters, Volume 4, Wantage, UK: Sean Kingston Publishing; Katherine Lepani, 2008, 'Mobility, violence, and the gendering of HIV in Papua New Guinea', *Changing Pacific Masculinities*, ed. John P. Taylor, special issue 20, *The Australian Journal of Anthropology* 19(2): 150–64; Vicki Luker and Sinclair Dinnen (eds), 2010, *Civic Insecurity: Law, Order and HIV in Papua New Guinea*, Canberra: ANU E Press.

11   Katherine Lepani, 2011, *Historical Analysis of the Australian Aid Program's Contribution to the National HIV Response in Papua New Guinea*, Annex 12, Evaluation of the Australian Aid Program's Contribution to the National HIV Response in Papua New Guinea, Canberra: AusAID Office of Development Effectiveness.

12   Susan Kippax and Niamh Stephenson, 2012, 'Beyond the distinction between biomedical and social dimensions of HIV prevention through the lens of a social public health', *American Journal of Public Health* 102(5): 789–99.

and HIV as twin epidemics positions human rights within a deficit paradigm, wherein women and children—also conjoined as a single category of vulnerability—are represented as passive victims in need of protection through the enforcement of 'negative rights',[13] or rights defined in terms of redressing harmful and abusive behaviour, but not in terms of challenging the hierarchies of power that structure sexual inequalities and delimit the expression of sexual agency and identity.[14] In significant ways, the conceptual application of such models, dissociated from lived experience, contribute to further stigmatisation, the othering of risk, and the silencing of the perils of gender violence in marital and sexual relationships.

Although the women's conversation on the aid post veranda did not incorporate the language of human rights, the woven narrative brought contextual nuance to the fore, thus inviting consideration of the 'social life of rights', including how cultural ideas of personhood, the body, and kinship obligations, for instance, inform notions of justice.[15] Such narratives of sociality are suggestive of potential avenues for 'vernacularization', to use Sally Engle Merry's term,[16] bringing the global human rights discourse into direct articulation with local knowledge. They invite closer consideration of how universal precepts and instruments of rights might be translated and activated in Papua New Guinea in ways relevant to local communities as well as national development, whether through replicated terminology made salient through distinct local content, or more interactive, hybrid forms that merge imported and local values and structures.[17]

---

13   Richard Parker, 2010, 'Reinventing sexual scripts: Sexuality and social change in the twenty-first century' (the 2008 John H. Gagnon Distinguished Lecture on Sexuality, Modernity and Change), *Sexuality Research and Social Policy* 7: 58–66, p. 62.

14   See also Alice M. Miller and Carole S. Vance, 2004, 'Sexuality, human rights, and health', *Health and Human Rights* 7(2): 5–15.

15   Richard A. Wilson, 2006, 'Afterword to "Anthropology and Human Rights in a New Key": The social life of human rights', *American Anthropologist* 108(1): 77–83, p. 78.

16   Sally Engle Merry, 2006, 'Transnational human rights and local activism: Mapping the middle', *American Anthropologist* 108(1): 38–51, p. 44.

17   Merry, 'Transnational human rights and local activism'; see also Margaret Jolly, 2012, 'Introduction—engendering violence in Papua New Guinea: Persons, power and previous transformations', in *Engendering Violence in Papua New Guinea*, ed. Margaret Jolly, Christine Stewart and Carolyn Brewer, pp. 1–45, Canberra: ANU E Press. See also Aletta Biersack and Martha Macintyre, 'Introduction: Gender violence and human rights in the western Pacific', this volume; and Jean Zorn, 'Translating and internalising international human rights law: The courts of Melanesia confront gendered violence', this volume.

Papua New Guinean contemporary artist, Jeffry Feeger, has produced a powerful visual statement about global discourse and textual representations of gender violence, and how these articulate with local perspectives, in a small A4 drawing superimposed on a page from a summary report on gender violence in PNG (see Figure 6). Feeger calls the piece *Physical Integrity* and he posted the following comment with the image on Facebook in February 2014: 'Felt frustrated the other day reading a report about violence against women. Decided to sketch over some of the text.'

Figure 6. Jeffry Feeger, *Physical Integrity*, ink and pencil on A4 paper, 2014
Source. Used with permission of the artist

Paying attention to the articulation of local narratives, global discourses, and the translational processes of meaning-making raises pertinent questions about terminology and the epistemological and ethical challenges of defining gender violence across a wide spectrum of values, beliefs, practices and linguistic contexts.[18] The conversation by my Trobriand interlocutors, which flowed between the vernacular and English, used the colloquial term 'wife-bashing' to describe the type of gender violence inflicted by the husband on the deceased

---

18   Margaret Jolly, 'Introduction—engendering violence in Papua New Guinea', p. 1.

woman. While standard definitions allow for some degree of consistency in meaning, and facilitate the instrumentalist objective of applying measurement tools for collecting prevalence and case data and assessing progress on implementation of preventive strategies,[19] the questions of applicability and relevance remain. An undated fact sheet produced by UN Women Australia, which makes specific reference to Papua New Guinea, identifies six different types of violence against women, including the category of HIV/AIDS and violence, which cover a range of acts and practices at different levels, from intimate to structural.[20] The definitions reveal the difficulty of specifying distinctions between various forms of violence, particularly in terms of domain and relationality. For example, sexual violence is defined as acts of assault perpetrated by non-partners, as distinct from domestic and intimate partner violence.[21] In this article, I focus primarily on sexual violence as a form of gender violence that has direct physiological links to HIV transmission, but I am mindful that individual acts of sexual violence emanate from complex and dynamic historical, social and cultural precedents regarding the meanings and values of sexuality and gender, and the relational inequalities of agency and power. Coerced sex, forced sex, genital trauma and rape, whether perpetrated by strangers or by marital or other intimate partners, are all acts of sexual violence; however, they are experienced differentially and register meaning in diverse ways, with different implications for defining and promoting human rights.

In what follows, I engage the concept of culture through a critical analytical lens to challenge the preponderance of negative representations of sexual practice and to highlight how such

---

19   See Sally Engle Merry, 2011, 'Measuring the world: Indicators, human rights, and global governance', *Current Anthropology* 52(S3): S83–93.
20   UN Women Australia, n.d., *Fact Sheet: Violence Against Women*, Canberra: UN Women Australia.
21   The World Health Organization (2012) makes the following distinction between intimate partner violence and sexual violence:

> Intimate partner violence refers to behaviour by an intimate partner or ex-partner that causes physical, sexual or psychological harm, including physical aggression, sexual coercion, psychological abuse and controlling behaviours. Sexual violence is any sexual act, attempt to obtain a sexual act, or other act directed against a person's sexuality using coercion, by any person regardless of their relationship to the victim, in any setting. It includes rape, defined as the physically forced or otherwise coerced penetration of the vulva or anus with a penis, other body part or object.

See World Health Organization, *Violence Against Women*, n.p.

perspectives delimit the contextual understanding of rights,[22] as well as to consider how different cultural codes are mediated by popular imaginaries in the dynamic national context. I make the general argument that approaches to human rights and HIV framed in the negative undermine the potential for transforming harmful practice and engendering positive change, particularly where heightened levels of movement and intimate exchanges between people from different cultural groups are generating new regional and national subjectivities in Papua New Guinea's contemporary social landscape.

Proclivity, prevalence and place

The social structures of male dominant gender relations and, specifically, men's proclivity for violence against women—indeed the 'pervasive *legitimacy* of violence' more broadly—are persistently emphasised in representations of Papua New Guinea, and have been the subject of considerable social research.[23] Sexual violence is recognised as a significant contributing factor to HIV transmission risk in the Papua New Guinea context, and increasingly is taking programmatic precedence in addressing the gender dimensions of the epidemic under the rubric of human rights, with greater efforts focused on generating evidence to account for sexual violence as a driver of the epidemic.[24] Sexual violence, including acts perpetrated by police and other state officials, is acknowledged as an important dimension of risk and vulnerability for sexual minorities and people involved in sex work.[25] Accounts of sexual violence tend to emphasise

---

22   See Jane K. Cowan, 2006, 'Culture and rights after *Culture and Rights*', *American Anthropologist* 108(1): 9–24.

23   Margaret Jolly, 'Introduction—engendering violence in Papua New Guinea', p. 3.

24   I. Lewis, B. Maruia, D. Mills and S. Walker, 2007, *Final Report on Links between Violence against Women and Transmission of HIV in 4 Provinces of Papua New Guinea*, Canberra: University of Canberra; Holly Buchanan et al., 2010, *Behavioural Surveillance Research in Rural Development Enclaves in Papua New Guinea 2010*, National Research Institute Special Publication No. 59, Waigani: Papua New Guinea National Research Institute; Holly Buchanan et al., 2011, *Behavioural Surveillance Research in Rural Development Enclaves in Papua New Guinea: A Study with the Oil Search Limited Workforce*, National Research Institute Special Publication No. 61, Waigani: Papua New Guinea National Research Institute; Angela Kelly et al., 2012, *Emerging HIV Risk in Papua New Guinea*, Goroka and Sydney: Papua New Guinea Institute of Medical Research and University of New South Wales.

25   Angela Kelly et al., 2011, Askim na Save *(Ask and Understand): People Who Sell and Exchange Sex in Port Moresby*, Goroka and Sydney: Papua New Guinea Institute of Medical Research and University of New South Wales; Kelly et al., *Emerging HIV Risk in Papua New Guinea*; Christine

the pervasiveness of acts of rape, including *lainap* (Tok Pisin for group rape or serial intercourse involving groups of men lining up to sexually penetrate a woman),[26] which produce highly conducive conditions for HIV transmission, not only between perpetrator and victim but among the participating men.[27] Yet there is strident evidence that the greatest risk of sexual violence and HIV transmission for many women is found within marriage and regular partnerships.[28] This evidence is reinforced by the general observation that bride price payments confer men's proprietary ownership of women, and hence give men the right to use violence as a means of asserting their control. Refusal of sex is reported as one of the main reasons for violence within marriage, with fear of HIV transmission an aspect of refusal in some instances.[29] The potential for HIV transmission through sexual partnering outside

Stewart, 2012, '"Crime to be a woman?" Engendering violence against female sex workers in Port Moresby, Papua New Guinea', in *Engendering Violence in Papua New Guinea*, ed. Margaret Jolly, Christine Stewart and Carolyn Brewer, pp. 213–38, Canberra: ANU E Press.

26   See Anou Borrey, 2000, 'Sexual violence in perspective: The case of Papua New Guinea', in *Reflections on Violence in Melanesia*, ed. Sinclair Dinnen and Alison Ley, pp. 105–18, Sydney: Hawkins Press and Asia Pacific Press; Fiona Hukula, 2012, 'Conversations with convicted rapists', in *Engendering Violence in Papua New Guinea*, ed. Margaret Jolly, Christine Stewart and Carolyn Brewer, pp. 197–212, Canberra: ANU E Press; *Human Rights Watch*, 2005, 'Making their own rules: Police beatings, rape, and torture of children in Papua New Guinea', Human Rights Watch, 31 August.

27   Carol Jenkins, 2007, 'HIV/AIDS, culture, and sexuality in Papua New Guinea', in *Cultures and Contexts Matter: Understanding and Preventing HIV in the Pacific*, ed. Carol Jenkins and Holly Buchanan-Aruwafu, pp. 5–69, Manila: Asia Development Bank, p. 45.

28   Philip Gibbs and Marie Mondu, 2010, *Sik Nogut o Nomol Sik. A Study into the Socio-cultural Factors Contributing to Sexual Health in the Southern Highlands and Simbu Provinces, Papua New Guinea*, Sydney: Caritas Australia; Hammar, *Sin, Sex and Stigma*; Lepani, 'Mobility, violence, and the gendering of HIV in Papua New Guinea'; Lewis et al., *Final Report on Links between Violence against Women and Transmission of HIV in 4 Provinces of Papua New Guinea*; Pacific Islands AIDS Foundation (PIAF), 2011, *Experiences and Perspectives of Women Living with HIV in Fiji and Papua New Guinea: A Qualitative Study*, Cook Islands: PIAF; Michell L. Redman-MacLaren et al., 2013, 'Women and HIV in a moderate prevalence setting: An integrative review', *BioMed Central Public Health* 13: 552–65; Holly Wardlow, 2007, 'Men's extramarital sexuality in rural Papua New Guinea', *American Journal of Public Health* 97(6): 1006–14; Holly Wardlow, 2009, '"Whip him in the head with a stick!" Marriage, male infidelity, and female confrontation among the Huli', in *The Secret: Love, Marriage, and HIV*, ed. Jennifer S. Hirsch et al., pp. 136–67, Nashville: Vanderbilt University Press. It is important to acknowledge the fluidity of marital status and household composition in Papua New Guinea, and that in many parts of the country marriage includes forms of polygamy. The issue of whether polygamous marriages heighten or lessen women's vulnerability to HIV is the source of considerable debate among practitioners involved in the response to HIV.

29   Gibbs and Mondu, *Sik Nogut o Nomol Sik*; Lewis et al., *Final Report on Links between Violence against Women and Transmission of HIV in 4 Provinces of Papua New Guinea*. Rape within marriage is now criminalised in Papua New Guinea with the amendments to the Criminal Code under the Sexual Offences and Crimes against Children Act 2002.

of marriage is also the rationale used by some HIV counsellors to encourage women to be sexually receptive to their husband to ensure fidelity.

At its core, the moral narrative about the deceased Trobriand woman illuminates the connection between gender violence, marriage and women's vulnerability to HIV transmission by appealing to the notion of 'place' as the embodied site of cultural identity, genealogical belonging, and moral location—a powerful construct in Melanesian personhood and sociality. The narrative also accentuates notions of cultural difference in the figure of the abusive Highlands husband, reinforcing the regional stereotypes of violent masculinity and oppressive patriarchal power that pervade popular imaginaries among Papua New Guineans and outsiders alike, and similarly are drawn in the representations of numerous ethnographic accounts, social mapping exercises and quantitative surveys. The importance of place and cultural difference are of particular concern for attending to generalised perceptions of gender violence in Papua New Guinea and how these perceptions influence the way sexuality is represented in relation to HIV risk. As the voices of my interlocutors suggest, the Trobriand context counters negative representations of violence as the defining feature of sexual practice in Papua New Guinea, underscoring the importance of comparative mapping of local diversities to inform HIV prevention strategies, as well as the need to resist stereotypical framing of difference.

Engaging the concept of culture through a critical analytical lens shifts the instrumentalist framing of human rights from a focus on the isolated individual toward the significance of relational personhood, where the person is 'the plural and composite site of the relationships that produced them'.[30] This refocusing offers sharper understanding of the way rights are realised or denied in the realm of social relations, of how 'vernacularization' succeeds or fails, often in contexts with marked incommensurability between the rhetoric of rights and the capacity of the state to ensure the protection and wellbeing of its citizens.[31] A vocabulary of rights was not employed in the deliberation

30   Marilyn Strathern, 1988, *Gender of the Gift: Problems with Women and Problems with Society in Melanesia*, Berkeley: University of California Press, p. 13.
31   Cowan, 'Culture and rights after *Culture and Rights*'; Mary Crewe, 2009, 'Cultures of response: Introductory essay', in *The Fourth Wave: Violence, Gender, Culture, and HIV in the 21st Century*, ed. Jennifer F. Klot and Vinh-Kim Nguyen, pp. 271–78, Paris: UNESCO.

of the circumstances of the Trobriand woman's death; however, strong sentiments about relationality and connectedness to place *were* articulated by the women on the veranda, and, by inference, the assertion of women's rights in Trobriand matrilineal society. Paradoxically, perhaps, by exercising individual agency and sexual autonomy beyond familiar cultural surrounds, the deceased found herself in a violent relationship, estranged from her place of belonging and unsupported by the institutional and social systems that provide protection from harm. Even though, by the women's accounts, the deceased had an extensive medical record of hospital admissions, it appears that the system failed to adequately uphold her rights through the sustained provision of ongoing case management and links to available support services. Social support was eroded not only because the deceased failed to maintain her matrilineal ties, but her husband as an outsider did not activate a productive exchange relationship with his male affines. Perhaps if he had, the violent abuse would not have been tolerated.[32] However, what was patently clear in the eventual resolution of the plight of the deceased was her inalienable right to be buried on clan land.

It was not clear, however, whether the women's assessment of the deceased's predicament was based primarily on a critique of moral individualism or on a collective sensibility about relational personhood. What does resonate in the narrative are the dialectical tensions between the two positions, the way culture grounded in 'place' sets parameters for individual agency—and the proclivity for violence—and how culture provides a conceptual and moral framework for mediating new social phenomena, including HIV, and evaluating 'incipient individualism'.[33] Hence, the importance of understanding the influence of culture on the deliberation of rights and how cultural values might be engaged strategically to transform the contexts and circumstances of sexual violence.[34]

---

32   It is interesting to note that the man's abusive behaviour does not uphold the common explanation in Papua New Guinea that male violence against women is perpetuated through bride price payments, which confer to the husband a sense of entitlement and ownership over his wife, since in this case bride price was not made because it is not a Trobriand marriage custom.

33   Holly Wardlow, 2006, *Wayward Women: Sexuality and Agency in a New Guinea Society*, Berkeley: University of California Press, pp. 3, 11–13.

34   Cf. Mirriam A. Dogimab, 2009, 'An examination of culture as a protective mechanism against gender based violence: A case study in Mt Bosavi, Papua New Guinea', M.Phil. (Development Studies), Palmerston North: Massey University.

Trobriand culture is exemplified by a resilient collective identity attached to place, both geographically and relationally, expressed through the constellation of beliefs and practices that define personhood and gender relations.[35] The sex-positive culture of the Trobriands offers a solid basis for HIV prevention and the mitigation of gender violence. Distinct from many places in Papua New Guinea,[36] Trobriand sexual culture does not privilege male sexual aggression and coercion, nor does it easily countenance intimate partner violence. Young people enjoy sexual freedom before marriage based on the values of mutual consent and pleasure. Sexual activity is not viewed as promiscuous or risky but as valued social practice. Becoming sexually active as a young person is an emergent and active process, a transition to a new stage of embodied sociality and relational personhood that connects individuals to broader social networks. Women have sexual autonomy and choose their sexual and marital partners. The Trobriand matrilineal kinship system venerates women's reproductive power, made visible by their social and economic agency as exemplified in *sagali*, the elaborate distribution of exchange valuables in mortuary feasts, which women organise and control; and women retain rights over matrilineal land and residence in their natal villages.[37] The Trobriands does not have a system of bride price that confers rights to the husband over a woman's sexuality, fertility, labour and offspring.

Domestic violence in marriage is uncommon and precipitates direct intervention and recourse. The respective clans of perpetrators and victims are obligated to assume responsibility for resolving grievances and particular acts of violence with the exchange of *lula*, or atonement gifts. Marriage is mutable and divorce not uncommon; if a couple is in a discordant relationship, the social expectation is that they will choose to separate or dissolve the marriage with no violent repercussions or protracted conflict. Rape is also a rare occurrence in the Trobriands,

---

35   Lepani, *Islands of Risk, Islands of Love*.

36   Borrey, 'Sexual violence in perspective'; Haley, 'Witchcraft, torture and HIV'; Martha Macintyre, 2012, 'Gender violence in Papua New Guinea and the problem of Millennium Development Goal No. 3', in *Engendering Violence in Papua New Guinea*, ed. Margaret Jolly, Christine Stewart and Carolyn Brewer, pp. 239–66, Canberra: ANU E Press; Wardlow, *Wayward Women*; Laura J. Zimmer-Tamakoshi, 1997, '"Wild pigs and dog men": Rape and domestic violence as "women's issues" in Papua New Guinea', in *Gender in Cross-Cultural Perspective*, ed. Caroline B. Brettel and Carolyn F. Sargent, pp. 538–53, Englewood Cliffs, NJ: Prentice-Hall.

37   Annette B. Weiner, 1976, *Women of Value, Men of Renown: New Perspectives in Trobriand Exchange*, Austin: University of Texas Press.

in contrast to other areas in Papua New Guinea where high levels of sexual violence are not only associated with rapid social change and urbanisation but with customary precedent.[38] Young women have the right to reject the advances of suitors they find undesirable and young men say they would feel shame to physically coerce, or 'pull', a sexual partner against their will. The prospect of shame associated with potential rejection mitigates coercion; it also holds gendered implications for sexual decision-making. Because the responsibility for averting shame is largely carried by the female as the recipient of solicitations, a young girl's response to a boy who is 'trying luck' may be diminished to passive submission rather than polite rejection. Her vulnerability to unwanted sexual advances is further increased by the possibility that he might retaliate with the use of love magic to *kivili nanola*, or 'turn her mind', so that she loses her sexual autonomy and becomes sick with desire for him.[39]

Sexual jealousy, commonly regarded as the cause and justification for intimate partner violence and rape in Papua New Guinea,[40] is considered an inappropriate expression of desire for young Trobrianders. Perceived as the antithesis of sexual autonomy and mobility, jealousy is the emotional preserve of couples in a steady relationship or those who are married.[41] Nonetheless, young people demonstrate strong group loyalty and are quick to criticise members of their cohort who are seen to deviate from established patterns of sexual networking between village groups. The protocol of youth sexuality has gendered implications for sexual autonomy, with boys generally more territorial and possessive about the movement of their female peers while privileging greater expansiveness for themselves. These gendered dimensions of sexual mobility can be the source of resentful tension between males and females of the same village regarding spatial boundaries and the frequency and distance of planned outings with sexual partners from other villages. Unendorsed group outings or

---

38   Jenkins, 'HIV/AIDS, culture, and sexuality in Papua New Guinea'; Luker and Dinnen (eds), *Civic Insecurity: Law, Order and HIV in Papua New Guinea*; Hukula, 'Conversations with convicted rapists'; Margaret Jolly, 'Introduction—engendering violence in Papua New Guinea'.
39   Katherine Lepani, 2015, '"I am still a young girl if I want": Relational personhood and individual autonomy in the Trobriand Islands', in *Gender and Person in Oceania*, ed. Anna-Karina Hermkens, Rachel Morgain and John P. Taylor, special issue of *Oceania* 85(1): 51–62.
40   Jolly, Stewart and Brewer (eds), *Engendering Violence in Papua New Guinea*.
41   Cf. Naomi McPherson, 2012, 'Black and blue: Shades of violence in West New Britain, PNG', in *Engendering Violence in Papua New Guinea*, ed. Margaret Jolly, Christine Stewart and Carolyn Brewer, pp. 47–72. Canberra: ANU E Press.

a secret rendezvous may precipitate a fight: either a planned ambush targeted at the party from another village or a confrontation when the party held accountable returns to their home village after an outing. Fights involving youths from different villages are typically restricted to the same sex, more often boys fighting boys as an expression of territorial pride. Physical confrontations over alleged waywardness and excessiveness are regarded generally as an acceptable punitive measure to restore respect for the village name. However, the potential for disruptive conduct is mitigated by the desire among young people to preserve amicable inter-village exchange relations.[42]

Fighting might also erupt if a steady relationship is perceived to be threatened by concurrent partnering. Usually in such cases, boys will fight each other to appeal to the girl's fidelity, and girls will fight each other to assert their claim over the attentions of the boy. It is considered unacceptable for a girl to fight her boyfriend if she discovers him with another partner; her retaliation is to fight the other girl or reject him outright. In some instances, a boy might 'punish' his steady girlfriend for having a concurrent partner by striking her legs with a stick or metal chain. Such an assault is generally viewed as justifiable in a long-term relationship, symbolising the cessation of female sexual mobility in marriage. A young girl has customary recourse against such treatment and may seek retaliatory support from her kinspeople or reassert her autonomy by ending the relationship.

The Trobriands have long been known as the 'Islands of Love', an eroticised geographical trope that can be traced to the work of anthropologist Bronislaw Malinowski, whose ethnography of Trobriand sexual culture influenced European fantasies of exotic and primal cultures in the Pacific, as well as the colonial and missionary agendas of reform and salvation.[43] 'Islands of Love' continues to play

---

42 A recent case of violent inter-village conflict related to sexual networking made national headline news in the *Post Courier*. Apart from its considerable scale and volatility, the significance of this event compared to many situations of group violence in Papua New Guinea was that the rule of law was swiftly and successfully enforced to resolve the conflict; over 70 arrests were made and all cases were heard in the district court within a matter of days. See 'Trobriand courtship ritual turns violent', 2013, *Post Courier*, 29 May. 'Village, food destroyed over girls', 2013, *Post Courier*, 30 May. See also Personal communication, Clerk of Court, Losuia District Court, 18 June 2013.

43 Bronislaw Malinowski, 1932 [1929], *The Sexual Lives of Savages in North-Western Melanesia: An Ethnographic Account of Courtship, Marriage and Family Life among the Natives of the Trobriand Islands, British New Guinea* (3rd edition), London: Routledge & Kegan Paul.

in the contemporary imagination and now features in Papua New Guinea's national HIV narrative, which marks the Trobriands as a 'high risk setting' and a 'hot spot' of transmission risk. The hot spot metaphor, introduced uncritically into the official language of the response, reflects the dominance of epidemiological constructs in HIV interventions. Like other metaphors of distancing, 'hot spot' externalises risk by mapping stigmatising boundaries around different places, settings, and groups of people in an attempt to target HIV risk behaviours. The hot spot delineation of the Trobriands is based on the Papua New Guinea National AIDS Council Secretariat's perception that 'cultural norms are spreading AIDS in the Trobriands unlike other parts of the country'.[44]

This delineation is telling of how epidemiology, and the global discourse on HIV, gender violence, and human rights more broadly, essentialise culture in terms of risk—a static variable in a linear cause and effect relationship.[45] Culture thus perceived is regarded as an impediment to the realisation of rights; indeed, culture represents the absence of rights in local contexts, if not the outright opposition to universal principles.[46] The delineation is also telling of the conceptual unease with which sexuality and sexual practice are positioned in Papua New Guinea's response to the epidemic. The hot spot metaphor of perceived sexual promiscuity aligns with the generalised narrative that presents violence as a defining feature of sexual practice. The emphasis on sexual violence in the discourse on gender and human rights, although important, tends to reinforce a moralistic and pathological framing of sexuality in relation to HIV. The application of such a deficit paradigm, where negative assumptions and dystopian representations of social practice determine interventions, precludes positive ways of speaking about sexuality and HIV prevention in terms of mutual dignity, respect, and pleasure, and shared rights.[47] Furthermore, it fails to recognise the plurality of meanings regarding

---

44   Maureen Gerawa, 2010, 'Cultural norms spreading HIV/AIDS', *Post Courier* (Port Moresby), 19 April.

45   Eileen Stillwaggon, 2003, 'Racial metaphors: Interpreting sex and AIDS in Africa', *Development and Change* 34(5): 809–32.

46   Cowan, 'Culture and rights after *Culture and Rights*'; Margaret Jolly, 'Introduction— engendering violence in Papua New Guinea'; Merry, 'Transnational human rights and local activism'.

47   Susie Jolly, 2007, 'Why the development industry should get over its obsession with bad sex and start to think about pleasure', IDS Working Paper 283, Brighton: University of Sussex.

sexual practice within diverse cultural contexts, including the relational dimensions of sexual control, force and coercion; and how sexual coercion and 'the complexity of its connections to gender-related norms, identities and aspirations'[48] is mediated differentially in relation to notions of rights.

Papua New Guinea policy response

The twin epidemics of gender violence and HIV dominate images of the development landscape in Papua New Guinea, epitomising the turbulent processes of social change and modernity, and together they provide the thematic focus for projects on human rights, gender equality and good governance.[49] Unequal gender relations are officially recognised as the key contributing factor to the environment of HIV risk and vulnerability. The three successive national strategy frameworks for responding to HIV over the last 15 years all articulate guiding principles on gender equity and human rights and acknowledge the particular significance of sexual violence for HIV transmission. Papua New Guinea is one of only a few countries to have put in place a specific *National Gender Policy and Plan for HIV and AIDS*, which identifies a comprehensive course of action for integrating a gender perspective into the national response and addressing gender inequalities that contribute to HIV transmission.[50] Awareness campaigns have combined Violence against Women messages with HIV prevention messages in ways that have thematically emphasised the importance of gender equality and rights, but which have also conjoined the issues to the extent that much of what is communicated is mere slogan and meets resistance and disengagement from intended audiences.[51]

---

48   Kate Wood, Helen Lambert and Rachel Jewkes, 2007, '"Showing roughness in a beautiful way": Talk about love, coercion, and rape in South African youth sexual culture', *Medical Anthropology Quarterly* 21(3): 277–300, p. 280.

49   Luker and Dinnen (eds), *Civic Insecurity: Law, Order and HIV in Papua New Guinea.*

50   National AIDS Council, 2006, *National Gender Policy and Plan on HIV and AIDS 2006–2010*, Waigani: National AIDS Council.

51   Katherine Lepani, 2008, 'Review of HIV messaging promoted during PM's XIII visits in Papua New Guinea', unpublished report for the PNG–Australia HIV and AIDS Program.

Increasingly, gender violence is taking programmatic precedence in HIV prevention strategies. The current *National HIV and AIDS Strategy 2011–2015*[52] prioritises gender violence as a key issue for strategic action, particularly in terms of the legal, judicial and medical services required to mitigate its impact. One of the top 10 interventions is: *Develop specific interventions to reduce HIV vulnerability associated with gender-based violence and sexual violence against women and girls.*[53] While this includes strategies for working with men to address the social and cultural factors that contribute to gender violence, the key focus is on the provision of services for survivors of violence, including post-exposure prophylaxis for all sexual assault cases. The ambitious target set for 2015 was to establish and operationalise 80 Family and Sexual Violence Action Committees throughout the country, roughly one per district, and Family Support Centres in all provincial hospitals.[54]

The global precedent for national governments to develop HIV programs within the framework of gender equity and human rights is related to the parallel push for 'evidence-based practice', which now dominates the fields of biomedicine and public health, and the mandate to intensify HIV prevention efforts based on evidence of transmission dynamics. The UNAIDS global catchcry, 'Know your epidemic, know your response', advocates improved efforts at generating evidence from bio-behavioural surveillance to map risk factors, including patterns of sexual violence, so that national programs of response are better 'targeted' to achieve desired outcomes.[55] Underlying this call is the push for better systems of program monitoring and evaluation based on performance indicators, largely in the interest of promoting greater 'ownership' of the epidemic—a concept that has taken centre stage in the global response in efforts to balance massive flows of donor funding and technical support with national leadership and commitment.[56]

---

52   National AIDS Council, 2010, *National HIV Prevention Strategy 2011–2015*, Waigani: National AIDS Council.

53   Ibid., p. 6.

54   Ibid., p. 7.

55   UNAIDS, 2007, *Practical Guidelines for Intensifying HIV Prevention*, Geneva: UNAIDS; David Wilson and Daniel T. Halperin, 2008, '"Know your epidemic, know your response": A useful approach, if we get it right', *The Lancet* 372(9637): 423–26.

56   See Macintyre, 'Gender violence in Papua New Guinea and the problem of Millennium Development Goal No. 3', pp. 258–62; see also Merry, 'Measuring the world'.

From the early years of the national response to HIV in Papua New Guinea, the trends in available data presented an increasingly serious, if uneven and limited, picture of the country's estimated HIV prevalence. Between 1997 and 2004, available data showed a rapid escalation of the number of confirmed HIV cases at the national level, which increased annually by 30 per cent,[57] prompting warnings by donors of an 'African-style' epidemic—a comparison rife with racialised connotations about sexuality, sexual violence, and risk.[58] In 2002, UNAIDS classified Papua New Guinea as the fourth country in the Asia Pacific region to have a 'generalised' HIV epidemic with prevalence estimated at 1 per cent of the adult population, based on surveillance testing of antenatal clinic attendees at Port Moresby General Hospital.[59] Then in 2010, official HIV prevalence estimates were adjusted to suggest that the epidemic was 'levelling off' at less than 1 per cent of the adult population—0.92 per cent to be exact, if such claims of accuracy can be taken seriously.[60] This was adjusted to 0.8 per cent in 2012, with regional estimates showing the highest prevalence in the Highlands region (0.91 per cent).[61] The most recent official estimates, released in 2014, further adjusted national prevalence down to 0.65 per cent.[62] While limitations are acknowledged regarding the quality, reliability, and scope of data used in these modelling exercises, the revised estimations are upheld by government officials and program managers as an indication of significant progress over recent years in improving the national HIV surveillance system and expanding prevention and treatment services.

The push for statistical data to map Papua New Guinea's epidemic and guide the response, and the concomitant effort to 'scale up' services, is apparent throughout the country, most notably signified

57   National AIDS Council and National Department of Health, 2004, *The Report of the 2004 National Consensus Workshop of Papua New Guinea*, Waigani: National AIDS Council Secretariat and National Department of Health, p. 7.

58   Stillwaggon, 'Racial metaphors'; Michael O'Keefe, 2011, 'Contextualising the AIDS epidemic in the South Pacific: Orthodoxies, estimates and evidence', *Australian Journal of International Affairs* 65 (2): 185–202.

59   National AIDS Council and National Department of Health, *The Report of the 2004 National Consensus Workshop of Papua New Guinea*, p. 7.

60   National Department of Health, 2010, *Papua New Guinea HIV Prevalence: 2009 Estimates*, Waigani: National Department of Health, p. 1.

61   National AIDS Council Secretariat, 2012, *HIV @ Glance*, Leaflet, Waigani: National AIDS Council Secretariat.

62   National AIDS Council Secretariat, 2014, *Papua New Guinea Interim Global AIDS Progress and Universal Access Reports*.

by the blue and yellow signs that designate Voluntary Confidential Counselling and Testing (VCCT) facilities. Since 2003, with the advent of Global Fund financing of antiretroviral therapies (ART) in Papua New Guinea, there has been a major 'roll-out' of testing services, to use the jargon of public health and HIV programming—an illusory phrase if ever there was one—smooth deployment, impediment free, as if Papua New Guinea doesn't have any pot holes. By the end of 2010, nearly 300 facilities throughout the country had been accredited for HIV testing, and records show that nearly 140,000 people nationwide had been tested for HIV.[63] The expanded provision of testing brings the human rights discourse into direct articulation with public health interventions.[64] The global theme for World AIDS Day 2010 was Universal Access to treatment. In Papua New Guinea this was translated as '*Testim na tritim—em rait bilong yu!*' (Tok Pisin for 'Get tested and get treated—it's your right!'). Yet this promise of individualised rights poses a serious ethical dilemma in contexts where uneven power relations exist between clients and service providers, and where the limited capacity of the health system does not guarantee the provision of adequate follow-up and ongoing ART services for all who qualify.[65]

It is of note that Papua New Guinea added 'confidential' to the acronym—the standard global term is simply VCT—voluntary counselling and testing. The deliberate addition reflected a concern to uphold the country's HIV/AIDS Management and Prevention Act to protect the rights of people living with HIV. However, the notion of confidentiality, based on individualist modes of service access and provision, coupled with an emphasis on patient responsibility to practise safe sex and adhere to treatment, has been the source of conceptual discomfort from the beginning of the national response in Papua New Guinea; in particular, the dissonance between confidentiality as an individual right and the promotion of community participation in HIV care and support. A further tension is emerging with the introduction of provider-initiated testing, which reclaims the health sector's central role in the national response and is consonant with the global trend toward medicalisation of HIV management

---

63   Ibid.

64   M.J. Heywood, 2005, 'The routine offer of HIV counseling and testing: A human right', *Health and Human Rights: An International Journal* 8(2): 13–19.

65   Angela Kelly, 2009, 'The role of HIV social research in the response efforts to the HIV epidemic in Papua New Guinea', *Papua New Guinea Medical Journal* 52(1/2): 35–43.

based on an individualist model of treatment and care.[66] The current national strategy has introduced a subtle semantic shift in all references to testing, dropping the V for voluntary to give more authority to provider-initiated testing, on which available evidence of practice suggests that the provision of counselling is also routinely dropped.[67]

The expanded provision of testing, particularly provider-initiated, raises serious questions about informed consent and disclosure of HIV status, particularly for people who are socially vulnerable and for women whose point of entry into the health system is through antenatal care.[68] Accessing resources and services, including the provision of post-exposure prophylaxis for rape victims, and drug therapies for the prevention of parent to child transmission, can create new contexts of risk mapped onto existing forms of gender inequality. There is evidence that disclosing test results to partners and family members, and even accessing testing in the first place, can precipitate violence.[69] The prospect of being subjected to HIV testing also is keeping some women away from antenatal clinics.[70] As a Catholic health worker observes, 'Telling partners about test results can cause family violence. We help at one end and create problems at the other.'[71]

The persistent drive to measure the epidemic numerically, and pin down prevalence to the decimal point, is now being pursued like never before through the planned HIV integrated bio-behavioural survey (IBBS) of 12,000 households nationwide. This is a much touted, hugely expensive undertaking, tendered by the World Bank with funding from a consortium of development partners, initially meant to be conducted

---

66   Jennifer F. Klot and Vinh-Kim Nguyen, 2009, 'Introduction', in *The Fourth Wave: Violence, Gender, Culture, and HIV in the 21st Century*, ed. Jennifer F. Klot and Vinh-Kim Nguyen, pp. 15–26, Paris: UNESCO.
67   Lewis et al., *Final Report on Links between Violence against Women and Transmission of HIV in 4 Provinces of Papua New Guinea*; Christine Bradley, 2009, 'Notes on gender issues in prevention of parent to child transmission', unpublished report to the Papua New Guinea – Australia HIV and AIDS Program; PIAF, *Experiences and Perspectives of Women Living with HIV in Fiji and Papua New Guinea*.
68   Heywood, 'The routine offer of HIV counseling and testing; Kelly, 'The role of HIV social research in the response efforts to the HIV epidemic in Papua New Guinea'.
69   Lewis et al., *Final Report on Links between Violence against Women and Transmission of HIV in 4 Provinces of Papua New Guinea*; Kelly, 'The role of HIV social research in the response efforts to the HIV epidemic in Papua New Guinea'.
70   Bradley, 'Notes on gender issues in prevention of parent to child transmission'.
71   Katherine Lepani and Emily Rudland, 2011, Annex 27, Madang Province, *Evaluation of the Australian Aid Program's Contribution to the National HIV Response in Papua New Guinea*, Canberra: AusAID Office of Development Effectiveness, p. 20.

in 2012 by an international agency which has carried out more than 100 such surveys in over 40 different countries. Apparently logistics and ethics proved insurmountable for the contracted agency, and for now the survey is suspended. But the magic of numbers is indeed seductive[72]—there is a sense that the national response has finally come of age with the planned IBBS and that, at last, it will be mounted from a solid base of evidence. The orthodoxy of statistical evidence will now hold the national response—and people's sexuality—accountable like never before. I only hope this exercise of biopower, to use Michel Foucault's term for the ongoing regulation and monitoring of populations,[73] does not undermine the important relationships of trust nurtured at the local level with people involved in the national response, nor diminish the importance of lived experience and the contribution of cultural knowledge.

I do not discount the considered thought and consultation that has gone into formulating Papua New Guinea's national strategies and indicators. However, the discursive framing of evidence-based policy frameworks imposes reductionist logic to the diversity of sexual meanings and practices, effectively silencing the realities of lived experience by configuring people as individuals aggregated into 'passive target populations' based on risk categories.[74] More importantly, it holds serious ethical implications for how the new relational spaces and practices of HIV service provision are operationalised. Strategies and services tend to re-inscribe men as perpetrators of violence and women and children as passive victims, inadvertently upholding existing gender inequalities and male sexual privilege.[75] The inverse effect of this 'rescue paradigm of response' reinforces perceptions that women are not only the sole target of interventions but the cause of HIV infection, while neglecting HIV prevention efforts for men.[76]

---

72   See Merry, 'Measuring the world'.
73   Michel Foucault, 1978, *The History of Sexuality: Volume 1. An Introduction*, trans. Robert Hurley, New York: Random House, p. 140.
74   Hakan Seckinelgin, 2009, 'Colonial silences, gender and sexuality: Unpacking international HIV and AIDS policy culture', in *The Fourth Wave: Violence, Gender, Culture, and HIV in the 21st Century*, ed. Jennifer F. Klot and Vinh-Kim Nguyen, pp. 279–94, Paris: UNESCO, p. 280.
75   Susie Jolly, 'Why the development industry should get over its obsession with bad sex and start to think about pleasure'.
76   Klot and Nguyen, 'Introduction', pp. 20, 22.

To counter this trend, HIV prevention programs and services must attend more closely to the needs of women and men whose identities and circumstances are not consonant with standardised notions of what constitutes 'proper' sexuality. Women who choose casual partnering, or choose to remain single over the prospect of being married an abusive partner, and to avoid the kind of sexual jealousy that intensifies in a steady relationship or marriage,[77] are effectively excluded from services defined in terms of maternity and the nuclear family. An ethnographic focus on the social spaces of service provision would enhance understanding of the range of sexual subjectivities, the place of violence in people's lives, and the ways in which people define and exercise their rights. The assumption that biomedical technologies of surveillance and testing hold the answer to determining the presence of HIV in local populations raises serious ethical questions about the quantitative measurement practices that dominate the global response, setting a dangerous precedent for further dislodging sexual practice—including harmful practice—from cultural meanings, embodied experience, and the social structures and spaces that shape sexual geographies.

New measures for accountability

The moral narrative from the Trobriands points to another dimension of social life that holds significant implications for the dynamics of sexual violence in contemporary Papua New Guinea. This is the growing trend of intercultural marriage and how it is reshaping gender relations, often with serious consequences for displacing traditional social constraints on interpersonal and family violence. On one level, the narrative can be seen as an example of the persistent 'othering' of risk—constructing risk in terms of difference and drawing safe boundaries around the familiar. The assessment of the deceased's marital circumstances imputes safety within Trobriand cultural norms and danger when individual choice is exercised outside of established affiliations. Furthermore, the construction of difference links violent

77   See Martha Macintyre, 2011, 'Money changes everything: Papua New Guinean women in the modern economy', in *Managing Modernity in the Western Pacific*, ed. Mary Patterson and Martha Macintyre, pp. 90–120, St Lucia: University of Queensland Press; Ceridwen Spark, 2011, 'Gender trouble in town: Educated women eluding male domination, gender violence and marriage in PNG', *The Asia Pacific Journal of Anthropology* 12(2): 164–79.

masculinity directly to the cultural other, the figure of the Highlands husband, and the unattainable prospect of a marriage free of abuse. Herein is a particular challenge for Papua New Guineans, as ethnic constructions impede the formation of shared national identity and create new inequalities and forms of dissonance, even as intermarriage between cultural groups becomes more prevalent and desired[78]— indeed, as 'ideas of culturally and ethnically distinct places become perhaps even more salient'[79] in the context of accelerated movement and relocation.

On a broader level, the tale can be understood as a 'moral narrative of modernity', to use Webb Keane's phrase,[80] where the individual is deemed solely responsible for determining the circumstances of their life, including willed displacement and estrangement.[81] It is debatable whether the scale of modernity is best measured by emergent forms of individualism that outweigh collective agency. Yet, in the deceased's case, her failure to honour kinship obligations by maintaining her connections to place, and to ensure that her children's rights to those connections are intact, was the source of an apparent immobilising personal shame. Such shame reveals the modern dilemma of individual agency and dislocation, and thwarts the potential for exercising human rights.

Nonetheless, the narrative relates how the desire for youthful adventure was palpable, made possible for the young woman in part by the relative gender equality and autonomy espoused by Trobriand culture. Modernity has widened the field of imaginable social interaction, and sexuality takes new expressions within this highly charged and exciting landscape. Accounting for sexual violence within the shifting domain of modernity requires closer examination of the relational dynamics that produce and disrupt subjectivities, both personal and collective, and how these are linked to, or disconnected from, established modes of social connection. Likewise, insights on HIV transmission dynamics can be found in the ways sexual networks take shape and operate within the larger social networks of reciprocal

---

78   See Macintyre, 'Money changes everything', pp. 109–10.
79   Akhil Gupta and James Ferguson, 1997, *Culture, Power, Place: Explorations in Critical Anthropology*, Durham, NC: Duke University Press, p. 39.
80   Phrase from Webb Keane, 2007, *Christian Moderns: Freedom and Fetish in the Mission Encounter*, Berkeley, Los Angeles and London: University of California Press, p. 4.
81   See Wardlow, *Wayward Women*.

exchange, which underpin subsistence and informal economies and provide the basis for engendering individual and group identities. Relational personhood continues to hold key significance in how social relations activate agency, both personal and collective, in fields of exchange, be it the exchange of body fluids, traditional wealth items, manufactured goods, or cash. Within these relational networks, sexuality as a valued resource activates the circulation and redistribution of exchange items, underscoring how intimate transactions are embedded in larger fields of exchange. These are the gendered intersections of people's daily lives which hold potential for HIV transmission;[82] where 'potent masculinity' is performed,[83] where female sexual agency is positively expressed as well as restricted and punished, where sexual jealousy is triggered and acts of violence perpetrated.[84]

That sex might be valued and practised as a form of relational personhood disturbs the moral underpinnings of HIV prevention discourse. Recognising gender violence as a dimension of relational personhood, and of sexual practice, creates further disruption to the evidence-based orthodoxy of responding to HIV under the rubric of an individualised notion of human rights. An ethnographic research agenda for understanding how violence becomes engendered and reproduced in Melanesian sexual cultures might seek to articulate the language of human rights in terms of sexual citizenship, or the rights and responsibilities of all people to have control over their sexual and reproductive health and to express sexual identity, desire and pleasure in healthy and safe ways, free of fear, harm and force, as an expected part of membership in a shared community.[85] While the question of vernacular translation remains, I contend that the concept of sexual citizenship helps to clarify the discourse on HIV and human rights, and brings into sharper focus the structural relations of power and control within intimate relationships and how these relations are situated within larger social fields, including that of service provision,

82   Elizabeth Reid, 2009, *Interrogating a Statistic: HIV Prevalence Rates in PNG*. State, Society and Governance in Melanesia, Discussion Paper 1. Canberra: The Australian National University.
83   Wardlow, '"Whip him in the head with a stick!"' p. 53.
84   Lepani, 'Mobility, violence, and the gendering of HIV in Papua New Guinea'.
85   Diane Richardson, 2000, 'Constructing sexual citizenship: Theorizing sexual rights', *Critical Social Policy* 20(1): 105–35; Ana Luisa Liguori and Marta Lamas, 2003, 'Gender, sexual citizenship and HIV/AIDS', *Culture, Health and Sexuality* 5(1): 87–90; Susie Jolly, 'Why the development industry should get over its obsession with bad sex and start to think about pleasure'.

access and use.[86] The concept helps to productively focus social research on new subjectivities being shaped by the provisions and services of donors, non-government organisations and the state, and on the emergent forms of national identity being forged in the context of accelerated mobility, intercultural mixing and the desires and pleasures of modernity.[87] Furthermore, the concept allows us to see the positive potential of the deep-rooted values of Melanesian sociality, relational personhood, and social reproduction for transcending the effects of stigma and fear, and indeed for transforming unequal gender relations, as people become accustomed to new forms of rights and responsibilities in relation to living with HIV.[88]

Papua New Guinea has contributed substantially to anthropological understandings of multiply constituted subjectivities and relational personhood, where gender and sexuality are not singular identities but shaped by dynamic networks of social relations, which increasingly involve moving and mixing between diverse cultural realms made permeable through heightened interaction and translocation. These spheres of connection and relationality might yet prove to be the most productive ground for defining and securing human rights and addressing the proclivity of sexual violence in the context of the HIV epidemic. The tragic paradox in the Trobriand woman's story is that this potential was not realised. Enmeshed in the structures that perpetuate inequalities and vulnerabilities, the woman was disconnected from her place of belonging and the social relations that enable support; her relatives found it difficult to act in her interest, even at the time of death. By extension, the story becomes a parable about the challenges of connecting human rights discourse and policies to the realities of everyday life, with a more direct focus on the mutual relations of care, respect and responsibility as the pivotal terms for engendering change.

---

86   Sonia Corrêa and Richard Parker, 2004, 'Sexuality, human rights, and demographic thinking: Connections and disjunctions in a changing world', *Sexuality Research & Social Policy* 1(1): 15–38; Andrea Cornwall, Sonia Corrêa and Susie Jolly, 2008, 'Development with a body: Making the connections between sexuality, human rights and development', in *Development with a Body: Sexuality, Human Rights and Development*, ed. Andrea Cornwall, Sonia Corrêa and Susie Jolly, pp. 1–21, London and New York: Zed Books.

87   See Hukula, 'Conversations with convicted rapists', p. 210.

88   See Angela Kelly et al., 2013, *HIV, Pregnancy and Parenthood: A Qualitative Study of the Prevention and Treatment of HIV in Pregnant Women, Parents and their Infants in Papua New Guinea*, Sydney: Papua New Guinea Institute of Medical Research and University of New South Wales.

Acknowledgements

I would like to thank my research collaborators, Ethel Jacob, Diana Siyotama Lepani and Florence Mokolava, for their support and guidance, and the many people in the Trobriands who welcomed us to their villages and participated in the research. I thank Margaret Jolly for her ongoing generous support of my work and for funding through her Australian Research Council Laureate Project, Engendering Persons, Transforming Things: Christianities, Commodities and Individualism in Oceania (FL100100196), for my attendance at the 2011 Annual Meeting of the American Anthropological Association, where I presented the first version of this paper. Thanks also to Margaret Jolly, Martha Macintyre and Aletta Biersack for organising the panel on Gender Violence in Melanesia and their helpful comments on earlier drafts of this paper.

References

Borrey, Anou. 2000. 'Sexual violence in perspective: The case of Papua New Guinea'. In *Reflections on Violence in Melanesia*, ed. Sinclair Dinnen and Alison Ley, pp. 105–18. Sydney: Hawkins Press and Asia Pacific Press.

Bradley, Christine. 2009. 'Notes on gender issues in prevention of parent to child transmission'. Unpublished report to the Papua New Guinea – Australia HIV and AIDS Program.

Brettel, Caroline B. and Carolyn F. Sargent (eds). 1997. *Gender in Cross-Cultural Perspective*. Englewood Cliffs, NJ: Prentice-Hall.

Buchanan, Holly, Frances Akuani, Francis Kupe, Angelyn Amos, Kayleen Sapak, Francis Be, Thomas Kawage, Rei Frank and Murray Couch. 2011. *Behavioural Surveillance Research in Rural Development Enclaves in Papua New Guinea: A Study with the Oil Search Limited Workforce*. National Research Institute Special Publication No. 61. Waigani: Papua New Guinea National Research Institute.

Buchanan, Holly, Frances Akuani, Thomas Kawage, Kayleen Sapak, Angelyn Amos, A. Naemon and Murray Couch. 2010. *Behavioural Surveillance Research in Rural Development Enclaves in Papua New Guinea 2010*. National Research Institute Special Publication No. 59. Waigani: Papua New Guinea National Research Institute.

Cornwall, Andrea, Sonia Corrêa and Susie Jolly (eds). 2008. *Development with a Body: Sexuality, Human Rights and Development*. London and New York: Zed Books.

Cornwall, Andrea, Sonia Corrêa and Susie Jolly. 2008. 'Development with a body: Making the connections between sexuality, human rights and development'. In *Development with a Body: Sexuality, Human Rights and Development*, ed. Andrea Cornwall, Sonia Corrêa and Susie Jolly, pp. 1–21. London and New York: Zed Books.

Corrêa, Sonia and Richard Parker. 2004. 'Sexuality, human rights, and demographic thinking: Connections and disjunctions in a changing world'. *Sexuality Research & Social Policy* 1(1): 15–38.

Cowan, Jane K. 2006. 'Culture and rights after *Culture and Rights*'. In *Anthropology and Human Rights in a New Key*, ed. Mark Goodale. *American Anthropologist* 108(1): 9–24.

Crewe, Mary. 2009. 'Cultures of response: Introductory essay'. In *The Fourth Wave: Violence, Gender, Culture, and HIV in the 21st Century*, ed. Jennifer F. Klot and Vinh-Kim Nguyen, pp. 271–78. Paris: UNESCO.

Dogimab, Mirriam A. 2009. 'An examination of culture as a protective mechanism against gender based violence: A case study in Mt. Bosavi, Papua New Guinea'. M.Phil. (Development Studies), Palmerston North: Massey University.

Dunkle, Kristin L. and Michele R. Decker. 2013. 'Gender-based violence and HIV: Reviewing the evidence for links and causal pathways in the general population and high-risk groups'. *American Journal of Reproductive Immunology* 69(1): 20–26.

Foucault, Michel. 1978. *The History of Sexuality: Volume 1. An Introduction*, trans. Robert Hurley. New York: Random House.

Gerawa, Maureen. 2010. 'Cultural norms spreading HIV/AIDS'. *Post Courier* (Port Moresby) 19 April.

Gibbs, Philip and Marie Mondu. 2010. *Sik Nogut o Nomol Sik. A Study into the Socio-cultural Factors Contributing to Sexual Health in the Southern Highlands and Simbu Provinces, Papua New Guinea.* Sydney: Caritas Australia.

Global Coalition on Women and AIDS. 2005. 'Concerted action required to address the twin epidemics of violence against women and AIDS'. Press statement, 25 November. Geneva: UNAIDS.

Gupta, Akhil and James Ferguson. 1997. *Culture, Power, Place: Explorations in Critical Anthropology.* Durham, NC: Duke University Press.

Haley, Nicole. 2010. 'Witchcraft, torture and HIV'. In *Civic Insecurity: Law, Order and HIV in Papua New Guinea*, ed. Vicki Luker and Sinclair Dinnen, pp. 219–35. State, Society and Governance in Melanesia Program, Studies in State and Society in the Pacific, No. 6. Canberra: ANU E Press. Online: press.anu.edu.au/publications/series/state-society-and-governance-melanesia/civic-insecurity (accessed 4 February 2016).

Hammar, Lawrence. 2010. *Sin, Sex and Stigma: A Pacific Response to HIV and AIDS.* Anthropology Matters, Volume 4. Wantage, UK: Sean Kingston Publishing.

Heywood, M.J. 2005. 'The routine offer of HIV counseling and testing: A human right'. *Health and Human Rights: An International Journal* 8(2): 13–19.

Hirsch, Jennifer S., Holly Wardlow, Daniel Jordon Smith, Harriet M. Phinney, Shanti Parikh and Constance A. Nathanson (eds). 2009. *'The Secret: Love, Marriage, and HIV.* Nashville: Vanderbilt University Press.

Hukula, Fiona. 2012. 'Conversations with convicted rapists'. In *Engendering Violence in Papua New Guinea*, ed. Margaret Jolly, Christine Stewart and Carolyn Brewer, pp. 197–212. Canberra: ANU E Press. Online: press.anu.edu.au/publications/engendering-violence-papua-new-guinea (accessed 29 October 2014).

Human Rights Watch. 2005. 'Making their own rules: Police beatings, rape, and torture of children in Papua New Guinea'. Human Rights Watch. 31 August.

Jenkins, Carol and Holly Buchanan-Aruwafu (eds). 2007. *Cultures and Contexts Matter: Understanding and Preventing HIV in the Pacific*. Manila: Asia Development Bank.

Jenkins, Carol. 2007. 'HIV/AIDS, culture, and sexuality in Papua New Guinea'. In *Cultures and Contexts Matter: Understanding and Preventing HIV in the Pacific*, ed. Carol Jenkins and Holly Buchanan-Aruwafu, pp. 5–69. Manila: Asia Development Bank.

Jolly, Margaret, Christine Stewart and Carolyn Brewer (eds). 2012. *Engendering Violence in Papua New Guinea*. Canberra: ANU E Press. Online: press.anu.edu.au/publications/engendering-violence-papua-new-guinea (accessed 29 October 2014).

Jolly, Margaret. 2012. 'Introduction—engendering violence in Papua New Guinea: Persons, power and previous transformations'. In *Engendering Violence in Papua New Guinea*, ed. Margaret Jolly, Christine Stewart and Carolyn Brewer, pp. 1–45. Canberra: ANU E Press. Online: press.anu.edu.au/publications/engendering-violence-papua-new-guinea (accessed 29 October 2014).

Jolly, Susie. 2007. 'Why the development industry should get over its obsession with bad sex and start to think about pleasure'. IDS Working Paper 283. Brighton: University of Sussex.

Keane, Webb. 2007. *Christian Moderns: Freedom and Fetish in the Mission Encounter*. Berkeley, Los Angeles and London: University of California Press.

Kelly, Angela, Bradley Mathers, Thomas Kawage and Andrew Vallely. 2012. *Emerging HIV Risk in Papua New Guinea*. Goroka and Sydney: Papua New Guinea Institute of Medical Research and University of New South Wales.

Kelly, Angela, Heather Worth, Martha Kupul, Voletta Fiya, Lisa Vallely, Ruthy Neo, Sophie Ase, Priscilla Ofi, Glen Mola, Grace Kariwiga, Yves-Laurent Jackson, Tarcisia Hunahoff and John Kaldor. 2013. *HIV, Pregnancy and Parenthood: A Qualitative Study of the Prevention and Treatment of HIV in Pregnant Women, Parents and their Infants in Papua New Guinea.* Sydney: Papua New Guinea Institute of Medical Research and University of New South Wales.

Kelly, Angela, Martha Kupul, Wing Young Nicola Man, Somu Nosi, Namarola Lote, Patrick Rawstorne, Grace Halim, Claire Ryan and Heather Worth. 2011. *Askim na Save (Ask and Understand): People Who Sell and Exchange Sex in Port Moresby.* Goroka and Sydney: Papua New Guinea Institute of Medical Research and University of New South Wales.

Kelly, Angela. 2009. 'The role of HIV social research in the response efforts to the HIV epidemic in Papua New Guinea'. *Papua New Guinea Medical Journal* 52(1/2): 35–43.

Kippax, Susan and Niamh Stephenson. 2012. 'Beyond the distinction between biomedical and social dimensions of HIV prevention through the lens of a social public health'. *American Journal of Public Health* 102(5): 789–99.

Klot Jennifer F. and Vinh-Kim Nguyen (eds). 2009. *The Fourth Wave: Violence, Gender, Culture, and HIV in the 21st Century.* Paris: UNESCO.

Klot, Jennifer F. and Vinh-Kim Nguyen. 2009. 'Introduction'. In *The Fourth Wave: Violence, Gender, Culture, and HIV in the 21st Century*, ed. Jennifer F. Klot and Vinh-Kim Nguyen, pp. 15–26. Paris: UNESCO.

Klot, Jennifer F., Judith D. Auerbach and Miranda R. Berry. 2013. 'Sexual violence and HIV transmission: Summary proceedings of a scientific research planning meeting'. *American Journal of Reproductive Immunology* 69(1): 5–19.

Lepani, Katherine. 2008. 'Mobility, violence, and the gendering of HIV in Papua New Guinea'. *Changing Pacific Masculinities*, ed. John P. Taylor. Special Issue 20. *The Australian Journal of Anthropology* 19(2): 150–64.

——. 2008. 'Review of HIV messaging promoted during PM's XIII visits in Papua New Guinea'. Unpublished report for the PNG–Australia HIV and AIDS Program.

——. 2011. *Historical Analysis of the Australian Aid Program's Contribution to the National HIV Response in Papua New Guinea*. Annex 12, Evaluation of the Australian Aid Program's Contribution to the National HIV Response in Papua New Guinea. Canberra: AusAID Office of Development Effectiveness.

——. 2012. *Islands of Love, Islands of Risk: Culture and HIV in the Trobriands*. Nashville: Vanderbilt University Press.

——. 2015. '"I am still a young girl if I want": Relational personhood and individual autonomy in the Trobriand Islands'. In *Gender and Person in Oceania*, ed. Anna-Karina Hermkens, Rachel Morgain and John P. Taylor. Special issue of *Oceania* 85(1): 51–62.

Lepani, Katherine and Emily Rudland. 2011. Annex 27, Madang Province. *Evaluation of the Australian Aid Program's Contribution to the National HIV Response in Papua New Guinea*. Canberra: AusAID Office of Development Effectiveness.

Lewis, I., B. Maruia, D. Mills and S. Walker. 2007. *Final Report on Links between Violence against Women and Transmission of HIV in Four Provinces of Papua New Guinea*. Canberra: University of Canberra.

Liguori, Ana Luisa and Marta Lamas. 2003. 'Gender, sexual citizenship and HIV/AIDS'. *Culture, Health and Sexuality* 5(1): 87–90.

Luker, Vicki and Sinclair Dinnen (eds). 2010. *Civic Insecurity: Law, Order and HIV in Papua New Guinea*. State, Society and Governance in Melanesia Program, Studies in State and Society in the Pacific, No. 6. Canberra: ANU E Press. Online: press.anu.edu.au/publications/series/state-society-and-governance-melanesia/civic-insecurity (accessed 4 February 2016).

Macintyre, Martha. 2011. 'Money changes everything: Papua New Guinean women in the modern economy'. In *Managing Modernity in the Western Pacific*, ed. Mary Patterson and Martha Macintyre, pp. 90–120. St Lucia: University of Queensland Press.

——. 2012. 'Gender violence in Papua New Guinea and the problem of Millennium Development Goal No. 3'. In *Engendering Violence in Papua New Guinea*, ed. Margaret Jolly, Christine Stewart and Carolyn Brewer, pp. 239–66. Canberra: ANU E Press.

Malinowski, Bronislaw. 1932 [1929]. *The Sexual Lives of Savages in North-Western Melanesia: An Ethnographic Account of Courtship, Marriage and Family Life among the Natives of the Trobriand Islands, British New Guinea* (3rd edition). London: Routledge & Kegan Paul.

Mallett, Shelley. 2003. *Conceiving Cultures: Reproducing People and Places on Nuakata, Papua New Guinea*. Ann Arbor: University of Michigan Press.

McPherson, Naomi. 2012. 'Black and blue: Shades of violence in West New Britain, PNG'. In *Engendering Violence in Papua New Guinea*, ed. Margaret Jolly, Christine Stewart and Carolyn Brewer, pp. 47–72. Canberra: ANU E Press.

Merry, Sally Engle. 2006. 'Transnational human rights and local activism: Mapping the middle'. *American Anthropologist* 108(1): 38–51.

——. 2011. 'Measuring the world: Indicators, human rights, and global governance'. *Current Anthropology* 52(S3): S83–93.

Miller, Alice M. and Carole S. Vance. 2004. 'Sexuality, human rights, and health'. *Health and Human Rights* 7(2): 5–15.

National AIDS Council and National Department of Health. 2004. *The Report of the 2004 National Consensus Workshop of Papua New Guinea*. Waigani: National AIDS Council Secretariat and National Department of Health.

National AIDS Council Secretariat. 2012. *HIV @ Glance*. Leaflet. Waigani: National AIDS Council Secretariat.

——. 2014. *Papua New Guinea Interim Global AIDS Progress and Universal Access Reports*. Online: www.unaids.org/sites/default/files/country/documents//PNG_narrative_report_2014.pdf (accessed 5 September 2015).

National AIDS Council. 2010. *National HIV Prevention Strategy 2011–2015*. Waigani: National AIDS Council.

———. 2006. *National Gender Policy and Plan on HIV and AIDS 2006–2010*. Waigani: National AIDS Council.

National Department of Health. 2010. *Papua New Guinea HIV Prevalence: 2009 Estimates*. Waigani: National Department of Health.

O'Keefe, Michael. 2011. 'Contextualising the AIDS epidemic in the South Pacific: Orthodoxies, estimates and evidence'. *Australian Journal of International Affairs* 65(2): 185–202.

Pacific Islands AIDS Foundation (PIAF). 2011. *Experiences and Perspectives of Women Living with HIV in Fiji and Papua New Guinea: A Qualitative Study*. Cook Islands: PIAF.

Parker, Richard. 2010. 'Reinventing sexual scripts: Sexuality and social change in the twenty-first century' (the 2008 John H. Gagnon Distinguished Lecture on Sexuality, Modernity and Change). *Sexuality Research and Social Policy* 7: 58–66.

Patterson, Mary and Martha Macintyre (eds). 2011. *Managing Modernity in the Western Pacific*. St Lucia: University of Queensland Press.

Redman-MacLaren, Michelle L., Jane Mills, Rachel Tommbe, David J. MacLaren, Richard Speare and William J.H. McBride. 2013. 'Women and HIV in a moderate prevalence setting: An integrative review'. *BioMed Central Public Health* 13: 552–65. Online: bmcpublichealth. biomedcentral.com/articles/10.1186/1471-2458-13-552 (accessed 16 November 2016).

Reid, Elizabeth. 2009. *Interrogating a Statistic: HIV Prevalence Rates in PNG*. State, Society and Governance in Melanesia, Discussion Paper 1. Canberra: The Australian National University.

Richardson, Diane. 2000. 'Constructing sexual citizenship: Theorizing sexual rights'. *Critical Social Policy* 20(1): 105–35.

Seckinelgin, Hakan. 2009. 'Colonial silences, gender and sexuality: Unpacking international HIV and AIDS policy culture'. In *The Fourth Wave: Violence, Gender, Culture, and HIV in the 21st Century*, ed. Jennifer F. Klot and Vinh-Kim Nguyen, pp. 279–94. Paris: UNESCO.

Spark, Ceridwen. 2011. 'Gender trouble in town: Educated women eluding male domination, gender violence and marriage in PNG'. *The Asia Pacific Journal of Anthropology* 12(2): 164–79.

Stewart. Christine. 2012. '"Crime to be a woman?" Engendering violence against female sex workers in Port Moresby, Papua New Guinea'. In *Engendering Violence in Papua New Guinea*, ed. Margaret Jolly, Christine Stewart and Carolyn Brewer, pp. 213–38. Canberra: ANU E Press. Online: press.anu.edu.au/publications/engendering-violence-papua-new-guinea (accessed 29 October 2014).

Stillwaggon, Eileen. 2003. 'Racial metaphors: Interpreting sex and AIDS in Africa'. *Development and Change* 34(5): 809–32.

Strathern, Marilyn. 1988. *Gender of the Gift: Problems with Women and Problems with Society in Melanesia*. Berkeley: University of California Press.

'Trobriand courtship ritual turns violent'. 2013. *Post Courier*, 29 May. Online: www.facebook.com/TheLeniataLegacy/posts/175250975973761 (accessed 16 November 2016).

UN Women Australia. n.d. *Fact Sheet: Violence Against Women*. Canberra: UN Women Australia. Online: unwomen.org.au/sites/default/files/UNW_VAW_web%20(3).pdf (site discontinued).

UNAIDS. 2007. *Practical Guidelines for Intensifying HIV Prevention*. Geneva: UNAIDS.

'Village, food destroyed over girls'. 2013. *Post Courier*, 30 May. Online: www.postcourier.com.pg/20130530/news05.htm (site discontinued).

Wardlow, Holly. 2006. *Wayward Women: Sexuality and Agency in a New Guinea Society*. Berkeley: University of California Press.

——. 2007. 'Men's extramarital sexuality in rural Papua New Guinea'. *American Journal of Public Health* 97(6): 1006–14.

——. 2009. '"Whip him in the head with a stick!" Marriage, male infidelity, and female confrontation among the Huli'. In *The Secret: Love, Marriage, and HIV*, ed. Jennifer S. Hirsch, Holly Wardlow, Daniel Jordon Smith, Harriet M. Phinney, Shanti Parikh and Constance A. Nathanson, pp. 136–67. Nashville: Vanderbilt University Press.

Weiner, Annette B. 1976. *Women of Value, Men of Renown: New Perspectives in Trobriand Exchange*. Austin, TX: University of Texas Press.

Wilson, David and Daniel T. Halperin. 2008. '"Know your epidemic, know your response": A useful approach, if we get it right'. *The Lancet* 372(9637): 423–26.

Wilson, Richard A. 2006. 'Afterword to "Anthropology and Human Rights in a New Key": The social life of human rights'. *American Anthropologist* 108(1): 77–83.

Winskell, Kate, Peter J. Brown, Amy E. Patterson, Camilla Burkot and Benjamin C. Mbakwem. 2013. 'Making sense of HIV in Southeastern Nigeria'. *Medical Anthropology Quarterly* 27(2): 193–214.

Wood, Kate, Helen Lambert and Rachel Jewkes. 2007. '"Showing roughness in a beautiful way": Talk about love, coercion, and rape in South African youth sexual culture'. *Medical Anthropology Quarterly* 21(3): 277–300.

World Health Organization. 2012. *Violence Against Women: Intimate Partner and Sexual Violence Against Women*. WHO Fact sheet No. 239, November. Online: www.who.int/mediacentre/factsheets/fs239/en/ (accessed 31 October 2014).

Zimmer-Tamakoshi, Laura J. 1997. '"Wild pigs and dog men": Rape and domestic violence as "women's issues" in Papua New Guinea'. In *Gender in Cross-Cultural Perspective*, ed. Caroline B. Brettel and Carolyn F. Sargent, pp. 538–53. Englewood Cliffs, NJ: Prentice-Hall.

5

Sorcery Talk, Gender Violence and the Law in Vanuatu

John P. Taylor and Natalie G. Araújo
both at La Trobe University

In her 1996 paper *'Woman Ikat Raet Long Human Raet O No?'*
(Do women have the right to human rights or not?), Margaret Jolly
reported on a conference on Violence and the Family in Vanuatu
held in Port Vila in 1994 and attended by a wide range of women's
rights activists, NGO representatives, development practitioners and
politicians.[1] As Jolly described, the conference raised familiar issues
that might be expected of similar conferences elsewhere:

> What is domestic violence—is it only physical abuse or does it
> include psychological torture? Does it have to be intended? Who are
> the perpetrators and who are the victims? How does male violence
> compare with female violence? Are they sequentially linked? What
> about violence towards children? What makes violence 'domestic'
> or private rather than public? Is domestic violence acceptable to some,
> even legitimate? Is domestic violence increasing? If so, why?[2]

---

1   Margaret Jolly, 1996, *'Woman Ikat Raet Long Human Raet O No?* Women's rights, human
rights and domestic violence in Vanuatu', *Feminist Review* 52: 169–90.
2   Ibid., p. 175.

As Jolly also noted, however, there was a great deal of discussion around less familiar questions that 'might seem strange to Europeans or Anglo-Australians (though perhaps less so to Aboriginal Australians and many migrants to Australia)'. The first of those questions was, 'Is sorcery violence?' This was followed by further questions, 'Has violence increased as people have moved into towns? Is the growth of the cash economy and the increased isolation of the family to blame?'[3]

As we demonstrate in this chapter, the raising of such concerns regarding the link between sorcery or witchcraft (*nakaemas* in Vanuatu's lingua franca, Bislama)[4] and gender violence, including psychological violence, was far from unreasonable, especially when considered from the local perspective. Nor was their framing within a broader context of modernity. Manifesting as a frequent topic of casual conversation and gossip, fear and conjecture surrounding sorcery pervades everyday life in Vanuatu. As several commentators have noted,[5] concerns regarding the presence of sorcery as a malignant component of everyday sociality are intimately associated with transformations of modernity in the contemporary context. More especially, they are readily associated with new inequalities arising within the context of a rapidly transforming capitalist political economy, with urbanisation, and the breakdown of pre-colonial structures of kinship and authority. Concerns about sorcery are also perpetually regenerated in dynamic entanglement with ever-transforming expressions of Christianity, including most recently the emergence of evangelical forms of Pentecostalism.

---

3   Ibid.
4   Typically blending learned and inherited powers, *nakaemas* in this generalised sense blurs classic anthropological definitions of 'witchcraft' and 'sorcery', but corresponds to the broadly agreed upon definition of both; i.e., 'the belief, and those practices associated with the belief, that one human being is capable of harming another by magical or supernatural means'. Mary Patterson, 1974, 'Sorcery and witchcraft in Melanesia', *Oceania* 45(2): 132–60, p. 132. Terry Crowley's definition in *A New Bislama Dictionary* therefore reads as follows: 'nakaemas (n) sorcery, witchcraft, evil force directed by humans that can be used to harm and kill people'. Terry Crowley, 1995, *A New Bislama Dictionary*, Suva, Fiji: Institute of Pacific Studies, p. 155.
5   Knut Rio, 2010, 'Handling sorcery in a state system of law: Magic, violence and *kastom* in Vanuatu', *Oceania* 80(2): 182–97; Jean Mitchell, 2011, '"Operation restore public hope": Youth and the magic of modernity in Vanuatu', *Oceania* 81(1): 36–50; Miranda Forsyth, 2006, 'Sorcery and the criminal law in Vanuatu', *Lawasia Journal* 1: 1–27; John P. Taylor, 2016, 'Two baskets worn at once: Christianity, sorcery and sacred power in Vanuatu', in *Christianity, Conflict, and Renewal in Australia and the Pacific*, ed. Fiona Magowan and Carolyn Schwarz, pp. 139–60, Leiden: Brill Publishers (under contract); Taylor, 2015, 'Sorcery and the moral economy of agency: An ethnographic approach', in *Gender and Person in Oceania*, ed. Anna-Karina Hermkens, Rachel Morgain and John P. Taylor, special issue of *Oceania* 85 (1): 38–50.

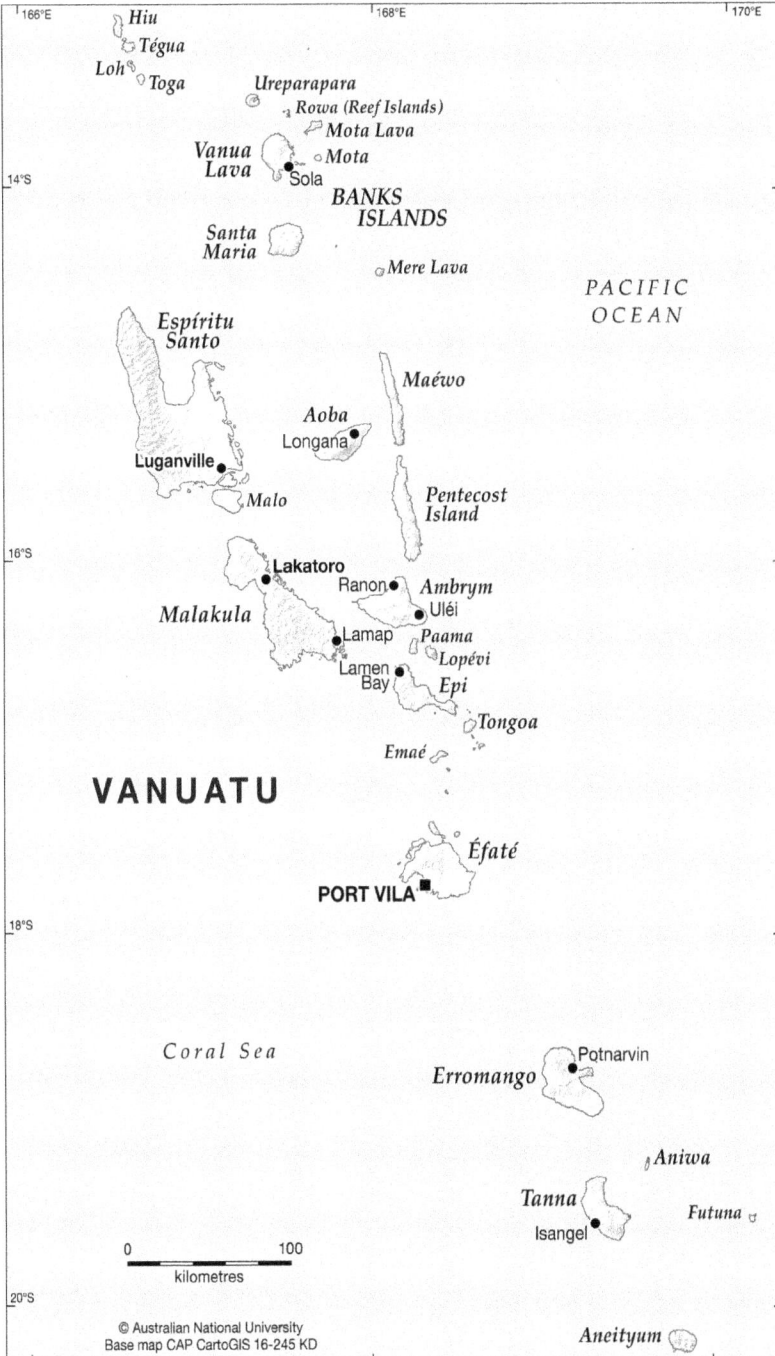

Map 4. Vanuatu

Source. © The Australian National University. Base Map. CAP CartoGIS ANU 16-245 KD

Within this context, and as this chapter demonstrates, sorcery narratives circulate as ambiguous expressions of power and gendered agency. Focusing primarily on several specific sorcery-related narratives recorded by John P. Taylor while conducting fieldwork in Vanuatu's 'second town', Luganville, in 2006–2007,[6] we demonstrate how talk about sorcery articulates and reinscribes relations of power in two key ways. First, we consider narratives concerning the transformation of social context and uses of *nakaemas* during colonialism. Highlighting as they do the positive value of sorcery as a legitimate mechanism of chiefly authority and juridical power in the past, these oral-historical analyses speak to a lamented breakdown of *kastom* (loosely, indigenous knowledge and practice). More especially they express the perceived demise of central hierarchies of masculine power associated with the 'graded society', a hierarchical system of leadership based on competitive exchange and porcine sacrifice, such that occurred within the context of colonialism and is perpetuated in the form of the nation state.[7] Within the context of this historical rupture, sorcery is understood to have become dangerously unbound from 'traditional' structures of male authority. Through the introduction of a Christian morality of 'good' and 'evil', rather than appearing as a useful mechanism of social control, it now became cast as a malignant force of modern chaos. Far from simply articulating a loss of male agency in the face of colonial and state power, however, sorcery in this transformed context is understood to have proliferated into new forms that may be used to challenge the powers of colonialism and the state. Second, while such narratives can thus be read positively as expressions of indigenous agency, we are also attentive to the crucial gendering of sorcery beliefs and their associated narrative tropes in Vanuatu. This is not to say that women are not believed to use sorcery in Vanuatu. Indeed, while men appear to be the main practitioners of sorcery, this is not exclusively the case.[8] More especially, focusing on sex-related accounts of sorcery activity, including what we tentatively refer to as 'sexual assault sorcery', we argue that much sorcery-related discourse reifies gender-based inequalities. Such discourse is often

---

6   John P. Taylor, 2010, 'Janus and the siren's call: Kava and the articulation of gender and modernity in Vanuatu', *Journal of the Royal Anthropological Institute* 16(2): 279–96; Taylor, 'Two baskets worn at once'; Taylor, 'Sorcery and the moral economy of agency'.

7   See also Knut Rio, 2002, 'The sorcerer as an absented third person: Formations of fear and anger in Vanuatu', *Social Analysis* 46(3): 129–54.

8   For example, Forsyth, 'Sorcery and the criminal law in Vanuatu'.

aimed at curtailing female agency by normalising the use of violence against women, including sexual violence, as a form of punitive social justice.

Background

With approximately 110 languages spoken across a current population of around 250,000 people, Vanuatu is an archipelago of stunning linguistic and cultural diversity. Since gaining independence in 1980 from joint British and French colonial rule, it has also become a place of increasing economic inequalities. Like the majority of the Pacific's so-called least developed countries, being relatively isolated in geographical terms, Vanuatu has struggled to build up a strong commodity economy and instead relies heavily on foreign aid. At the same time, within Vanuatu there is often a marked contrast between rural and urban livelihoods. Rural settlements typically consist of dispersed hamlets of around 50 to 300 people. While subsistence agriculture is the primary economic activity in rural areas, this is supplemented by cash incomes typically derived from copra, timber, cocoa and increasingly kava production. By contrast, for those living in one of the two main urban centres, Port Vila and Luganville, dependence on the cash economy is more especially marked. Without easy access to land for gardens or dwellings, and in a context in which conspicuous consumption is of increasing cultural importance, for most urbanites participation in wage labour and entrepreneurship is vital. With jobs remaining relatively scarce, and with an increasingly educated and youthful population, this is a highly competitive sphere of engagement. At the same time, with an increasing dependence on imported foods—especially rice, instant noodles and tinned fish—ni-Vanuatu in urban contexts especially are facing new health challenges such as obesity and diabetes.[9]

Sorcery beliefs, discourses and sorcery-related actions are ubiquitous throughout Vanuatu but assume a particular character and intensity in town. Indeed, as the present discussions from Luganville indicate, within the urban context sorcery is often tied to economic and marital or romantic jealousies. By contrast, sorcery accusations in rural contexts

---

9   Kelsey Needham Dancause et al., 2013, 'Behavioral risk factors for obesity during health transition in Vanuatu, South Pacific', *Obesity* 21(1): E98–E104.

are more often tied to land disputes. In all contexts, however, they are not only closely tied to violence, including gender violence, but also to health-seeking strategies and issues of law and governance. Sorcery accusations are a key factor in much gender-based and other forms of violence.[10] Sorcery impacts negatively on local responses to illness, that incorporate traditional, Christian and biomedical healthcare systems. The question of how to practically confront sorcery through legal or other mechanisms is a continually fraught concern,[11] as demonstrated in a recent conference on Sorcery and Witchcraft-Related Killings in Melanesia at The Australian National University in Canberra.[12]

Sorcery beliefs and practices are not uniform across Vanuatu. Indeed, contemporary sorcery-related anxieties are linked to human mobility and the 'mixing' of different island-based or language-based populations, including their diverse forms and knowledge of sorcery. For this reason, urban settlements, places of employment, and public spaces such as hospitals, kava bars and cargo ships used for inter-island transport represent particularly dangerous sites of sorcery-related activity. At the same time, stereotypes exist across class and ethnicity, with sorcery practice being attributed especially to particular islands (such as Ambrym, Malakula and Maewo) and also to poorer, 'grassroots' groups.[13] There are also discernible differences in the gendered experience of sorcery, that accord with more generalised patterns of gender inequality and gender violence.[14] For example, while both men and women may be subject to attacks on wealth and property, women may also fall victim to sex-related sorcery attacks. Speaking more generally, the literature on Vanuatu suggests a strong link between sorcery and masculine power, with men maintaining their place in political hierarchies by strategically comingling benevolent leadership with the ever-present threat of a dangerous capacity to harm, including the use of spiritual power

---

10   Rio, 'Handling sorcery in a state system of law'; Taylor, 'Sorcery and the moral economy of agency'.
11   Forsyth, 'Sorcery and the criminal law in Vanuatu'.
12   Conference on Sorcery and Witchcraft-Related Killings in Melanesia, 5–7 June 2013, The Australian National University, Canberra.
13   Mitchell, '"Operation restore public hope"'.
14   Chakriya Bowman, Jozefina Cotura, Amanda Ellis and Clare Manuel, 2009, *Women in Vanuatu: Analyzing Challenges to Economic Participation*, Washington DC: The World Bank.

wielded either by themselves or their followers.[15] At the same time, male religious leaders and chiefs often campaign against sorcery, thereby demonstrating their moral capacities, while protecting themselves from the threat of sorcery accusation.[16] Such moral campaigns serve to reinforce both fears of sorcery and fears of being accused. The threat of such masculine power is especially apparent among the growing numbers of new Pentecostal churches, but is also palpable among Anglicans and other established churches.[17]

In this chapter, we contribute to the growing discussion of sorcery and sorcery-related beliefs and practices in Vanuatu, and in the broader region, particularly as these intersect with questions regarding gender violence, the law and human rights concerns more generally. As acknowledged in a UNIFEM report (2010),[18] sorcery is clearly linked to violence, including gender violence, and sorcery-related violence appears to be increasing in Vanuatu and across Melanesia.[19] Indeed, results of a large-scale statistical survey (2,326 respondents) into the status of women in Vanuatu found that of all forms of violence, 'violence due to sorcery' was of the greatest

---

15   William L. Rodman, 1973, 'Men of influence, men of rank: Leadership and the graded society on Aoba, New Hebrides', PhD thesis, University of Chicago; Jolly, '*Woman Ikat Raet Long Human Raet O No?*'; Tim Curtis, 1999, 'Tom's Tambu house: Spacing, status and sacredness in South Malakula, Vanuatu', *Oceania* 70(1): 56–71; Rio, 'Handling sorcery in a state system of law'; John P. Taylor, 2010, 'The troubled histories of a stranger god: Religious crossing, sacred power, and Anglican colonialism in Vanuatu', *Comparative Studies in Society and History* 52(2): 418–46.
16   On the 'moral economy of agency' that surrounds sorcery and expressions of personhood, see Taylor, 'Sorcery and the moral economy of agency'.
17   Taylor, 'Two baskets worn at once'.
18   UNIFEM, 2010, 'Ending violence against women and girls: Evidence, data and knowledge in the Pacific Island Countries. Literature review and annotated bibliography', Suva: UNIFEM Pacific Sub-Regional Office.
19   See, for example, Richard Eves, 2000, 'Sorcery's the curse: Modernity, envy and the flow of sociality in a Melanesian society', *Journal of the Royal Anthropological Institute* 6(3): 453–68; Rio, 'Handling sorcery in a state system of law'; Philip Gibbs, 2012, 'Engendered violence and witch-killing in Simbu', in *Engendering Violence in Papua New Guinea*, ed. Margaret Jolly, Christine Stewart with Carolyn Brewer, pp. 107–35. Canberra: ANU E Press.

overall concern for women (at 49 per cent).[20] In 2007 the international press reported on a high-profile case that resulted in rioting in Port Vila.[21] This incident was not only suggestive of the links between sorcery and gender violence, as well as inter-ethnic violence, but also of the role that Christian and *kastom*-based institutions play in encouraging sorcery beliefs, as manifestations of 'dark powers'. The violence was sparked by allegations that sorcery was used to kill a woman following a marital dispute, with people from the victim's home island (Tanna) attacking the accused husband's island community (Ambrym). Police were unable to control the situation and three people were killed. The Malvatumauri National Council of Chiefs finally settled the dispute and called on members of the Melanesian Brotherhood, a male sect of the Anglican Church,[22] to remove the malignant spiritual powers at work.[23]

While Papua New Guinea has repealed its Sorcery Act, sorcery practice is criminalised in Vanuatu according to state law, and in 2012 the first sorcery conviction occurred under section 151 of the Penal Code. Debate about the effectiveness of such legislation in Vanuatu nevertheless persists, with questions being raised as to whether the existence of sorcery legislation entrenches sorcery belief through legitimating it, and whether the introduction of laws against sorcery accusations might help reduce sorcery-related violence or merely drive it underground.[24] However, while sorcery cases do very occasionally go to trial in Vanuatu,[25] they are typically handled by chiefs through state-sanctioned mechanisms of *kastom* law. More often still they are

---

20 Vanuatu Women's Centre/Vanuatu National Statistics Office, 2011, *Vanuatu National Survey on Women's Lives and Family Relationships*, Port Vila: Vanuatu Women's Centre, p. 54. While certainly praiseworthy for reporting this important statistic, broader questions concerning the nature of these concerns were not discussed elsewhere in the 246-page document. This includes such crucial issues as whether women are concerned about sorcery itself as a form of violence, or about physical violence resulting from sorcery accusations. While certainly praiseworthy for taking steps towards acknowledging sorcery's negative impact on human security by including questions regarding sorcery in the research question, the failure of any attempt to understand the significance of these findings points to a general incapacity within development industry approaches and analytic perspectives concerning sorcery.

21 Emma O'Brian, 2007, 'Vanuatu chiefs ban black magic after riot over woman's death', *Bloomberg*, 27 March.

22 Taylor, 'The troubled histories of a stranger god'.

23 Rio, 'Handling sorcery in a state system of law.

24 Forsyth, 'Sorcery and the criminal law in Vanuatu'; and cf. Nicholas Herriman, 2006, 'Fear and uncertainty: Local perceptions of the sorcerer and the state in an Indonesian witch-hunt', *Asian Journal of Social Sciences* 34(3): 360–87.

25 Forsyth, 'Sorcery and the criminal law in Vanuatu', pp. 21–22.

handled through mechanisms based in Christian churches including processes of dispute resolution, counselling and the exorcism of suspected sorcerers. As the following examples demonstrate, sorcery is related to governance mechanisms in other ways: for example, in pervasive beliefs that *nakaemas* can be used to influence legal outcomes, the strength of sorcery is often considered greater than that of the law. For this reason, anyone involved in court trials, including chiefs, lawyers and judges, presents a potential target for sorcery attack by those wishing to affect legal outcomes. Disturbingly, several anthropologists have suggested that Police Force personnel are often believed to 'act like sorcerers'.[26] Indeed, like many Christian spiritual leaders, such as the members of the Anglican Melanesian Brotherhood, who are said to work on the 'frontline' against such 'dark powers',[27] police officers occupy a dangerously ambiguous position with regard to malignant sacred powers.

Although most individuals in Vanuatu are able to describe personal encounters with sorcery, most sorcery-related activity does not take the form of sorcery *per se*, nor indeed of sorcery-related violence. Rather, and along with the everyday embodied fears of sorcery that individuals carry throughout their daily lives, sorcery primarily appears discursively, in the constant flow of talk, comingled in everyday intrigue, gossip and conjecture. For this reason, the focus in this chapter is to present a preliminary analysis of the ways in which such *sorcery talk* is imbricated with changing relations of power, first in relation to modernity as rupture consequent on the experience of colonialism, and second in relation to novel inequalities in gender relations.[28]

As Hannah Arendt noted, the stories we tell ourselves, about ourselves and others, form an essential component of identity-making and of the constitution and transformation of private and public life.[29] As such, the sorcery-related narratives explored here represent complex, socially and historically embedded expressions of relational agency. Here we focus on an analysis of sorcery narratives as complex articulations of agency occurring within the context of political

---

26   Rio, 'Handling sorcery in a state system of law', p. 134.
27   See Taylor, 'Two baskets worn at once'.
28   Also John P. Taylor, 2008, 'The social life of rights: Gender antagonism, modernity and *raet* in Vanuatu', *The Australian Journal of Anthropology* 19(2): 165–78.
29   Hannah Arendt, 1998 [1958], *The Human Condition*, Chicago: University of Chicago Press.

and gender-based inequalities. Our analysis concentrates attention on three specific historically constituted and gendered sorcery narratives. In the first, two well-respected older men lament the demise of sorcery as a legitimate expression of masculine authority. In this pre-colonial context, sorcery is understood to operate as a realm of esoteric power that works to uphold social order, including hierarchical relations between different kinds of men within society. By contrast, in the second a young man recounts his own experience of having utilised sorcery to aid in the carrying out of a gang rape. In this case sorcery is understood to have fallen into the hands of young, relatively disempowered men. Rather than appearing as an integrated mechanism of chiefly legal authority, as in the previous example, here sorcery is used to express a form of masculine agency that is subversive, anti-authoritarian and counter-hegemonic, both of chiefly justice and state law. All the while, however, in the present context such narratives work to uphold what R.W. Connell has called the 'patriarchal dividend',[30] an assumed set of rights and privileges that structure unequal power relations between men and women. Finally, and in conclusion, we apply these insights to a high-profile legal case concerning sorcery and gender-based violence, as described by Miranda Forsyth.[31]

Masculine authority and the unbinding of sorcery from chiefly power

For our first example we present at length an extract from an interview conducted with two well-educated and respected men, both in their 50s that took place in Luganville. The two men, referred to simply as Michael and Paul for reasons of anonymity, hail from Ambrym and Malakula respectively, the former being a place with a reputation for producing particularly strong sorcery and sorcerers.

---

30 R.W. Connell, 1995, *Masculinities*, Berkeley: University of California Press.
31 Forsyth, 'Sorcery and the criminal law in Vanuatu'.

Michael: On Ambrym we have two societies: one that we call the 'common society' and the other the 'seclusion society'. This thing, *nakaemas*, or black magic, it resided in the seclusion society and was controlled by them [high-ranking men, or today, 'chiefs'] from above.[32]

Paul: Black Mafia!

Michael: And in the *kastom* ranking system, if you take a rank without following the proper road, there will be questions and you must straighten it [i.e., correct it]. But if you don't straighten it, they [chiefs] use this thing [*nakaemas*] to return things to how they were before. At the same time, they use it [*nakaemas*] to keep peace, law and order inside society. A man who disobeys? He won't be able to escape it. Everyone must obey.

JT: So this kind of magic, is it like a form of security for the community?

Paul: Yes, they [chiefs] used it to provide security, to make sure that there is order at all times. However, it is always the last resort. If someone does something that they're not supposed to do, maybe first they'll warn him. The second time, their family will act. And the third time—usually when someone does something wrong the parents or chief will try to solve the problem—but if things continue and it reaches a stage where he no longer obeys, the chief, we say, 'he tells' [*hemi telem*: to notify, or secretly inform, see discussion below].

Paul: Black Mafia!

Michael: Now the talk is out. If you do something wrong, you're told to fix it, for instance by paying a fine. All the leaders or chiefs will come and say, 'You, my child, it's best that you see and understand [*luk save*] that you've done something wrong, and that you fix it and make it straight. Then you can go back, play and live well.' But if you go and do it again, and go out of control, they'll say the following words: 'I see this child is too willful and disobedient [*stronghed tumas*].' That's it—finished now. They'll say those words, and then there will be people around him who will just affect them [*makem hem*, that is, to harm, or otherwise affect someone by supernatural means]. But it would be wrong to blow this up and say that when this occurs, this is an issue for every man. If you're a good man, it's not your issue—it's not your concern.

---

32   In a follow-up interview, Michael further explained the punitive workings of *nakaemas* by using English legal terminology, stating that it works 'like a penalty system' made up of 'judgments' within a 'justice system'. Interview conducted by John P. Taylor, Luganville, 2007.

JT: So you can walk around freely, and you'll be alright?

Paul: That's correct. It's not your concern—they don't poison indiscriminately.

JT: So where did this go wrong? How did this go wrong?

Michael: Cash! Because society in the past was small and its power was enough to keep the peace in that small place. But that small population grew, and more culture came in, and it destroyed that fragile system. And when it was destroyed, people had no other option but to resort to these things [that is, using *nakaemas* inappropriately].

The interview material presented here shows that, in contemporary understandings, sorcery in the past was valued as a largely positive mechanism of masculine chiefly hierarchy and social control, and seen as an integral component of *kastom* law. By contrast, according to local narratives of cultural and masculine loss associated with the breakdown of *kastom* structures of governance during the colonial period, sorcery today represents a largely negatively valued agency. Unbound from previously integrated chiefly structures, and as demonstrated further below, sorcery today is understood to operate in a dangerously liminal space that lies beyond the reach of both state and *kastom* law. These narratives suggest that sorcerers are beyond legal prosecution not only due to ontological incompatibilities concerning evidence, but more so because their powers are seen as so much greater than those of the law.

As well as asserting the legitimacy of indigenous forms of knowledge and power displaced through colonialism, such conversations reflect Robert Tonkinson's claim that, prior to colonialism, 'sorcery was considered a legitimate institution', one that 'kept people in line'.[33] As he suggests further, throughout the ensuing colonial period, and as a part of the demise of male chiefly power and legitimacy through processes of missionisation and 'pacification', there occurred a profound 'democratisation of sorcery'. As Knut Rio describes:

---

33   Robert Tonkinson, 1981, 'Sorcery and social change in Southeast Ambrym, Vanuatu', *Social Analysis* 8: 77–88, p. 79.

The practice became available to all people through inter-island exchange. In the highly mobile era of colonialism, people brought back sorcery from plantations on other islands and from the urban cultural conglomerate. Sorcery became the tool of everyone and everybody. Those who had purchased sorcery could now pose a threat to others without being legitimately known as *vanten hanglam* (high men).[34]

In the above transcript, Michael in particular asserts that sorcery in the past did not constitute an offence to be controlled and legislated against, as it is in the present. By contrast, while certainly dangerous, it is considered by him to have constituted a positively valued legal mechanism in and of itself, one that was used by high-ranking chiefs to bring about justice, law and order.[35] Law and sorcery are in this way understood to have been entwined socially and institutionally within what are typically referred to in the anthropological literature as 'secret societies'—a ritualised system of male initiation cults[36]—and the related 'graded society'—a more public sphere of competitive exchange and porcine sacrifice through which ni-Vanuatu men and women rose in status by moving through a hierarchy of named grades.[37] Indeed, linked in this way to social hierarchy, leadership and juridical control, sorcery appears as a defining feature in the distinction between what Michael instructively describes as the 'common society' and a masculine, chiefly and spiritually powerful 'seclusion society'. Speaking more generally, sorcery is understood to have been incorporated as a part of a normative juridical framework, having been used to support a sanctions-based model of social order and moral duty presided over by high-ranking men.

---

34   Rio, 'The sorcerer as an absented third person', p. 132.

35   The allusion here, including in the metaphoric association of height with masculine power, is to the so-called 'secret men's cults' that occur across Northern Vanuatu. See Michael R. Allen, 1967, *Male Cults and Secret Initiations in Melanesia*, Melbourne: Melbourne University Press. More specifically in Ambrym where they are also linked to esoteric powers including sorcery, see Rio, 'The sorcerer as an absented third person'.

36   See especially Allen, *Male Cults and Secret Initiations in Melanesia*.

37   Rodman, 'Men of influence, men of rank'; Michael Allen (ed.), 1981, *Vanuatu: Politics, Economics, and Ritual in Island Melanesia*, Sydney: Academic Press; Peter Blackwood, 1981, 'Rank, exchange and leadership in four Vanuatu societies', in *Vanuatu: Politics, Economics and Ritual in Island Melanesia*, ed. Michael R. Allen, pp. 35–84, Sydney: Academic Press; Margaret Jolly, 1994, 'Hierarchy and encompassment: Rank, gender and place in Vanuatu and Fiji', *History and Anthropology* 7(1–4): 133–67; on this point also see Rio, 2010, 'Handling sorcery in a state system of law', pp. 137–38.

The decoupling of sorcery from exclusive chiefly juridical control clearly corresponds to a narrative concerning the breakdown of the graded hierarchies of male chiefly power during colonialism. Indeed, this breakdown is understood to have been made possible by the unbinding of *nakaemas* as a legitimate form of social control, and more especially as a mechanism of indigenous law, from the social and political structure. The criminalisation of sorcery in state law during the colonial period and at independence can be seen to have contributed to the breakdown of male chiefly authority and power within the 'seclusion society'. Ironically, colonialism can in this way be seen to have unwittingly propelled rather than reduced sorcery beliefs, especially by allowing for the dispersal of sorcery powers across society at large. Indeed, according to this narrative, previously restricted as an extension of the authority of high ranking men, the power of *nakaemas* was now dangerously set loose, potentially extending everywhere as a largely uncontrolled and widely dispersed sphere of concealed agency.

As the following discussion indicates, however, while forming what might be considered an expression of anticolonial agency, particularly through challenging introduced codes of legality and juridical authority, in this so-called 'democratisation', the power of sorcery was and is still largely controlled by men, and indeed became used in acts of violence against women. At the same time, sorcery remains linked to power and authority, and for this reason an ambivalent link exists in contemporary Vanuatu between sorcery and Christianity, sorcery and the law, and sorcery and masculine power more generally. This comes as no surprise when we consider the oral-historical link that is often made between sorcery and pre-colonial systems of male authority and justice. On this point it is particularly interesting to note the significance of Paul's description of the so-called 'seclusion society' as a 'Black Mafia!' This richly suggestive cross-cultural metaphor, drawn from popular culture and commonly used to describe Ambrym sorcerers in particular, aptly calls to mind the present association of sorcery with a pre-Christian time of 'heathen darkness', while at the same time describing the secretive sphere of masculine power by which sorcery operates, both in the past and in the present. Indeed, the obscure chiefly acts of 'telling' and 'making' described here reflect broader understandings concerning the authoritative and disciplinary power of chiefly talk, found for example in Lamont Lindstrom's

Foucauldian analysis of the John Frum movement on Tanna.[38] In colonial and contemporary times the potentially dangerous power of oblique or indirect speech is also harnessed by Christian priests, including missionaries, in powers of cursing, for instance.[39] Today obscure magical speech is understood to be more widely distributed among men, especially in a form of *nakaemas* known as *swit maot* (sweet mouth), a beguiling talk that is especially used by young men to seduce women and by politicians to win votes.

Sorcery and gender violence

One of the strongest narratives associated with modernity in Vanuatu is that *kastom* has remained more robustly intact in rural contexts than in urban ones, which are typically seen to have been more thoroughly exposed to the ravages of externally derived technologies and socioeconomic forces of change through the colonial period and after. Relating to this is an understanding that indigenous leadership systems, including present manifestations of *kastom* law, are more strongly represented in island villages than in town. Correspondingly, the idea of sorcery as a force unbounded from social structures and institutions, including the law, is often seen to be more closely associated with urban life.[40] With modernity, and especially in towns where people live in communities that are dangerously 'mixed' in terms of island or place-based identity, use of *nakaemas* is believed to have proliferated into multiple forms. Far from comprising mechanisms of chiefly law, these contemporary forms of *nakaemas* are associated with antisocial and criminal behaviour. Terms in Bislama describing these forms include *nakaemas*, which is used as a generalised term for what generally accords to sorcery/witchcraft in anthropological vocabulary. More specifically it describes the ability to change one's form into a spirit animal, such as a shark or a hawk, and to evade

---

38   Lamont Lindstrom, 1990, *Knowledge and Power in a South Pacific Society*, Washington, DC: Smithsonian Institution Press.

39   See, for example, Taylor, 'The troubled histories of a stranger god', p. 59; Taylor, 'Two baskets worn at once'; Knut Rio and Annelin Eriksen, 2013, 'Missionaries, healing and sorcery in Melanesia: A Scottish evangelist in Ambrym Island, Vanuatu', *History and Anthropology* 24(3): 398–418.

40   For a counter-example, see Annelin Eriksen, 2012, *Gender, Christianity and Change in Vanuatu: An Analysis of Social Movements in North Ambrym*, Aldershot and Burlington VT: Ashgate Publishing, p. 60.

the law or commit law-breaking acts such as theft. Other magical forms in Bislama include *bibi*, also known as *kilim tinting* (to kill thought), which describes mental suggestion and memory erasure; *posen* (poison) and sometimes *masin* (from medicine), which describe magically assisted acts of poisoning; *swit maot* (sweet mouth), a form of beguiling talk (see above); and *su*, the ability to move invisibly and imperceptibly through physical space, or as one Pastor described it to Taylor, the ability to 'walk around in the spirit of another power' (*spirit blong narafala power*).

As the following discussion indicates, however, sorcery remains an important component of male chiefly power, including as an expression of what Siobhan McDonnell has described for Efate as 'Masters of Modernity' in land disputes and business enterprise.[41] Yet in the post-independence period it is young men who are understood to have benefited most from sorcery's so-called 'democratisation'. In particular, according to local narratives, young men in town have appropriated and creatively transformed *nakaemas* for two main purposes: stealing money and engaging in illicit sexual activity. *Su* is in this way especially associated with the activities of wayward young men and in gender-related forms of violence. As the Pastor quoted above described it further:

> At this time, now, *nakaemas* is like—many young men play with these rubbish things. It's like, sometimes they think it's a good thing, and they take hold of it, and they're glad. But then they hurt someone else. For instance, to get girls, or to go inside of the house of another man to spoil their wife. To walk around like this, with *su*.

In a very graphic account of what might be called 'sexual assault sorcery', one male interlocutor in his early twenties, also from Ambrym and whom we here call David (also a pseudonym), openly claimed to be a practitioner of *nakaemas*. In the following transcript, David describes how he and a group of male companions once employed such magic to engage in sexual assault as disciplinary social justice on a young woman. Narratives relating to such punitive acts, particularly directed at transgressions of gendered norms and expectations relating to patriarchy, are relatively common. Whether

---

41 Siobhan McDonnell, 2015, '"The land will eat you": Land and sorcery in North Efate, Vanuatu', in *Talking it Through: Responses to Sorcery and Witchcraft Beliefs and Practices in Melanesia*, Miranda Forsyth and Richard Eves, pp. 137–60. Canberra: ANU Press.

or not the narrated events are to be considered 'real' in any material sense, such stories circulate widely in Vanuatu as expressions of masculine agency—including especially, albeit not exclusively, the agency of male youths—and can be seen as part of more generalised processes involving the oppression and surveillance of women, as well as violence against women generally. As such, they reflect other, non-sorcery-related scenarios, whereby women are punished for transgressing gender-based norms and expectations, in acts of shaming, physical violence, and surveillance, or in other means of enforcing male hegemony. This can be seen in recent analyses of chiefly and other social injunctions placed on female behaviour, including especially in prohibitions against the drinking of kava or in personal adornment,[42] such as chiefly bans on the wearing of 'trousers'.[43] It can also be seen in male reactions to women's rights movements, whereby women's empowerment is interpreted relationally as an infringement of male 'rights'.[44] Furthermore, this example shows how sorcery today represents expressions of agency that operate specifically outside or beyond the reach of the law, both Western and *kastom*. Not only are lawbreaking sorcerers unable to be prosecuted due to reasons of evidence and causality, but also, as this account suggests, their strength is often considered greater than the strength of the laws of the state. The following conversation began with a description that mirrors closely those of Michael and Paul (above) with regard to the view of sorcery as intimately tied to chiefly law in the past. This similarly included how chiefly power and authority is directed through chiefly injunctions and enacted as a function of hierarchical relations between men in a concealed manner.

> **David:** On Ambrym, people use it [*nakaemas*] for punishment. Now they use Police. Before, they didn't use Police. It's like Chief Willy Bongmatur told me one time: before, there were no Police. You make trouble the first time, you go the *nakamal* [men's house] for a meeting, and when it's finished, they give you a chance. Okay, next time at the meeting, when they see that you've done the same thing time

---

42   Taylor, 'Janus and the siren's call'.
43   Benedicta Rousseau, 2004, 'The achievement of simultaneity: *Kastom* in contemporary Vanuatu', PhD thesis, Cambridge University; Maggie Cummings, 2008, 'The trouble with trousers: Gossip, kastom, and sexual culture in Vanuatu', in *Making Sense of AIDS: Culture, Sexuality, and Power in Melanesia*, ed. Leslie Butt and Richard Eves, pp. 133–49, Honolulu: University of Hawai'i Press.
44   Taylor, 'The social life of rights'.

and again, they proclaim now that 'it would be best if you go out of society' [*yu aot long sosaeti*]. When they say this—'it would be best if you go out of society'—this is a form of talk by which they mean, 'it would be best if you were simply dead'.

JT: And when that happens, someone will *makem* you [harm/affect by supernatural means]?

David: Yes, there are men for this present already. You and I will not know who kills him, but the poison will happen. You'd think there must be a witness—an eyewitness. But if I come to kill you, you won't see me.

Speaking hurriedly, David abruptly changed the direction of the conversation to explain how sorcery represents a secretive sphere of masculine competition that operates beyond the grasp of the common or Western-style law. Importantly, and underlining the argument that sorcery narratives represent counter-hegemonic expressions of agency, according to David's reckoning, the reason why it is so difficult to bring sorcery cases or carry out sorcery convictions within the context of Western law is not due to ontological incompatibility, especially concerning theories of causality. Rather, this incapacity of Western law to apprehend contemporary sorcerers is due to the unbound capacity of sorcery and to its ability to overpower the force of the law:

> **David:** There's never been a court case for *posen* [poison, or poisoning through sorcery], or someone winning a court case against someone using *posen* against them. Never! If you talk against someone who uses *posen*, you must either shoot him dead, or whatever [i.e., physically murder them], but you will never be able to beat them in court. As we see it, we might know that 'this man has done it', but to tell it out publicly? You can't win. Because once you tell it out publicly, saying, 'this man has done it', you must know [i.e., possess the esoteric knowledge of] much more protection than that man. If he tries to use whatever [form of *nakaemas*], you must know you have many ways to protect yourself from him. Because if you want to talk against him, saying 'you hold something' [for the purposes of *nakaemas*], but you don't have anything to protect yourself, you won't say anything. Because when you say anything in public, he will start to *makem* you, and he'll never stop.

In narratives such as these, sorcery-related acts are described as acts of concealed agency that exist in a competitive sphere that lies both beyond the grasp of the law and the visible 'openness' of public space. In Vanuatu, according to our preliminary analysis at least, such exchanges are typically understood to take place between men, or groups of men. Over the course of such exchanges, acts of sorcery and accusations of sorcery are entangled with acts of physical violence, with the only ultimate equivalent of the power of sorcery being murder.

Changing the direction of conversation again, David went on to describe a personal example in which young men employed *nakaemas* to engage in non-consensual and therefore illegal sexual activity with an unsuspecting young woman. In this instance such sorcery was used to facilitate what was described as a brutal gang rape, one that was enacted as a punitive expression of masculine power. In the narrative David began by observing that 'in town, young men use *nakaemas* especially for women'. He then went on to describe an occurrence in which one of his classificatory brothers, a young man like himself, had been slighted and offended by a girl who had spurned his advances. After returning home to tell of the incident, one of the two young men's classificatory fathers (also in his twenties, and for whom he used the term 'Daddy') suggested that they teach her a lesson, especially as the woman had allegedly spoken badly of their Ambrymese island identity in brushing off the advances of David's brother.

> **David:** So, do you know what happened? We jumped on a truck. We went down into town and brought markers—writing markers. We went to the house of the girl. It was still early. But, regarding the *nakaemas* where you go inside of houses for women, there are two. One—this brother who the woman swore at carried the first. He hid close to the house. Okay, this Daddy carried the second one. With the second one, you can't hurry. You must walk around slowly. If you hurry—once you get in the house, you and I and everyone in the house will die. You must walk around slowly with it, because it makes everyone in the house sleep. Because its power makes everyone sleep.
>
> So, when this second one started working, we could hear everyone inside saying 'goodnight', 'goodnight', and the light switched off. They went to sleep. Then, quickly, the other one who held the first one, he held the one for opening doors. He opened the door. We went

inside—these two things, they're called 'su'. So, su, when you use them, you can't place it close to a person's heart. If you put it on someone's heart, they'll die.

JT: What is it? A leaf? Stone?

David: It's something that the old men make, and you can pay them for it.

JT: Can it be anything?

David: No, it's something special. Some are similar to a flying fox. Sometimes when you've finished using them they fly and then hang all about, especially in banyan trees. Have you seen? I've seen! Because mostly they're so powerful you can't see them. But some are just stones. The first one we used [for opening the door] was a stone, but the second one that he took to use—if you want to carry one on a ship, you have to bury it in a tin, buried in some dirt, and then you can ship it. Because if you carry it on the ship uncovered, the ship will sink. Its power is strong.

So, we went inside, carried out this girl—everyone inside slept, and knew nothing. We carried her and lay her outside. Okay, all the boys did their work on her now—took off all her clothes. One had sex with her, then finished—then another one—another one. Once all of us had finished, we used the markers. Wrote names on whatever part of the body you wanted to—we just wrote it. She slept, and didn't know anything. But in the morning? They found out she'd slept outside—and she was greatly ashamed for having slept outside.

JT: And all the writing?

David: Yes, with all the writing. She read this writing, and she could tell that the sounds of the writing were the sounds of Ambrym. So, she understood that 'No, I said something no good to them all'.

Okay, time passed, and one day we went into town and ran into her. Okay, we met her and talked to her. After, she talked, but she cried. She talked and cried and we asked, 'What's going on?' She said, 'You all used something on me.' We said, 'Yes, we did it because of your behaviour. If you didn't agree last time, you should have just said so. There's no need for you to swear, because you know what kind of a place we come from.' So after, she apologised, and we said 'sorry' to her back. Okay, now we are reconciled.

So, mostly we use it for women, and also we use it to steal.

Given the persuasive and pervasive circulation of such narratives, it is no surprise that the above-mentioned report on violence against women found statistical evidence for widespread fear of sorcery amongst ni-Vanuatu women.[45] Indeed, anecdotal evidence suggests that women routinely switch their phones off at night to avoid their potential use as a conduit for *nakaemas*. Young women especially are encouraged to remain in the company of close female relatives and not to stray to unfamiliar places or at unfamiliar times.[46] Even so, as David's narrative demonstrates, the power of *nakaemas* is such that it can be used to secretly infiltrate even the most familiar of domestic spaces.

Unlike the use of sorcery in chiefly justice, such punitive acts by young men are not socially sanctioned or positively valued. Indeed, at a later point in the interview David explained how he had been counselled and prayed over by members of the Melanesian Brotherhood (see above) on account of his nefarious *nakaemas* activities, especially following a public revelation of his activities from one of the other men involved in the events described above. As David explained, after exorcising him of the evil demons they believed were causing him to undertake such activities, the Melanesian Brothers had allowed him to continue using his magical powers, so long as he only used them to do good.

As well as demonstrating the entanglement of *nakaemas* with Christian understandings and expressions of sacred power,[47] be it in the form of *nakaemas* or in Christian 'cursing', this also suggests something of the juridical role that is played by Christianity in contemporary Vanuatu. Indeed, if the legal environment of Vanuatu is to be described as 'plural' rather than simply dual as is often the case, such pluralism clearly needs to include a wide range of Christian and other responses, including the once legitimate and still quasi-juridical sphere of sorcery. While sorcery-related conflicts and cases often fall under the purview of *kastom* law, they are more often handled by Christian means. Church leaders often intervene in sorcery-related cases through a mixture of

---

45   Vanuatu Women's Centre/Vanuatu National Statistics Office, *Vanuatu National Survey on Women's Lives and Family Relationships*.

46   On the differential value of male and female mobility, and the sexualisation of the latter, see Margaret Jolly, 1999, 'Another time, another place', *Oceania* 69(4): 282–99.

47   Taylor, 'The troubled histories of a stranger god'; Taylor, 'Two baskets worn at once'; Taylor, 'Sorcery and the moral economy of agency: An ethnographic approach'.

spiritual intervention (including by performing divinations, exorcisms and 'clearances' of malignant spiritual forces, counselling, and dispute management) that includes processes of restorative justice. It also suggests that sorcery is not simply a component of *kastom* or even of strictly indigenous cosmology and practice, as is often supposed. Rather its contemporary transmutations are intimately linked both to the largely male hierarchies of Christianity[48] and (as we soon explain) to introduced, hegemonic Western legal frameworks.[49] Indeed, this may come as no surprise in consideration of the ambivalent unbinding of sorcery from localised social and juridical structures, including male graded hierarchies, but also the crossing over of those hierarchies into broader Christian ones.[50]

The mechanisms of both state and *kastom* law and governance are heavily monopolised by men in Vanuatu,[51] as are the hierarchies of Christianity and the magical powers of *nakaemas*. Indeed, according to the local perspectives and analyses presented above, while tied in the past to male hierarchies as a mechanism for the maintenance of law and order, the *nakaemas* of today has become dangerously unbound from the law, both state and *kastom*, and as such has been harnessed for the purposes of more generalised expressions of masculine agency. In this sense, while the use of *nakaemas* by young and sometimes disempowered men discussed here may be viewed positively as an expression of the 'weapons of the weak', it must also be seen as much more negatively engaged in the enactment of violence against women and in the curbing of women's freedoms more generally.

Conclusions

Since the 1994 conference attended by Jolly, a great deal of development resources and capacity building have been directed at women's empowerment in Vanuatu, with many positive results.[52] Despite these efforts, however, pressing questions relating to the

---

48   See Taylor, 'The troubled histories of a stranger god'; Taylor, 'Two baskets worn at once'.
49   Rio, 'Handling sorcery in a state system of law'.
50   See Taylor, 'The troubled histories of a stranger god'.
51   Margaret Jolly, 2011, 'Flying with two wings? Justice and gender in Vanuatu', *The Asia Pacific Journal of Anthropology* 12(2): 195–201, p. 196.
52   See Aletta Biersack, 'Human rights work in Papua New Guinea, Fiji and Vanuatu', this volume.

role of sorcery, sorcery beliefs and fears, and sorcery violence—including gender violence—have since that time remained largely unasked. Indeed, despite being clearly implicated in development concerns—especially relating to health and gender violence—sorcery has to this point remained a problematic 'development taboo' within development and health-related discourses and practice in Vanuatu.[53] While sorcery and religion are classic areas of anthropological interest, issues related to the sacred and especially the negative 'supernatural' are often systematically avoided in development and health industry policy and practice. While possibly bolstered by concerns of cultural relativism, the avoidance of issues regarding belief in the supernatural is continuous with the colonial legacy whereby diverse forms of indigenous agency are only recognised if they conform to biomedical conceptions of causation and reality.[54] While lip service is occasionally paid to the important role played by Christian and indigenous spiritual beliefs and practices in healthcare, present healthcare-related literature suggests that such refusals to acknowledge or attempt to understand the value of indigenous healing methods, including those aimed at combatting the negative health effects of *nakaemas*, are still very much the case. Similarly, while international development programs often seek to bolster 'traditional' governance methods and mechanisms, including male chiefly systems,[55] the pressing issue of how to confront the negative effects of sorcery beliefs and discourse in sorcery-related violence remains unexamined.

This, however, looks set to change. In June 2013, a wide range of scholars, development workers and political and legal representatives met at The Australian National University to discuss the pressing issue of 'Sorcery and witchcraft-related killings in Melanesia: Culture, law and human rights perspectives'. This forum, convened by the State, Society and Governance in Melanesia Project and funded by AusAID, was prompted by a recent and dramatic increase in gruesome

---

53   Kurt Alan Ver Beek, 2000, 'Spirituality: A development taboo', *Development in Practice* 10(1): 31–43, p. 31.

54   Alexandra Widmer, 2007, 'Genealogies of biomedicine: Formations of modernity and social change in Vanuatu', PhD thesis, Toronto: York University, p. 30.

55   Volker Boege, 2008, *A Promising Liaison: Kastom and State in Bougainville*, Brisbane: Australian Centre for Peace and Conflict Studies (ACPACS), University of Queensland; Peter Westoby and Anne M. Brown, 2007, 'Peaceful community development in Vanuatu: A reflection on the Vanuatu *kastom* governance partnership', *Journal of Peacebuilding and Development* 3(3): 77–81; Anne Brown, 2007, 'Gender and customary governance in Vanuatu', paper presented at the 10th Pacific Islands Political Studies Association, Port Vila, Vanuatu, 7–8 December.

gender-related 'witch killings' in Papua New Guinea[56] that gained media attention internationally and apparently prompted the Papua New Guinea Government not only to revoke its 1971 Sorcery Act but also to reintroduce and broaden death penalty laws for murder, including sorcery-related murder and aggravated rape.[57] While largely focused on Papua New Guinea, as conference conveners Richard Eves and Miranda Forsyth observed, the reason for the instigation of that forum was to address a lack of engagement by development industry practitioners with broader legal and human rights concerns relating to sorcery across the region as a whole. More specifically, and as signalled in a wide-ranging opening address by Forsyth, many of the discussions and debates raised in that forum concerned legal responses to sorcery and sorcery-related violence. This included debates about the role of the law in dealing with practices for which there is an unreliable evidence base. Questions were also raised as to whether sorcery legislation might negatively affect sorcery-related beliefs and practices at a local level, for instance by adversely promoting belief in sorcery or by driving the activities of sorcerers underground. Alongside these discussions ran a stream of detailed descriptive accounts suggesting that fear of sorcery and sorcery-related violence is endemic across the region.

Leaving aside difficult and perhaps unanswerable questions concerning the effectiveness or appropriateness of legal mechanisms in reducing sorcery-related violence, these accounts strongly reinforced the observations concerning sorcery and human rights suggested almost 20 years earlier by women in Vanuatu, as reported by Jolly: that sorcery-related fears and violence are human rights concerns; that, looked at from the local perspective, sorcery itself does constitute a form of violence;[58] and that sorcery beliefs and sorcery-related violence are invariably if not always structured by locally specific social hierarchies and relations of gender.[59]

---

56 See Aletta Biersack and Martha Macintyre, 'Introduction: Gender violence and human rights in the western Pacific', this volume; and Biersack, 'Human rights work in Papua New Guinea, Fiji and Vanuatu', this volume; Gibbs, 'Engendered violence and witch-killing in Simbu'.
57 'Amnesty International, 2013, 'Papua New Guinea repeals Sorcery Act while moving closer to executions', News bulletin, 28 May.
58 Jolly, '*Woman Ikat Raet Long Human Raet O No?*'
59 Gibbs, 'Engendered violence and witch-killing in Simbu'.

While acknowledging that the present chapter is based on just a handful of interviews and that further research is required in this area, through engaging a gender-focused analysis with respect to sorcery-related narratives in Vanuatu, it becomes apparent that sorcery beliefs in this context are structured in such a way that both challenge and uphold hegemonic relations of power. In particular, and in contrast to Papua New Guinea, sorcery in this context is typically—although indeed not exclusively[60]—understood to be controlled by men, and to be used in such a way as to produce and reproduce hierarchical relations between men and, crucially in the contemporary context, between men and women. This can be clearly seen in what is perhaps the most high-profile sorcery legal case for Vanuatu, the so-called 'Malsoklei case',[61] as summarised by Forsyth.[62]

> A young and possibly mentally unbalanced adolescent wanted to join a group of men who were reputed to engage in sorcery. He was told that they would accept him if he named someone for them to sacrifice and so he named his sister, Roslyn, during an initiation ceremony. Arrangements were made and she was brought to a clearing at night where she was raped by all the men and then one of them killed her and removed her intestines by using a pandanus leaf pushed up her anus. The leader of the group then cut a piece of her liver or heart and gave it to the brother to eat. Another member of the group then had a leaf waved over him and magical words were said to make him resemble Roslyn and he was then sent home in Roslyn's place. A few days later the leader of the group came to her home and asked 'Roslyn' to go to the local nightclub with him and at the nightclub they started to dance. Then suddenly 'Roslyn' fell down and the body was replaced by that of the real Roslyn, who was taken to the local hospital where she was pronounced to be dead, but no autopsy was carried out. In April 1996 the brother went to the police and talked to them about the death of his sister and events which had occurred in the days prior to her death. Four years later, each of the defendants was committed by the Senior Magistrates' Court at Lakatoro to the Supreme Court in 2000. The reason provided for this long delay was that the police did not investigate the matter immediately but waited for five years because they wanted time to let the issue cool down.

---

60   For example, Forsyth, 'Sorcery and the criminal law in Vanuatu'.
61   *Malsoklei* v Public Prosecutor [2002] VUCA 28.25.
62   Forsyth, 'Sorcery and the criminal law in Vanuatu', pp. 13–14.

In this instance it is notable that the violent rape and murder of a young woman occurs as an expression of male power, in particular as an act performed in the production of competitive hierarchical relations between men. Further, while distributing what Connell has termed the 'patriarchal dividend' through masculine acts of physical violence and *nakaemas*,[63] here the ambivalent power of sorcery is such that it overpowers the effectiveness of the rule of law. Whether through fear of themselves becoming targets of such malicious *nakaemas*, both the police and the court appear unable to respond to the crimes committed. Finally, the issue of Rosalyn's brutal murder not only remains unresolved but is subsumed by ambivalent questions about legal process concerning *nakaemas* itself.

As Eves argues with regard to local knowledge surrounding HIV/AIDS in Papua New Guinea, if we are to understand the broader context of gender violence, we must seriously and respectfully take account of the local contexts of belief and discourse that structure such behaviour, including how they have changed and continue to change with modernity.[64] Here we have argued that contemporary sorcery beliefs and associated narratives often represent ambivalent performative expressions of male agency. Such narrative expressions have been demonstrated to be dynamically engaged within multiple spheres of hegemony, first in subverting the effects of state power and its legal mechanisms in particular, and second by reinscribing unequal relations between men and women. This is particularly seen in that, while both men and women are potential victims of health- or fortune-related sorcery attacks, women also live in fear of sex-related sorcery attacks, which often appear as expressions of punitive gender violence. Indeed, in this respect examination of sorcery-related narratives shows *nakaemas* to represent a largely negative force in society. In the hands of young men, for example, it may be used to subvert the authority of chiefly and state justice. At the same time it works to uphold patriarchy and the generalised subjugation and surveillance of women, including through naturalising sexual violence as a form of social justice.

---

63   Connell, *Masculinities*.
64   Richard Eves, 2012, 'Resisting global AIDS knowledges: Born-again Christian narratives of the epidemic from Papua New Guinea', *Medical Anthropology* 31: 61–76.

Acknowledgements

We give thanks first and foremost to the individuals and communities with whom this research was carried out. We are grateful to ARC Laureate Professor Margaret Jolly, and support received from the ARC Laureate project 'Engendering Persons, Transforming Things: Christianities, Commodities and Individualism in Oceania' (FL100100196). This chapter was completed as a part of Dr John Taylor's ARC Discovery Project 'Sorcery and Human Security in Vanuatu' (DP140104244).

References

Allen, Michael R. 1967. *Male Cults and Secret Initiations in Melanesia*. Melbourne: Melbourne University Press.

Allen, Michael (ed.). 1981. *Vanuatu: Politics, Economics, and Ritual in Island Melanesia*. Sydney: Academic Press.

Amnesty International. 2013. 'Papua New Guinea repeals Sorcery Act while moving closer to executions'. News bulletin, 28 May. Online: www.amnesty.org/en/latest/news/2013/05/papua-new-guinea-repeals-sorcery-act-while-moving-closer-executions/ (accessed 16 November 2016).

Arendt, Hannah. 1998 [1958]. *The Human Condition*. Chicago: University of Chicago Press.

Blackwood, Peter. 1981. 'Rank, exchange and leadership in four Vanuatu societies'. In *Vanuatu: Politics, Economics and Ritual in Island Melanesia*, ed. Michael R. Allen, pp. 35–84. Sydney: Academic Press.

Boege, Volker. 2008. *A Promising Liaison: Kastom and State in Bougainville*. Brisbane: Australian Centre for Peace and Conflict Studies (ACPACS), University of Queensland.

Bowman, Chakriya, Jozefina Cotura, Amanda Ellis and Clare Manuel. 2009. *Women in Vanuatu: Analyzing Challenges to Economic Participation*. Washington DC: The World Bank.

Brown, Anne. 2007. 'Gender and customary governance in Vanuatu'. Paper presented at the 10th Pacific Islands Political Studies Association, Port Vila, Vanuatu, 7–8 December.

Butt, Leslie and Richard Eves (eds). 2008. *Making Sense of AIDS: Culture, Sexuality, and Power in Melanesia*. Honolulu: University of Hawai'i Press.

Conference on Sorcery and Witchcraft-Related Killings in Melanesia, 5–7 June 2013. Canberra: The Australian National University.

Connell, R.W. 1995. *Masculinities*. Berkeley: University of California Press.

Crowley, Terry. 1995. *A New Bislama Dictionary*. Suva, Fiji: Institute of Pacific Studies.

Cummings, Maggie. 2008. 'The trouble with trousers: Gossip, kastom, and sexual culture in Vanuatu'. In *Making Sense of AIDS: Culture, Sexuality, and Power in Melanesia*, ed. Leslie Butt and Richard Eves, pp. 133–49, Honolulu: University of Hawai'i Press.

Curtis, Tim. 1999. 'Tom's Tambu house: Spacing, status and sacredness in South Malakula, Vanuatu'. *Oceania* 70(1): 56–71.

Dancause, Kelsey Needham et al. 2013. 'Behavioral risk factors for obesity during health transition in Vanuatu, South Pacific'. *Obesity* 21(1): E98–E104.

Eriksen, Annelin. 2012. *Gender, Christianity and Change in Vanuatu: An Analysis of Social Movements in North Ambrym*. Aldershot and Burlington VT: Ashgate Publishing.

Eves, Richard. 2000. 'Sorcery's the curse: Modernity, envy and the flow of sociality in a Melanesian society'. *Journal of the Royal Anthropological Institute* 6(3): 453–68.

——. 2012. 'Resisting global AIDS knowledges: Born-again Christian narratives of the epidemic from Papua New Guinea'. *Medical Anthropology* 31: 61–76.

Forsyth, Miranda. 2006. 'Sorcery and the criminal law in Vanuatu'. *Lawasia Journal* 1: 1–27. Online: heinonline. org/HOL/LandingPage?handle=hein.journals/lawasiaj7 &div=5&id=&page= (accessed 19 November 2014).

Forsyth, Miranda and Richard Eves. 2015. *Talking it Through: Responses to Sorcery and Witchcraft Beliefs and Practices in Melanesia*. Canberra: ANU Press.

Gibbs, Philip. 2012. 'Engendered violence and witch-killing in Simbu'. In *Engendering Violence in Papua New Guinea*, ed. Margaret Jolly, Christine Stewart and Carolyn Brewer, pp. 107–35. Canberra: ANU E Press. Online: press.anu.edu.au/publications/engendering-violence-papua-new-guinea (accessed 17 November 2014).

Herriman, Nicholas. 2006. 'Fear and uncertainty: Local perceptions of the sorcerer and the state in an Indonesian witch-hunt'. *Asian Journal of Social Sciences* 34(3): 360–87.

Jolly, Margaret. 1994. 'Hierarchy and encompassment: Rank, gender and place in Vanuatu and Fiji'. *History and Anthropology* 7(1–4): 133–67.

——. 1996. '*Woman Ikat Raet Long Human Raet O No?* Women's rights, human rights and domestic violence in Vanuatu'. *Feminist Review* 52: 169–90.

——. 1999. 'Another time, another place'. *Oceania* 69(4): 282–99.

——. 2011. 'Flying with two wings? Justice and gender in Vanuatu'. *The Asia Pacific Journal of Anthropology* 12(2): 195–201.

Jolly, Margaret, Christine Stewart and Carolyn Brewer (eds). 2012. *Engendering Violence in Papua New Guinea*. Canberra: ANU E Press. Online: press.anu.edu.au/publications/engendering-violence-papua-new-guinea (accessed 17 November 2014).

Lindstrom, Lamont. 1990. *Knowledge and Power in a South Pacific Society*. Washington, DC: Smithsonian Institution Press.

McDonnell, Siobhan. 2015. '"The land will eat you": Land and sorcery in North Efate, Vanuatu', in Forsyth, Miranda and Richard Eves, *Talking it Through: Responses to Sorcery and Witchcraft Beliefs and Practices in Melanesia*. pp. 137–160. Canberra: ANU Press.

Mitchell, Jean. 2011. '"Operation restore public hope": Youth and the magic of modernity in Vanuatu'. *Oceania* 81(1): 36–50.

O'Brian, Emma. 2007. 'Vanuatu chiefs ban black magic after riot over woman's death'. *Bloomberg*, 27 March.

Patterson, Mary. 1974. 'Sorcery and witchcraft in Melanesia'. *Oceania* 45(2): 132–60.

Rio, Knut and Annelin Eriksen. 2013. 'Missionaries, healing and sorcery in Melanesia: A Scottish evangelist in Ambrym Island, Vanuatu'. *History and Anthropology* 24(3): 398–418.

Rio, Knut. 2002. 'The sorcerer as an absented third person: Formations of fear and anger in Vanuatu'. *Social Analysis* 46(3): 129–54.

——. 2010. 'Handling sorcery in a state system of law: Magic, violence and kastom in Vanuatu'. *Oceania* 80(2): 182–97.

Rodman, William L. 1973. 'Men of influence, men of rank: Leadership and the graded society on Aoba, New Hebrides'. PhD thesis, University of Chicago.

Rousseau, Benedicta. 2004. 'The achievement of simultaneity: *Kastom* in contemporary Vanuatu'. PhD thesis, Cambridge University.

Taylor, John P. 2008. 'The social life of rights: Gender antagonism, modernity and *raet* in Vanuatu'. *The Australian Journal of Anthropology* 19(2): 165–78.

——. 2010, 'Janus and the siren's call: Kava and the articulation of gender and modernity in Vanuatu'. *Journal of the Royal Anthropological Institute* 16(2): 279–96.

——. 2010. 'The troubled histories of a stranger god: Religious crossing, sacred power, and Anglican colonialism in Vanuatu'. *Comparative Studies in Society and History* 52(2): 418–46.

——. 2015. 'Sorcery and the moral economy of agency: An ethnographic approach'. In *Gender and Person in Oceania*, ed. Anna-Karina Hermkens, Rachel Morgain and John P. Taylor. Special issue of *Oceania* 85(1): 38–50.

——. 2016. 'Two baskets worn at once: Christianity, sorcery and sacred power in Vanuatu'. In *Christianity, Conflict, and Renewal in Australia and the Pacific*, ed. Fiona Magowan and Carolyn Schwarz, pp. 139–60. Leiden: Brill Publishers (under contract).

Tonkinson, Robert. 1981. 'Sorcery and social change in Southeast Ambrym, Vanuatu'. *Social Analysis* 8: 77–88.

UNIFEM. 2010. 'Ending violence against women and girls: Evidence, data and knowledge in the Pacific Island Countries. Literature review and annotated bibliography'. Suva: UNIFEM Pacific Sub-Regional Office. Online: www.unicef.org/pacificislands/evaw.pdf (accessed 6 November 2014).

Vanuatu Women's Centre/Vanuatu National Statistics Office. 2011. *Vanuatu National Survey on Women's Lives and Family Relationships*. Port Vila: Vanuatu Women's Centre. Online: www. spc.int/nmdi/nmdi_documents/VanuatuWomensCentreSurveyWo mensLives2011.pdf (accessed 16 November 2016).

Ver Beek, Kurt Alan. 2000. 'Spirituality: A development taboo'. *Development in Practice* 10(1): 31–43.

Westoby, Peter and Anne M. Brown. 2007. 'Peaceful community development in Vanuatu: A reflection on the Vanuatu kastom governance partnership'. *Journal of Peacebuilding and Development* 3(3): 77–81.

Widmer, Alexandra. 2007. 'Genealogies of biomedicine: Formations of modernity and social change in Vanuatu'. PhD thesis. Toronto: York University.

6

Translating and Internalising International Human Rights Law: The Courts of Melanesia Confront Gendered Violence

Jean G. Zorn

City University of New York School of Law

Stories

Discrimination against women takes many forms. In Fiji, a sister and her improvident brothers argued over the disposition of their dead father's estate. The brothers had already disposed of a good deal of it, in the worst ways possible, running a once prosperous sugar cane business into the ground and stripping a formerly thriving farm of all its top soil. The sister, afraid—and for good reason—that her brothers would fritter away what was left, asked the court to appoint her administrator of the estate in their place. But the laws of Fiji provided, in no uncertain terms, that the courts were to appoint sons, not daughters, to administer the estates of their deceased parents.

In Kiribati, a young woman was brutally raped. As with most rapes, however, no one was there to see it happen except the woman and her rapist. And he said she was lying. In most courts today—not just in the Pacific, but around the world—that would have all but put an end to the trial, because, in most countries, a rapist cannot be convicted on the uncorroborated testimony of his victim. A court is free to convict defendants charged with robbery or fraud or assault, even when there is no evidence beyond the word of the victim. But rape—that most private of crimes—is in many jurisdictions an exception.

And, in Vanuatu, a husband claimed in divorce proceedings that the businesses he had started during the marriage belonged to him alone, despite the fact that, throughout their marriage, she had taken full charge of their home and children, had worked herself, had paid for all the household expenses and had contributed to the businesses. Since the Vanuatu legislature had never invalidated the 19th-century British statutes governing the allocation of property in divorce, the court could well have given the businesses to him, leaving him wealthy and her with virtually nothing.

What do these three stories have in common? One point of similarity is obvious: all involve a woman subjugated, exploited or endangered. But that is not the whole story. Another common thread in their stories is that each of the women found herself in court and, in each case, despite local laws that discriminated against women and would have held against them, the court or legislature was able, using international human rights treaties and conventions, to fashion a new, liberating remedy.

Introduction

In 1979, when the Convention to Eliminate All Forms of Discrimination against Women (CEDAW) was adopted, it was a groundbreaking instrument, the first international treaty to recognise that women's rights are human rights. But that original version of CEDAW contained no mention of rape or domestic violence. It took another decade for gender violence to be included among the discriminatory laws, customs and actions that CEDAW outlaws.

The realisation that gender violence is a human rights issue, and that CEDAW requires states to take steps to end it, has had a positive impact on Melanesian women. It has energised women's groups and given them new tools and ideas to work with. Women in Papua New Guinea, fresh from attendance at world conferences on women in Copenhagen (1980) and Nairobi (1985), formed a coalition that produced books, pamphlets, posters, legislation and even a film promoting gender equality and calling for an end to gendered violence. A decade later, women in Vanuatu attended their first UN women's meeting (in Beijing, in 1995), and with a new appreciation of the world's willingness to help them, they actively, and ultimately successfully, campaigned for CEDAW to be ratified by Vanuatu.[1]

Despite those gains, however, women in Melanesian societies continue to occupy a subordinate status, and violence against women remains an intransigent problem. Politicians, journalists and scholars have given numerous reasons for CEDAW's less than absolute success. Two of the leading CEDAW scholars, Sally Engle Merry and Bonita Meyersfeld, come at their studies from differing, though overlapping, perspectives—Merry is a legal anthropologist; Meyersfeld is a specialist in international law—and arrive at differing, though not entirely different, conclusions: while both agree that CEDAW has to date hardly been implemented, they disagree about where the responsibility lies for its implementation, how it gets implemented, and therefore how effective it has been to date, and how likely it is to be effective in the future.[2]

Merry, in her 2006 study of the impact of CEDAW, saw a relative lack of progress in ending violence against women, despite the mobilisation of international organisations, and suggested that one reason for it is the disconnect between the rarefied corridors of the United Nations headquarters in New York and Geneva and the variable, variegated, ever-changing local cultures that CEDAW is supposed to affect.[3] Merry posits that the legal culture of international human rights workers is so different from the cultures of women's groups and other local organisations within nation-states that they misunderstand and often talk past one another.[4]

---

1   Jean Zorn, 2003, 'Custom then and now: The changing Melanesian family', in *Passage of Change: Law, Society and Governance in the Pacific*, ed. Anita Jowitt and Tess Newton Cain, pp. 95–124, Canberra: Pandanus Books.

2   The results vary from country to country, from researcher to researcher, and depend on what each study denotes as indicia of changing norms. Merry finds less than total acceptance of CEDAW's goals in Fiji and India. See Sally Engle Merry, 2006, *Human Rights and Gender Violence: Translating International Law into Local Justice*, Chicago: University of Chicago Press, pp. 103–33. Meyersfeld finds significant changes, in the direction of making domestic violence a higher profile state concern, in Sweden, Nicaragua and Mexico. See Bonita Meyersfeld, 2012, *Domestic Violence and International Law*, Oxford: Hart Publishing, pp. 291–316.

3   Merry, *Human Rights and Gender Violence*, p. 1.

4   Ibid., p. 103.

Meyersfeld's perspective is more traditionally legal. She describes CEDAW, like other examples of international law, as operating primarily on states (on national governments), not on individuals or groups within state boundaries. Finding many examples of changed state behaviour—that is, of governmental initiatives such as the addition to national criminal codes of domestic violence as a crime, the creation of governmental panels and commissions to study and find ways of combatting domestic violence, and the use by courts of CEDAW as a source of judicial decision-making—she pronounces CEDAW a qualified success.[5]

Their disparate perspectives are important to an understanding of how CEDAW might succeed in the Pacific. Merry describes two failures of vision that have hindered the Committee's attempts to change domestic laws and customs: first, the failure of both CEDAW's supporters and its detractors to understand the flexible and changing nature of the customs or culture of the reporting countries; and, second, the failure to understand that the world of international human rights experts is itself a culture, with its own beliefs, values and blind spots—a world that needs to be translated if it is to have an impact on the other world of domestic law and lifestyles.

Merry believes that CEDAW could be employed more effectively if the experts on the CEDAW Committee and other international actors took into account the ever-changing nature of custom in making their recommendations. With sufficient time and resources to make a thorough study of each reporting country's situation, the Committee could make recommendations that were more tailored to local circumstances, recommendations that would make use of local customs, circumstances and politics in effecting change. Culture and custom can become, in Merry's words, a resource for, rather than a barrier to, change.[6]

---

5   Meyersfeld, *Domestic Violence and International Law*.
6   Merry, *Human Rights and Gender Violence*, p. 9. To be fair to the international human rights workers, their essentialist view of culture and custom is also held by their opposition, conservatives within reporting states who wish to retain the status quo, despite or because of its subordination of women. They, too, reify custom, declaring that the UN's attempts to impose supposedly universal values will serve only to destroy local cultures.

Merry's second point is that, despite the assumption of the international elites that culture is something that exists only in insular and isolated places, the meetings and reports and discussions, most of which take place in far-off capitals like New York or Geneva, of NGOs and other groups that make up the international human rights community, is itself a culture, with customs and values of its own:

> Culture defined only as tradition or as national essence implies that villages are full of culture but that there is no culture in the conference halls of New York and Geneva. Yet, culture is as important in shaping human rights conferences as it is in structuring village mortuary rituals ... UN meetings are deeply shaped by a culture of transnational modernity, one that specifies procedures for collaborative decision-making, concepts of global social justice, and definitions of gender roles. Human rights law is itself primarily a cultural system.[7]

The particular culture of the international human rights world is centred not just on a firm conviction about the universal value of human rights, but also on a shared belief in the rule of law: 'The [CEDAW and other human rights] experts are applying the law. They are acting as a legal body to enforce compliance with the terms of a treaty ratified by the country. The human rights system is a legal system committed to the universal application of a code of conduct to myriad particular situations.'[8] This is a culture that drafts, lobbies for and attempts to enforce written laws. The enforcement mechanisms available to the CEDAW Committee differ from those that a judge in a state court can wield. Judges hand down verdicts, mete out sentences; except for the parties' right to appeal, their word is, well, law. Conversely, 'The impact of human rights law is a matter of persuasion rather than force, of cultural transformation rather than coercive change'.[9] Still, the two cultures have much in common. The experts on the CEDAW Committee share with judges in state courts a value system characterised by a deeply held belief that reason ought to trump bias, anger and other emotions and that the best and safest norms are those that are uniformly, impartially and universally applied.

---

7   Ibid., p. 16.
8   Ibid., p. 130.
9   Ibid.

Merry's insistence that it is the task of the CEDAW Committee to come to a better understanding of the variations in local culture overlooks the basic truth that the achievement of CEDAW's aim of overcoming discrimination might be best served by ignoring the differences in local cultures and focusing on the ways in which all can meet this goal. Further, she places the major responsibility for carrying out CEDAW's requirements on non-governmental organisations, and perhaps social agencies within government, overlooking the role that other actors, particularly actors within national governmental and legal institutions—and, most particularly, legislators in parliament and judges in national courts—can play in translating CEDAW's principles for national consumption. Meyersfeld offers a beneficial corrective and addendum to Merry's study in viewing CEDAW as a law, not as a rallying cry, and in recognising that CEDAW is at its most effective in legal settings.

Merry focuses on legal cultures; Meyersfeld on legal institutions, pointing out that there are two ways in which international law can improve states' responses to domestic violence. First (as Merry also notes), international law has an expressive value: it stipulates norms, which define the contents of rights, and concomitant state obligations. The second function of international law (and here is where Meyersfeld's theory diverges from Merry's) is its implementing capability. International laws act on states, urging them to modify their laws in accordance with international standards.[10]

Meyersfeld posits, first, that 'international law is a legal structure, which regulates state behaviour', not individual behaviour.[11] Even when an international covenant, such as CEDAW, purports to regulate the affairs of individuals within states, it is not actually addressing those individuals; it is telling the state to address those individuals. Its aim is to change the behaviour of states, and only through that, to reach the behaviour of individuals. Thus, CEDAW does not say that individuals should stop engaging in gender discrimination; it says that states should prohibit individuals from engaging in it.

---

10 Meyersfeld, *Domestic Violence and International Law*, p. xxxiv.
11 Ibid., p. 254.

Meyersfeld's second premise is that, by its very nature, international law can have no enforcement mechanisms. Short of war, sovereign states do not enforce the law on one another; they act by agreement. Meyersfeld's third premise follows closely on the heels of her second: 'Despite the absence of an international legislature, judiciary or policing institution … international law remains effective. The fact that it is not obeyed some of the time, does not mean that it is never obeyed at any time.'[12] To explain how international law is effective, Meyersfeld borrows from Harold Hongju Koh and others the theory of 'infiltration': 'Its method of enforcement … is by infiltrating … international norms through national courts, legal systems and political lobbying.'[13] The interactive process by which international law infiltrates national law and becomes 'internalized into a nation's domestic legal system' is the work of all the agencies of government, especially of the courts, which, by (interacting with CEDAW), then interpreting CEDAW's doctrines, gives them a domestic meaning, so that they can be 'integrated into national law and assume the status of internally binding domestic legal obligations'.[14] Legislators and judges are the most able, and most likely, to be able to translate CEDAW into local practice, because they are themselves members both of the legal culture and, at the same time, of the local culture. Moreover, that is their job.

In this chapter I examine the many ways that lawyers and judges in Melanesian courts quite consciously and purposely go about the job that Merry describes as transplantation and translation and Meyersfeld describes as infiltration and implementation. I begin by describing CEDAW, what it provides, and how it is enforced, and then analyse a number of recent cases in which judges have discussed and even used CEDAW.[15]

---

12   Ibid.
13   Ibid., p. 256; see also Harold Hongju Koh, 1997, 'Why do nations obey international law?' *Yale Law Journal* 106: 2599–611; and the chapters in S. McDougal Myres, Harold D. Lasswell and Lung-chu Chen (eds), 1977, *Human Rights and the World Public Order: The Basic Policies of an International Law of Human Dignity*, New Haven: Yale University Press.
14   Koh, 'Why do nations obey international law?' p. 626, quoted in Meyersfeld, *Domestic Violence and International Law*, p. 258.
15   The list of databases can be accessed on the website of the Pacific Islands Legal Information Institute. All cases discussed in this article can be accessed there.

As there have been too few cases in Melanesian courts using CEDAW to make a meaningful sample, I have extended my net to include cases from many of the Pacific Islands nations represented in the database of the Pacific Islands Legal Information Institute. The Pacific Islands Legal Information Institute's database of statutes and cases includes all the Anglophonic postcolonial nations of the Pacific, as well as Nouvelle-Calédonie. It does not include Australia, New Zealand, Hawai'i, or the Pacific Rim nations. I have limited my search to Anglophonic nations that were British, New Zealand and Australian colonies, territories and protectorates. Although there are many social, political and cultural differences among the Pacific Islands nations, there are also, I believe, enough continuities to make the study meaningful. Equally important, any Pacific Islands judge, finding insufficient precedents amongst the cases from his or her own jurisdiction, would be well-advised to look for analogies in decisions of the courts of other Pacific Islands states rather than such inapposite jurisdictions as Australia or England. Indeed, the Papua New Guinea Constitution, as well as the PNG Underlying Law Act, expressly recommend this course, as do the laws of other Pacific Islands jurisdictions.[16]

CEDAW: Gender violence as a violation of human rights under international law

Starting in the 1970s, and impelled, in large part, by women's NGOs, the member states of the United Nations began to recognise that women needed and deserved the protection and support of international law. A major consequence of this was the promulgation by the UN General

---

16 *Papua New Guinea Consolidated Legislation.*

If in any particular matter before a court there appears to be no rule of law that is applicable and appropriate to the circumstances of the country, it is the duty of the National Judicial System, and in particular of the Supreme Court and the National Court, to formulate an appropriate rule as part of the underlying law having regard – (c) to analogies to be drawn from relevant statutes and custom; and (d) to the legislation of, and to relevant decisions of the courts of, any country that in the opinion of the court has a legal system similar to that of Papua New Guinea.

Assembly in 1979 of the Convention on the Elimination of All Form of Discrimination against Women (CEDAW).[17] CEDAW defines discrimination against women as:

> Any distinction, exclusion or restriction made on the basis of sex which has the effect or purpose of impairing or nullifying the recognition, enjoyment or exercise by women, irrespective of their marital status, on a basis of equality of men and women, of human rights and fundamental freedoms in the political, economic, social, cultural, civil or any other field.[18]

CEDAW marks a radical change from 20th-century international law orthodoxy in a number of ways: first, by being among the first to include gender violence in its definition of human rights violations. But, when CEDAW was first promulgated, gender violence was not expressly included in it, and for almost a decade there was no certainty that it would be. CEDAW came into being in 1979 and, though women's groups and sympathetic NGOs had foregrounded gender violence by then, it was not until the late 1980s, after a great deal of work and effort, that there was sufficient consensus within the United Nations in support of the idea that gender violence was also a form of discrimination against women, deserving of international law protection, to guarantee its addition to CEDAW. The General Assembly issued two non-binding Resolutions declaring freedom from gender violence a human right, one in 1985, the second in 1990.[19] The UN Committee created to interpret and enforce CEDAW, the Committee on the Elimination of Discrimination against Women (the 'Committee'), announced in 1989 that it would treat gender violence as a form of discrimination outlawed by CEDAW. By 1992, the Committee had promulgated General Recommendation No. 19, which corrected for the absence of an express CEDAW provision about gender violence by stating, 'the definition of discrimination includes gender-based

---

17   CEDAW was adopted by the United Nations General Assembly on 18 December 1979, opened for signature by the member nations of the UN on 1 March 1980, and came into force on 3 September 1981, 30 days after ratification by the requisite 20 nations. See Convention on the Elimination of All Forms of Discrimination against Women, G.A. Res. 34/180, U.N. GAOR, 34th Sess. Suppl. No. 46, at 193, U.N. Doc. A/34/46 (1979).

18   CEDAW, Article 2.

19   The 1985 UN Resolution (n 76) Art. 2 provides that states should 'take specific action urgently in order to prevent domestic violence and to render the appropriate assistance to the victims thereof'. See also 1990 Resolution (n 85).

violence'.[20] General Recommendation 19 defines 'gender-based violence' as 'violence that is directed against a woman because she is a woman or that affects women disproportionately'.[21]

The recognition of discrimination against women in general, and of gender violence in particular, as human rights violations are not the only ways in which CEDAW significantly enlarged the scope of international law. Traditionally, international law consisted of normative agreements between states, concerning the actions of those states towards one another and towards each other's citizens. Only in the 20th century, in such multilateral agreements as the Geneva Convention on Human Rights, did the scope of international law enlarge to include the relations of states towards their own citizens. CEDAW goes a step further. In calling for an end to discrimination and violence by individuals against one another, CEDAW is the first international law to concern itself with the actions of citizens within a state towards other citizens of the same state.[22] But CEDAW cannot reach inside a state to hold the individuals who disobey it personally responsible; the most that CEDAW, like any other international law, can do is to hold the state responsible for the acts of its citizens. Nevertheless, the very fact that CEDAW does do that is a change to international law of paradigmatic proportions.

Predictably, from its beginnings CEDAW has stirred strong reactions— both in opposition and in support. CEDAW provides that equal treatment for women should prevail not only over state laws and individual actions, but also over custom, and some of its strongest opposition has come from those who argue that, in questioning custom, CEDAW is yet another example of the West enforcing its own morality on other cultures, and consequently trampling on the

---

20 Meyersfeld, *Domestic Violence and International Law*, p. 34.

21 Committee on the Elimination of Discrimination Against Women, General Recommendation No. 19, 11th Sess., Agenda Item 7, U.N. Doc. CEDAW/C/1992/L.1/Add. 15 (1992). In 1995, the General Assembly passed the Declaration on the Elimination of Violence against Women. Although it is a persuasive statement in support of General Recommendation No. 19, it is, as the title 'Declaration' suggests, not binding.

22 It is, of course, not always true that individuals, and not states, are the perpetrators of gender violence. The international community has recognised that rape and other forms of violence against women are sometimes overt elements of state policy, particularly during wartime. As such, they are among the crimes punishable by the International Criminal Court. See *Cour Pénal Internationale / International Criminal Court*, 13 November 2011.

sensibilities of third world nations.[23] CEDAW's critics are correct in saying that CEDAW takes direct issue with custom. Articles 2 and 5 are key provisions for the nations of the Pacific, because they expressly obligate states to end customary norms and practices that involve gender discrimination. Under Article 5(a), ratifying states agree 'to take all appropriate measures' 'to modify the social and cultural patterns of conduct of men and women, with a view to achieving the elimination of prejudices and customary and all other practices which are based on the idea of the inferiority or the superiority of either of the sexes or on stereotyped roles of men and women'. Article 2(f) is aimed even more directly at abolishing discriminatory customs; it requires states 'to take all appropriate measures, including legislation, to modify or abolish existing laws, regulations, customs and practices which constitute discrimination against women'. And, at section 23(e), Recommendation No. 19, which added gender violence to the discriminatory acts CEDAW outlaws, CEDAW explicitly includes custom in the list of major causes of gender violence and proposes that states act to change or abolish these customs: 'States parties in their reports should identify the nature and extent of attitudes, customs and practices that perpetuate violence against women and the kinds of violence that result. They should report on the measures that they have undertaken to overcome violence and the effect of those measures.'[24]

CEDAW and other international women's human rights laws, covenants and treaties have had considerable effect worldwide. It would be difficult to find any prominent institution or agency, within or without government, in any country today that is not aware of CEDAW and the standards it sets. But violence against women continues to be endemic

---

23   Jean Zorn, 1999. '"Women's rights are human rights": International law and the culture of domestic violence', in *To Have and To Hit: Cultural Perspectives on Wife Beating* (2nd edition), ed. Dorothy Counts, Judith Brown and J. Campbell, pp. 286–302, Urbana and Chicago: University of Illinois Press.
24   Convention on the Elimination of All Forms of Discrimination against Women: General recommendations made by the Committee on the Elimination of Discrimination against Women, n.d., *UN Women*.

to most cultures, not least in the countries that make up Melanesia. Anthropologists, feminists and international law scholars have all put forward theories and speculations about why this might be so.[25]

One answer is that, because of the peculiar nature of international law, CEDAW's effectiveness is limited. First, because it is an international convention, a form of treaty, it applies only to those states that have ratified it.[26] And, making CEDAW's reach even more limited, a number of the ratifying states have done so with reservations, by which they opt out of certain provisions, sometimes even including key requirements, like the state's promise to abolish customs or laws that promote gender discrimination.[27] However, although it looked, for a while, as if this would be a major obstacle in the Pacific, CEDAW has now been ratified, without reservation, by every Pacific Islands nation except Tonga and Palau.[28]

But, even those states that have ratified CEDAW have few duties under it. CEDAW contains neither penalties for states that fail to follow it, nor enforcement methods to make them do it. The most that CEDAW actually requires of the signatory states is that they report every four years to the Committee about the extent of the state's compliance,

---

25   See especially the articles collected in Counts, Brown and Campbell (eds), *To Have and To Hit: Cultural Perspectives on Wife Beating*; Sinclair Dinnen and Allison Ley (eds), 2000, *Reflections on Violence in Melanesia*, Annandale NSW/Canberra: Hawkins Press/Asia Pacific Press; and Margaret Jolly, Christine Stewart and Carolyn Brewer (eds), 2012, *Engendering Violence in Papua New Guinea*, Canberra: ANU E Press.

26   For a list of all the countries that have ratified CEDAW, together with the dates of ratification, see *United Nations Treaty Collection*. For information about country reports to CEDAW, see *Office of the United Nations High Commission for Human Rights*.

27   A list of signatory, acceding and ratifying nations, including notes about reservations made by them, may be found at the *United Nations Treaty Collection*.

28   By 1991, only two Pacific island nations—Cook Islands and Niue—had signed, and they only because New Zealand, which was, at the time, responsible for their foreign affairs, had done it for them. Throughout the 1990s, however, propelled by the South Pacific Forum's support for the Convention, most of the rest of the nations of the Pacific signed on: Samoa in 1992; Papua New Guinea, Fiji and Vanuatu in 1995; Tuvalu in 1999. They were followed, in the next decade, by Solomon Islands in 2002, Kiribati and Federated States of Micronesia in 2004, and the Marshall Islands in 2006. The State of Palestine is, as of this writing, the most recent signatory, having been permitted to accede to the Convention in June of 2014, leaving only Tonga and Palau as Pacific nations that have not ratified CEDAW. Palau signed CEDAW on 20 September 2011, but has not ratified it, which means Palau is not bound by it. Tonga has neither signed nor ratified. The only other nations that have not yet ratified CEDAW are the Vatican, Iran, Somalia, Sudan, South Sudan and the United States. Even ratification may not be enough; governments are permitted to ratify with reservations and, of the Pacific island countries that ratified CEDAW, Cook Islands originally reserved in part as to Articles 2(f) and 5(a). Fiji originally reserved as to Articles 5(a) and 9. Both, however, have since withdrawn their reservations.

if any, with CEDAW's aims.[29] And there is no penalty if a ratifying state fails to report.[30] Indeed, Papua New Guinea, which ratified CEDAW in 1995, did not draft its first report until 2008, and did not present it to the CEDAW Committee until 2010. That report, prepared under the direction of Dame Carol Kidu, who was at the time Papua New Guinea's Minister for Community Development, was titled Papua New Guinea's 'combined first, second, third and fourth reports'. Fiji, similarly, ratified the convention in 1995, but has filed just two reports: the first one, dated 2000, was brought up for discussion by the Committee in 2002; and the second report (which was titled a combined second, third and fourth report) is dated November 2008, and was discussed by the Committee in 2010. Vanuatu's combined initial, second and third reports were discussed in 2007; Vanuatu did file another report in 2015 and is scheduled for Committee review in 2016. Solomon Islands, whose first report was due in 2003, filed its first, and only, report in 2014.[31]

---

29   CEDAW, Article 18. The CEDAW Committee is made up of 23 experts in gender issues, selected from among the UN member nations. In the 30 years since the Committee began its work, it has progressed from being a mostly overlooked corner of UN activity to being a highly sought-after post. UN member nations vie to get their candidates appointed. Every member of the Committee reads each country report prior to meeting with country representatives, and asks questions during the meeting. Usually, countries then file a written set of responses to the questions. Sometimes, there is a follow-up meeting. The Committee then draws up its 'Concluding Observations', which are phrased in carefully generous terms. The Committee never condemns. It commends the country for good work; it shows 'concern', sometimes 'deep concern'. Nor does it require the country to change; it requests or urges.

30   Article 2 of an Optional Protocol to the Convention, adopted by the General Assembly on 15 October 1999, would give more authority to the Committee, by permitting people or groups who claimed to be victims of 'a violation of any of the rights set forth in the Convention' to bring their complaint to the Committee. Article 8 of the Optional Protocol would enable the Committee to act upon 'reliable information indicating grave or systematic violations by a State Party of rights set forth in the Convention'. However, the extent of the Committee's response to these seems still to be limited to reporting the violations to the state involved and asking for a response from the state (Optional Protocol, Articles 2 and 8, 1999).

31   Convention on the Elimination of All Forms of Discrimination against Women, 63rd Session (15 Feb 2016 – 4 Mar 2016). The slowness of small countries to file reports is not necessarily a sign of their unwillingness to promote gender equality. The reporting process is a major undertaking, requiring time, resources and information from many governmental departments and ministries. Moreover, representatives from reporting countries are supposed to travel to UN headquarters in New York to present their reports, and most countries do demonstrate their respect for the CEDAW Committee by sending a high-ranking team. For example, the 2010 PNG delegation was headed by Dame Carol Kidu, Minister for Community Development, and included the State Solicitor, PNG's Ambassador to the United Nations, a Principal Advisor to the Prime Minister, and the heads or deputy heads of the Departments of Labour and Employment, National Planning, Community Development, Education, Health, Foreign Affairs, and Agriculture, or of key divisions of those departments.

The potential shortcomings of the implementation process are not singular to CEDAW; non-enforceability is a characteristic of international law. Much like pre-colonial customary law in Melanesia, international law is not supported by institutionalised enforcement mechanisms: there are, for all intents and purposes, no courts and no police charged with the authority to enforce international law.[32] How, then, are the principles of international law turned into effective action by and within states? One way is through the agency of judges in state courts. In the next section of this chapter, I describe the methods judges in Melanesia are using to interact with and interpret CEDAW's doctrines in order to integrate CEDAW into state law and turn it into a binding domestic legal obligation.

The approaches of Pacific Islands courts to CEDAW

Despite their different approaches, Merry and Meyersfeld concur on one point. Both recognise that, for international norms to have an effect within states, they must be, in Merry's words, 'translated', and, in Meyersfeld's words, 'interpreted and internalized'. Judges of the state courts of the Pacific Islands nations are uniquely placed to translate the culture of international human rights law into the local context, because the judges themselves partake of both cultures. As judges, they have been socialised into a legal culture that, like the culture of international agencies, foregrounds the values of universality and rationality. In addition, as members of their local communities, they ought to have some feel for the frictions, tensions and possibilities provided by local cultures, and they ought to be more able than are the faraway CEDAW experts to understand how to meld the two, and how to use their own cultures' malleability to CEDAW's advantage.

We can trace with some degree of accuracy the interactions of CEDAW and the courts, as well as the results of those interactions, because the judges write about it for us. The written judicial decision exists for many reasons. Most immediately, its purpose is to convince the parties

---

32   The recent establishment of international and multilateral human rights and criminal law courts prove the point. The courts have jurisdiction only over those states that voluntarily accept their jurisdiction; many states, including the United States, have not. And their decisions, while formally like those of state courts, are unenforceable absent the agreement of the subject state.

to the case that the court decided it correctly. A second, equally key reason is to explain the new law to lower courts and lawyers, so in future they will interpret and apply it similarly. Judges are not supposed to decide disputes on the basis of who is nicer, or more sympathetic, or more like the judge; they are not even supposed to decide on the basis of what would be the best outcome for the parties or for their community. Judges are supposed to apply the law, and to do this they need to know just what the law is and how it applies. Statutes go only so far; they give rules, but they don't interpret them. That's what judicial opinions do; they become precedents, that courts and lawyers can rely on to shape the outcome of later cases.[33]

However, precedent does not work with an iron hand; the common law admits, even encourages, responsiveness to changing circumstances, as long as the changes are neither too precipitate nor too extensive. And that is another of the reasons why judges write opinions. Judges who wish to alter the interpretation or application of a long-standing norm, so as to make it better fit the present, can find, in the words and thoughts, the analogies and allusions, of earlier opinions, support for doing so.[34] And, in their own decisions, they can explain their reasons for adopting a new or slightly different interpretation, in ways that may persuade, or at least deflect some of their readers' criticism.[35]

The recognition that gender violence is not only wrong but unlawful, presents such a moment for judges in Pacific Islands nations: a moment when it might be up to them to reinterpret or reapply old common-law doctrines in new ways, perhaps even to make new common law. CEDAW gives judges both a reason to do so and support for doing it. Judges in Pacific Islands courts have sometimes acknowledged CEDAW's existence and used it to support their decisions, sometimes refused to, in a variety of different contexts, ranging from the expected (including cases involving marriage and the custody of children, domestic violence, and rape) to the surprising (such as disputes over customary land, the enforcement of collective bargaining agreements, and deportation proceedings). A court's choice not to use CEDAW is just as telling as a choice to use it.[36]

---

33   James Boyd White, 1995, 'What's an opinion for?' *University of Chicago Law Review* 62(4): 1363–69, pp. 1363–64; see also Patricia M. Wald, 1995, 'The rhetoric of results and the results of rhetoric: Judicial writings', *University of Chicago Law Review* 62(4): 1371–419, p. 1376.

34   Wald, 'The rhetoric of results and the results of rhetoric: Judicial writings', p. 1400.

35   Ibid., pp. 1394–98.

36   Ibid., p. 1376.

How the courts justify their adoption of CEDAW into domestic law

An international treaty or convention, such as CEDAW, is meant to be enforceable by the courts and law enforcement authorities of each ratifying state as if it were the law of that state. But, technically, that enforcement cannot occur merely because the executive arm of the state government has ratified the convention. It becomes enforceable, as part of the state's law, only after the state's legislative body has expressly adopted it as such. Very few legislatures have taken that second, crucial step of enacting CEDAW into domestic legislation.

That, supposedly, leaves the courts without the power to enforce the treaty or covenant; unable, that is, to hold people accountable if they do something that conflicts with or violates the convention. But courts have found ways to incorporate international covenants or conventions into their decisions, even when parliaments have not expressly adopted them. One method is for the court to rule that, while not precisely or expressly enacting an adopting statute, the legislature has done something that can be characterised as close enough to such an enactment to justify the court in treating the convention as if it were statutory. Another way is for the court to decide that the legislature's express adoption of the Convention in one area of law implies that the legislature intended it to be adopted and enforced in other areas as well. These and other methods are more fully described below.

A case from Fiji illustrates how judges can sometimes find a way to introduce an international convention into their opinions, even when the particular domestic law that the court is enforcing contains no mention of it. Courts are supposed to obey and apply their nation's statutes; they can't ignore them or make a decision that flouts the applicable statute. But, in order to apply statutes, courts first have to interpret them, have to figure out just what the statute requires. And courts are authorised to make up their own rules of interpretation. *Prakash v. Narayan* [2000] FJHC 145 involved the UN Convention on the Rights of the Child (the CRC), not CEDAW, but it illustrates a method of statutory interpretation that can accommodate itself equally well to CEDAW and other international agreements. The case concerned a dispute between a divorcing couple over which of them should have temporary custody of their children during the divorce proceedings. Fiji's Maintenance and Affiliation Act was not clear, the court found, on whether the magistrate deciding the divorce action had the authority to make an interim custody order. The CRC contained definitions that would resolve the ambiguity, but counsel pointed out that Fiji's legislature had not yet adopted the CRC into domestic law; for the court to use the CRC in this manner, counsel argued, would be improper, because the court would be usurping the legislature's prerogative. The appellate court held that, to the contrary, it could search for an interpretation of the Act in the CRC, even though it had not been adopted into Fijian domestic law, because, as the judges of the High Court of Australia had said, when faced with a similar choice,

> If the language of the legislation is susceptible of a construction which is consistent with the terms of the international instrument and the obligations which it imposes … then that construction should prevail. So expressed, the principle is no more than a canon of construction and does not import the terms of the treaty or convention into our municipal law as a source of individual rights and obligations.[37]

A neat, and very judicial, splitting of hairs.[38]

But the courts are not always willing to split those particular hairs. *Tepulolo v. Pou* [2005] TVHC 1 was a Tuvaluan case that also centred on a custody dispute. The Island Court gave custody to the father, and the mother appealed, saying that the statute in question, the Native Lands Ordinance, violated both the CRC and CEDAW by providing

---

37 *Minister of State for Immigration and Ethnic Affairs v. Ah Hin Teoh* [1995] HCA 20.

38 A similar method was employed in *Fijian Teachers Association v. President of the Republic of Fiji Islands* [2008] JFHC 59. Here, the controversy was between the union and a post-coup government that wanted to introduce by fiat new labour legislation, which would abrogate the collective bargaining agreement in place between the union and the government. The union wanted the decree stayed, at least until a court could rule on its validity. Justice Scutt stated that, in order to decide whether to stay the effect of the decree, she must balance the public interests for and against a stay. One of the key provisions of the new decree was the award of generous, paid maternity leave. Although the Fijian Parliament had not made CEDAW generally applicable, it had, in the Family Law Act of 2003, provided specifically that courts should have regard to CEDAW in carrying out the provisions of that Act. Among CEDAW's provisions is a requirement that states grant women adequate maternity leave. Justice Scutt held, 'If it is in the public interest to affirm these rights under the *Family Law Act*, then it appears to me that it would, could or should be accepted as in the public interest to affirm them as relevant under employment or industrial law also' (p. 49). She did not go so far as to treat CEDAW as if it had become part of Fijian law, which she could do only if Parliament had adopted it for all purposes. She held merely that courts could look to certain provisions of CEDAW as examples of topics, like maternity leave, that the government considered to be matters of public interest. Because the edict covered maternity leave, it was, on balance, more in the public interest to allow it to proceed than to stay its effectiveness, pending more court hearings.

that, after the age of two, the child of 'a father being a native' shall reside with the father or his relations and shall in accordance with native customary law inherit land and property from his father in the same way as the father's legitimate children. Although the Government of Tuvalu had ratified both Conventions, parliament had yet to enact any law to bring 'those obligations into effect'.[39] The appellate court noted that Tuvalu's Interpretation Act provides, 'A construction of a written law which is consistent with the international obligations of Tuvalu is to be preferred to a construction which is not'.[40] But the court stated that 'will only be relevant where there is an apparent ambiguity in the laws of Tuvalu which requires the court to determine the true construction of the law'.[41]

And the court held there is no ambiguity in the Native Lands Ordinance; contrary to the principles of international law it might be; unclear it is not. Judges focus on the effect that the case they are deciding will have on the law; the parties to those cases, however, focus on the effect that the law—and the judge—has on them. In this case, a judge's interpretation of the law resulted in a Tuvaluan mother losing not only custody of, but almost all contact with, her six-year-old son, because the father took him to live in New Zealand.

When judges declare that they will not apply CEDAW, it is usually because of some other value inherent in the legal culture that the judge finds more important. Thus, in *Hatilia v. Attorney General* [2012] SBHC 101, a Solomon Islands case, the plaintiff's husband had earlier lost a court case in which he tried to stave off deportation; the plaintiff then brought suit, claiming that her husband's deportation would harm the rights guaranteed to her by the Solomon Islands Constitution and CEDAW. The court responded that the arguments had been fully aired in the earlier case, which, though it was brought by her husband, focused on the same Constitutional provisions as she was presenting, and that, since the CEDAW provisions were simply analogues of the Constitutional guarantees, those had, for all intents and purposes, already been litigated as well.

---

39   *Tepulolo v. Pou* [2005] TVHC 1, p. 8.
40   Ibid.
41   Ibid.

Sometimes, though, one can detect in the judge's approach to the case that the reason she is not applying CEDAW is because she, personally, disagrees with CEDAW. For example, in *Police v. Apelu* [2010] WSSC 178, a Samoan case, the defendant was a woman, accused of performing abortions—a crime still in Samoa. Her counsel argued, 'quite passionately' the court noted, 'that while abortion is against the law of this country, there exists a social need for it'.[42]

> Counsel also pointed out that Samoa's approach to this complex issue is contradictory. This country is party on the one hand to the United Nations Convention on the Rights of the Child which focuses on safeguarding of children and a child's right to life and co-existence but on the other hand it is also party to CEDAW or the United Nations Convention on the Elimination of all forms of Discrimination against Women which advocates the right of a women to decide what is in her best interests.[43]

The court was moved neither by counsel's passion nor by his arguments:

> Notwithstanding our beliefs in relation to what I concede is a complicated and controversial subject it is a criminal offence to do what the defendant did. People in any societal grouping are not free to decide whether or not to follow the law depending on their personal views. No one is free to say I will follow that law because I think it is a good law but not that law because I think it's a bad law. If we went down that path we would end up in a society subject to a lot of chaos. This country through its elected representatives namely Parliament has chosen to take a pro-life stand and have legislated against abortion except when it is necessary to preserve the life of the mother ... Parliament having enacted that law, the court's duty is beyond question, it is required to enforce the laws of the land. The rightness, wrongness or morality of such a law is debated in the building next door [in Parliament], not in this one.[44]

The court seems to be saying that, at least for purposes of Samoan criminal law, CEDAW does not exist. If it did, then as defendant's counsel had attempted to argue, she would not be acting solely out of personal belief; she'd be acting in line with the law.

---

42 *Police v. Apelu* [2010] WSSC 178, p. 2.
43 Ibid.
44 Ibid.

Courts can be effective translators of the norms and values of international law, implanting international norms into their country's domestic legal system, even when parliament has failed to enact a statute expressly adopting the international law. Occasionally, a court will take wing, and dare to put itself way out ahead of parliament. Such was a recent Papua New Guinea National Court decision by Justice Cannings. In *Sukuramu v. New Britain Palm Oil Ltd* [2007] PGNC 21, an employee was fired for threatening his supervisor and, in a rage after that argument, damaging the company's property. Good cause to dismiss him, perhaps—except, he argued, the implied terms of his employment contract required that he be given a hearing before he could be dismissed. However, the contract contained no provisions requiring that an employer be fair or just. The errant employee argued that the common law of Papua New Guinea (which is referred to in the Papua New Guinea legal system as the 'underlying law') ought to be changed from its faraway English beginnings; it ought, the employee argued, to reflect the circumstances and values of Papua New Guinea. And how to find what those circumstances and values are in a case involving the termination of an employee contract? Look, the employee said, to the Convention of the International Labour Organization, to which Papua New Guinea is a signatory, and which, among other things, prohibits the termination of employees before they are given an opportunity to defend themselves. Justice Cannings agreed with the erstwhile employee, and held that, based on that treaty, the employee ought to have been granted a hearing. Parliament had not yet acted to give that treaty the status of domestic law. But, Justice Cannings held, that was not an impediment:

> In the present case there is no Constitutional Law or Act of the Parliament that gives ILO Convention … the status of municipal law. Therefore the question of whether its provisions have been breached is non-justiciable. However, its significance lies elsewhere. PNG is a party to it and has an obligation as a matter of international law to make laws to give it effect, except to the extent that its provisions are given effect in some other manner, including by court decisions. If I formulate a rule of law, as a court decision, that gives effect to ILO Convention No 158 I will be helping PNG discharge its international law obligations. I will be developing the underlying law in a manner consistent with those obligations. PNG's municipal law will be made consistent with international standards.[45]

---

45   *Sukuramu v. New Britain Palm Oil Ltd* [2007] PGNC 21, p. 41.

This decision goes very far afield from the maxim that international agreements become domestic law only when the legislature has acted expressly to give them that status. But, even here, the judge feels called upon to explain himself in conventionally legal terms. He is not anarchically changing that rule, he says; he is, indeed, following it—just in a rather eccentric way.

How the courts use CEDAW

In the preceding section, we looked at the various arguments courts make to justify their decision to use CEDAW as if it had the force of local law, even where the legislature has not formally given it that force. Having decided that they will use CEDAW, courts go on to make use of it in a variety of different ways. There are at least four ways in which a court can make use of CEDAW and other international laws. First, the court can use CEDAW as a precedent—much as if it were the ruling in an earlier case—helping the court to interpret and apply the common law, Constitutional law or statutory law. Second, the court can cite CEDAW as an authority for making changes in the common law. Third, if statutes or custom contain provisions or norms that conflict with CEDAW, the court can declare those no longer in effect. And, finally, the court can treat CEDAW as it would any domestic statute, making a breach of any of its provisions, either by an individual or by the government, unlawful. In each of these circumstances, as Meyersfeld says, the courts are engaging in a process of infiltration, by which CEDAW is internalised into the country's domestic legal system. And, in each of these circumstances, as Merry points out, the international law undergoes a process of translation and change.

CEDAW as precedent

The court can use an international convention as precedent, to buttress the court's view of the way in which a statute or constitutional provision should be interpreted. In *State v. S.N.M.* [2011] FJHC 26, for example, Justice David Goundar of the Fiji High Court had to decide whether to issue a restraining order, prohibiting a husband convicted of wife-beating from approaching his de facto wife. The husband argued earnestly that he'd learnt his lesson by going to prison and was willing to undergo counselling; his wife, however, did not want anything to do with him. The Domestic Violence Decree, which had recently been issued by the Prime Minister, provided that one of its objects was 'to implement the Convention on the Elimination of All Forms of Discrimination against Women' which was promulgated 'to ensure the protection, safety and wellbeing of victims of domestic violence'.[46] The judge decided this gave him the authority to issue an order prohibiting the man from going anywhere near his wife.

CEDAW as authority to change the common law

In *Estate of Chinsami Reddy* [2000] FJHC 134, the Fiji High Court referenced CEDAW as authority to change the common law. A sister and her two brothers disputed which of them should administer their deceased parents' estate; the sister was considerably more responsible than her devil-may-care brothers, but they pointed out to the court that the common law of England, which Fijian courts are supposed to follow (no matter how ancient the precedent might be), preferred males over females.[47] The Fijian judge could have found in the sister's favour and, at the same time, upheld hoary precedent, just by pointing out that the brothers' behaviour (one of them had assaulted their father; and then, after his death, ran his sugar cane business into the ground and stripped the farm of its top soil) would cause anyone to have 'substantial objections' to their service as administrators. The Fiji court, however, chose instead to change Fiji's common law, voiding the rule that disfavoured women, and the court cited to CEDAW as the major source allowing it to do so:

> Formerly, males were preferred over females … Fortunately, the law no longer gives effect to such a negative inference about the ability of women to administer an estate, and with the widespread ratification of international human rights instruments such as the United Nations Convention Against the Elimination of Discrimination Against Women, this last principle is of no persuasive value at all.[48]

CEDAW emboldened a Fiji court to make a change in the common law—a change that makes women a little more equal under Fiji common law.

---

46   Republic of Fiji Islands, Domestic Violence Decree (Decree No. 33 of 2009), Part I, section 6(c).
47   *In the Estate of Chinsami Reddy* [2000] FJHC 134 (22 December 2000] p. 8, citing *Chittendon v. Knight* [1758] 2 Cas. Temp. Lee 559.
48   *In the Estate of Chinsami Reddy* [2000] FJHC 134 (22 December 2000] pp. 8–9.

CEDAW used as if it were domestic legislation

In a Vanuatu case, *Joli v. Joli* [2003] VUSC 63, the judge treats CEDAW essentially the same as he would any Vanuatu domestic statute. A Francophone couple, neither of whom is ni-Vanuatu, are divorcing. They aren't subject to custom, and no Vanuatu statute or common law rule applies. There is an 1882 British statute, but Justice Coventry finds it inapplicable, both because of its Victorian assumption of female inferiority and because the parties, being French, were never subject to British law. The judge turns, instead, to CEDAW, and turns it into a statute, noting that Article 16 provides that:

> States Parties shall take all appropriate measures to eliminate discrimination against women in all matters relating to marriage and family relations and in particular shall ensure, on a basis of equality of men and women … The same rights for both spouses in respect of ownership, acquisition, management, administration, enjoyment and disposition of property, whether free of charge or for a valuable consideration.[49]

Applying that rule to the numerous business and personal assets that the parties held, most of which were in the husband's name, the court found that:

> In a marriage of any duration there will be assets which have been bought, created or acquired during the currency of the marriage. In my judgment there is a presumption that all such assets are beneficially owned jointly, no matter whose name they are in or who in fact paid for them, made them or acquired them … Upon reading the affidavits of both parties and hearing the evidence it is clear that indeed in this case they regarded their contributions and activities as building up the family assets and the use of those assets as being for the advancement of the welfare of the family as a whole … I cannot find on the evidence anything to rebut the presumption that all the assets in dispute are beneficially owned by both parties. Accordingly I rule that all the assets listed as being in dispute are matrimonial assets for the purposes of negotiation for a settlement.[50]

The cases reviewed in this section demonstrate that judges do use international law as if it was domestic law. They use it, as they would the common law, as precedent for their decisions; they use it, as they

---

49   *Joli v. Joli* [2003] VUSC 63, p. 4, citing CEDAW Article 16(1).
50   *Joli v. Joli* [2003] VUSC 63, p. 7.

would a statute, as the rule that they are supposed to apply to the parties before them. By shaping their decisions according to the rules of international law, they change the outcomes for the parties. If, for example, the Vanuatu court had not chosen, in *Joli v. Joli*, to treat CEDAW as if it were a governing statute, Mr Joli might have ended up with practically all the couple's property, because most of it was held in his name. Similarly, if the Fijian court had not chosen, in *Estate of Reddy*, to treat CEDAW as precedent, the improvident brothers might have become administrators of their father's estate. Instead, their caring and responsible sister was put in charge of the farm. Sometimes, the parties know that the judge has used international law to decide the case; often, the lawyers know, but the parties don't. But the result is the same. A domestic rule of law has been changed, and the outcome for the parties is different from what it might have been. A principle of international law has become domestic law.

Nor are these merely changes to the law itself. Changes to the law do ultimately affect behaviour and even values. Will the mere adoption by a court of rules against domestic violence significantly decrease wife beating? Probably not on its own. But, gradually, and to a greater or lesser extent, individuals do shape their expectations to match what the law will allow them. As divorce lawyers and their clients learn that the courts will award to the wife a share of the property acquired during the marriage, more women will ask for their share; more women might even decide to divorce. As the word spreads that women can be administrators and executors of estates, more of them will ask for the job—and for similar jobs. In Meyersfeld's perfect choice of a descriptive term, international law 'infiltrates' national legal systems and culture through the medium of judge-made law.

CEDAW in different circumstances

We have now seen the different ways in which courts can use— or refuse to use—CEDAW. The next question that requires answering is whether courts use CEDAW differently depending on the area of law and culture involved—depending, in particular, on whether the case involves state law or custom. In this section, I will analyse the different ways in which state courts use CEDAW in response to three different areas in which gender discrimination occurs: in the rules governing title to customary land, in the rules about who gets to choose the person a young man or woman will marry, and in the rules about the kind of evidence needed to prove a rape case. The first two areas involve conflicts between CEDAW and custom; the third involves conflicts between CEDAW and state law.

CEDAW and customary land tenure

In cases involving customary land tenure, the Vanuatu courts insist that they are changing custom to make it comport with CEDAW. In fact, however, in these cases, custom is altered very little, and women's position remains subordinate to men's.

CEDAW has been used in a number of Vanuatu cases involving dispute over customary land. In each of the reported cases, the clearest and most persuasive evidence of customary ownership would require the court to recognise the right of a woman to inherit the land and, in each case, one or more of the (male) disputants argued that customary law prohibited women from inheriting land. The court responded that CEDAW required custom to change, and gave the land to the woman's clan. In one of the cases, *Awop v. Lapemal* [2007] VUIC 2, one of the witnesses was an older man; the judge described the old man's testimony:

> In his concluding words he stressed that the basis for land ownership in the island of Malekula is based on a monarchy type of system whereby a daughter marrying another tribe cannot claim land ownership. He accuses the Convention on Elimination of all Forms of Discrimination Against Woman (CEDAW) to have caused serious conflict and disruption with the custom system long practiced.[51]

The ni-Vanuatu judge dealt with this argument, summarily:

> It is apparent that those advanced submissions are culturally oriented upon the patrilineal structure patronising men over women. Unfortunately, such a standard norm cannot bypass the applicable laws of this country as discussed below ... Firstly, Vanuatu has ratified the Convention on the Elimination on Discrimination Against Women by the Ratification Act of Parliament no. 3 of 1995. This international law requires that every signatories [*sic*] to it must take all necessary steps to condemn and wipe away [all] forms of discrimination against females. This court cannot allow custom to discriminate against women.[52]

---

51 *Awop v. Lapemal* [2007] VUIC 2, p. 10.
52 Ibid., p. 17.

But, in fact, the court did not go so far. It held only that '*if, there are no more surviving male descendants*' of the original ancestor then 'ownership will pass on to the matrilineal offspring'.[53] The court is allowing the winning clan to trace its rights through a woman only when no men are alive at the time. And the woman in question does not herself gain any control over the land; that went to her male children, thus continuing the ownership of the land in their father's line. Still, the case does mark one small step in the direction of gender equality trumping custom.

CEDAW and arranged marriages

There are at least five cases concerning the custom among Fiji's Indian community of arranged marriages.[54] All five cases were decided in 2008 and 2009 by a single judge, Justice Jocelynne Scutt of the High Court of Fiji, Family Division. Dr Scutt is a leading scholar, teacher and barrister in Australia, specialising in women's issues; she has written extensively on issues of women's equality and gender violence.[55] It is, therefore, not surprising that, in each of these cases, she voided the arranged marriage on the grounds that it violated CEDAW.

All the cases involved Fijians in their 20s who had been married at the behest of their parents and relatives, and who wanted out; they were looking not for a divorce (none of them wanted to be known as a divorced person) but for an annulment (which, at law, means the marriage never happened). There are only a few grounds for annulment; one of them is duress or coercion. The courts of both England and Fiji had interpreted the statute to require a party who wanted an annulment on the ground of duress or coercion to prove that they had been physically beaten, injured, terrorised, or put in fear of such treatment. Justice Scutt changed that statutory interpretation; she held that no proof of physical injury or threat was needed, because the custom of marriages arranged by parents is itself coercive, especially for young people who want to do what their family and society ask of them.

---

53 Ibid., p. 4.
54 *FJN and MRK* [2009] FJHC 94. *LK and JVR* [2009] FJHC 60. *NK and ZMR* [2009] FJHC 95. *PP and RP* [2009] FJHC 72. *RPN v. SPP* [2008] FJHC 166. *TZS and FSB* [2009] FJHC 97. *VDC and VNS* [2009] FJHC 69.
55 Jocelynne Scutt, 2012, 'Leadership interviews: Interviews about the glass ceiling', Australian Centre for Leadership for Women.

She also held that the Fijian courts ought not to be supporting arranged marriages, because 'in Fiji, [annulment] applications are heard against the backdrop of section 26 of the Family Law Act', which incorporates CEDAW into the law of Fiji, and requests courts to take CEDAW into account in reaching their decisions:

> The international conventions and instruments emphasise the importance of agency in entering into the marriage relationship. Referred to explicitly in the Family Law Act, the Convention on the Elimination of All Forms of Discrimination against Women is emphatic as to a woman's 'right to choose a spouse and enter freely into marriage', this right to choose and the freedom of entering into marriage being 'central to her life and her dignity and equality as a human being'.[56]

CEDAW and rape

CEDAW has been cited in a number of cases involving convictions for rape. One of these cases, *State v. Bechu* [1999] FJMC 3, from Fiji, involved custom, or at least customary attitudes. The defendant admitted in his testimony that the victim had struggled, had said she did not want sex with him, and that he had had to punch her to get her to give in—and then he pleaded not guilty on the grounds she'd consented. In sentencing the defendant to a five-year prison term, the judge felt called upon to explain to the defendant that, when a woman says no, she means no:

> Women are your equal and therefore must not be discriminated on the basis of gender. Men should be aware of the provision of 'Convention on the Elimination of all forms of Discrimination against Women' (CEDAW), which our country had ratified in 1981 ... The old school of thoughts, that women were inferior to men; or part of your personal property, that can be discarded or treated unfairly at will, is now obsolete and no longer accepted by our society.[57]

The judge did not rule that CEDAW had made any particular customary norm or practice unlawful, but he enlisted international law on the side of social change.

---

56 *NK and ZMR* [2009] FJHC 95, p. 9, citing CEDAW Article 16(1)(b).
57 *State v. Bechu* [1999] FJMC 3, p. 9.

In most of the rape cases, however, CEDAW has played a more substantive role. Until very recently, statutory and common-law rules regarding rape contained many gender-biased elements. For example, most courts required there be evidence that a woman was beaten, or threatened with serious physical harm, in order to convict a man of rape. A woman who did not fight with her assailant might find the court declaring her assailant not guilty. Similarly, courts refused to convict a defendant on the word of the victim alone; her testimony had to be corroborated by other evidence, such as the testimony of a witness or a hospital examination.[58] CEDAW has aided Pacific Islands courts to free themselves from these discriminatory doctrines—but only, it seems, when the court is already disposed to discard the rule.

In *Republic v. Timiti & Robuti* [1998] KIHC 1, a Kiribati judge refused to do away with the corroboration rule, though he left the door open for doing so in the future. In Kiribati, as in PNG,[59] courts may convict a rapist on the uncorroborated testimony of his victim, but only if the judge has first reminded himself that he must be very cautious about believing women who cry rape. The prosecutor argued that this rule, which allows many rapists to go free, should be discarded, because it applies only to rape and sexual abuse; the courts do not question the uncorroborated testimony of robbery victims, victims of attempted murder, assault or, for that matter, any other crime of violence. And rape, the prosecutor pointed out, is almost always a crime perpetrated on a woman. Therefore, the prosecutor concluded, the corroboration rule 'violates the rights of women in that it denies them the equal protection of the law guaranteed by section 3 of the Constitution'.[60] Furthermore, the prosecutor continued, 'In interpreting the law on this point', the judge 'ought to follow the principles formulated in the Convention on the Elimination of All Forms of Discrimination against Women'.[61] The judge refused to give up the 'uncorroborated testimony' rule. However, he did not defend the rule, did not try to argue that it was not discriminatory. Instead, he performed a favourite judicial sleight of hand: in this case, the judge pointed out, the woman's testimony had been corroborated—there were witnesses who had seen her and

---

58   Jean Zorn, 2010, 'The paradoxes of sexism: Proving rape in the Papua New Guinea Village Courts', *LawAsia Journal* 2010: 17–58.
59   Ibid.
60   *Republic v. Timiti & Robuti* [1998] KIHC 1, p. 4.
61   Ibid.

talked to her right after the rape, when she was still dishevelled, distraught and dazed. Since that was the situation, the judge said, he had in fact not used the 'uncorroborated testimony' rule. So this was not, the judge concluded, the appropriate case in which to contest its validity.

But in *Balelala v. State* [2004] FJCA 49, Fiji's Court of Appeal took the opposite position. The defendant had been convicted of rape and appealed on the ground that, contrary to the rule then in force, he had been convicted despite the fact that the victim's testimony had not been corroborated. The three-judge appellate panel found that there had been corroboration; the defendant had confessed to the rape, and that, the panel held, is corroboration enough. Having found corroboration, the court could have stopped there, as the Kiribati court had done in *Republic v. Timiti & Robuti*. It had done all it needed to do to uphold that defendant's conviction.

But the court went further. It discussed the history of the corroboration rule, not only in Fiji, but in England, New Zealand and Canada as well, pointing out that the rule existed because of gender discrimination: 'The rule of practice which required corroboration ... in cases of sexual assault, depended on a generalisation that female evidence in such cases is intrinsically unreliable.'[62] The court also noted that in these jurisdictions, as well as in many others, the rule has been abrogated, because it 'is counter productive, confusing and both discriminatory and demeaning of women'.[63] The practice of other jurisdictions gave the court support for repealing the rule, but it found its most urgent support in section 38(1) of the 1997 Fiji Constitution, which provided, 'a person must not be unfairly discriminated against ... on the ground of his or her ... gender'. Did the uncorroborated testimony rule unfairly discriminate against women? The court held that it did, because section 43(2) of the 1997 Constitution required courts to interpret the Constitution with 'regard to public international law', and the court found: 'All major human rights instruments establish standards for the protection of women, including a prohibition on any form of discrimination against them: e.g. the Convention on the Elimination of All Forms of Discrimination against Women.'[64] CEDAW had given

---

62   *Balelala v. State* [2004] FJCA 49, p. 14.
63   Ibid., p. 22.
64   Ibid., p. 24.

the Fiji Court of Appeal the interpretive tools it needed to conclude that the 1997 Fiji Constitution required an end to the uncorroborated testimony rule.

CEDAW and child sexual abuse

In Papua New Guinea, a new statute increasing the penalties for child sexual abuse, and making convictions easier to obtain, was enacted in 2002. Its backers drew their inspiration from CEDAW. Thus, in this area of law, the courts have the necessary legislative backing to enforce CEDAW, and do not need to resort to the kinds of arguments I've outlined earlier in this chapter.

Dame Carol Kidu played the key role in translating into domestic law some of the key provisions of CEDAW on rape and the sexual abuse of children, when she introduced the Sexual Offences and Crimes Against Children Act of 2002 into parliament, and shepherded it to enactment. Although she was a Cabinet member, she had so little support from government for the bill that she had to introduce it as a private member's bill.[65] The Act has changed the law on child sexual abuse, making the sexual penetration of a child under the age of 16 an offence punishable by a prison term of up to life imprisonment, and adding the offence of sexual touching, which does not require penetration, and is punishable by a prison term of up to 12 years if the child is below the age of 12, and also if the child is between the ages of 12 and 16 and the offender was in a relationship of trust, authority or dependency with the child.

---

65   The Act does not itself mention CEDAW, but Dame Carol Kidu stressed CEDAW's influence when she introduced the bill into parliament:

In 1995, Papua New Guinea ratified the United Nations Convention [on the Elimination of] All Forms of Discrimination and Violence Against Women. As a nation we have both a regional and international commitment to address this important issue … Mr. Speaker, we as parliamentarians must speak out loudly against all violent sexual assaults because they not only can cause us physical injury; they also destroy our self-dignity and pride. Declaring acts as criminal … gives us a moral denunciation of the unacceptable conduct. This can have a very significant impact on shaping the changing values of our young nation. We as parliamentarians have an extremely important role to play in this regard; passing, drafting or clarifying laws that criminalize violence particularly against women and children but also to all violence is an important step in re-defining the limits of acceptable behaviour (as quoted in *The State v. William Patangala* [2006] PGNC 43; N3027).

In two leading Papua New Guinea cases, Justice Salatiel Lenalia of the Papua New Guinea Supreme Court not only applied the stringent new provisions, but quoted Dame Carol's Act approvingly when he did so. Thus, the Act and Dame Carol's support of it have had both an expressive and an implementing effect.

Both cases involved the 'sexual touching' of a young girl by an older relative with whom the girl was living and who was, in effect, the girl's guardian. Though two years apart (one case was heard in 2006, the other in 2008), both were tried in the National Court in Kokopo, before Justice Lenalia. By citing CEDAW when she introduced the bill, Dame Carol began the political work that Merry calls translation, pointing out to parliament and NGOs the key transformative role that CEDAW could play in helping to end Papua New Guinea's culture of violence against women and girls. And when Justice Lenalia picked up the idea from her, first by interacting with CEDAW and interpreting its doctrines 'to give them a domestic meaning', he completed the process of integrating CEDAW into domestic law, giving CEDAW the status of an 'internally binding domestic legal obligation'.[66]

The first of the cases to be decided by Justice Lenalia was *The State v. William Patangala* [2006] PGNC 43; N3027.[67] The defendant pleaded guilty to the crime of sexually touching[68] a 14-year-old girl; Justice Lenalia's task was to decide on a sentence. He could have sentenced the defendant to 12 years; after all, a relationship of trust existed: the victim was the defendant's niece, the daughter of his wife's sister.[69] Leaning toward a shorter sentence were the defendant's freely given confession and his payment to the victim's family of twice the amount of money and shell compensation ordered by the village councillor. On

---

66   Koh, 'Why do nations obey international law?' p. 262, quoted in Meyersfeld, *Domestic Violence and International Law*, p. 258.

67   Actually, *State v. Patangala* was not the first case involving the sexual touching of a minor to come before Justice Lenalia. He'd decided another such case a year earlier—*The State v. Adrian Amos*, CR No. 701 of 2005—but that case was not published.

68   The new law provides two levels of sexual crimes against children: those involving penetration and those involving only touching. The crime of 'sexually touching' a child is defined in section 229B of the Criminal Code: 'when a person, for a sexual purpose, touches with any part of his/her body, the sexual parts of a child under the age of 16 years, or compels a child under that age to touch the sexual parts of that person with any part of his/her body.'

69   Section 6A(2)(c) of the Criminal Code contains a list of persons in positions of trust, authority or dependency, including teachers, parents, guardians, aunts or uncles and a number of others.

the side of a longer sentence were the existence of that relationship of trust and the fear of the victim and her parents that, if the defendant were not suitably punished, he would assault her again.

In weighing these competing concerns, Justice Lenalia took into account social and legal considerations. First, he noted that the Act was new; it had come into operation less than three years before. Parliament had enacted it in response to the disturbing prevalence in Papua New Guinea of 'sexual abuse of our children both very young girls and boys', and it was imperative, the judge said, to publicise the existence of the new law and to make sure it was applied.[70] Papua New Guinea had entered a new reality, he pointed out, one characterised by a new respect for the human rights of women and children. And, here, he quoted Dame Carol's speech when she presented the Act to parliament. At the moment that Justice Lenalia quoted that speech in a judicial decision, the integration of CEDAW's provisions into the domestic culture had taken a major step forward. Dame Carol, parliament and the courts were now united in translating CEDAW's provisions from general principles of international law into doctrines with 'a domestic meaning'.[71]

Justice Lenalia ultimately decided to sentence the defendant to a total of four years, with only the first year to be served in prison, the next three, subject to good behaviour, on parole. Not a lengthy sentence; but Justice Lenalia was making a start.

The next step was to actually integrate CEDAW's requirements into a common law principle, turning CEDAW into an 'internally binding domestic legal obligation'.[72] Justice Lenalia did so in *State v. Narakavi* [2009] PGNC 109; N 3737, the next of the sexual touching cases that he decided. That case also involved the sexual touching of a 14-year-old girl by an older man. In this case, however, the relationship was even closer than that of uncle and niece. The victim, a first cousin of the defendant's wife, had been raised from the age of four by the defendant and his wife. That made her, Justice Lenalia said, for all intents and purposes, the defendant's daughter, and no relationship of trust, authority and dependency could be closer than that. The defendant

---

70   *The State v. William Patangala* [2006] PGNC 43, p. 6.
71   Meyersfeld, *Domestic Violence and International Law*, p. 258.
72   Koh, 'Why do nations obey international law?' p. 262, quoted in Meyersfeld, *Domestic Violence and International Law*, p. 258.

had pleaded guilty, so Justice Lenalia's task was to decide how long a prison sentence he should impose. He needed legal support if he was to sentence this defendant to a term longer than had been the norm, and he found it in two places: in the Criminal Code and in CEDAW. First, he noted the rule from the Criminal Code, section 229B(5), that sexual touching in the context of a relationship of trust, authority and dependency should be met with a longer prison term. He added, 'If the relationship of trust, authority and dependency is very close, like in [this] case, the more serious the case becomes and the higher the penalty should be'.[73] Second, he said that the integration of CEDAW into the underlying law of Papua New Guinea authorises judges to respond to the widespread problem of sexual violence with longer prison sentences. And, to make sure his audience understood the link, he then quoted Dame Carol's speech again. In the end, Justice Lenalia sentenced the defendant to a term of five years. He also required the defendant to pay compensation to the victim and her family in 'an amount of K1,000.00 and one live pig'.[74]

Afterthoughts and conclusions

These cases illustrate the various ways in which judges translate international law precepts into terms accessible to domestic cultures. In the cases involving customary land tenure, the courts' response was more expressive than instrumental: although the change to customary inheritance norms that the courts decreed was itself scarcely momentous, it was a key harbinger of greater changes to come, especially when accompanied by the judges' lectures about the law's recognition of women's equal status. In the arranged marriage cases, Justice Scutt attempted to jettison a customary practice entirely, a clear example of the internalisation of the international norm in the domestic legal system; whether her rulings will be followed by other Fijian judges remains to be seen.

It is in the rape and child abuse cases that CEDAW seems to have had its greatest impact. We do not have enough data to know whether the difference between the land cases and the rape cases is because judges are, with some notable exceptions (such as Scutt on arranged

---

73   *State v. Narakavi* [2009] PGNC 109, p. 9.
74   Ibid., p. 11.

marriages), treading more lightly when it comes to changes in custom than in changes to state law. Or, perhaps, it results from the articulate presence of women's groups, which have been speaking out against rape, wife beating and other forms of gender violence. If so, then internalisation, at least in this area of law, was the result of a fertile cross-breeding, with the activities of NGOs and the opinions of judges strengthening one another.

CEDAW has had a salutary effect on the island nations of the South Pacific, including Papua New Guinea. To say that, however, is not to say very much. To date, CEDAW's effect has been limited— and the problems of women's subordination and of widespread, systemic violence against women remain obdurate and intractable. Nevertheless, it is a beginning. Guided by the analyses of Meyersfeld and Koh, who pointed out that the first impact of an international law on the politics, economy and social ordering of any culture will most likely be found in the legal practices of that culture, I sought for evidence of CEDAW in the decisions handed down by judges of the state courts. And, indeed, I found a number of cases—still scattered, but potentially influential—in which judges have not only mentioned CEDAW's existence, but have actually relied upon it in framing the common law and in applying domestic statutes. In other words, in the Meyersfeld/Koh terminology, judges are aiding the infiltration of this crucially important piece of international law into the domestic legal system.

To date, it would be difficult to argue that CEDAW has had more than that limited effect on the legal systems of the Melanesian states. In Papua New Guinea, for example, despite continued activism by women's groups and other concerned organisations, there has been no legislation implementing any of the provisions of CEDAW since the 2002 enactment of the Sexual Offences and Crimes Against Children Act. The 2013 amendments to the Criminal Code, providing the death penalty for rape, and repealing the Sorcery Act provisions that gave defendants who believed in sorcery a partial defence to the murder of an alleged sorcerer, are cited by some as much needed attempts to put a stop to gendered violence in Papua New Guinea.

Dame Carol's tenure as Minister for Community Development ended in August 2011, when a change of government impelled her into the opposition. That was barely a year after she had shepherded Papua

New Guinea's 2008 Report to the CEDAW Committee. Under Article 18 of CEDAW, states are expected to report every four years, and the CEDAW Committee, in its Concluding Observations in July 2010, therefore invited Papua New Guinea to submit another report in July 2014. To date, the government has not complied.

The effect of the judicial decisions implementing CEDAW has not gone much beyond the legal system itself. Domestic law has not yet had a significant effect on culture and mores. Throughout Melanesia, and in Papua New Guinea in particular, women are, if anything, more subordinated, more the subjects of violence, less able to compete with any equality in politics or the economy, less likely to receive an education, less likely to receive adequate health care, than ever. The dismal statistics quoted in Papua New Guinea's Report to CEDAW are, if anything, worse. Girls are educated at less than half the rate of boys; village and settlement women die of untreated STDs, such as HIV/AIDS, in alarming numbers; the 2012 general election resulted in a parliament including only four women members. Although women who are the victims of rape and other sexual assaults can now expect some support in the formal state courts, the expense, location and cultural distance of these courts effectively closes them to attempts by women to redress wrongs committed against them. Village Courts are closer and more accessible financially, but their record at responding to women's concerns is questionable at best.[75] I, like most lawyers, wholeheartedly believe that the law does change behaviour, somewhat, over some period of time, eventually, and can point to numerous instances supporting that belief. So, I am optimistic about the future impact of CEDAW. One wishes that the future would not take so long to arrive.

Acknowledgements

I wish to acknowledge the help and support of Christine Stewart, whose serious readership took me seriously, which emboldened me to do the same.

---

75 Jean Zorn, 1994–95. 'Women, custom and state law in Papua New Guinea', Symposium on Women's Rights and Traditional Law: A Conflict, *Third World Legal Studies*, 1994–95: 169–205.

References

Belshaw, Cyril S. 1957. *The Great Village: The Economic and Social Welfare of Hanuabada, an Urban Community in Papua*. London: Routledge & Kegan Paul.

Counts, Dorothy, Judith Brown and J. Campbell (eds). 1999. *To Have and To Hit: Cultural Perspectives on Wife Beating* (2nd edition). Urbana and Chicago: University of Illinois Press.

Cour Pénal Internationale / International Criminal Court. 13 November 2011. Online: www.icc-cpi.int/en_menus/icc/situations%20and%20 cases/Pages/situations%20and%20cases.aspx (accessed 1 October 2015).

Crenshaw, Kimberlé. 1991. 'Mapping the margins: Intersectionality, identity politics, and violence against women of color'. *Stanford Law Review* 43(6): 1241–99.

Dinnen, Sinclair and Allison Ley (eds). 2000. *Reflections on Violence in Melanesia*. Annandale NSW/Canberra: Hawkins Press/Asia Pacific Press.

Inglis, Amirah. 2009 [1974]. *Not a White Woman Safe: The White Women's Protection Ordinance*. Port Moresby: University of Papua New Guinea Press (reprint edition).

Jolly, Margaret, Christine Stewart and Carolyn Brewer (eds). 2012. *Engendering Violence in Papua New Guinea*. Canberra: ANU E Press. Online: press.anu.edu.au?p=182671 (accessed 3 November 2014).

Jowitt, Anita and Tess Newton Cain (eds). 2003. *Passage of Change: Law, Society and Governance in the Pacific*. Canberra: Pandanus Books.

Koh, Harold Hongju. 1997. 'Why do nations obey international law?' *Yale Law Journal* 106: 2599–611.

Luluaki, John Y. 2003. 'Sexual crimes against and exploitation of children and the law in Papua New Guinea'. *International Journal of Law, Policy and the Family* 17(3): 275–307.

Merry, Sally Engle. 2006. *Human Rights and Gender Violence: Translating International Law into Local Justice*. Chicago: University of Chicago Press.

Meyersfeld, Bonita. 2012. *Domestic Violence and International Law*. Oxford: Hart Publishing.

Myres, S. McDougal, Harold D. Lasswell and Lung-chu Chen (eds). 1977. *Human Rights and the World Public Order: The Basic Policies of an International Law of Human Dignity*. New Haven: Yale University Press.

Pacific Islands Legal Information Institute. Online: www.paclii.org (accessed 1 October 2015).

Papua New Guinea Consolidated Legislation. Online: www.paclii.org/pg/legis/consol_act/cotisopng534/ (accessed 1 October 2015).

Scutt, Jocelynne. 2012. 'Leadership interviews: Interviews about the glass ceiling', Australian Centre for Leadership for Women (23 May). Online: www.leadershipforwomen.com.au/empowerment/leadership/item/dr-jocelynne-scutt-2 (accessed 1 October 2015).

Toft, Susan (ed.). 1985. *Domestic Violence in Papua New Guinea*. Monograph No. 3. Port Moresby: Papua New Guinea Law Reform Commission.

Wald, Patricia M. 1995. 'The rhetoric of results and the results of rhetoric: Judicial writings'. *University of Chicago Law Review* 62(4): 1371–420.

White, James Boyd. 1995. 'What's an opinion for?' *University of Chicago Law Review* 62(4): 1363–71.

Wolfers, Edward P. 1975. *Race Relations and Colonial Rule in Papua New Guinea*. Ann Arbor: University of Michigan Press.

Zorn, Jean. 1994–95. 'Women, custom and state law in Papua New Guinea', Symposium on Women's Rights and Traditional Law: A Conflict. *Third World Legal Studies*, 1994–95: 169–205.

———. 1999. *Women, Custom and International Law in the Pacific*. Occasional Paper No. 5, Port Vila: University of the South Pacific School of Law Faculty Colloquium.

———. 2010. 'The paradoxes of sexism: Proving rape in the Papua New Guinea Village Courts'. *LawAsia Journal* 2010: 17–58.

———. 2012. 'Engendering violence in the Papua New Guinea Courts: Sentencing in rape trials'. In *Engendering Violence in Papua New Guinea*, ed. Margaret Jolly, Christine Stewart and Carolyn Brewer, pp. 163–96. Canberra: ANU E Press. Online: press.anu.edu.au/publications/engendering-violence-papua-new-guinea (accessed 3 November 2014).

United Nations Documents

Committee on the Elimination of Discrimination against Women (CEDAW), Thirty-eighth Session, Concluding Observations: Vanuatu (CEDAW/C/VUT/CO/3) (11 June 2007).

———. Forty-sixth Session, Summary Record of the 940th Meeting, Held 22 July 2010 (CEDAW/C.SR.940) (October 2010).

———. Forty-sixth Session, Concluding Observations: Papua New Guinea (CEDAW/C/PNG/CO/3) (30 July 2010).

———. 2009. 'Consideration of reports submitted by States parties under article 18 of the Convention on the Elimination of All Forms of Discrimination against Women: Combined initial, second and third periodic report of State parties: Papua New Guinea'. CEDAW/C/PNG/3, p. 28, item 2.2. Online: www.bayefsky.com//reports/papua_cedaw_c_png_3_2008.pdf (accessed 24 November 2014).

———. List of issues and questions with regard to the consideration of periodic reports: Papua New Guinea, CEDAW/C/PNG/Q/3 (15 September 2009).

Convention on the Elimination of All Forms of Discrimination against Women, G.A. Res. 34/180, U.N. GAOR, 34th Sess. Suppl. No. 46, at 193, U.N. Doc. A/34/46 (1979).

Convention on the Elimination of All Forms of Discrimination against Women, Sixty-third Session (15 Feb 2016 – 04 Mar 2016). Online: tbinternet.ohchr.org/_layouts/treatybodyexternal/SessionDetails1.aspx?SessionID=1007&Lang=en (accessed 18 April 2016).

Convention on the Elimination of All Forms Discrimination against Women, General recommendations made by the Committee on the Elimination of Discrimination against Women. n.d. *UN Women*. Online: www.un.org/womenwatch/daw/cedaw/recommendations/recomm.htm (accessed 1 October 2015).

Declaration on the Elimination of Violence against Women, G.A. Res. 48/104, U.N. Doc. A/RES/48/104 (1994). Online: www.un.org/documents/ga/res/48/a48r104.htm (accessed 30 December 2015).

Office of the United Nations High Commission for Human Rights. Online: www2.ohchr.org/english/bodies/cedaw/sessions.htm (accessed 1 October 2014).

Office of the High Commissioner, Convention on the Rights of the Child, G.A Res. 44/25 (1989). Online: www.ohchr.org/en/professionalinterest/pages/crc.aspx (accessed 18 April 2016).

Papua New Guinea Responses to the list of issues and questions [from the Committee on the Elimination of Discrimination against Women] with regard to the consideration of the combined initial, second and third periodic reports, CEDAW/C/PNG/Q/3/Add.1 (10 March 2010).

Report of the Committee on the Elimination of Discrimination against Women, General Recommendation No. 19, 11th Sess., Agenda Item 7, U.N. Doc. CEDAW/C/1992/L.1/Add. 15 (1992).

The Permanent Mission of Papua New Guinea to the United Nations, Delegation to the Forty-sixth Session of the Committee on the Elimination of Discrimination against Women to be Held from 12 to 30 July 2010 (PNG/084/2010).

United Nations Treaty Collection. Online: treaties.un.org/ (accessed 16 November 2016).

Universal Declaration of Human Rights, G.A. Res. 271A(III), U.N. GAOR, 3d Sess., U.N. Doc. A/810 (1948). Online: www.un.org/en/universal-declaration-human-rights/ (accessed 18 April 2016).

Cases

Awop v. Lapemal [2007] VUIC 2. Online: www.paclii.org/vu/cases/VUIC/2007/2.html (accessed 5 October 2015).

Balelala v. State [2004] FJCA 49. Online: www.paclii.org/fj/cases/FJCA/2004/49.html (accessed 16 November 2016).

Chittendon v. Knight [1758] 2 Cas. Temp. Lee 559.

Estate of Chinsami Reddy [2000] FJHC 134. Online: www.paclii.org/fj/cases/FJHC/2000/134.html (accessed 16 November 2016).

Fijian Teachers Association v. President of the Republic of Fiji Islands [2008] JFHC 59. Online: www.paclii.org/cgi-bin/disp.pl/fj/cases/FJHC/2008/59.html (accessed 5 October 2015).

Hatilia v. Attorney General [2012] SBHC 101. Online: www.paclii.org/cgi-bin/disp.pl/sb/cases/SBHC/2012/101.html (accessed 5 October 2015).

Joli v. Joli [2003] VUSC 63. Online: www.paclii.org/vu/cases/VUSC/2003/63.html (accessed 5 October 2015).

Minister of State for Immigration and Ethnic Affairs v. Ah Hin Teoh [1995] HCA 20, cited in *Prakash v. Narayan* [2000] FJHC 145. Online: www.paclii.org/cgi-bin/disp.pl/fj/cases/FJHC/2000/144.html (accessed 5 October 2015).

NK and ZMR [2009] FJHC 95. Online: www.paclii.org/fj/cases/FJHC/2009/95.html (accessed 16 November 2016).

Police v. Apelu [2010] WSSC 178. Online: www.paclii.org/cgi-bin/disp.pl/ws/cases/WSSC/2010/178.html (accessed 5 October 2015).

Prakash v. Narayan [2000] FJHC 145. Online: www.paclii.org/cgi-bin/disp.pl/fj/cases/FJHC/2000/144.html (accessed 5 October 2015).

Republic v. Timiti & Robuti [1998] KIHC 1. Online: www.paclii.org/cgi-bin/disp.pl/ki/cases/KIHC/1998/35.html (accessed 5 October 2015).

State v. A.V. [2009] FJHC 18. Online: www.paclii.org/cgi-bin/disp.pl/fj/cases/FJHC/2009/ (accessed 5 October 2015).

State v. Basa [2011] FJHC 446. Online: www.paclii.org/cgi-bin/disp.
pl/fj/cases/FJHC/2011/446.html (accessed 5 October 2015).

State v. Bechu [1999] FJMC 3. Online: www.paclii.org/cgi-bin/disp.pl/
fj/cases/FJHC/1999 (accessed 5 October 2015).

State v. Narakavi [2009] PGNC 109; N 3737. Online: www.paclii.org/
cgi-bin/disp.pl/pg/cases/PGNC/2009/109.html (accessed 5 October
2015).

State v. Patangala [2006] PGNC 43; N3027. Online: www.paclii.org/
cgi-bin/disp.pl/pg/cases/PGNC/2006/43.html (accessed 5 October
2015).

State v. S.N.M. [2011] FJHC 26. Online: www.paclii.org/cgi-bin/disp.
pl/fj/cases/FJHC/2011/26.html (accessed 5 October 2015).

Sukuramu v. New Britain Palm Oil Ltd [2007] PGNC 21. Online: www.
paclii.org/cgi-bin/disp.pl/pg/cases/PGNC/2007/21.html   (accessed
5 October 2015).

Tepulolo v. Pou [2005] TVHC. Online: www.paclii.org/cgi-bin/disp.pl/
tv/cases/TVHC/2005/1.html (accessed 13 September 2016).

Vaai v. Leni [1996] WSCA 8.

7

Human Rights Work in Papua New Guinea, Fiji and Vanuatu

Aletta Biersack

University of Oregon

Papua New Guinea (PNG), Fiji and Vanuatu emerged between 1970 and 1980, as they gained independence from their respective colonisers: Australia, Britain and France. As ratifiers of the Convention for the Elimination of All Forms of Discrimination against Women (CEDAW) and the Convention on the Rights of the Child (CRC), they participate in the international human rights regime outlined in the introduction to this volume, the bureaucratic machinery for which lies half way around the world. This UN-anchored network is itself augmented by international non-governmental organisations (INGOs), which pressure ratifying countries and their citizens to conform to the human rights norms they consider universal. Additionally, civil society NGOs devoted to the promotion of women's and girls' rights inform the general public of laws designed to advance women's rights, provide succour and assistance to survivors of gender violence, train citizens in human rights ideology and human rights work, and pressure states to honour their 'due diligence' obligations. Articulating with rights-based international NGOs and partially funded by ex-colonial regional powers, these civil society organisations are indispensable to the advancement of human rights in the western Pacific.

The three histories offered here trace the strategies and instruments developed by both state and civil society in PNG, Fiji and Vanuatu to curb violence against women and girls. These histories offer insights into the dynamics of the globalising 'ideoscape' (to use Appadurai's term) of human rights,[1] as human rights ideology streams out from its Euro-American birthplace and heartland[2] towards peoples and places beholden to alternative principles and values. 'Human rights promote ideas of individual autonomy, equality, choice, and secularism', ideas that do not transfer easily to cultural zones that are 'less individualistic and more focused on communities and responsibilities'[3]—the western Pacific, for example. Jonathan Xavier Inda and Renato Rosaldo have warned about the inadequacy of the 'hypodermic' model of how globalisation works,[4] which assumes, implausibly, direct, unmediated 'penetration' by the foreign. 'Cultural materials just do not transfer in a unilinear manner ... They always entail interpretation, translation, and customization on the part of the receiving subject. In short, they can only be understood in the context of their complex reception and appropriation.'[5] As these three histories attest, human rights doctrine may 'infiltrate' in the form of new, rights-based legislation and policies at the national level and 'grassroots awareness campaigns' at the village level,[6] but in all three cases reducing gender violence has proved difficult, suggesting that alternative ideologies compete with human rights ideology. Nevertheless, these histories also support Sally Engle Merry's contention that culture is not ossified but contested from within and from without, amenable to change.

1   Arjun Appadurai, 1996, *Modernity at Large: Cultural Dimensions of Globalization*, Minneapolis: University of Minnesota Press, pp. 33, 35–38.

2   Lynn Hunt, 2007, *Inventing Human Rights: A History*, New York and London: W.W. Norton & Company.

3   Sally Engle Merry, 2006, *Human Rights and Gender Violence: Translating International Law into Local Justice*, Chicago: University of Chicago Press, p. 4.

4   Jonathan Xavier Inda and Renato Rosaldo, 2008, 'Tracking global flows', in *The Anthropology of Globalization: A Reader* (2nd edition), ed. Jonathan Xavier Inda and Renato Rosaldo, pp. 3–46, Malden, MA and Oxford: Wiley-Blackwell, p. 20.

5   Inda and Rosaldo, 'Tracking global flows', p. 20.

6   See Jean G. Zorn, 'Translating and internalising international human rights law: The courts of Melanesia confront gendered violence', this volume.

I begin with Papua New Guinea, which celebrated its 40th anniversary of independence recently and which is, for some, the poster child for gender violence in the western Pacific.[7] I go on to highlight milestones in Fiji's and Vanuatu's struggles to curb gender violence. Despite a turbulent recent political and military history, a history that George shows in her contribution to this volume has negatively impacted on Fijian women, Fiji has developed powerful civil society institutions to combat gender violence and continues to exercise regional leadership in promoting women's rights. All three countries have dual systems of justice: a system of informal justice tied to village or chiefly courts, which emphasises the reconciliation of disputing parties rather than the punishment of offenders, and a formal or state justice system, which enforces national laws by trying and incarcerating offenders in the interest of justice for the victim[8] and deterrence. In all three countries the duality of the justice system hampers the enforcement of the national laws that are designed to advance the cause of women's and girls' rights. While the tension between these two systems is evident in all three countries, it is not directly addressed here until the third account, which chronicles Vanuatu's efforts to stem gender violence and which is in part guided by Miranda Forsyth's excellent book *A Bird that Flies with Two Wings: The* Kastom *and State Justice Systems in Vanuatu*.

Papua New Guinea

Early statistics

PNG became independent in 1975, five years later than Fiji and five years before Vanuatu's independence. The PNG Constitution guarantees gender equality. In its 'Basic Rights' section, all citizens, 'whatever their race, tribe, places of origin, political opinion, colour, creed or sex',[9] are assured '(a) life, liberty, security of person and the

---

7   Margaret Jolly, 2012, 'Prologue: The place of Papua New Guinea in contours of gender violence', in *Engendering Violence in Papua New Guinea*, ed. Margaret Jolly, Christine Stewart and Carolyn Brewer, pp. xvii–xxvii, Canberra: ANU E Press.
8   In this writing, I sometimes use the word *victim* to keep before the reader the suffering of those who have experienced gender violence.
9   GoPNG, Constitution of the Independent State of Papua New Guinea, 1975, 'Basic Rights', p. 5.

protection of the law' and '(c) freedom from inhuman treatment'.[10] PNG also ratified CEDAW, although not immediately, as some considered CEDAW 'not consonant with [PNG's] diverse cultural traditions'.[11] Indeed, realities on the ground contrast sharply with the show of support for women's rights in the PNG Constitution.

The most comprehensive survey of domestic violence to date was conducted by the PNG Law Reform Commission (LRC) between 1982 and 1986. The report's 'Summary and Recommendations' noted that in PNG 'domestic violence is a widespread problem affecting over two-thirds of families in the country … A certain amount of domestic violence is accepted as normal in most parts of the country, with brideprice seen as justifying a husband's right to beat his wife in many … societies. Reducing or eliminating the problem therefore means changing attitudes as well as behaviour.'[12] Although the incidence of violence was somewhat lower in urban rather than in rural areas, its severity was greater in major towns,[13] where, in contrast to village life, it may be speculated husbands had access to alcohol and wives were economically dependent on their husbands and were not able to leave violent husbands. However, 'there is considerable variation across the country, with figures of close to 100% from some of the Highlands villages surveyed, and half that level' in two coastal provinces: Oro and New Ireland provinces.[14]

---

10   Ibid., pp. 5–6.
11   Martha Macintyre, 2000, '"Hear us, women of Papua New Guinea!": Melanesian women and human rights', in *Human Rights and Gender Politics: Asia-Pacific Perspectives*, ed. Anne-Marie Hilsdon, Martha Macintyre, Vera Mackie and Maila Stivans, pp. 147–71, London and New York: Routledge, p. 149.
12   PNG Law Reform Commission, 1992, *Final Report on Domestic Violence. Report No. 14.* Boroko, N.C.D., Papua New Guinea.
13   Christine Bradley with Jane Kesno, 2001, *Family and Sexual Violence in PNG: An Integrated Long-Term Strategy*, Port Moresby: Institute of National Affairs, p. 8.
14   Ibid. See also Richard Eves, 2010, 'Masculinity matters: Men, gender-based violence and the AIDS epidemic in Papua New Guinea', in *Civic Insecurity: Law, Order and HIV in Papua New Guinea*, ed. Vicki Luker and Sinclair Dinnen, pp. 47–79, Studies in State and Society in the Pacific, no. 6, State, Society and Governance in Melanesia Program, Canberra: ANU E Press, p. 54. On the gender *non*violence of Trobriand Islanders, see Katherine Lepani, 'Proclivity and prevalence: Accounting for the dynamics of sexual violence in the response to HIV in Papua New Guinea', this volume.

Repeatedly mentioned as the cause of high rates of gender violence was the notion that 'a husband has the right to hit his wife as a way to discipline her if she does something to upset him'.[15] Indeed, gender violence in PNG has enjoyed 'pervasive legitimacy' since at least the 1980s,[16] when the LRC study was conducted. PNG is 'a country where violence in general and gender violence in particular is both expected and accepted by women and men alike'.[17] Christine Bradley, the author of the LRC's *Final Report on Domestic Violence*, concluded in her 2001 study, *Family and Sexual Violence in PNG*, that, although there was less support for domestic violence in urban than in rural areas, domestic violence was accepted as 'part of normal life',[18] something she attributed to the 'common attitude that the payment of brideprice entitles a man to control his wife and to discipline her forcefully if he thinks it necessary'.[19]

Given the shame associated with sexual violence, sexual violence is underreported, and statistics on it are harder to come by. The most commonly cited data were published in 1994 by the PNG Medical Research Institute[20] and were based on 423 interviews with men and women and 61 focus groups—in total representing 82 per cent of the population.[21] Fifty-five per cent of the women questioned said they had been forced into sex.[22] Male participants indicated that gang rape was a common practice, and 60 per cent of them admitted to having engaged in it.[23] The findings 'established that women and girls experience a very high level of sexual violence, ranging from unwanted touching

15   Rashida Manjoo, 2013, 'Report of the Special Rapporteur on violence against women, its causes and consequences, on her mission to Papua New Guinea', A/HRC/23/49/Add.2, p. 6, item 19.
16   Margaret Jolly, 2012, 'Introduction—engendering violence in Papua New Guinea: Persons, power and perilous transformations', in *Engendering Violence in Papua New Guinea*, ed. Margaret Jolly, Christine Stewart and Carolyn Brewer, pp. 1–45, Canberra: ANU E Press, p. 3. See also Laura Zimmer-Tamakoshi, 2001 [1997], '"Wild pigs and dog men": Rape and domestic violence as "women's issues" in Papua New Guinea', in *Gender in Cross-Cultural Perspective*, ed. Caroline B. Brettell and Carolyn F. Sargent, pp. 565–80, Upper Saddle River, NJ: Prentice-Hall, p. 574.
17   Jolly, 'Introduction—engendering violence in Papua New Guinea', p. 4.
18   Bradley with Kesno, *Family and Sexual Violence in PNG*, p. 10.
19   Ibid.
20   Carol Jenkins (and the National Sex and Reproduction Research Team), 1994, *National Study of Sexual and Reproductive Knowledge and Behaviour in Papua New Guinea*, Monograph 10, Goroka: Papua New Guinea Institute of Medical Research.
21   Amnesty International, 2009, 'Briefing to the UN Committee on the Elimination of Discrimination Against Women: Violence Against Women', p. 8, n. 5.
22   Ibid., p. 8.
23   Ibid.

of their bodies and being made to engage in various forms of sexual activity against their will, through to forced sexual intercourse with one or many men at the extreme but still very common end of the spectrum'.[24] Nor is sexual violence restricted to adults. PNG's first report to the committee responsible for reviewing and critiquing reports filed by state party ratifiers of the CRC acknowledged that 'rape, sexual assault and harassment, indecent assault, rape, carnal knowledge, incest and sodomy where children are the victims are common occurrences in contemporary Papua New Guinean society'.[25]

The Family and Sexual Violence Action Committee

Had PNG acted upon the 54 recommendations of the LRC's final report on domestic violence in 1992,[26] domestic violence might have been curbed. Between 1986 and 2000, PNG did take some steps to mitigate gender violence,[27] but these steps were insufficient to quell domestic violence, which had reached epidemic proportions. Instead of acting upon the LRC's recommendations, 'government focus on domestic violence substantially decreased and the momentum for change dissipated'.[28]

The follow-up to the LRC's recommendations would not come until 1999, when Lady Carol Kidu, an expatriate who was married to a prominent PNG citizen and who was the only female Member of Parliament, convened workshops to review the LRC recommendations. Emerging out of these workshops was the Family and Sexual Violence Action Committee (FSVAC), formed 'to bring together government agencies, private sector and civil society partners to develop policy and directly influence government decision making' in the area of family and sexual violence.[29] The FSVAC promotes legal reform, disseminates knowledge of new laws, provides services to victims, upgrades community prevention and response, collects relevant

---

24 Bradley with Kesno, *Family and Sexual Violence in PNG*, p. 11.
25 Committee on the Rights of the Child, 2003, 'Consideration of reports submitted by States parties under article 44 of the Convention: Initial reports of State parties due in 2000: Papua New Guinea', 21 July. CRC/C/28/Add.20, p. 99, item 396.
26 PNG LRC, 'Summary and Recommendations', in *Final Report on Domestic Violence*.
27 See Bradley with Kesno, *Family and Sexual Violence in PNG*, pp. 21–25.
28 Amnesty International, 2006, 'Papua New Guinea—Violence against women: Not inevitable, never acceptable!' p. 27.
29 Consultative Implementation and Monitoring Council (CIMC)/Family and Sexual Violence Action Committee (FSVAC), 2008.

data, develops materials for advocacy and training, and runs national awareness campaigns. Funded by such international donors as the Australian Government, the British High Commission, UNICEF and the UN Population Fund (UNFPA), the FSVAC pursues an 'integrated approach' in seven areas, including law and traditional justice, services for victims, community prevention, and male advocacy for women's rights and the ending of gender violence.[30] Since its inception in 2000, it has established branch committees in most PNG provinces.[31] It has also taken the lead in training male advocates for women's rights in its 'focus area': 'Men as Champions and Partners against Violence'.[32]

The Criminal Code (Sexual Offences and Crimes Against Children) Act

In 2002, the National Parliament passed the Criminal Code (Sexual Offences and Crimes Against Children) Act (henceforth, Criminal Code Act).[33] The bill was introduced by Lady Carol Kidu, who was at the time the Minister for Community Development, the only governmental bureau attentive to women's and children's issues. In the previous five years, there had been a sharp increase in sexual violence against women. In presenting the bill, Lady Kidu stated that it was 'an important step in re-defining the limits of acceptable behavior' because the bill would shape 'the changing values of our young nation'.[34]

The new law abandoned the archaic term 'carnal knowledge' of older legal language and replaced it with the more graphic term 'sexual penetration'; it defined sexual penetration broadly, to encompass the use of non-penile means of vaginal, anal and oral penetration, including the use of the tongue, fingers and other objects; for the first time it criminalised marital rape; and it acknowledged that females as well as males could be sex offenders. The Criminal Code Act established penalties for sexual penetration without consent that were graduated according to the age of the victim and whether the

---

30   Ibid.
31   Ibid.
32   Ibid.; see also CIMC/FSVAC, 2014, 'Final Stage for male advocacy training—Fiji', *Hadibaiatok* vol. 1, January–June, p. 5.
33   CIMC/FSVAC, n.d. 'Rape, incest, child abuse: The PNG laws have changed!!!'
34   Carol, Lady Kidu, quoted in John Y. Luluaki, 2003, 'Sexual crimes against and exploitation of children and the law in Papua New Guinea', *International Journal of Law Policy and the Family* 17(3): 275–307, p. 277.

victim was in 'a relationship of trust with the perpetrator'.[35] Other provisions criminalised sexual transgressions short of 'penetration': for example, touching a child in a sexual way, forcing a child to touch in a sexual way, exposing oneself to a child in a sexual way, or causing a child to expose himself or herself in a sexual way. Anyone committing these crimes against children would be imprisoned for up to 25 years depending upon the age of the victim, whether the victim and perpetrator was in a relationship of trust, and the number of times the offence was committed.[36] The new law also modified the evidence laws so that victims of sex crimes no longer had to produce medical evidence or a witness to the act to prove the accusation, making pressing charges less daunting for survivors.[37]

In criminalising sexual offences, the Criminal Code Act aimed to shift cases of rape from the village courts to district and national courts, where the stiff penalties called for in national laws would be imposed upon any defendant found to be guilty. PNG's dual justice system opposes village courts, on the one hand, to district and national courts, on the other. The latter enforce the PNG Constitution and national laws, but village courts function under 'the principles of restorative (rather than punitive) justice',[38] reconciling disputing parties 'in a manner that restores "peace and harmony"'.[39] Although village courts were restricted from hearing rape cases, they often did, acting beyond their jurisdiction[40] by resolving incidents of rape through reconciliation, the offender giving bridewealth or other compensation to his victim's kin to reestablish harmonious relationships. Based on her 2012 visit to PNG, the UN Special Rapporteur on Violence against Women noted in her 2013 report: 'cases of violence against women

---

35   CEDAW Committee, 2009, 'Consideration of reports submitted by States parties under article 18 of the Convention on the Elimination of All Forms of Discrimination against Women: Combined initial, second and third periodic report of States parties: Papua New Guinea, CEDAW/C/PNG/3, p. 28, item 2.2.

36   CIMC/FSVAC, 'Rape, incest, child abuse: The PNG Laws have changed!!!'

37   Ibid. See also the summary of The Criminal Code (Sexual Offences and Crimes Against Children) Act in CEDAW Committee, 2009, 'Consideration of reports submitted by States parties under article 18 of the Convention on the Elimination of All Forms of Discrimination against Women: Combined initial, second and third periodic report of State parties: Papua New Guinea', CEDAW/C/PNG/3, pp. 27–29, section 2.2.

38   Department of Justice and Attorney General (DJAG), 2001, 'Village Courts Policy', Port Moresby, p. 3.

39   Ibid.

40   Michael Goddard, 2009, *Substantial Justice: An Anthropology of Village Courts in Papua New Guinea*, Oxford: Berghahn, pp. 87–88.

rarely reach the district courts or the National Court. Such cases are mainly being resolved through mediation processes and compensation payments at the village court level'.[41] In this way, national laws are bypassed, and customary justice—with its focus upon healing relationships, especially between men—prevails.[42]

The Lukautim Pikinini Act

In 2009, the PNG Government passed the Lukautim Pikinini (Child Welfare) Act (LPA), which was informed by the CRC and written and sponsored by Carol Kidu, now Dame Carol and still then the Minister of Community and Development. Children were granted their constitutional rights as well as the right granted in domestic laws and the CRC,[43] upon whose principles the act was based. The child was defined as anyone under 18 instead of under 16, as in previous legislation.[44] It gave responsibility for enforcing the law and protecting children from abuse (verbal, physical and sexual) to newly established Child Protection Officers and Community Development Officers, mandating them to provide guidance and counselling to families in support of their parental responsibilities, to investigate allegations that a child is in need of protection and to provide that protection, and to identify, raise awareness, and work with communities 'to change harmful social, economic and customary practices', among other responsibilities.[45] It criminalised child abuse, including emotional and psychological harm, imposing a fine of K2,000 ($US800) and/ or imprisonment for the offence.[46] Also, it put in place a system of councils and committees: a National Lukautim Pikinini Council to oversee the enforcement of the law; Lukautim Pikinini Councils in every province; and Lukautim Pikinini Committees in every district, to ensure the enforcement of the LPA at all levels.[47] The intention of the LPA, with its system of councils and committees, was to make

---

41   Manjoo, 'Report of the Special Rapporteur on violence against women', p. 19, item 84.

42   See discussion in Sarah Garap, 1999, 'Struggles of women and girls in Simbu Province', *Development Bulletin* 50 (October): 47–50, p. 48.

43   GoPNG, 2009, Lukautim Pikinini (Child) Act (LPA), Part II, p. 6, item 5.

44   Ibid., p. 2.

45   Ibid., Part IV, p. 17, item 32.

46   Ibid., pp. 65–66, Part XVI, items 132–33; ibid., Part V, pp. 18–20.

47   'Lukautim Pikinini Act soon to be enforced', 2009, *Post-Courier*, 29 June. See UNICEF and the GoPNG, 2010, *Lukautim Pikinini: Training Manual*, Module 10: Child Protection Laws and Policies, 154–63.

community participation in 'ensuring the protection of children under the law'[48] mandatory and to encourage all citizens to take ownership of this mission.[49] Importantly, 'Village Courts would have no jurisdiction under the law to hear child abuse [cases] or other matters relating to children' but were expected to refer such matters to a national Lukautim Pikinini Court.[50]

A revised LPA was passed in parliament. It renders marriage of a male and/or female under the age of 18 illegal.[51] The primary motivation for revising the LPA was an alarming increase in orphans and 'street kids'—homeless children or children who remain in the family but are neglected there and who beg and steal and who are vulnerable to sexual exploitation.[52] Like the original Act, the revised LPA emphasises children's rights (to protection from abuse and neglect and to equal opportunity and education) but also parental responsibilities and duties. Children who are neglected or abused in their family situation may be removed and placed in the care of the Office for Child and Family Services, which the Department of Community Development will create to implement the revised LPA.[53] Provincial-level child and family service committees will be formed to assure children's welfare throughout the country.[54]

---

48   'Lukautim Pikinini Act soon to be enforced'.

49   Ibid.

50   HELP Resources Inc., 2005, 'A situational analysis of child sexual abuse and the commercial sexual exploitation of children in Papua New Guinea', Port Moresby: UNICEF PNG, p. 104; see also LPA, Part V, pp. 18–20.

51   Gorethy Kenneth, 2015, 'Under-age marriage ban', *Post-Courier*, 13 March, pp. 1–2; Nellie Setepano, 2016, 'PNG marriage laws to be amended as part of reform bundle to legally recognize traditional marriage and protect minors', *Pacific Islands Report*, 22 August.

52   'PNG defines marriage age', 2015, *Radio New Zealand International*, 14 March.

53   Ibid. See also Simon Bomai, 2015, 'NEC endorsement of the PNG national Lukautim Pikinini Bill', Ministry of Community Development, Religion and Youth, 24 May.

54   'Lukautim Pikinini Act—passed in Parliament', 2015, Ministry of Community Development, Religion and Youth, 8 June.

Family Support Centres, Family Sexual Violence Units, and the PNG Family and Sexual Violence Case Management Centre

Legislation is crucial in the effort to curb gender violence, but institution building is required to help survivors medically, psychologically and legally. This section summarises recent institutional innovations designed to assist survivors of gender violence in PNG.

The PNG National Department of Health and the non-profit Digicel PNG Foundation have both, albeit independently, promoted hospital-based Family Support Centres (FSCs) to provide short-term shelter, counselling and legal support for victims of gender violence.[55] Digicel's initiative was undertaken in partnership with the FSVAC and included, along with hospital-based FSCs, women's safe houses (*Meri Saif Haus*) 'within hospitals and through other service providers'.[56] In a parallel development, Médecins Sans Frontières (MSF) or Doctors Without Borders has developed hospital-based FSCs that combine medical with 'psychosocial' assistance at its three hospital-based support centres (Lae, Tari and Port Moresby).[57] The PNG Department of Health has committed to establishing such centres in all PNG hospitals.[58]

Whereas FSCs offer survivors of domestic and sexual violence medical and psychosocial assistance, Family and Sexual Violence Units (FSVUs) provide police and prosecutorial support to these same victims, opening up a pathway to the state court system for would-be complainants in legal cases involving family and sexual violence. After a pilot phase in 2008, with Australian support, police stations across the country have opened FSVUs, assisting survivors in 'lodging complaints, seeking Interim Protection Orders from the District Court, and linking to safe emergency housing and health services'.[59] The staff of FSVUs are, as the Commissioner of the PNG police force, the Royal

---

55   Manjoo, 'Report of the Special Rapporteur on violence against women', p. 18, item 77; Digicel PNG, 2010, 'Signing of financial MOU between INA CIMC-FSVAC, UNICEF and Digicel PNG Foundation', 2 February.

56   Digicel PNG, 'Signing of financial MOU'.

57   Médecins Sans Frontières (MSF) (Doctors Without Borders), 2013, 'Papua New Guinea: A comprehensive response to family and sexual violence is crucial', 25 November.

58   Helen Davidson, 2013, 'Papua New Guinea takes first steps to combat "epidemic" of abuse', *Guardian Australia*, 26 November.

59   Australian High Commission, PNG, 2014, 'Ambassador opens Family and Sexual Violence Unit in Boroko', 8 April.

Papua New Guinea Constabulary, put it, 'frontline service providers in the law and justice sector'[60] and as such receive training in how to respond sensitively and effectively to the needs of victims of domestic and sexual violence.

> It is extremely difficult in cases of family and sexual violence for victims of these crimes to find a way from the rural villages and towns into the courtroom where justice is found. There are many obstacles. However, the police stand at the door of the courtroom and can open it for victims by giving awareness, gaining the trust of the people, responding to people in need of assistance, investigating reported crimes quickly and offering compassionate support to victims of violence. That is the task of the Family and Sexual Violence Unit.[61]

The FSVU operates under the PNG police force, the Royal Papua New Guinea Constabulary (RPNGC). A late December 2015 evaluation of the then existing 15 FSVUs concluded that, even though the FSVU provided a point of entry into the state justice system for complainants, few complaints brought to the FSVU are investigated and even fewer prosecuted because of case overload and a general lack of FSVU resources, the tendency of complainants to withdraw and accept compensation in lieu of adjudication, and the disinterest of the police.[62]

At the beginning of 2014, the Australian Government, which prioritises women's empowerment and the cessation of violence against women and girls in PNG,[63] announced it would provide AU$3 million over three years to fund the PNG Family and Sexual Violence Case Management Centre (CMC) in Lae, the country's second largest city.[64] The award signalled a shift in the Australian Government's PNG aid policy. No longer funding the initiatives of the PNG Government only, the Australian Government would also support PNG civil society initiatives—the development of NGOs such as the CMC, for example.[65]

---

60   Ibid.
61   Voice of ToRot, 2014, 'Madang police fight domestic sexual violence', 1 July.
62   AusAID, 2015, Evaluation of the RPNGC Family and Sexual Violence Units, 31 December.
63   Statement by Julie Bishop, Australia's Foreign Minister, as quoted in Jo Chandler, 2014, 'Violence against women in PNG: How men are getting away with murder', Lowy Institute for International Policy, 29 August.
64   Helen Davidson, 2014, 'Australia pledges $3m for Papua New Guinea Centre for victims of violence', Guardian Australia, 7 February.
65   Ashlee Betteridge and Kamalini Lokuge, 2014, 'Combatting the family and sexual violence epidemic in Papua New Guinea', Devpolicy blog, Development Policy Centre, 30 June.

The Lae CMC was designed by the ANU Development Policy Centre.[66] It is run by Femili PNG, a local NGO,[67] and managed by a committee of Australian and PNG stakeholders, in partnership with The Australian National University (ANU) and Oxfam, the 'implementing partner'.[68] CMC targets 'women, men or children who are survivors of intimate partner violence, sexual violence and/or child abuse'.[69]

The need for such a case management centre was highlighted in a May 2013 address at ANU given by Ume Wainetti, the national coordinator of the FSVAC. Women who have been treated at FSCs and who have stayed at safe houses have sometimes been brutalised, even murdered, upon returning home, Wainetti said.[70] The CMC is designed to integrate the medical and counselling support afforded by FSCs with other available services—'police, courts, hospitals, women's refuges, health and domestic and family violence support services'[71]— and the FSVUs, for example, are to deliver 'a full spectrum of services'[72] to gender violence survivors in the hope of averting such outcomes. Provincial service providers will receive training at the Lae centre 'and take the knowledge back to regional areas with oversight and support from Lae'.[73] In this way the Lae CMC strives to have a national impact and will serve as a model for CMCs to be built elsewhere in the country in the future.

---

66   'Family and sexual violence', 2014, *Ruby.Connection*, 24 March; see also Femili PNG, 2014, 'Introducing Femili PNG and the Case Management Centre'.
67   Femili PNG, 'Introducing Femili PNG and the Case Management Centre'.
68   Ibid. See also Betteridge and Lokuge, 'Combatting the family and sexual violence epidemic in Papua New Guinea', p. 10.
69   Ume Wainetti, the National Coordinator of the FSVAC, quoted in Betteridge and Lokuge, 'Combatting the family and sexual violence epidemic in Papua New Guinea', p. 5.
70   Stephen Howes, Kamalini Lokuge, Daisy Plana and Ume Wainetti, 2013, 'Responding to family and sexual violence in PNG: The case for a Case Management Centre', *Devpolicy Blog*, 11 July.
71   Ibid.
72   Ibid.
73   Davidson, 'Australia pledges $3m for Papua New Guinea Centre for victims of violence'.

The resurgence of sorcery accusation-related homicides

Retaliations against alleged sorcerers or witches have grabbed the headlines within PNG and abroad in recent years, and sorcery- and witchcraft-related violence is on the rise.[74] In most PNG societies, if a person dies unexpectedly and/or is in his or her prime, prominent and/or wealthy, sorcery may be suspected and accusations against alleged sorcerers made. If a death is attributed to these occult forces, either compensation will be demanded of the alleged perpetrator or the accused will be targeted for 'payback' punishment, typically involving torture and/or execution.[75]

Does such activity involve violence against women? In a summary of her 2012 visit to PNG, the UN Special Rapporteur on Violence against Women stated that more women than men are tortured and murdered as a result of sorcery accusations.[76] Reporting on fieldwork in Goroka, PNG, where sorcery accusations and related homicides are rampant, Richard Eves and Angela Kelly-Hanku indicated that most of the victims of attacks on alleged sorcerers—30 out of 32 people—were females.[77] It is frequently noted that women who lack male protection—widows and older women with no offspring, women born out of wedlock, and women living at a distance from kin—tend to be vulnerable to sorcery accusations.[78] Not all researchers agree

---

74   Following earlier ethnographic work in Africa, some social scientists distinguish witchcraft from sorcery. As Miranda Forsyth and Richard Eves write in their introduction to *Talking it Through*, published in 2015 by ANU Press, 'Witches are seemingly possessed of an innate and unconscious propensity to harm others, whereas sorcery involves the conscious and deliberate manipulation of objects and/or spells to achieve a desired outcome' (p. 4). However, for present purposes I use the word *sorcery* to refer to *all* beliefs and alleged practices pertaining to supernatural homicide. See John P. Taylor and Natalie G. Araújo's contribution to this volume, 'Sorcery talk, gender violence, and the law in Vanuatu', for a Vanuatu example of the spectre of sorcery.

75   Amnesty International, 'Papua New Guinea—violence against women', p. 22; see also Manjoo, 'Report of the Special Rapporteur on Violence against Women', p. 8, item 31.

76   Manjoo, 'Report of the Special Rapporteur on Violence against Women', pp. 8–10. See also Amnesty International, 2011, 'Papua New Guinea: Violence against women, sorcery-related killings, and forced evictions', Amnesty International submission to the UN Universal Periodic Review.

77   Richard Eves and Angela Kelly-Hanku, 2014, 'Witch-hunts in Papua New Guinea's Eastern Highlands Province: A fieldwork report', in Brief 2014/4, State, Society and Governance in Melanesia, Canberra: The Australian National University.

78   For example, Manjoo, 'Report of the Special Rapporteur on Violence against Women', p. 9, items 34 and 36. See also, Philip Gibbs, 2012, 'Engendered violence and witch-killing in Simbu', in *Engendering Violence in Papua New Guinea*, ed. Margaret Jolly, Christine Stewart and Carolyn Brewer, pp. 107–35, Canberra: ANU Press.

that women are more likely than men to be the targets of sorcery accusations.[79] Practices vary from place to place. However, in general, the perpetrators of revenge killings are overwhelmingly male. It is also telling that the techniques used to torture alleged sorcerers, at least in some places, are sexualised in patently misogynist ways. It seems clear, then, that some, perhaps the majority, of sorcery accusation-related homicides constitute especially heinous instances of violence against females.

The most notorious recent incident of sorcery accusation-related revenge violence occurred on 6 February 2013, when Kepari Leniata, a 20-year-old mother who was accused of ensorcelling a six-year-old boy, was publicly tortured and burned alive in Mt Hagen, the largest town in the PNG highlands.[80] In rapid response, the UN Office of the High Commissioner for Human Rights entreated the PNG Government 'to take urgent action to prevent further cases',[81] as did Amnesty International, which stated that sorcery beliefs were being used as 'a pretext to mask abuse of women'.[82]

The public torture and immolation in broad daylight of Kepari Leniata galvanised the PNG Government and citizenry as no other incident had. In the wake of this brutal murder, Women Arise, a coalition of women's groups and NGOs, formed to combat violence against women. At the UN in March 2013, H.E. Robert G. Aisi, the PNG Permanent Representative to the UN, addressed the 57th session of the Commission on the Status of Women on behalf of the PNG

---

79   Miranda Forsyth, 2013, 'Summary of main themes emerging from the conference on Sorcery and Witchcraft-Related Killings in Melanesia, 5–7 June 2013, ANU, Canberra', *Outrigger: Blog of the Pacific Institute*, The Australian National University. See also Dan Jorgensen, 2014, 'Preying on those close to home: Witchcraft violence in a PNG village', *The Australian Journal of Anthropology* 25: 267–86.

80   That alleged sorcerers may be tortured much less killed makes contemporary sorcery a violation of the International Covenant on Civil and Political Rights and the Convention Against Torture, which prohibits both torture and extrajudicial killing. To the extent that females and/or children are singled out for sorcery accusations and retributions, sorcery-related violence contravenes CEDAW and/or CRC, see Nancy Robinson, then Regional Representative of the UN Office of the High Commissioner for Human Rights, 2013, 'Statement on sorcery-related killings and impunity in Papua New Guinea', Paper presented at the Sorcery and Witchcraft-related Killings in Melanesia: Culture, Law and Human Rights Perspectives Conference, The Australian National University, Canberra, 5–7 June.

81   Peter Kumer, 2013, 'UN urges Papua New Guinea to take action after woman burned alive for witchcraft', United Nations Association of Slovenia, 8 February.

82   Amnesty International, 2013, 'Papua New Guinea must end "sorcery" killings and harassment', 8 February.

Government, mentioning specifically the murder of Kepari Leniata, a symbol, he said, of 'the savagery' of violence against women and girls in PNG,[83] as he vowed to eradicate this violence. 'The Government of Papua New Guinea acknowledges that violence against women and girls in the country is a … human rights concern that must not be tolerated any more. We are therefore committed to combat gender-based violence and also entrench gender equality and empowerment in the country.'[84]

A 'Remembering Kepari Leniata Campaign' erupted on Facebook and, with the help of Women Arise, an overnight *haus krai* or 'house of mourning' event occurred in Port Moresby, beginning on the night of 14 May and continuing into 15 May 2013, 'to advocate against the unacceptably high rate of violence against women in Papua New Guinea'.[85] Similar *haus krai* events occurred elsewhere in PNG, and sympathetic public protests were held in Australia, New Zealand, the US, the UK, Ireland, Japan, the Philippines, Italy and Fiji.[86] One thousand people came to the Port Moresby *haus krai*. There, Prime Minister Peter O'Neill apologised to women for the 'despicable violence' against them 'in our communities and throughout the country',[87] and he pledged tougher laws and penalties and the use of the death penalty to stem gender violence.[88] Also at the Port Moresby *haus krai*, the Australian High Commissioner Deborah Stokes, the first female to hold that post, addressed the crowd and pledged solidarity with 'the men and women of Papua New Guinea who are speaking out against violence against women' and with 'those who are taking part in similar Haus Krai events around the globe, to condemn all acts of violence against women'.[89]

83   Robert G. Aisi, 2013, 'Statement By H.E. Mr Robert G. Aisi Permanent Representative of Papua New Guinea to the United Nations at the Fifty-Seventh Session of the Commission on the Status of Women', New York, 11 March.
84   Ibid., p. 3, item xii.
85   Nellie Setepano, 2013, 'PNG "Haus Krai" movement gains support abroad', *Pacific Islands Report*, East-West Center, Honolulu: University of Hawai'i.
86   Ibid.
87   Peter O'Neill, quoted in Eoin Blackwell, 2013, 'PNG says sorry for violence against women', *Sydney Morning Herald*, 15 May.
88   Heretofore, the death penalty had been reserved for crimes such as treason and piracy.
89   Deborah Stokes, 2013, 'Speech by Australian High Commissioner Ms Deborah Stokes at the "Haus Krai" condemning violence against women, 15 May 2013', Australian High Commission Papua New Guinea, 16 May.

Recent governmental measures

Leniata's murder was not an isolated incident. Around the same time there were other attempted and actual tortures and/or murders in retaliation for alleged sorcery homicides in Mt Hagen, the Southern Highlands Province and Bougainville, and there have been sorcery accusation-related revenge murders that have made national and international headlines ever since.[90] These events partake of a broader pattern of escalation that has been ongoing since the 1980s. In fact, sorcery accusation-related violence in PNG, and especially in the highlands, is 'rapidly becoming one of the world's most urgent human rights issues'[91]—so much so that nearby countries have expressed fear that sorcery-related violence will spread into Pacific countries hitherto free of sorcery.[92]

Kepari Leniata's death has served as an important catalyst. The ongoing Remembering Kepari Lenaita Campaign (also referred to as the *Haus Krai* Movement) has mobilised significant support for clamping down on gender violence. In late May 2013, the PNG Parliament repealed the Sorcery Act,[93] which recognised allegations of sorcery as a defense in the murder of an alleged sorcerer and which also criminalised sorcery. Also, new provision was made in the Criminal Code Act of 1974 that wilful murder, including sorcery-related executions, would draw the death penalty.[94] Parliament also replaced the milder penalties for rape imposed by the Criminal Code Act of 2002 with the death penalty for aggravated rape (typically gang rape).[95]

---

90   For example, Sorcha Pollak, 2013, 'Woman burned alive for witchcraft in Papua New Guinea', *Time Magazine*, 7 February.

91   Aaron Fernandes, 2014, 'A war on witches', *Aljazeera*, 1 May.

92   Karen Barlow, 2013, 'Fears sorcery-killings may be spreading from PNG', ABC Radio Australia, 5 June.

93   Matt Siegel, 2013, 'Papua New Guinea acts to repeal sorcery law after strife', *New York Times*, 29 May.

94   Miranda Forsyth, 2014, 'New draft national action plan to address sorcery accusation-related violence in PNG', in Brief 2014/18, State, Society and Governance in Melanesia, Canberra: The Australian National University.

95   Siegel, 'Papua New Guinea acts to repeal sorcery law after strife'. The international reaction to this repurposing of the death penalty has been mixed at best. Some see in the death penalty the ultimate denial of human rights in that it empowers the state to take a life. Executing rapists or murderers of alleged sorcerers would also have the unintended consequence of perpetuating rather than quelling violence wherever custom requires the eye-for-an-eye justice of retaliation.

Especially significant, within four months of the Port Moresby *Haus Krai* and two decades after the bill was first drafted,[96] parliament passed unanimously the Family Protection Act (FPA), which criminalises domestic violence in an effort to 'promote safe, stable and strong families; and to prevent and deter domestic violence at all levels of society'.[97] Amnesty International attributed the passage of the bill 'to the collective action of grassroots organisations and a multitude of women human rights defenders in PNG' and to the *Haus Krai* Movement.[98] The FPA asserts that 'freedom from violence is every person's right'[99] and defines violence in broad terms, including physical assault and psychological and sexual abuses. A key significance of the FPA is that it criminalises domestic violence, referring cases to district courts in the state justice system, which will award stiff fines and sentences—up to K5,000 (about $US2,000) and/or a prison term of up to two years—for acts of domestic violence.[100] The act explicitly states that payment of bridewealth is not a justification for domestic violence.[101] Complainants may seek an enforceable physical separation from a family member by applying for a 'Family Protection Order' (FPO) if they feel threatened by that family member.[102] They may also apply for an 'Interim Protection Order' (IPO), which lasts 30 days and which can be renewed for another 30 days.[103] Domestic violence survivors do not always report the offence. With the FPA, someone other than the victim—neighbours and kinsfolk, even children— may report the offence, triggering police and court penal action and reducing the degree of impunity that domestic offenders tend to enjoy.[104] Almost 30 years after the initial LRC study, the statistics on domestic violence and rape had not improved. Yet, as Prime Minister O'Neill proclaimed, with the FPA, 'The lid over domestic violence is now removed and the problem exposed as a national issue needing government intervention'.[105]

---

96 Chandler, 'Violence against women in PNG', p. 4.
97 GoPNG, 2013, Family Protection Bill, 2013, preamble, 3a and 3b.
98 Amnesty International, 2013, 'Good news: Family protection laws passed in PNG', 26 September.
99 Family Protection Bill, Part I, 4a.
100 Ibid., Part II, 6.1.
101 Ibid., Part II, 6.2.
102 Ibid., Part III, 9.
103 Ibid., Part III, 14.2.
104 Eoin Blackwell, 2013, 'PNG govt backs domestic violence laws', *The Australian*, News, 2 April.
105 Ibid.

But has the PNG Government, through state actors such as judges, prosecutors, and the police, actually intervened? A September 2015 Human Rights Watch (HRW) report noted that, as of June 2015, when HRW conducted the research on which this report was based: (1) the FPA has not been implemented,[106] (2) police and prosecutors are 'rarely prepared to pursue investigations or criminal charges against people who commit family violence, even in cases of attempted murder, serious injury, and repeated rape',[107] (3) victims have difficulty obtaining IPOs[108] and (4) victims and their children have no shelter or other assistances if they wish to leave their abusers.[109] These observations are repeated in HRW's November 2015 report, *Bashed Up*.[110]

Beyond the state: Towards multi-sectoral coalitions and grassroots activism

The most recent PNG initiative in regard to violence against females is the Sorcery National Action Plan or SNAP. SNAP was developed in June 2014 in a Port Moresby workshop. This was a follow-up to a Goroka, PNG, conference that was held in December 2013, which developed out of an ANU conference in June 2013. A national plan, SNAP nonetheless constitutes a marked departure from state and legislation-centred initiatives in that it relies on a 'holistic', 'comprehensive' approach involving governmental but also non-governmental actors and entities, including representation of national and international NGOs (for example, the FSVAC and Oxfam), the UN and academic and faith-based organisations and international partners such as the Australian Department of Finance and Trade (which allocates aid money to PNG).[111] The National Executive Committee approved SNAP in July 2015.[112] SNAP signals a shift away from a reliance upon government alone towards an investment in

---

106 Human Rights Watch (HRW), 2015, 'Papua New Guinea: Universal Periodic Review Submission 2015', summary, item 7, 21 September.
107 Ibid., summary, item 8.
108 Ibid., summary, item 9.
109 Ibid., summary, item 10.
110 HRW, 2015, *Bashed Up: Family Violence in Papua New Guinea*, 4 November. See also MSF, 2016, 'Return to abuser: Gaps in services and a failure to protect survivors of family and sexual violence in Papua New Guinea'.
111 Forsyth, 'New draft national action plan to address sorcery accusation-related violence in Papua New Guinea'.
112 Maria, 2015, 'Papua New Guinea needs its Sorcery National Action Plan as soon as possible!' 24 October.

hybrid coalitions that integrate public with private and national with international entities in collaborative governance projects. Working with such hybrid coalitions at the community and provincial levels has also been recommended in the effort to thwart violence flowing from sorcery accusations.[113]

Also participating in this hybrid governance project are citizen-activists such as members of the Highland Women Human Rights Defenders Movement (HWHRDM), which 'is an umbrella organisation for different grassroots and community-based organisations working to defend human rights in the seven Highlands provinces'.[114] The work of these women is 'linked to the broader goals of the international human rights movement',[115] as they offer counselling and practical assistance to survivors of gender violence, 'monitor and document human rights violations ... hold gender and human rights trainings and workshops ... raise awareness ... and work with the law and justice sectors to improve access to justice for victims'.[116]

HWHRDM signals ever-greater activism among ordinary citizens, especially among women themselves. As Margaret Jolly has observed of PNG today, 'gender violence is increasingly being seen as an important problem by many Papua New Guineans and ... it is possible to mobilise large congregations of women and men in protest'.[117] Tacitly acknowledging this incipient social movement, Amnesty International uses the term 'human rights defenders' more broadly, to signify PNG women's rights supporters who may not identify as human rights defenders but who are nonetheless:

> on the frontline of the struggle to stop violence against women [as they] provide temporary shelter for women escaping abusive partners ... offer para-legal advice to women attempting to obtain maintenance orders ... provide counselling, support and advice to victims of gender-based violence ... conduct training on human rights ... who lobby the

113 Philip Gibbs, 2015, 'Confronting sorcery accusation violence in PNG: Will PNG's Sorcery National Action Plan be able to stop the torture and murder of those accused of witchcraft?' *Asia and the Pacific Policy Society*, Policy Forum, November.
114 Highlands Women Human Rights Defenders Movement website, n.d., 'About us'.
115 Ibid.
116 Ibid., 'Themes'.
117 Jolly, 'Prologue', p. xix.

police to investigate incidents of sexual violence and violence within the home and who provide medical assistance to the battered, bruised and broken.[118]

PNG, the poster child for gender violence in the western Pacific, may be coming of age.

Fiji

Bashed Up, Human Rights Watch's most recent exposé of human rights violations in PNG, opens with the alarming statement that 'Family violence in Papua New Guinea is an emergency'.[119] But 'there are some signs of progress'.[120] Among these are government plans for establishing a national human rights commission, the establishment of a new hotline to help direct survivors toward existing services, and other steps, most of which have already been covered in this discussion.[121] Nevertheless, the constant refrain of the report is that much more needs to be done. While PNG struggles to operate effectively within the globalised space of human rights work, Fiji continues to exercise regional leadership in this arena. But it, too, strives, with only partial success, to eradicate violence against women and children, as a 2011 survey published at the end of 2013 and discussed below makes clear.

Civil society responses to gender violence

The Fiji Women's Crisis Centre (FWCC) is renowned throughout the Pacific for its women's rights work. Originally called the Women's Crisis Centre,[122] it was established in 1984 at a time when the level of sexual violence in Suva was escalating and a new local research centre, the Action Centre for Women in Need, issued 'Rape in Fiji', a report calling for the creation of an entity that could respond to the needs of rape survivors.[123] That entity would be the FWCC.

---

118 Amnesty International, 2006, 'Papua New Guinea: Women human rights defenders in action'.
119 HRW, *Bashed Up*, p. 2.
120 Ibid.
121 Ibid., pp. 2–3.
122 Nicole George, 2012, *Situating Women: Gender Politics and Circumstance in Fiji*, Canberra: ANU E Press, p. 80.
123 Ibid., pp. 80–81. See also George, '"Lost in translation"', this volume; and Ruby Taylor-Newton, 2009, 'Twenty-five years on, Fiji Women's Crisis Centre stands as a beacon of hope for women', *Womensphere*, 4 September.

It soon became evident that female victims suffered additionally from other forms of gender violence, and the scope of FWCC operations expanded to include domestic violence, among other abuses.[124] Conducting awareness campaigns, distributing pamphlets and posters, and running training sessions on gender violence, the FWCC provoked opposition from conservative groups, including other women's organisations, who 'often argued that the [FWCC's] discussion of domestic violence threatened the integrity of the family ... and promoted an agenda that was essentially "anti-men"'.[125] Some governmental figures also felt that using terms like *crisis* (not to mention the topic of gender violence itself) tarnished Fiji's reputation as a 'tropical paradise' tourist destination.[126] Regardless, the FWCC has been from its inception 'the main institution providing psychological, human rights–based crisis counselling and practical support for women and children who have experienced violence in Fiji'.[127] The Suva-based FWCC has branches in Ba, Nadi and Rakiraki, all on Viti Levu, where Suva is, and Labasa on Vanua Levu, the central island in the Fijian archipelago.[128] There are plans to open a fifth branch in Savusavu on Vanua Levu.[129] On the regional level the FWCC is the Secretariat for the Pacific Women's Network on Violence Against Women, a network of human rights organisations devoted to combatting violence against women in the Pacific, which the FWCC was instrumental in establishing and for which it is the coordinating body.[130] As the Secretariat, the FWCC offers a four-week Regional Training Program (RTP) twice a year for men and women working in the areas of lobbying, counselling, advocacy and community awareness of violence against women and girls in the Pacific.[131]

---

124 Ibid., p. 81.
125 Ibid.
126 Ibid.
127 AusAID, 2009, *Stop Violence: Responding to Violence Against Women in Melanesia and East Timor*, p. 76.
128 'About us', n.d., Fiji Women's Crisis Centre: Eliminating Violence Against Women in Fiji and the Pacific (FWCC), website.
129 Fiji Women's Crisis Centre, 2013, *Somebody's Life, Everybody's Business! National Research on Women's Health and Life Experiences in Fiji (2010/2011): A survey exploring the prevalence, incidence and attitudes to intimate partner violence in Fiji*, Suva: FWCC, p. 12.
130 Edwina Kotoisuva, 2007, 'Fiji Women's Crisis Centre: Organising against violence against women', paper presented at Pacific Women, Pacific Plan: Stepping up the Pace to 2010, Secretariat of the Pacific Community, 10th Triennial Conference of Pacific Women, Noumea, New Caledonia, 27–31 May.
131 Fiji Women's Crisis Centre website, n.d., 'Regional training program (RTP)'.

A sister organisation called the Fiji Women's Rights Movement (FWRM) was formed in Suva in 1986. 'Members of the FWCC were … realising that … they were facing an uphill battle when it came to the patriarchal structures of national governance. Changing attitudes to women was one thing; dealing with a legal and judicial system that was blind to the realities and experiences of women was another.'[132] And so, according to Shamima Ali, Coordinator of the FWCC and one of the founders of the FWRM, 'We decided that there was an immediate need for another group, a more academically inclined group, to draft policies and advocate for legislative reform'.[133] This would become a 'feminist human rights organisation that combines local concerns with a global perspective'.[134] Together with the FWCC, the FWRM would work 'within a rights-based approach to women's issues'.[135]

At first the FWRM addressed sexual violence, conducting an anti-rape campaign in partnership with an Australian NGO.[136] In 1987, it organised the first anti-rape march in Fiji, delivering to the parliament a 5,000-signature petition endorsing stiffer sentences for convicted sexual violence offenders.[137] As the petition suggested, the FWRM's ultimate goal was legal reform. Not surprisingly, the FWRM was an important advocate for the adoption of CEDAW region-wide.[138] It also lobbied for a progressive Bill of Rights in the 1997 Constitution that protected and promoted women's rights.[139]

In addition to promoting legal reforms, the FWRM provides 'a free legal information and referral service for women in Suva and delivers feminist training to groups and organisations, including developing school and institution-based education and awareness-raising'.[140] In this effort it works in tandem with the Suva-based Regional Rights and Resources Team (RRRT), which provides 'training, advocacy and

132 Fiji Women's Rights Movement (FWRM), 2012, 'Herstory: Celebrating 25 Years of Balancing the Scales, 1986–2011', Suva: FWRM.
133 Quoted in FWRM, 'Herstory', p. 2.
134 Ibid., p. 1.
135 Ibid., p. 2.
136 George, Situating Women, p. 109.
137 Ibid., p. 119.
138 Ibid.
139 FWRM, 'Herstory', p. 30.
140 AusAID, 2008, Violence Against Women in Melanesia and East Timor: Building on Global and Regional Promising Approaches, Report prepared by the Office of Development Effectiveness, p. 155.

resourcing on human rights issues relating to violence against women to the police, the judiciary and community-based organisations' for the entire Pacific.[141] The RRRT and the FWRM train police officers, magistrates, judges and prosecutors on violence against women.[142] The FWCC, the FWRM and the RRRT were 'the first in Melanesia to tackle violence against women from a human-rights perspective'[143] as well as the first 'to create broad community acceptance that violence should be viewed through a human rights framework'.[144]

State responses to gender violence

Together with the National Council of Women Fiji, the FWCC and the FWRM lobbied successfully for the bureaucratisation of the government's response to women's concerns. In 1987, just three years after the FWCC was formed and one year after the FWRM came into existence, the Department for Women and Culture was created.[145] This would become the Ministry for Women, Children and Poverty Alleviation (henceforth, Ministry for Women).[146] The Ministry for Women combines the Department of Women, which advises the Fijian Government on public policy bearing on issues of women and gender, and the Department of Social Welfare, which is responsible for children's welfare.

In 1998, the Ministry for Women spearheaded the effort to put in place a National Women's Plan of Action (WPA), which was in effect from 1999 to 2008. The WPA designated the elimination of violence against women and children as one of five areas of concern. It acknowledged that there was an 'ingrained bias against women'[147] and that Fiji had been slow to recognise violence against women as a problem because it was 'identified as a family matter that should remain in the private domain, in the belief that intervention would have an adverse effect

---

141 AusAID, *Stop Violence*, p. 80.
142 AusAID, *Violence Against Women in Melanesia and East Timor*, p. 155; AusAID, *Stop Violence*, p. 74.
143 AusAID, *Violence Against Women in Melanesia and East Timor*, p. 152.
144 Ibid.
145 Ministry for Social Welfare, Women and Poverty Elimination, 2014, 'Fiji's national report on the 20-year review of the implementation of the Beijing Platform for Action', p. 3.
146 This ministry has operated under a number of appellations: Ministry for Social Welfare, Women and Poverty Elimination and Ministry for Women and Culture, for example.
147 Ministry for Women and Culture, 1998, 'The Women's Plan of Action 1999–2008', vol. 2, section on violence against women and children, 'Executive summary'.

on the family unit'.[148] In addition, violence against women in the family was said to be 'entrenched' and either tolerated as disciplinary or ignored.[149] Yet the plan did not argue that present day violence against women reflected the practices of the past. The importance of family relationships has indeed been longstanding, but 'the dynamics that determine family relationships have changed',[150] resulting in myriad problems, including poverty, drug abuse, crime and violence against women and children.[151] A revised WPA came into effect in 2009, effective through 2018. Also, a National Gender Policy was put in place in 2014 to promote gender equality and sustainable development, which was thought to depend on achieving gender equality.[152] In 2009, the Ministry for Women would launch the first Zero Tolerance Violence Free Community (ZTVFC) at Koroipita,[153] a community outside the Viti Levu city of Lautoka, the second largest urban centre in Fiji. As will be discussed, the ZTVFC initiative has assumed tremendous importance in Fiji's war against gender violence.

The Fijian Police Force has taken important steps towards aiding victims of domestic and sexual violence. Beginning in 1995, it has opened up Sexual Offences Units (SOUs). Like PNG's FSVUs, Fiji's SOUs are designed to give direct assistance to the victims of domestic violence and sexual assault and also to direct them towards the state justice system, bypassing the village courts of the informal justice system.[154] Each SOU takes statements from survivors, transports them to medical facilities, and refers them to other agencies (the FWCC, for example) for counselling and other support.[155] They do so under a 'no drop' policy that requires police to record and pursue a charge of domestic violence once it is filed, even if the accuser changes (usually) her mind and wants to withdraw the charge.[156] Before the 'no drop' policy was instituted, 'women who reported domestic abuse cases to the police often faced severe pressure from family, in-laws and

---

148 Ibid., vol. 2, section on violence against women and children, 'Overview'.
149 Ibid.
150 Ibid.
151 Ibid.
152 Fijian Government, 2014, 'Fiji's national gender policy approved', 25 February.
153 Fijian Government, 2013, 'Violence free campaigns paying dividends for communities', press release, 6 July.
154 AusAID, *Violence Against Women in Melanesia and East Timor*, p. 152.
155 AusAID, *Stop Violence*, p. 74. However, Fiji's SOUs appear to suffer from inadequate resources and demanding workloads.
156 AusAID, *Violence Against Women in Melanesia and East Timor*, p. 156.

community members, and often returned to the police station shortly afterward to withdraw their complaints'.[157] In fact, 'the police and courts ["overwhelmingly male"][158] have been reluctant to prosecute violence against women and impose penalties … Both police and courts find … cases [of domestic violence] embarrassing and often do not support women who complain.'[159]

Fiji's Family Law Act (FLA) was passed in 2003.[160] The passage of the Act was 'the culmination of a 15-year process that had frequently been stalled by Fiji's coups'.[161] The law aimed to provide 'a level playing field for women and men' in regard to divorce, maintenance and custody of children.[162] Divorcées were afforded 'enforced spousal maintenance should they be raising children as single parents',[163] thus helping women 'escape violent domestic relationships through no-fault divorce provisions'. Courts could also issue restraining orders against a violent partner, and the police were granted powers to enforce such orders.[164] Those exercising jurisdiction under the terms of the FLA were instructed to 'have regard to' the two treaties discussed here, CRC and CEDAW.[165] While women's rights advocates hailed the new law, opponents derided its corrosive effects on the grounds that it made obtaining a divorce easier, thus undermining 'indigenous conceptions of leadership, property rights and inheritance and threatened the religious sanctity of marriage'.[166]

The intention of the police's 'no drop' policy, like the work of the police's SOUs, was to direct cases of domestic violence towards the state justice system. Consistent with that goal, the Domestic Violence Decree (DVD) of 2009 prohibited the use of reconciliation practices (principal of which was the *bulubulu* process described in Newland's contribution to this volume) to resolve instances of domestic violence. Henceforth instances of domestic violence would require prosecution and sentencing in the state courts, although evidence of the perpetrator

---

157 Ibid.
158 Merry, *Human Rights and Gender Violence*, p. 144.
159 Ibid.
160 Republic of Fiji Islands, 2003, Family Law Act.
161 George, '"Lost in translation"', this volume.
162 Fiji Women's Rights Movement, n.d., 'Fiji: Family Law Bill passed'.
163 George, '"Lost in translation"', this volume.
164 Republic of Fiji Islands, 2003, Family Law Act, items 202(1) and 203.
165 Ibid., item 26(e).
166 George, *Situating Women*, p. 181.

and victim having been reconciled could be used as a mitigating factor in determining the offender's sentence.[167] The DVD also enabled family members, co-residents, neighbours, police and welfare officers, and any entity—rights-based NGOs, for example—to apply for a protection order on behalf of the victim to protect (typically her) from further harm.[168]

Also in 2009, the Fiji Parliament passed the Crimes Decree (CD). The CD replaced the earlier definition of rape as the 'forced penile penetration of the female organ' with a definition of rape as nonconsensual 'sexual penetration', broadly defined, as penetration of genitalia, anus or mouth by means of a finger or other object.[169] Cases that were tried as 'indecent assault'[170] would now be tried as rape, drawing the stiffer penalty of 25 years[171] to life.[172] A child younger than 13 years of age was deemed incapable of giving consent.[173] In addition, a home or property owner who suspects that a person under 13 or a girl under 16 has been defiled on his (typically) property and who fails to report the crime, would be charged.[174]

How effective?

Fiji ratified CRC in 1993 and CEDAW in 1995, albeit with two reservations. The more important of these concerned CEDAW's article 5a, which requires states to 'modify the social and cultural patterns of conduct of men and women' to promote gender equality. Fiji objected to this article 'on the grounds that it "impinges on our cultural values and social norms of behavior that are the mainstay of traditional societies like Fiji"'.[175] However, the Constitutional Amendment Act of 1997 granted equal rights to female and male citizens alike,[176] and Fiji

---

167 Nazhat Shameem, 2012, 'The Domestic Violence Decree 2009, Fiji', pp. 10–11.

168 Ibid., p. 4.

169 Republic of Fiji, 2009, 'Crimes Decree 2009', in *Republic of Fiji Islands Government Gazette* 10(95) (5 November), p. 1061, item 88.5.

170 'New crime decree in Fiji to assist fight against sexual abuse', 2010, *Solomon Times Online*, 25 January.

171 Republic of Fiji, 'Crimes Decree 2009', p. 1063, item 93(1).

172 Ibid., p. 1097, item 207(1).

173 Ibid., p. 1097, item 207(3).

174 'New crime decree in Fiji to assist fight against sexual abuse'.

175 CEDAW Committee, 2000, 'Initial report of States parties: Fiji Islands', CEDAW/C/FJI/1, p. 4.

176 CEDAW Committee, 2008, 'Consideration of reports submitted by States parties under article 18 of the Convention on the Elimination of All Forms of Discrimination against Women. Combined second, third and fourth periodic reports of States parties: Fiji', CEDAW/C/FJI/2-4, p. 8.

withdrew its CEDAW reservations in 2000, filing its first report with the committee that reviews and critiques state party reports that same year.

Fiji's combined second, third and fourth report would follow eight years later. It made it abundantly clear that, despite Fiji's civil society organisations, laws and state institutions, gender violence remained a serious problem. Given the 'patriarchal' nature of Fijian society,[177] 'gender inequality infiltrates all aspects of life including the tacit acceptance of violence against women in the home'.[178] A 2008 report from the UNFPA concurred, noting that violence is used by men to keep '"women in their place", especially if women show signs of going beyond the traditional gender roles accorded them by society. Ideas and attitudes on traditional gender roles are so engrained in Fiji that cases of sexual harassment and abuse are often not thought of as criminal offenses'.[179] Of the women the UNFPA surveyed, 66 per cent were the victims of domestic violence, 30 per cent were repeatedly abused, and 74 per cent of female victims neither sought medical attention nor reported the incident to the police.[180] Women who reported violent husbands to the police were seen to be 'disrespectful of their marriage vows … or seen to be challenging cultural norms that strive to keep the family together, despite adverse and dangerous situations'.[181] A similar kind of pressure was placed on incest victims. 'When the victim chooses to pursue the case through the justice system [instead of informal mediation], family members sometimes step in to defend the reputation of the offender, and put pressure on the victims not to "tarnish the family name" or "break up the family"'.[182] Indeed, 'There is a lot of pressure on women to reconcile with their husbands/partners following incidents of domestic violence, rather than seek access to justice. This pressure can come from traditional, community and religious leaders, the Police, the Family Court and other Courts.'[183] In regard to the police's 'no drop' policy, this may have 'improved police response to violence against women overall',

---

177 Ibid., p. 48, item 128.
178 Ibid., p. 48, item 127.
179 UN Population Fund (UNFPA), 2008, 'An assessment of the state of violence against women in Fiji', Suva: UNFPA Pacific Sub Regional Office, p. 19.
180 Ibid., p. 13.
181 Ibid.
182 Ibid., p. 19.
183 FWCC, *Somebody's Life, Everybody's Business!*, p. 17.

but police insensitivity to domestic violence and its impacts remain.[184] In fact, the 'no drop' policy has had the unintended consequence of discouraging women from coming forward lest their assailant be sentenced and incarcerated.[185] All in all, reporting to the police had become 'a last resort'.[186]

Whether because of police indifference, women's fear of reprisals or both, the same fate awaited the Domestic Violence Decree (DVD) of 2009. According to Madam Nazhat Shameem—the first woman to be appointed judge of the High Court of Fiji[187] and who is presently Fiji's first Permanent Representative to the UN Office in Geneva, where she now resides[188]—'most cases of domestic violence ... never come to the attention of the media, or the High Court. Sadly most cases of rape and incest within a family do not lead to ... a domestic violence sentence. This is so, even in the High Court.'[189] As a result, the purpose of the DVD, 'which was to promote gender equality in the courts, and to promote gender competence within the judiciary, is defeated'.[190] The predominant mechanism for resolving domestic conflict remains reconciliation, which the Penal Code allows but does not favour.[191] Women who succumb to the 'pressure ... to reconcile with their husbands/partners following incidents of domestic violence, rather than seek access to justice'[192] expose themselves to '[r]e-victimisation'.[193] Despite progressive legislation, the previous status quo largely prevails.

---

184 AusAID, *Violence Against Women in Melanesia and East Timor*, p. 154.
185 Ibid., p. 156.
186 Ibid.
187 Australian Centre for Leadership for Women, 2012, 'Nazhat Shameem', 1 June.
188 Fijian Government, 2014, 'Nazhat Shameem to be Fiji's Permanent Representative to the UN Office in Geneva', 8 May.
189 Shameem, 'The Domestic Violence Decree 2009', p. 12.
190 Ibid.
191 AusAID, *Violence Against Women in Melanesia and East Timor*, p. 158.
192 FWCC, *Somebody's Life, Everybody's Business!*, p. 17.
193 Ibid.

Community-based advocacy

In 2002, the FWCC began a Male Advocacy Program in partnership with the Ministry of Women.[194] The program is based in a human rights framework and, much like the program Philip Gibbs describes in his contribution to this volume, helps men recognise their complicity in patterns of behaviour that undermine women's rights and reform their behaviour. Male advocates advocate for women's rights and serve as role models to other men and boys. Many participants in the Male Advocacy Program experience behavioural and attitudinal changes.[195]

As already indicated, the Ministry for Women piloted one of its most important programs in 2008. The Zero Tolerance Violence Free Communities (ZTVFC) Campaign emphasises changing attitudes and behaviours through human rights education and awareness programs[196] within indigenous (*iTaukei*) communities for the purpose of promoting women's rights and eliminating violence against women and children. The aim is to 'empower women, men and children through human rights education using media campaigns and community training'.[197] Participation in the program is entirely voluntary. After a successful pilot, the ZTVFC began in earnest. As of July 2014, 87 communities were participating in the program, with another 29 readying for awareness trainings.[198] The number of communities participating or wanting to participate continues to rise. A 'gatekeeper committee' comprised of village leaders, including women and youth, is chosen by the village to monitor violence against women and children in the village. The committee serves as the 'eyes and ears' of the local campaign as it operates in particular locations.[199] Committee members are trained in human rights and how to respond to cases of abuse in their village. Once the community becomes free of violence, a billboard is erected in front of the village announcing its violence-

194 AusAID, *Violence Against Women in Melanesia and East Timor*, p. 161; Felix Chaudary, 2015, 'Call for commitment', *Fiji Times Online*, 23 March.
195 Seeds Theatre Group Inc., 2015, 'Male advocacy for human rights'.
196 AusAID, *Stop Violence*, pp. 80–81.
197 Ibid., p. 80.
198 Elizabeth Rokosuka, 2014, 'Zero tolerance violence free communities to report on crimes', *Fijivillage.com*, 6 July.
199 Fijian Government, 2013, 'Violence free campaigns paying dividends for communities', press release, 6 July.

free status.[200] Mobilising the public as gender violence watchdogs, the ZTVFC campaign empowers survivors by offering them human rights–informed communal support and in the process renders gender violence no longer a private but, instead, a most public matter.

How to explain the popularity of the ZTVFC, which has seen community after community queuing up to participate? Perhaps this way: gatekeeper committees are able to reconcile those whose relationships are marred by sexual abuse and domestic violence before particular incidents are reported to the police for prosecution, in effect rehabilitating reconciliation practices. This is despite the fact that the DVD, which village-based actors find 'a bit too harsh particularly when couples are able to reconcile almost immediately after an abuse experience',[201] requires prosecution of domestic violence in the state justice system. Staffed predominantly by male leaders, gatekeeper committees 'mediate between the community and the police department',[202] possibly bridging the difference between traditional or neo-traditional practices, on the one hand, and rights-informed legal practices, on the other. Operating under governmental agencies devoted to women's rights, participants in these 'zero tolerance' communities are in effect recruited to the global human rights movement, albeit as community-based activists.

At the dawn of the 'post-2015' era

The brutal execution of Kepari Leniata in February 2013 galvanised PNG to clamp down on sorcery accusation-related gender violence. More than two years later, in April 2015, another brutal murder focused attention on the persistence of violence against women in Fijian society. Losana McGowan, a Fijian journalist and women's rights advocate, was bludgeoned to death by her partner. Those associated with the cause of women's rights argued that the death, otherwise pointless, could '"reinvigorate", focus and discussion on women's abuse in Fiji'.[203] The FWRM saluted Losana for her 'exuberant personality and zest

---

200 A photograph of such a billboard appears in Rokosuka, 'Zero tolerance violence free communities to report on crimes'.

201 Geraldine Coutts, 2012, 'Fiji women's minister defends domestic violence decree', ABC Radio Australia, 6 December.

202 Ibid.

203 Alistar Kata, 2015, 'Death of Losana McGowan opens door for wider talks on domestic abuse', *Fiji Sun Online*, 19 April.

for life' and pledged to 'recommit to fighting gender-based violence in all its forms'.[204] But it was the response of Fiji's Prime Minister, the Honourable Voreqe (Frank) Bainimarama, that mattered the most. 'For too long, Fijian society in common with other Pacific societies has turned a blind eye to what goes on in the privacy of people's homes. Worse, we've tolerated, even encouraged, a culture in which spouses or partners are entitled to use violence to resolve disputes or bring supposedly errant family members into line',[205] he said. He went on to issue a clarion call for the Fijian public to tackle domestic violence. Indeed, the time for action 'to bring this scourge to an end is long overdue',[206] he said. Within months, the Minister for Women would deride Fiji's violence against women as a 'national shame'.[207]

The event occurred about 18 or 19 months after the FWCC had released the findings of its national survey of violence against women and girls, which was conducted with the cooperation of the Fiji Islands Bureau of Statistics and paid for with Australian aid money, in the form of a 300+-page report called *Somebody's Life, Everybody's Business!* The survey was based on interviews conducted in 3,538 households, including 3,193 interviews with individual women.[208] It found that 64 per cent of the Fijian women surveyed who had at some time been in an intimate relationship ('ever-partnered women', as the report called them) had experienced sexual and/or physical violence by a husband or intimate partner,[209] a rate that is twice the global prevalence for physical and/or sexual abuse for ever-partnered women.[210] Moreover, 29 per cent of women were forced to have their first sexual experience.[211] Overall, 71 per cent of women had experienced physical and/or sexual violence at the hands of someone (partner or not) at some point in their life.[212] In fact, every day '43 women are injured, 1 is permanently

---

204 'FWRM pays tribute to former journalist and women human rights defender', 2015, *The Jet*, 9 April.
205 Reginald Chandar, 2015, 'Fiji Government has "zero tolerance" for domestic violence: PM', *Pacific Island Reports*, 29 April.
206 Ibid.
207 Niklas Pedersen, 2015, 'Fiji women's minister calls gender violence a "national shame"', *Pacific Island Reports*, 10 September.
208 FWCC, 2013, *Somebody's Life, Everybody's Business!*, p. 2.
209 Ibid.
210 Ibid., p. 3.
211 Ibid.
212 Ibid.

disabled, and 71 lose consciousness'.[213] The report noted that physical and/or sexual violence among *iTaukei* or Indigenous Fijians, the ethnic group treated in Newland's contribution to this volume, was almost twice as much as the physical and/or sexual violence among Indo-Fijian women.[214]

The senseless murder of Losana McGowan put an exclamation point on the survey's findings. Fiji could not rest on its laurels as the premier advocate for women's and children's rights in the western Pacific; there was more work to be done. In September 2015, the Ministry for Women announced that it was working towards strengthening its partnership with the police to enhance women's access to the state justice system.[215] This and other recent initiatives have been undertaken in the context of the Interagency Taskforce on Elimination of Violence Against Women (hereafter, EVAW taskforce), which was convened to support the two iterations of the Women's Plan of Action under the leadership of the Minister for Women. The EVAW taskforce pursues 'holistic' means to develop 'new strategies to eliminate violence against women and children'.[216] The EVAW taskforce convenes agents from government, civil society, faith-based organisations, multilateral organisations and the Australian Department of Foreign Affairs and Trade, a principal sponsor of women's rights initiatives in the western Pacific.[217] 'The taskforce is working collaboratively to have the best practice responses by police and other service providers when working with Domestic Violence Decree, Child Welfare Decree and other legislation that addresses crimes of violence and sexual violence against women and children. There is political will and a sense of urgency to protect the rights of women and children in Fiji.'[218] The first order of business for the EVAW taskforce would be to review the Zero Tolerance Violence Free Communities program.[219] In these and other ways, Fiji continues to exert regional leadership, developing human rights concepts, practices and institutions that neighbouring countries may well emulate.

---

213 Ibid., p. 4.
214 Ibid., p. 42, Figure 4.10.
215 Talebula Kate, 2015, 'Rethink on strategies to curb violence against women', *Fiji Times Online*, 14 September.
216 Ibid.
217 Ibid.
218 Fijian Government, 2015, 'EVAW taskforce to meet next week', 4 September.
219 Ibid.

Vanuatu

In Vanuatu, a sprawling Y-shaped archipelago lying southeast of the Solomon Islands, 'political and social life including gender roles and power relations between male and female are greatly influenced by traditional cultural attitudes and practices – kastom',[220] the Bislama word many translate as custom or culture even though it is 'not simply customary'[221] but a historical product that evokes 'not so much the totality of ancestral practices as a particular selection of such practices for the present'.[222] Some see *kastom* as superior to Western ways and resist change. But given 'the widespread open-mindedness of the chiefs and their willingness to embrace new ideas',[223] *kastom* is also open to change. This tension between resistance and openness to change governs the unfolding history of women's rights in Vanuatu. It is manifested most immediately in Vanuatu's two justice systems, discussed in the next section. This sets the stage for an examination of governmental and civil society efforts to realise constitutional guarantees of human rights and gender equality and the sometime opposition to these values. The final segment uses the 2011 survey conducted by the Vanuatu Women's Centre (VWC) to gauge the efficacy of these efforts. Just as the FWCC's *Somebody's Life, Everybody's Business!* provided a reality check for Fiji's women's rights advocates, the VWC's *Vanuatu National Survey on Women's Lives and Family Relationships* tells a dark story of progressive initiatives thwarted and of unmet rights-based goals.

220 Peggy Fairbairn-Dunlop, 2009, *Pacific Prevention of Domestic Violence Programme: Vanuatu Report*, prepared for the New Zealand Government, Wellington: Victoria University of Wellington, p. 18.
221 Lamont Lindstrom, 1997, 'Chiefs in Vanuatu today', in *Chiefs Today: Traditional Pacific Leadership and the Postcolonial State*, ed. Geoffrey M. White and Lamont Lindstrom, pp. 211–28, Stanford: Stanford University Press, p. 212.
222 Margaret Jolly, 1997, 'Woman–nation–state in Vanuatu: Women as signs and subjects in the discourses of *kastom*, modernity and Christianity', in *Narratives of Nation in the South Pacific*, ed. Ton Otto and Nicholas Thomas, pp. 133–62, Amsterdam: Harwood Academic Publishers, p. 139. See also discussion in Forsyth, *A Bird that Flies with Two Wings*, Chapter 3.
223 Forsyth, *A Bird that Flies with Two Wings*, p. 111.

The bird that flies with two wings

Vanuatu's Constitution proclaims all citizens to be 'entitled to … fundamental rights and freedoms of the individual without discrimination on the grounds of race, place of origin, religious or traditional beliefs, political opinions, language or sex',[224] and that among these 'fundamental rights and freedoms of the individual' are life, liberty, security of person, and protection of, and equal treatment from, the law.[225] Here, as in the constitutions of Papua New Guinea and Fiji, there is a strong flavour of 18th-century American and French revolutionary ideals.

But the Vanuatu Constitution also valorises *kastom*. 'Customary law shall continue to have effect as part of the law of the Republic of Vanuatu.'[226] If no 'rule of law' is applicable, then the court will decide the matter 'wherever possible in conformity with custom';[227] children are to be reared in such a way that they understand custom;[228] village and island courts will have 'jurisdiction over customary … matters and shall provide for the role of chiefs in such courts'.[229] To bolster *kastom* ideology and practice, the Vanuatu Constitution created the National Council of Chiefs (NCC) or Malvatumauri, a body composed of 'custom chiefs' elected by their peers and representing the various ethnic and linguistic groups of Vanuatu. The identity 'custom chief' (*kastom jif*), like *kastom* itself, is not 'simply customary'[230] but has been 'shaped by the events and interests of postcontact, colonial society'.[231] Nevertheless, the NCC is believed to have a 'general competence' in regard to 'all matters of tradition and custom and [makes] recommendations for the preservation and promotion of ni-Vanuatu culture and languages'.[232] In fact, the Vanuatu Parliament may consult with the NCC in regard to any bill under consideration,[233] softening any boundary between the two systems.

---

224 Constitution of the Republic of Vanuatu, Chapter 2, Part 1, article 5[1].
225 Ibid.
226 Ibid., Chapter 15, article 95[3].
227 Ibid., Chapter 8, article 47[1].
228 Ibid., Chapter 2, Part 2, article 7[h].
229 Ibid., Chapter 8, article 52.
230 Lindstrom, 'Chiefs in Vanuatu today', p. 212.
231 Ibid.
232 Constitution of the Republic of Vanuatu, Chapter 5, item 30[1].
233 Ibid., Chapter 5, item 30(2).

In actual practice, the two systems often compete for jurisdiction in criminal cases, all of which should be heard in state rather than *kastom* courts.[234] A recent gang rape allegation, made 34 years after Vanuatu achieved independence and the Constitution came into effect, helps make the point. Extramarital rape is a crime in Vanuatu, punishable by up to life imprisonment by state courts.[235] A 28-year-old woman from Tanna, an island in the southern part of the archipelago, alleged she was gang raped by six Tanna males. Although the crime was reported, the survivor and her chief each brought a letter to the prosecutor's office in May 2014 requesting that charges be dropped on the grounds that the assailants had been fined and had performed a *kastom* ceremony, paid a fine, and been beaten, albeit 'lightly', by men appointed by the chief to do so. The perpetrators had thus met the *kastom* conditions for a pardon and should not be punished twice, the survivor and her chief argued.[236] The prosecutors for the cases 'insisted' that the case was 'now a state case and not to be dealt with in a customary way'.[237] Jenny Ligo, a women's rights activist, vehemently protested against the plan to remove the case from the courts. 'It is totally degrading to the women of Vanuatu when you look at the records of the rape case, maltreatment to wives and young women ... that are either never properly addressed or simply ignored by male leaders in high positions of the government.'[238] Tanna chiefs themselves were divided. The victim's chief wanted the case dismissed, but the main chiefly body on Tanna (the Nikoletan Council of Chiefs) upheld the principle that 'the law of the nation'[239] should be applied. In fact the president of the Nikoletan Council of Chiefs averred that 'every criminal case needs to be dealt with in court not through custom'.[240] The jurisdiction of *kastom* courts is officially narrow: a matter of hearing cases involving theft, land and family disputes. Yet chiefs often do hear cases of incest and other kinds of sexual assault,[241] and not always with the rights

---

234 See discussion in Miranda Forsyth, 2004, 'Beyond case law: *Kastom* and courts in Vanuatu', *Victoria University of Wellington Law Review* 35(2): 427–46, pp. 434–35.

235 United States Department of State, 2013, '2012 Country Reports on Human Rights Practices—Vanuatu', 19 April.

236 'Vanuatu chief wants gang rape case dropped', 2014, *Radio New Zealand International*, 12 May.

237 Ibid.

238 'Women should protest, not celebrate', 2014, *Vanuatu Daily Post*, 16 May.

239 'Chiefs in Vanuatu's Tanna overrule colleague on rape charges', 2014, *Radio New Zealand International*, 19 May.

240 Ibid.

241 AusAID, *Violence Against Women in Melanesia and East Timor*, p. 177.

of the survivor in mind. Chiefs acting in *kastom* courts sometimes fine a raped girl 'for being in the wrong place or even make the girl marry the rapist',[242] as one ni-Vanuatu women's rights activist put it.

As with Fiji's *bulubulu* reconciliation practices as described in Newland's contribution to this volume, the Vanuatu *kastom* system has been 'focused on peace and harmony in the community rather than on individual justice'.[243] It is not unheard of that a chiefly court will make a woman return to an abusive husband 'for the sake of community stability'.[244] Moreover, women feel disadvantaged in *kastom* hearings,[245] which typically take place in village *nakamals*— meetings from which women are typically excluded, and presided over by village chiefs, who are male.[246]

Dislodging the authority of *kastom* in the arena of gender violence has proved difficult. Merrin Mason worked for the Vanuatu Women's Centre (VWC) for 18 months in 1995 and 1996, providing legal advice to women who were victims of domestic violence. In that period, domestic violence perpetrators were not pursued in the state courts because, Mason suggests, judicial officers and police alike[247] saw themselves as mediators, seeking a reconciliation between husband and wife and exhorting female victims to return to their husbands instead of pressing charges and sending perpetrators to jail.[248] Besides, getting women to press charges has proven difficult as wives fear being embarrassed and what vengeful spouses and their kin might do to retaliate if they go to the police.

Contemporary constructions of gender underwrite gender inequality, despite the Vanuatu Constitution. Grace Molisa, a well-known ni-Vanuatu leader who died in 2002, once observed that 'a female of the human species in Vanuatu traditional society is viewed as secondary and inferior to men. In childhood, a boy is allowed to assert himself,

---

242 Ibid.
243 Forsyth, *A Bird that Flies with Two Wings*, p. xviii; see also Fairbairn-Dunlop, *Pacific Prevention of Domestic Violence Programme: Vanuatu Report*, p. 21.
244 Forsyth, *A Bird that Flies with Two Wings*, p. 109.
245 AusAID, *Violence Against Women in Melanesia and East Timor*, p. 176.
246 Ibid.
247 Merrin Mason, 2000, 'Domestic violence in Vanuatu', in *Reflections on Violence in Melanesia*, ed. Sinclair Dinnen and Allison Ley, pp. 119–38, Annandale, NSW: Hawkins Press; Canberra: Asia Pacific Press, p. 119.
248 Ibid., p. 130.

while a girl is continuously taught subservience'.[249] The exchange of customary valuables upon marriage, at least in some parts of the archipelago, is sufficient to place a wife under her husband's supervision and control,[250] and husbands sometimes justify domestic violence on the grounds that they have given bridewealth.[251] Indeed, the customary view tolerates domestic violence, which many find 'an acceptable aspect of marriage or cohabitation'.[252] This, according to Mason, 'is not a fringe or extreme position in Vanuatu. Public figures often make statements excusing men's violence and asserting men's right to dominance in Vanuatu society.'[253] In fact, 'violence against Women … is often justified as a part of kastom'.[254] Nevertheless, females no less than males often prefer chiefly mediation to the foreign standards and procedures of the formal judicial system.[255] Chiefly reconciliation practices do what many want: mend rather than further strain relationships, and restoring peace is what chiefly courts promise and plaintiffs and defendants often seek. And so, chiefly courts, not state courts, tend to handle most disputes.[256] And so the 'strictures of *kastom* permeate all aspects of society, and customary practices and rules decreed by local chiefs, or by the national Malvatumauri Council of Chiefs, have the status of law, particularly in rural areas'.[257] Little wonder that it took the Vanuatu Government a long time to

---

249 Quoted in CEDAW Committee, 2004, 'Consideration of reports submitted by States parties under Article 18 of the Convention on the Elimination of All Forms of Discrimination against Women. Combined initial, second and third periodic reports of States parties, Vanuatu', CEDAW/C/VUT/1-3, p. 26, item 53.

250 Whether this is true everywhere, and to the same degree, are empirical questions. Based on what seems to have been fieldwork in the 1990s, Bronwen Douglas comments that gender relations in Aneityum, the southernmost island in the archipelago, are 'mostly benign'. Bronwen Douglas, 1998, 'Traditional individuals? Gendered negotiations of identity, Christianity and citizenship in Vanuatu', State, Society and Governance in Melanesia, Research School of Pacific and Asian Studies, Discussion papers 98/6, Canberra: The Australian National University. Roselyn Tor and Anthea Teka make it clear that there is no such thing as *kastom blong Vanuatu* (a culture that is uniform throughout Vanuatu) because of the archipelago's cultural diversity. See Roselyn Tor and Anthea Teka, 2004, *Gender, Kastom & Domestic Violence: A Research on the Historical Trend, Extent and Impact of Domestic Violence in Vanuatu*, Port Vila: Department of Women's Affairs, p. 18.

251 Tor and Teka, *Gender, Kastom & Domestic Violence*, p. 31.

252 Mason, 'Domestic violence in Vanuatu', p. 119.

253 Ibid.

254 AusAID, *Violence Against Women in Melanesia and East Timor*, p. 172.

255 Forsyth, *A Bird that Flies on Two Wings*, pp. 140–41.

256 Ibid., p. 97.

257 AusAID, *Violence Against Women in Melanesia and East Timor*, p. 172.

ratify CEDAW. 'Successive governments' dragged their feet, male politicians citing 'ancestral values or *kastom*' as the source of their reservations.[258]

Institution building

Despite the continuing authority of *kastom*, both the Vanuatu Government and Vanuatu civil society have developed institutions supportive of women's rights.

In 1980, the Vanuatu Government established what would become the Department of Women's Affairs (DWA) 'to monitor the government's decisions on issues concerning women and … advocate for women to have improved access to justice, health services and literacy'.[259] In 2004, the DWA was tasked 'to "implement" CEDAW, presumably as a result of … slow progress'.[260] In that capacity, the DWA is 'the lead government agency in gender equity, domestic violence and other CEDAW related issues'.[261] In 2009 a Child Desk Office was placed in the Ministry of Justice and Community Services to implement the CRC, which Vanuatu had ratified in 1992.[262]

Vanuatu civil society has arguably been more robust than the Vanuatu Government in developing institutions and programs supportive of women and children and their rights. The Vanuatu National Council of Women (VNCW), a civil society NGO, was founded just before independence in 1980 'to provide a forum for women's issues, to serve in an advisory capacity to Government on women's issues and to provide specific services for women'.[263] Area councils have been established throughout the archipelago, with VNCW representatives in all six provinces as well as in Port Vila and Luganville.[264]

---

258 Margaret Jolly, '*Woman ikat raet long human raet o no*? Women's rights, human rights and domestic violence in Vanuatu', *Feminist Review* 52: 169–90, p. 180.

259 DWA, 'Focus: Department of Women's Affairs'.

260 CEDAW Committee, 'Consideration of reports submitted by States parties under Article 18 of the Convention on the Elimination of All Forms of Discrimination against Women, Combined initial, second and third periodic reports of States parties, Vanuatu', 2004, CEDAW/C/VUT/1-3, p. 32, item 62.

261 Fairbairn-Dunlop, *Pacific Prevention of Domestic Violence Programme*, p. 44.

262 Ministry of Justice and Community Services, 'Child Desk Office'.

263 Tor and Teka, *Gender, Kastom & Domestic Violence*, p. 57.

264 Ibid., p. 61.

Vanuatu's most important civil society organisation dedicated to women's rights is the Vanuatu Women's Centre (VWC), established in 1992. The VWC participates in the rights-based trainings offered by the Fiji Women's Crisis Centre (FWCC), which serves in a managerial capacity vis-à-vis the VWC,[265] training most VWC staff. Headquartered in Port Vila, the VWC has three branches that are supported with Australian funding. They are (in the order of their founding) the Sanma Counselling Centre on Santo Island in Sanma Province; the Tafea Counselling Centre on Tanna Island in Tafea Province; and, the last to be opened, the Torba Counselling Centre on Vanua Lava Island in Torba Province.[266] The purpose of these branches is substantially the same as that of the Port Vila parent organisation: to counsel children and women who are the victims of violence, to conduct awareness campaigns and community education concerning women's and children's rights, and to educate survivors in their legal rights and how to exercise them.

Committees Against Violence Against Women

The VWC's signature creation is the community-based Committee Against Violence Against Women (CAVAW), the members of which 'receive training in legal literacy and counselling skills and are available to provide support to community women suffering domestic abuse or sexual assault'.[267] CAVAWs are similar to the 'gatekeeper communities' the FWCC deploys in its Zero Tolerance Violence Free Campaign. Locally prominent men and women sit on the CAVAWs and are trained by the staff of the VWC in basic counselling skills, community education and human rights. The number of CAVAWs has mushroomed. In 2010, 35 CAVAWs were distributed throughout Vanuatu's six provinces.[268] By 2013, this number had grown to forty-one.[269] Although community based, CAVAWs operate with respect to the entire VWC network, referring serious cases to VWC branches and to VWC headquarters in Port Vila, as well as to the Vanuatu police,

---

265 Sue Finucane and Roselyn Tor, 2010, 'Mid term review of the Vanuatu Women's Centre phase 5, July 2007 – June 2012, final report', 30 April, p. 5.
266 'About', Vanuatu Women's Centre website.
267 AusAID, *Violence Against women in Melanesia and East Timor*, p. 179.
268 Finucane and Tor, 'Mid term review of the Vanuatu Women's Centre', p. 10.
269 'Australia increases support for Vanuatu Women's Center', 2013, *Pacific Islands Report*, 20 February.

who also participate in CAVAWs.[270] Through this referral system, the CAVAWs participate in district and national law and justice networks. At the same time, as members of *local* committees, CAVAW personnel provide 'a local contact so that victims can make an initial approach to a trusted community member'.[271] CAVAWs appear to be especially effective with respect to sexual assault. 'The girls and young women who have been sexually assaulted have placed enough trust in the CAVAWs to come forward and seek assistance.'[272]

Dovetailing with the CAVAWs, the VWC's 'Male Advocates Programme' trains men who are already in leadership positions (chiefs, police officers, religious and other community leaders) in women's rights and rights-based advocacy. The program emulates the FWCC's training of male advocates in requiring that advocates address their own violent behaviour. Many male advocates also participate in CAVAWs.[273] Taken together, the Male Advocates Programme and the CAVAWs 'have greatly increased women's access to support and justice, particularly in rural areas where there are few other services'.[274] The males serving on CAVAWs set a standard of male conduct that other men find difficult to ignore. As one leader of a CAVAW observed in 2002, 'Men are beginning to respect their wives because there is now a body in place that will support the women and punish the men for mistreating them'.[275] Testimonies to the effectiveness of the training that male advocates receive abound in the literature. Sgt Davis Saravanu, who is in charge of the Port Vila Family Protection Unit soon to be described, vouched for the quality of the training he had received in a speech he made at a 2013 celebration of International Women's Day at the UN. 'I am a [ni-Vanuatu] Male Advocate for ending violence against women and girls. ... I didn't used to be like this before I became a Male Advocate, I had a terrible attitude towards victims and did not see the importance or need to go out of my way to help them.'[276] Collaborating with Vanuatu chiefs, some of whom have become male advocates, has proved important to this initiative. One female CAVAW

270 Fairbairn-Dunlop, *Pacific Prevention of Domestic Violence Programme: Vanuatu Report*, p. 33.
271 Finucane and Tor, 'Mid term review of the Vanuatu Women's Centre', p. 26.
272 Ibid., p. 23.
273 AusAID, *Violence Against Women in Melanesia and East Timor*, p. 180.
274 Ibid.
275 Ibid., p. 179.
276 Dorosday Kenneth, Vola Mata and Davis Saravanu, n.d., 'Vanuatu', Pacific Islands Forum Secretariat, p. 3.

leader in West Vanua Lava reached an agreement with the local chief that 'if a husband repeats violence after a report was brought to the attention of the chief, the chief will allow the CAVAW to help the wife file charges with the police',[277] thus transferring the case from chiefly to state courts.[278]

Through CAVAWs and male advocates, the international human rights regime reaches deep into Vanuatu's rural areas, where 80 per cent of the Vanuatu population lives and where *kastom* still holds sway. A 2010 review of the VWC praised the VWC for all it had accomplished since its founding in 1992.[279] It concluded that there was 'widespread support'[280] for the VWC's program against violence against women and observed that VWC initiatives had at times 'resulted in emergent gender equality and transformed gender relations in some areas'.[281] With its archipelago-wide network and its linkages to the FWCC, the VWC constitutes a subversive tool for undermining patriarchal aspects, if not character, of Vanuatu *kastom*. And yet, as the opposition to the passage of the Family Protection Act of 2008 discussed in the next section makes clear, patriarchal norms persist, despite the efforts of the VWC.

The Vanuatu Family Protection Act

The most significant piece of legislation in recent years has been Vanuatu's Family Protection Act (FPA) of 2008, which criminalised domestic violence, strategically widening the jurisdiction of the state justice system. The bill was first drafted in 1997[282] but, despite vigorous advocacy by the VWC and the Department of Women's Affairs, was opposed by the NCC and religious groups, 'who argued that it would erode the authority of chiefs in *kastom* courts and promote the breakdown of families'.[283] 'Based on traditional values of Vanuatu and

---

277 AusAID, *Violence Against Women in Melanesia and East Timor*, p. 179.
278 Miranda Forsyth points out that transferring cases from chiefly or informal courts to state courts may be difficult as 'the state system is often inaccessible for victims of domestic violence for a variety of reasons (geographic, financial etc.) and often the police will just send the case back to the chiefs as they see it as a family issue'. Email message to author, 28 July 2014.
279 Finucane and Tor, 'Mid term review of the Vanuatu Women's Centre', p. 5.
280 Ibid., p. 6.
281 Ibid.
282 AusAID, *Violence Against Women in Melanesia and East Timor*, p. 173.
283 Ibid.

on Christian principles',[284] the Act mandated that police investigate anyone the officer has good reason to believe has committed domestic violence and charge the person if the investigation substantiated the accusation.[285] Offenders could face prison terms of up to five years or a fine of up to 100,000 vatu (about $US890) or both.[286] If an offender gave bridewealth, this could not be used as a justification for his wife bashing.[287] Also, and very much like PNG's FPA, if a defendant is found guilty of domestic violence or if a spouse is judged likely to engage in domestic violence, a Family Protection Order (FPO) can be issued against the offender to safeguard family members.[288] Anyone who violates an FPO will be imprisoned for up to two years or required to pay a fine not to exceed 50,000 vatu (about $US445) or both.[289] This is again regardless of whether the person against whom the FPO is issued paid bridewealth to the victim and her family.[290]

Although the bill claimed to be based on Christian values and traditional principles, it was opposed, as said, by the pro-*kastom* NCC, which unanimously argued that it was 'a Western bill and did not suite [*sic*] Vanuatu Society [emphasis removed]'.[291] Some saw it as a 'Women's Rights Movement charade designed to grant women more power to destabilise the status quo in Melanesian society'.[292] After parliament passed the bill, the Vanuatu Christian Council challenged the bill on the grounds that it was unconstitutional, but the Vanuatu Supreme Court determined that the bill was constitutional,[293] making it the law of the land.

A striking example of insurgency against the bill is the backlash movement that John Taylor, one of the contributors to this volume, has described elsewhere: the Violence Against Men (VAM) movement of Luganville mentioned in the introduction to this volume.[294] In 2005,

---

284 Republic of Vanuatu, 2008, Family Protection Act, item 1(2).
285 Ibid., item 44.
286 Ibid., item 10(1).
287 Ibid., item 10(2).
288 Ibid., item 11(1).
289 Ibid., item 21(1).
290 Ibid., item 21(2).
291 Fairbairn-Dunlop, *Pacific Prevention of Domestic Violence Programme: Vanuatu Report*, p. 23.
292 *The Ni Vanuatu*, 26 August 2004, quoted in Fairbairn-Dunlop, *Pacific Prevention of Domestic Violence Programme: Vanuatu Report*, p. 23.
293 AusAID, *Stop Violence*, p. 93.
294 John P. Taylor, 2008, 'The social life of rights: "Gender antagonism", modernity and *raet* in Vanuatu', *The Australian Journal of Anthropology* 19(2): 165–87.

during Taylor's extended fieldwork in Vanuatu, some Luganvillean men denounced human rights as a foreign, neocolonial and anti-male discourse,[295] embracing *kastom* and Christianity for their perceived benign hierarchical and patriarchal values instead. The movement crystallised very much in the context of the Family Protection Bill and the rights-based measures taken by the Vanuatu Government to compensate for the protracted delay in its passage. The VAM movement opposed these measures, the Family Protection Bill itself, and women's rights more generally. The backlash nature of the movement is clear from its purposes, which included to 'protect married men whose wives don't respect their married lives' and to 'make sure that men are always the head of the family'.[296] Taylor argues that the movement was attractive to those ni-Vanuatu who believed that women's rights were 'unrealistic and unsuited to both the *kastom* and Christian values and life-ways' of '"ordinary" "ni-Vanuatu grassroots" people'.[297] Participants particularly objected to the fact that the bill brought domestic violence, which VAM members considered a private matter, within the purview of the state justice system.

Given the level of controversy the bill inspired before and after its passage, just how effective has the FPA been? While support for and knowledge of the FPA was relatively high within VWC networks, outside those networks the law has remained controversial and, like PNG's FPA, has lacked implementation. Reporting six months after the passage of the act, Peggy Fairbairn-Dunlop of Auckland University of Technology noted that even in Port Vila, the national capital and headquarters of the VWC, there was still 'considerable controversy about … whether domestic violence should be addressed within a family focussed or a rights based framework',[298] reflective of what she described as 'a fierce ambivalence as to whether domestic violence is a family or a legal issue',[299] fuelled in part by the constitutional recognition of customary law.[300] Abused women themselves continued to seek out reconciliation through local chiefs rather than filing a complaint with the police or state courts. Nor were the police on board. In fact, the ones who Fairbairn-Dunlop interviewed 'believed

295 Ibid., p. 167.
296 Ibid., p. 168.
297 Ibid., p. 169.
298 Fairbairn-Dunlop, *Pacific Prevention of Domestic Violence Programme: Vanuatu Report*, p. 15.
299 Ibid., p. 22.
300 Ibid., p. 40.

domestic violence should be dealt with within the family, village or church and in the customary way',[301] not through the state system of justice, to which women living in rural areas had little access anyway. Two years after Fairbairn-Dunlop's study, an article in the *Vanuatu Daily Post* noted that the FPA was not being used outside Port Vila because people did not know about it and because ni-Vanuatu preferred informal *(kastom)* to formal modes of conflict resolution where domestic violence was concerned.[302] Practically speaking, there is no viable nationwide alternative to informal systems of justice in domestic violence cases because the Vanuatu Police Force is insufficiently equipped to deal with it, especially in rural areas.

Family Protection Unit

In late 2010, the police opened the first Family Protection Unit (FPU) in Port Vila.[303] The initiative was developed in collaboration with the VWC, the Australian Federal Police and the New Zealand Police, among other law enforcement bodies. The Port Vila FPU has an officer-in-charge, the aforementioned male advocate Sgt Davis Saranavu, and six police officers working under him, and it operates five days a week from 7:30 a.m. to 4:30 p.m.[304] The FPU targets domestic and sexual violence, and is housed with the Vanuatu Police Force,[305] allowing 'a victim or a potential victim to feel safe with the official support' of the police.[306] In this way, and like PNG's FSVUs and Fiji's SOUs, Vanuatu's FPUs involve police and the state justice system, of which they are a part, in domestic violence proceedings. As of 2014, there were FPUs in four of six Vanuatu provinces.[307]

---

301 Ibid.

302 'Impacts of the Family Protection Act', 2011, *Vanuatu Daily Post*, 16 September.

303 Tom Schermer, 2010, 'Police open "Family Protection Unit"', *Vanuatu Daily Post*, 26 November.

304 Ibid.

305 United Nations General Assembly, 2014, 'Report of the working group on the Universal Periodic Review: Vanuatu', 4 April, A/HRC/26/9, item 15.

306 Schermer, 'Police open "Family Protection Unit"'.

307 UNGA, 'Report of the working group on the Universal Periodic Review: Vanuatu', A/HRC/26/9, item 15.

The VWC national survey of 2011

In 2011, the year that Fiji undertook the survey reported in *Somebody's Life, Everybody's Business!* the VWC, in partnership with the Vanuatu National Statistics Office, conducted a systematic survey of gender violence in Vanuatu, targeting all six provinces. The survey utilised two questionnaires—one for the household and one for individual women—which, like the 2011 FWCC survey, were adapted from the *WHO Multi-country Study on Women's Health and Domestic Violence against Women.*[308] The study covered several islands in each of Vanuatu's six provinces and 3,619 randomly chosen households.[309]

The devastating findings were reported in the *Vanuatu National Survey on Women's Lives and Family Relationships.* Concerning women, 'There are very high rates of all forms of violence against women across all provinces, islands, age groups, education levels, and religions'.[310] 'The prevalence of intimate partner violence in Vanuatu is among the highest in the world ... For most women who experience physical or sexual violence, it occurs frequently, and it is often very severe.'[311] Non-partner violence is also high. 'Almost half of the women interviewed had experienced non-partner physical or sexual violence or both since they turned 15.'[312] The statistics on the sexual abuse of girls are no less startling. 'The prevalence of sexual abuse of girls under the age of 15 is also one of the very highest in the world. Almost 1 in 3 women were sexually abused before the age of 15 years';[313] 54 per cent of these had been abused 'many times.'[314] Incest was also a factor. With respect to girls under 15 who had been sexually abused, the majority of perpetrators were either male family members or boyfriends.[315]

As elsewhere in the western Pacific, many ni-Vanuatu women acquiesce in intimate partner violence. 'The use of violence as a form of punishment and discipline is accepted as a normal part of behaviour within many families and communities ... some women say that they

---

308 VWC, 2011, *Vanuatu National Survey on Women's Lives and Family Relationships*, p. 14.
309 Ibid.
310 Ibid., p. 55.
311 Ibid., p. 181.
312 Ibid., pp. 181, 95.
313 Ibid., p. 181. See also Table 5.5, p. 100.
314 Ibid., p. 104, Table 5.9.
315 Ibid., pp. 181–82.

have not sought help because the violence was "normal".'[316] Sixty per cent of all respondents agreed with one or more of the stock justifications for intimate partner violence,[317] such as disobedient women should be disciplined, the wife was infertile, the wife refused intercourse, the wife was unfaithful, and bridewealth had been paid.[318] Despite the fact that the FPA explicitly precludes using payment of bridewealth as a justification for domestic violence, 32 per cent of the women interviewed believed that men's payment of bridewealth justified wife bashing.[319]

Conclusion

The trajectory in these three histories is frustratingly non-linear. What is worked out textually, in law, lacks implementation. It is easy to be pessimistic—to conclude, for example, that nothing much has changed in the western Pacific since the Beijing 'Platform for Action' of 1995 and that significant change is unlikely, since reducing gender violence would require that men relinquish the power they have long cultivated and safeguarded. Some progress has clearly been made, however, especially in Fiji and Vanuatu, where communities are participating in national initiatives that are themselves embedded in the initiatives of the international human rights regime described in the introduction and that are designed to decrease gender violence. Although the FWCC survey, conducted in 2011 and reported in *Somebody's Life, Everybody's Business!*, found evidence of a 'shocking' level of violence against women and children, it also noted that, because of the women's movement, 'attitudes to this problem are changing … there is now considerable support within the community in favour of women's rights and opposition to the use of violence'.[320] Moreover, 'younger women are less likely than older women to agree with statements that negate women's rights',[321] suggesting a generational rift that augurs well for the advancement of women's rights. Even in PNG, institutions and laws (however imperfectly implemented) have been put in place to

---

316 Ibid., p. 182.
317 Ibid., p. 80.
318 Ibid., pp. 80–82.
319 Ibid., p. 55.
320 FWCC, *Somebody's Life, Everybody's Business!*, p. 146.
321 Ibid., p. 151.

combat gender violence, and community-based activism now emerges as a key factor in the protection of women and girls and the pursuit of their rights.

It is often said that one of the more devastating consequences of the rapid change to which PNG, Fiji and Vanuatu have been subjected in recent decades is the loss of the authority of older, married men, who in the past had exercised power over and monitored and regulated the behaviour of boys and young men. Fiji's gatekeeper committees, Vanuatu's CAVAWs, and the male advocate programs in all three countries create spaces within which the authority of older, married males can be reasserted vis-à-vis those actors—typically male youth—whom village moral majorities denounce for their deviation from local norms. The men involved in Fiji's gatekeeper committees and Vanuatu's CAVAWs are doubly beholden: to the human rights principles they have been trained to promote but also to communal standards of decency (a point that is not often made). Such committees, along with the male advocates who sometimes serve on these committees, help constitute the interstitial element so crucial to the 'vernacularization' of human rights doctrine, according to Merry.[322] In this, they are far more than a conduit of exogenous norms, importing human rights principles across cultural borders. They are active synthesisers of local and international norms. The result is not 'pure' human rights principles but a viable merger of 'local structures' and norms with 'imported ideas such as women's human rights'.[323] The *inter*normative, *inter*cultural spaces these actors occupy are spaces of global Northern–Southern engagement, through which hybrid principles and practices are spawned.

This blending of normative systems can be seen in the collaborations between the Vanuatu chief and the female head of his village's CAVAW alluded to earlier. The two agreed 'that if a husband repeats violence after a report [of domestic violence] was brought to the attention of the chief, the chief will allow the CAVAW to help the wife file charges with the police'.[324] In this way, given circumstances the chief and the head of the village CAVAW have themselves stipulated, the machinery

---

322 Sally Engle Merry, 2006, 'Transnational human rights and local activism: Mapping the middle', in *Anthropology and Human Rights in a New Key*, ed. Mark Goodale, *American Anthropologist* 108(1): 38–51.
323 Ibid., p. 48.
324 AusAID, *Violence Against Women in Melanesia and East Timor*, p. 179.

of 'reconciliation' is brought to bear upon the first offence (albeit in contravention of national law) but scuttled with the second offence, which will be referred to the state justice system, with its harsh penalties. National law is honoured in the long but not in the short run, which belongs instead to customary practices and values. In effect, Vanuatu's CAVAWs are key nodes in a complex social justice network through which international and national laws are brought into dialogue with *kastom* and made to mesh in ways place-based actors decide are practical and just.

Such practices do not result in a 'hypodermic'-style transfer of ideology[325] but, rather, in 'customization on the part of the receiving subject'.[326] This customisation has been ongoing for decades, as Daniel Evans, Michael Goddard and Don Paterson make clear in their recent discussion of the 'hybrid' courts of Melanesia: courts that 'manage a fruitful compromise between the introduced law and customary systems, and between the individual rights-oriented justice of Western societies and the sociocentric orientation of traditional notions of dispute settlement'.[327] The 'custom' honoured in such courts is an '"adapted" form of custom',[328] reflecting 'the presence and importance of influential local mores'[329] among western Pacific peoples but also 'intermingled with Western processes and procedures'.[330] If this is

---

325 Inda and Rosaldo, 'Tracking global flows', p. 20.

326 Ibid.

327 Daniel Evans, Michael Goddard with Don Paterson, 2010, 'The hybrid courts of Melanesia: A comparative analysis of Village Courts of Papua New Guinea, Island Courts of Vanuatu and Local Courts of Solomon Islands', Justice and Development working paper series, 13/2010, p. 2.

328 Ibid., p. 18.

329 Ibid.

330 Ibid., p. 17. Such hybridisations involve 'legal pluralism'. See Evans, Goddard and Paterson, 'The hybrid courts of Melanesia', p. 2. The larger project is then to study the contexts within which such pluralistic systems emerge and the principles and practices undergirding their functionality and/or dysfunctionality. See Jonathan Aleck, 1986, 'Law reform as development policy: Customary law and the modern legal system in Papua New Guinea', MA thesis, Department of Political Science, University of Oregon; Jonathan Aleck and Jackson Rannells (eds), 1995, *Custom at the Cross-Roads: The Future of Customary Law in Papua New Guinea*, Port Moresby: University of Papua New Guinea; Forsyth, *A Bird that Flies with Two Wings*; Sally Engle Merry, 1988, 'Legal pluralism', *Law and Society Review* 22(5): 869–96.

true, then human rights doctrine does indeed have a 'social life'[331] as it enters various indigenous discursive and sociopolitical fields and engages in transcultural dialogue with its other.[332]

Here, then, is fertile empirical and interpretive terrain wherein social scientists may enquire into how conflicting legal and moral systems do or do not find common ground.[333] Who are the key agents in this process, who are their opponents, and what are the varying perspectives of the contending parties? How are human rights doctrines 'mobilized, vernacularized, resisted, reinterpreted … transformed',[334] and by whom and for what reasons? While crucial to our understanding of the complexity, pragmatics, cultural politics and semantics of human rights work in the Pacific, such investigations would also provide a nuanced, on-the-ground understanding of the cultural and historical specificities of the dynamics of globalisation, together with the corollary of those dynamics: despite claims of universality, an inevitable proliferation of difference.

Acknowledgements

I would like to thank Jonathan Aleck, Christine Bradley, Miranda Forsyth, Margaret Jolly, Dan Jorgensen, Kathy Lepani, Martha Macintyre, Signe Poulsen, Howard Van Trease and Richard Eves for the information, writings, and/or critiques they shared with me in the course of writing this chapter.

---

331 Richard Ashby Wilson and Jon P. Mitchell, 2003, 'Introduction: The social life of rights', in *Human Rights in Global Perspective*, ed. Wilson and Mitchell, pp. 1–15, London: Routledge. See also Richard A. Wilson, 2006, 'Afterword to "Anthropology and human rights in a new key": The social life of human rights', ed. Mark Goodale, *American Anthropologist* 108(1): 77–83.

332 Jane Cowan, Marie-Bénédicte Dembour and Richard A. Wilson, 2001, 'Introduction', in *Culture and Rights: Anthropological Perspectives*, ed. Jane Cowan, Marie-Bénédicte Dembour and Richard A. Wilson, pp. 1–26. Cambridge and New York: Cambridge University Press.

333 See Aletta Biersack and Martha Macintyre, 'Introduction: Gender violence and human rights in the western Pacific', this volume.

334 Jane K. Cowan, 2006, 'Culture and rights after *Culture and Rights*', *American Anthropologist* 108(1): 9–24, p. 9.

References

Aisi, Robert G. 2013. *Statement BY H.E. Mr Robert G. Aisi Permanent Representative of Papua New Guinea to the United Nations at the Fifty-Seventh Session of the Commission on the Status of Women.* New York, 11 March. Online: www.un.org/womenwatch/daw/csw/csw57/generaldiscussion/memberstates/png.pdf (accessed 11 December 2015).

Aleck, Jonathan. 1986. 'Law reform as development policy: Customary law and the modern legal system in Papua New Guinea'. MA thesis, Department of Political Science, University of Oregon.

Aleck, Jonathan and Jackson Rannells (eds). 1995. *Custom at the Cross-Roads: The Future of Customary Law in Papua New Guinea.* Port Moresby: University of Papua New Guinea.

Amnesty International. 2006. 'Papua New Guinea: Women human rights defenders in action'. Online: www.refworld.org/docid/4517a2ff4.html (accessed 28 November 2015).

——. 2006. 'Papua New Guinea: Violence against women: Not inevitable, never acceptable!' Online: www.refworld.org/docid/4517a4184.html (accessed 27 November 2015).

——. 2009. 'Papua New Guinea: Briefing to the UN Committee on the Elimination of Discrimination Against Women: Violence Against Women'. Online: www.amnesty.org/en/library/info/ASA34/002/2009/en (accessed 12 December 2015).

——. 2011. 'Papua New Guinea: Violence against women, sorcery-related killings, and forced evictions'. AI submission to the UN Universal Periodic Review. Online: www.amnesty-frauen.de/Main/Papua-Neuguinea?action=download&upname=asa340052010en.pdf (accessed 27 November 2015).

——. 2013. 'Good news: Family protection laws passed in PNG', 26 September. Online: www.amnesty.org.au/features/comments/32844 (accessed 28 November 2015).

——. 2013. 'Papua New Guinea must end "sorcery" killings and harassment', 8 February. Online: www.amnestyusa.org/news/press-releases/papua-new-guinea-must-end-sorcery-killings-and-harassment (accessed 13 December 2015).

Appadurai, Arjun. 1996. *Modernity at Large: Cultural Dimensions of Globalization*. Minneapolis: University of Minnesota Press.

AusAID. 2008. *Violence Against Women in Melanesia and East Timor: Building on Global and Regional Promising Approaches*. Report prepared by the Office of Development Effectiveness. Online: www.pacificwomen.org/wp-content/uploads/vaw_cs_full_report1.pdf (accessed 3 February 2016).

——. 2009. *Stop Violence: Responding to Violence Against Women in Melanesia and East Timor*. Online: dfat.gov.au/about-us/publications/Pages/stop-violence-responding-to-violence-against-women-in-melanesia-and-east-timor.aspx (accessed 20 December 2015).

——. 2015. *Evaluation of the RPNGC Family and Sexual Violence Units*, 31 December. Online: dfat.gov.au/about-us/publications/Documents/png-family-sexual-violence-units-evaluation.pdf (accessed 24 April 2016).

'Australia increases support for Vanuatu Women's Center'. 2013. *Pacific Islands Report*, 20 February. Online: pidp.eastwestcenter.org/pireport/2013/February/02-21-16.htm (accessed 5 December 2015).

Australian Centre for Leadership for Women. 2012. 'Nazhat Shameem', 1 June. Online: www.leadershipforwomen.com.au/empowerment/leadership/nazhat (accessed 26 December 2015).

Australian High Commission, PNG. 2014. 'Ambassador opens Family and Sexual Violence Unit in Boroko', 8 April. Online: www.png.embassy.gov.au/pmsb/235.html (accessed 13 December 2015).

Barlow, Karen. 2013. 'Fears sorcery-killings may be spreading from PNG'. ABC Radio Australia, 5 June. Online: www.radioaustralia.net.au/international/2013-06-05/fears-sorcerykillings-may-be-spreading-from-png/1141104 (accessed 27 November 2015).

Betteridge, Ashlee and Kamalini Lokuge. 2014. 'Combatting the family and sexual violence epidemic in Papua New Guinea'. *Devpolicy blog*. Development Policy Centre, 30 June. Online: devpolicy. org/in-brief/combatting-the-family-and-sexual-violence-epidemic-in-png-a-submission-to-the-joint-standing-committee-inquiry-20140630/ (accessed 13 December 2015).

Blackwell, Eoin. 2013. 'PNG govt backs domestic violence laws'. *The Australian*, News, 2 April. Online: www.theaustralian.com.au/news/latest-news/png-govt-backs-domestic-violence-law/story-fn3dxix6-1226611122873 (accessed 13 December 2015).

——. 2013. 'PNG says sorry for violence against women'. *Sydney Morning Herald*, 15 May. Online: news.smh.com.au/breaking-news-world/png-says-sorry-for-violence-against-women-20130515-2jmj9.html (accessed 13 December 2015).

Bomai, Simon. 2015. 'NEC endorsement of the PNG national Lukautim Pikinini Bill'. Ministry of Community Development, Religion and Youth, 24 May. Online: ministryofcomdev.blogspot.com/2015_05_01_archive.html (accessed 11 December 2015).

Bradley, Christine with Jane Kesno. 2001. *Family and Sexual Violence in PNG: An Integrated Long-Term Strategy*. Port Moresby: Institute of National Affairs. Online: www.popline.org/node/265152 (accessed 11 December 2014).

Chandar, Reginald. 2015. 'Fiji Government has "zero tolerance" for domestic violence: PM'. *Pacific Island Reports*, 29 April. Online: pidp.eastwestcenter.org/pireport/2015/April/04-30-07.htm (accessed 2 December 2015).

Chandler, Jo. 2014. 'Violence against women in PNG: How men are getting away with murder'. Lowy Institute for International Policy, 29 August. Online: www.lowyinstitute.org/files/violence_against_women_in_png.pdf (accessed 26 November 2015).

Chaudary, Felix. 2015. 'Call for commitment'. *Fiji Times Online*, 23 March. Online: www.fijitimes.com/story.aspx?ref=archive&id=299126 (accessed 2 December 2015).

'Chiefs in Vanuatu's Tanna overrule colleague on rape charges'. 2014. *Radio New Zealand International*, 19 May. Online: www.radionz. co.nz/international/pacific-news/244808/chiefs-in-vanuatu% 27s-tanna-overrule-colleague-on-rape-charge (accessed 2 December 2015).

Consultative Implementation and Monitoring Council (CIMC)/Family and Sexual Violence Action Committee (FSVAC). 2008. Online: 10toeacontribution.wordpress.com/2013/04/05/what-is-family-sexual-violence-action-committee-fsvac/ (accessed 16 November 2016).

———. 2014. 'Final Stage for male advocacy training—Fiji'. *Hadibaiatok* vol. 1, January–June, p. 5.

———. n.d. 'Rape, incest, child abuse: The PNG laws have changed!!!' Online: www.inapng.com/cimc/pdf_files/LEGAL%20 REFORM%20BROCHURE.pdf (site discontinued).

Coutts, Geraldine. 2012. 'Fiji women's minister defends domestic violence decree'. ABC Radio Australia, 6 December. Online: www. radioaustralia.net.au/international/radio/program/pacific-beat/ fiji-womens-minister-defends-domestic-violence-decree/1056742 (accessed 2 December 2015).

Cowan, Jane K. 2006. 'Culture and rights after *Culture and Rights*', *American Anthropologist* 108(1): 9–24.

Cowan, Jane K., Marie-Bénédicte Dembour and Richard A. Wilson (eds). 2001. *Culture and Rights: Anthropological Perspectives*. Cambridge and New York: Cambridge University Press.

Cowan, Jane K., Marie-Bénédicte Dembour and Richard A. Wilson. 2001. 'Introduction'. In *Culture and Rights: Anthropological Perspectives*, ed. Jane Cowan, Marie-Bénédicte Dembour and Richard A. Wilson, pp. 1–26. Cambridge and New York: Cambridge University Press.

Davidson, Helen. 2013. 'Papua New Guinea takes first steps to combat "epidemic" of abuse'. *Guardian Australia*, 26 November. Online: www.theguardian.com/society/2013/nov/26/papua-new-guinea-takes-steps-against-abuse (site discontinued).

———. 2014. 'Australia pledges $3m for Papua New Guinea Centre for victims of violence'. *Guardian Australia*, 7 February. Online: www.theguardian.com/world/2014/feb/07/australia-pledges-3m-for-papua-new-guinea-centre-for-victims-of-violence (accessed 13 December 2015).

Department of Justice and Attorney General. 2001. 'Village Courts Policy'. Port Moresby.

Department of Women's Affairs website. Online: dwa.gov.vu/ (accessed 9 November 2015).

Digicel PNG. 2010. 'Signing of financial MOU between INA CIMC-FSVAC, UNICEF and Digicel PNG Foundation', 2 February. Online: www.digicelpng.com/en/about/news/signing-of-financial-mou-between-ina-cimc-fsvac-unicef-and-digicel-png-foundation (accessed 13 December 2015).

Dinnen, Sinclair and Allison Ley (eds). 2000. *Reflections on Violence in Melanesia*. Annandale, NSW: Hawkins Press; Canberra: Asia Pacific Press.

Douglas, Bronwen. 1998. 'Traditional individuals? Gendered negotiations of identity, Christianity and citizenship in Vanuatu'. State, Society and Governance in Melanesia, Research School of Pacific and Asian Studies, Discussion papers 98/6, Canberra: The Australian National University. Online: ips.cap.anu.edu.au/publications/traditional-individuals-gendered-negotiations-identity-christianity-and-citizenship (accessed 27 December 2015).

Evans, Daniel, Michael Goddard with Don Paterson. 2010. 'The hybrid courts of Melanesia: A comparative analysis of Village Courts of Papua New Guinea, Island Courts of Vanuatu and Local Courts of Solomon Islands'. *J&D Justice & Development Working Paper Series 13/2010*. Online: documents.worldbank.org/curated/en/966011468286312445/pdf/620970REVISED0000public00BOX358362B.pdf (accessed 9 June 2016).

Eves, Richard. 2010. 'Masculinity matters: Men, gender-based violence and the AIDS epidemic in Papua New Guinea'. In *Civic Insecurity: Law, Order and HIV in Papua New Guinea*, ed. Vicki Luker and Sinclair Dinnen, pp. 47–79. Studies in State and Society in the

Pacific, no. 6. State, Society and Governance in Melanesia Program. Canberra: ANU E Press. Online: press.anu.edu.au/publications/series/state-society-and-governance-melanesia/civic-insecurity (accessed 4 December 2014).

Eves, Richard and Angela Kelly-Hanku. 2014. 'Witch-hunts in Papua New Guinea's Eastern Highlands Province: A fieldwork report'. In Brief 2014/4. State, Society and Governance in Melanesia. Canberra: The Australian National University. Online: ips.cap.anu.edu.au/publications/witch-hunts-papua-new-guineas-eastern-highlands-province-fieldwork-report (accessed 27 November 2015).

Fairbairn-Dunlop, Peggy. 2009. *Pacific Prevention of Domestic Violence Programme: Vanuatu Report*. Prepared for the New Zealand Government. Wellington: Victoria University of Wellington. Online: www.ppdvp.org.nz/wp-content/media/2010/01/PPDVP-Vanuatu-Final-Report-5-Nov-20093.pdf (accessed 19 December 2015).

'Family and sexual violence'. 2014. *Ruby.Connection*, 24 March. Online: rubyconnection.com.au/articles/2014/march/family-and-sexual-violence.aspx (accessed 13 December 2015).

Femili PNG. 2014. 'Introducing Femili PNG and the Case Management Centre'. Online: www.femilipng.org/introducing-the-png-family-and-sexual-violence-case-management-centre/ (accessed 13 December 2015).

Fernandes, Aaron. 2014. 'A war on witches'. *Aljazeera*, 1 May. Online: www.aljazeera.com/programmes/101east/2014/04/war-witches-20144299354589156.html (accessed 12 December 2015).

Fiji Women's Crisis Centre (FWCC). 2013. *Somebody's Life, Everybody's Business! National Research on Women's Health and Life Experiences in Fiji (2010/2011): A survey exploring the prevalence, incidence and attitudes to intimate partner violence in Fiji*. Suva: FWCC. Online: fijiwomen.com/wp-content/uploads/2014/11/1.pdf (accessed 5 November 2016).

——. n.d. 'About us'. Online: fijiwomen.com/?page_id=4500/#1 (accessed 13 December 2015).

——. n.d. 'Regional training program (RTP)'. Online: fijiwomen.com/?page_id=4222 (accessed 13 December 2015).

Fiji Women's Rights Movement. 2012. '*Her*story: Celebrating 25 Years of Balancing the Scales, 1986–2011'. Suva, Fiji: FWRM.

——. n.d. 'Fiji: Family Law Bill passed'. Online: www.wluml.org/node/1198 (accessed 10 June 2016).

Fijian Government. 2013. 'Violence free campaigns paying dividends for communities'. Press release, 6 July. Online: www.fiji.gov.fj/Media-Center/Press-Releases/VIOLENCE-FREE-CAMPAIGNS-PAYING-DIVIDENDS-FOR-COMMU.aspx (accessed 28 November 2015).

——. 2014. 'Fiji's national gender policy approved'. 25 February. Online: www.fiji.gov.fj/Media-Center/Cabinet-Releases/FIJI%E2%80%99S-NATIONAL-GENDER-POLICY-APPROVED.aspx (accessed 28 November 2015).

——. 2014. 'Nazhat Shameem to be Fiji's Permanent Representative to the UN Office in Geneva', 8 May. Online: www.fiji.gov.fj/Media-Center/Press-Releases/NAZHAT-SHAMEEM-TO-BE-FIJI%E2%80%99S-PERMANENT-REPRESENTATI.aspx?feed=news (accessed 26 December 2015).

——. 2015. 'EVAW taskforce to meet next week', 4 September. Online: www.fiji.gov.fj/Media-Center/Press-Releases/EVAW-TASKFORCE-TO-MEET-NEXT-WEEK.aspx (accessed 15 December 2015).

Finucane, Sue and Roselyn Tor. 2010. 'Mid term review of the Vanuatu Women's Centre phase 5, July 2007 – June 2012', final report, 30 April. Canberra: Department of Foreign Affairs and Trade, Australian Government. Online: aid.dfat.gov.au/countries/pacific/vanuatu/Documents/womens-centre-mid-term-review.pdf (accessed 19 December 2015).

'Focus'. n.d. Department of Women's Affairs website. Online: dwa.gov.vu/index.php/gender-protection-cluster/gender-protection-cluster (accessed 16 November 2016).

Forsyth, Miranda. 2004. 'Beyond case law: *Kastom* and courts in Vanuatu'. *Victoria University Wellington Law Review* 35(2): 427–46. Online: www.upf.pf/IMG/pdf/09_Forsyth.pdf (accessed 9 June 2016).

——. 2009. *A Bird that Flies with Two Wings: The* Kastom *and State Justice Systems in Vanuatu*. Canberra: ANU Press. Online: press.anu. edu.au/publications/bird-flies-two-wings (accessed 6 June 2016).

——. 2013. 'Summary of main themes emerging from the conference on Sorcery and Witchcraft-Related Killings in Melanesia, 5–7 June 2013, ANU, Canberra'. *Outrigger: Blog of the Pacific Institute*, The Australian National University. Online: pacificinstitute.anu.edu. au/outrigger/2013/06/18/summary-sorcery-witchcraft-related-killings-in-melanesia-5-7-june-2013/ (accessed 27 November 2015).

——. 2014. 'New draft national action plan to address sorcery accusation-related violence in PNG'. In Brief 2014/18. State, Society and Governance in Melanesia. Canberra: The Australian National University. Online: ips.cap.anu.edu.au/sites/default/files/ IB-2014-18-Forsyth-ONLINE.pdf (accessed 10 June 2016).

Forsyth, Miranda and Richard Eves. 2015. 'The Problems and victims of sorcery and witchcraft practices and beliefs in Melanesia: An introduction'. In *Talking it Through: Responses to Sorcery and Witchcraft Beliefs and Practices in Melanesia*, pp. 1–19. Canberra: ANU Press. Online: press.anu.edu.au/publications/series/pacific-series/talking-it-through (accessed 11 April 2016).

'FWRM pays tribute to former journalist and women human rights defender'. 2015. *The Jet*, 9 April. Online: www.thejetnewspaper. com/2015/04/09/fwrm-pays-tribute-to-former-journalist-and-women-human-rights-defender/ (accessed 15 December 2015).

Garap, Sarah. 1999. 'Struggles of women and girls in Simbu Province'. *Development Bulletin* 50: 47–50. Online: crawford.anu.edu.au/ rmap/devnet/devnet/db-50.pdf (accessed 22 December 2015).

George, Nicole. 2012. *Situating Women: Gender Politics and Circumstance in Fiji*. Canberra: ANU E Press. Online: press.anu. edu.au?p=154311 (accessed 28 November 2015).

Gibbs, Philip. 2012. 'Engendered violence and witch-killing in Simbu'. In *Engendering Violence in Papua New Guinea*, ed. Margaret Jolly, Christine Stewart and Carolyn Brewer, pp. 107–35. Canberra: ANU E Press. Online: press.anu.edu.au/publications/engendering-violence-papua-new-guinea (accessed 13 December 2015).

———. 2015. 'Confronting sorcery accusation violence in PNG: Will PNG's Sorcery National Action Plan be able to stop the torture and murder of those accused of witchcraft?' *Asia and the Pacific Policy Society*, Policy Forum, November. Online: www. policyforum.net/confronting-sorcery-accusation-violence-in-png/ (accessed 28 November 2015).

Goddard, Michael. 2009. *Substantial Justice: An Anthropology of Village Courts in Papua New Guinea*. Oxford: Berghahn.

GoPNG. 1975. Constitution of the Independent State of Papua New Guinea. Online: www.pngfacts.com/uploads/1/1/3/2/11320972/ papua_new_guinea_constitution.pdf (accessed 12 December 2015).

GoPNG. 2002. Criminal Code (Sexual Offences and Crimes Against Children) Act. Online: www.geneva-academy.ch/RULAC/pdf_state /PNG-Crim-Code-Sexual-Offences-Children-ccoacaca2002462.pdf (accessed 8 May 2016).

GoPNG. 2009. Lukautim Pikinini (Child) Act. Online: www.paclii.org/ pg/legis/num_act/lpa2009235.pdf (accessed 8 May 2016).

GoPNG. 2013. Family Protection Bill (PNG). Online: archive.org/ details/FamilyProtectionBillFinal19.4.13 (accessed 8 May 2016).

HELP Resources Inc. 2005. 'A situational analysis of child sexual abuse and the commercial sexual exploitation of children in Papua New Guinea'. Port Moresby: UNICEF PNG.

Highlands Women Human Rights Defenders Movement website. n.d. 'About us'. Online: womenrightsdefenders.wix.com/ papuanewguinea#!about_us/csgz (accessed 28 November 2015)'.

———. n.d. 'Themes'. Online: womenrightsdefenders.wix.com/ papuanewguinea#!themes/c21kz (accessed 28 November 2015).

Hilsdon, Anne-Marie, Martha Macintyre, Vera Mackie and Maila Stivens (eds). 2000. *Human Rights and Gender Politics: Asia-Pacific Perspectives*. London and New York: Routledge.

Howes, Stephen, Kamalini Lokuge, Daisy Plana and Ume Wainetti. 2013. 'Responding to family and sexual violence in PNG: The case for a Case Management Centre'. *DevPolicyBlog*, 11 July. Online: devpolicy. org/responding-to-family-and-sexual-violence-in-png-the-case-for-a-case-management-centre-20130711/ (accessed 13 December 2015).

Human Rights Watch. 2015. *Bashed Up: Family Violence in Papua New Guinea*, 4 November. Online: www.hrw.org/sites/default/files/report_pdf/png1115_4up.pdf (accessed 13 December 2015).

———. 2015. 'Papua New Guinea: Universal Periodic Review Submission 2015', 21 September. Online: www.hrw.org/news/2015/09/21/papua-new-guinea-upr-submission-2015 (accessed 28 November 2015).

Hunt, Lynn. 2007. *Inventing Human Rights: A History*. New York and London: W.W. Norton & Company.

'Impacts of the Family Protection Act'. 2011. *Vanuatu Daily Post*, 16 September.

Inda, Jonathan Xavier and Renato Rosaldo. 2008. 'Tracking global flows'. In *The Anthropology of Globalization: A Reader* (2nd edition), ed. Jonathan Xavier Inda and Renato Rosaldo, pp. 3–46. Malden, MA and Oxford: Wiley-Blackwell.

Jenkins, Carol (and the National Sex and Reproduction Research Team). 1994. *National Study of Sexual and Reproductive Knowledge and Behaviour in Papua New Guinea*. Monograph 10. Goroka: Papua New Guinea Institute of Medical Research.

Jolly, Margaret. 1996. '*Woman ikat raet long human raet o no?* Women's rights, human rights and domestic violence in Vanuatu', *Feminist Review* 52: 169–90.

———. 1997. 'Woman–nation–state in Vanuatu: Women as signs and subjects in the discourses of *kastom,* modernity and Christianity'. In *Narratives of Nation in the South Pacific*, ed. Ton Otto and Nicholas Thomas, pp. 133–62. Amsterdam: Harwood Academic Publishers.

———. 2012. 'Introduction—engendering violence in Papua New Guinea: Persons, power and perilous transformations'. In *Engendering Violence in Papua New Guinea*, ed. Margaret Jolly, Christine Stewart and Carolyn Brewer, pp. 1–45. Canberra: ANU E Press. Online: press. anu.edu.au/publications/engendering-violence-papua-new-guinea (accessed 10 December 2015).

———. 2012. 'Prologue: The place of Papua New Guinea in contours of gender violence'. In *Engendering Violence in Papua New Guinea*, ed. Margaret Jolly, Christine Stewart and Carolyn Brewer, pp. xvii–xxvii. Canberra: ANU E Press. Online: press.anu.edu.au/ publications/engendering-violence-papua-new-guinea (accessed 17 November 2014).

Jolly, Margaret, Christine Stewart and Carolyn Brewer (eds). 2012. *Engendering Violence in Papua New Guinea*. Canberra: ANU E Press. Online: press.anu.edu.au/publications/engendering-violence-papua-new-guinea (accessed 26 April 2016).

Jorgensen, Dan. 2014. 'Preying on those close to home: Witchcraft violence in a PNG village'. *The Australian Journal of Anthropology* 25: 267–86.

Kata, Alistar. 2015. 'Fiji: Death of Losana McGowan opens door for wider talks on domestic abuse'. *Fiji Sun Online,* 19 April. Online: www.pmc.aut.ac.nz/pacific-media-watch/fiji-death-losana-mcgowan-opens-door-wider-talks-domestic-abuse-9222 (accessed 15 December 2015).

Kate, Talebula. 2015. 'Rethink on strategies to curb violence against women'. *Fiji Times Online*, 14 September. Online: fijitimes.com/ story.aspx?id=321674 (accessed 15 December 2015).

Kenneth, Dorosday, Vola Mata and Davis Saravanu. n.d. 'Vanuatu'. Pacific Islands Forum Secretariat, p. 3. Online: www.forumsec.org/ resources/uploads/embeds/file/VANUATU%281%29.pdf (accessed 5 December 2015).

Kenneth, Gorethy. 2015. 'Under-age marriage ban'. *Post-Courier*, 13 March.

Kotoisuva, Edwina (Fiji Women's Crisis Centre). 2007. 'Fiji Women's Crisis Centre: Organising against violence against women'. Paper presented at Pacific Women, Pacific Plan: Stepping up the Pace to 2010. Secretariat of the Pacific Community, 10th Triennial Conference of Pacific Women. Noumea, New Caledonia, 27–31 May.

Kumer, Peter. 2013. 'UN urges Papua New Guinea to take action after woman burned alive for witchcraft'. United Nations Association of Slovenia, 8 February. Online: www.unaslovenia.org/en/node/2125 (accessed 11 December 2015).

Lindstrom, Lamont. 1997. 'Chiefs in Vanuatu today'. In *Chiefs Today: Traditional Pacific Leadership and the Postcolonial State*, ed. Geoffrey M. White and Lamont Lindstrom, pp. 211–28. Stanford: Stanford University Press.

'Lukautim Pikinini Act soon to be enforced'. 2009. *Post-Courier*, 29 June.

'Lukautim Pikinini Act—passed in Parliament'. 2015. *Ministry of Community Development, Religion and Youth*, 8 June. Online: ministryofcomdev.blogspot.com/2015/06/lukautim-pikinini-act-passed-in.html (accessed 22 December 2015).

Luker, Vicki and Sinclair Dinnen (eds). 2010. *Civic Insecurity: Law, Order and HIV in Papua New Guinea*. Studies in State and Society in the Pacific, no. 6. State, Society and Governance in Melanesia Program. Canberra: ANU E Press. Online: press.anu.edu.au?p=94091 (accessed 26 April 2016).

Luluaki, John Y. 2003. 'Sexual crimes against and exploitation of children and the law in Papua New Guinea'. *International Journal of Law, Policy and the Family* 17(3): 275–307.

Macintyre, Martha. 2000. '"Hear us, women of Papua New Guinea!": Melanesian women and human rights'. In *Human Rights and Gender Politics: Asia-Pacific Perspectives*, ed. Anne-Marie Hilsdon, Martha Macintyre, Vera Mackie and Maila Stivens, pp. 147–71. London and New York: Routledge.

Manjoo, Rahida. 2013. 'Report of the Special Rapporteur on violence against women, its causes and consequences, on her mission to Papua New Guinea (18–26 March 2012)'. *United Nations General Assembly, Human Rights Council*, A/HRC/23/49/Add.2. 2013. Online: reliefweb. int/report/papua-new-guinea/report-special-rapporteur-violence-against-women-its-causes-and-consequences (accessed 11 December 2015).

Maria. 2015. 'Papua New Guinea needs its Sorcery National Action Plan as soon as possible!' 24 October. Online: www.stopsorceryviolence. org/papua-new-guinea-needs-sorcery-national-action-plan-soon-possible/ (accessed 28 November 2015).

Mason, Merrin. 2000. 'Domestic violence in Vanuatu'. In *Reflections on Violence in Melanesia*, ed. Sinclair Dinnen and Allison Ley, pp. 119–38. Annandale, NSW: Hawkins Press; Canberra: Asia Pacific Press.

Médecins Sans Frontières (MSF) (Doctors Without Borders). 2013. 'Papua New Guinea: A comprehensive response to family and sexual violence is crucial', 25 November. Online: www.msf.org/en/ article/papua-new-guinea-comprehensive-response-family-and-sexual-violence-critical (accessed 16 November 2016).

——. 2016. 'Return to abuser: Gaps in services and a failure to protect survivors of family and sexual violence in Papua New Guinea', 1 March. Online: www.msf.org.za/msf-publications/return-to-abuser-abuse-survivors-family-sexual-violence (accessed 24 April 2016).

Merry, Sally Engle. 1988. 'Legal pluralism'. *Law and Society Review* 22(5): 869–96.

——. 2006. 'Transnational human rights and local activism: Mapping the middle'. In *Anthropology and Human Rights in a New Key*, ed. Mark Goodale. *American Anthropologist* 108(1): 38–51.

——. 2006. *Human Rights and Gender Violence: Translating International Law into Local Justice*. Chicago: University of Chicago Press.

Ministry for Social Welfare, Women and Poverty Elimination. 2014. 'Fiji's national report on the 20-year review of the implementation of the Beijing Platform for Action'. Online: www.unwomen. org/~/media/headquarters/attachments/sections/csw/59/national_ reviews/fiji_review_beijing20.ashx (accessed 28 November 2015).

Ministry for Women and Culture. 1998. 'The Women's Plan of Action 1999–2008'. Online: www.svri.org/fijinational.pdf (accessed 28 November 2015).

Ministry of Justice and Community Services. 'Child Desk Office'. Online: www.mjcs.gov.vu/index.php/justice-sector/child-desk-office (accessed 19 December 2015).

'New crime decree in Fiji to assist fight against sexual abuse'. 2010. *Solomon Times Online*, 25 January. Online: www.solomontimes. com/news/new-crime-decree-in-fiji-to-assist-fight-against-sexual- abuse/4844 (accessed 14 December 2015).

Otto, Ton and Nicholas Thomas (eds). 1997. *Narratives of Nation in the South Pacific*. Amsterdam: Harwood Academic Publishers.

Pedersen, Niklas. 2015. 'Fiji women's minister calls gender violence a "national shame"'. *Pacific Island Reports*, 10 September. Online: pidp.eastwestcenter.org/pireport/2015/September/09-11-11.htm (accessed 15 December 2015).

'PNG defines marriage age'. 2015. *Radio New Zealand International*, 14 March. Online: www.radionz.co.nz/international/pacific-news /268648/png-defines-marriage-age (accessed 12 December 2015).

PNG Law Reform Commission. 1992. 'Final Report on Domestic Violence. Report No. 14'. Boroko, N.C.D. Papua New Guinea.

Pollak, Sorcha. 2013. 'Woman burned alive for witchcraft in Papua New Guinea'. *Time Magazine*, 7 February. Online: newsfeed.time. com/2013/02/07/woman-burned-alive-for-witchcraft-in-papua- new-guinea/ (accessed 21 December 2015).

Republic of Fiji Islands. 2003. Family Law Act. Online: www.ilo. org/dyn/natlex/docs/ELECTRONIC/66125/69852/F1469246504/ FJI66125.pdf (accessed 8 May 2016).

Republic of Fiji Islands Government Gazette. 2009. Domestic Violence Decree, 14 August. Online: www.judiciary.gov.fj/images/dvro/Domestic %20Violence%20Decree%202009.pdf (accessed 16 November 2016).

Republic of Fiji Islands Government Gazette. 2009. Crimes Decree, 5 November. Online: www.fiji.gov.fj/getattachment/604e31fc-c7b1-41a0-9686-71377917b6eb/Decree-No-44---Crimes-Decree-2009 -(pdf).aspx (accessed 16 November 2016).

Republic of Vanuatu. 1980. Constitution of the Republic of Vanuatu. Online: www.wipo.int/wipolex/en/text.jsp?file_id= 195747 (accessed 19 December 2015).

Republic of Vanuatu. 2008. Family Protection Act. Online: www.ilo. org/dyn/natlex/docs/ELECTRONIC/88503/101220/F1853954544/ VUT88503.pdf (accessed 8 May 2016).

Robinson, Nancy. 2013. 'Statement on sorcery-related killings and impunity in Papua New Guinea'. Paper presented at the Sorcery and Witchcraft-related Killings in Melanesia: Culture, Law and Human Rights Perspectives Conference. The Australian National University, Canberra, 5–7 June. Online: un.org.au/files/2013/06/ Statement-on-Sorcery-related-Killings-and-Impunity-in-Papua-New-Guinea.pdf (accessed 27 November 2015).

Rokosuka, Elizabeth. 2014. 'Zero tolerance violence free communities to report on crimes'. *Fijivillage.com*, 6 July. Online: fijivillage.com/ news/Zero-Tolerance-Violence-Free-communities-to-report-on-crimes-s52r9k/ (accessed 15 December 2015).

Schermer, Tom. 2010. 'Police open "family protection unit"'. *Vanuatu Daily Post*, 26 November. Online: www.dailypost.vu/content/ police-open-%E2%80%98family-protection-unit%E2%80%99 (site discontinued).

Seeds Theatre Group Inc. 2015. 'Male advocacy for human rights', 25 June. Online: www.seedstheatre.org/male-advocacy-for-human-rights/ (accessed 8 June 2016).

Setepano, Nellie. 2013. 'PNG "Haus Krai" movement gains support abroad'. *Pacific Islands Report*, East-West Center, Honolulu: University of Hawai'i. Online: pidp.eastwestcenter.org/ pireport/2013/May/05-14-12.htm (accessed 19 September 2014). Originally published in the PNG *Post-Courier*, 13 May.

——. 2016. 'PNG marriage laws to be amended as part of reform bundle to legally recognize traditional marriage and protect minors'. *Pacific Islands Report*, 22 August. Online: www.pireport. org/articles/2016/08/22/png-marriage-laws-be-amended-part-reform-bundle-legally-recognize-traditional (accessed 1 December 2016).

Shameem, Nazhat. 2012. 'The Domestic Violence Decree 2009, Fiji'. Fiji Judiciary Criminal Law Workshop for Judges and Magistrates, 14 June. Online: www.fijileaks.com/uploads/1/3 /7/5/13759434/naz_on_the_domesticviolence-decree2009.pdf (accessed 14 December 2015).

Siegel, Matt. 2013. 'Papua New Guinea acts to repeal sorcery law after strife'. *New York Times*, 29 May. Online: www.nytimes. com/2013/05/30/world/asia/papua-new-guinea-moves-to-repeal-sorcery-act.html (accessed 27 November 2015).

Stokes, Deborah. 2013. 'Speech by Australian High Commissioner Ms Deborah Stokes at the "Haus Krai" condemning violence against women, 15 May'. *Australian High Commission Papua New Guinea*. Online: www.png.embassy.gov.au/pmsb/69.html (accessed 12 December 2015).

Taylor, John P. 2008, 'The social life of rights: "Gender antagonism", modernity and *raet* in Vanuatu'. *The Australian Journal of Anthropology* 19(2): 165–87. Online: www.academia.edu/1816894/ The_Social_Life_of_Rights_Gender_Antagonism_Modernity_ and_Raet_in_Vanuatu (accessed 7 December 2015).

Taylor-Newton, Ruby. 2009. 'Twenty-five years on, Fiji Women's Crisis Centre stands as a beacon of hope for women'. *Womensphere: Global Women's News, Views, and Issues*, 4 September. Online: womensphere.wordpress.com/2009/09/04/twenty-five-years-on-fiji-womens-crisis-centre-stands-as-beacon-of-hope-for-women/ (accessed 12 December 2015).

Tor, Roselyn and Anthea Teka. 2004. *Gender, Kastom & Domestic Violence: A Research on the Historical Trend, Extent and Impact of Domestic Violence in Vanuatu.* Port Vila: Department of Women's Affairs, Republic of Vanuatu.

UNICEF (United Nations Children's Fund) and the GoPNG. 2010. *Lukautim Pikinini: Training Manual*, Module 10: Child Protection Laws and Policies, pp. 154–63. Online: www.unicef.org/png/FBO_Manual_Part_4.pdf (accessed 6 June 2016).

United States Department of State. 2013. '2012 Country Reports on Human Rights Practices—Vanuatu', 19 April. Online: www.refworld.org/docid/517e6db71d.html (accessed 19 December 2015).

'Vanuatu chief wants gang rape case dropped'. 2014. *Radio New Zealand International*, 12 May. Online: www.radionz.co.nz/international/pacific-news/244103/vanuatu-chief-wants-gang-rape-case-dropped (accessed 19 December 2015).

Vanuatu Women's Centre. 2011. *Vanuatu National Survey on Women's Lives and Family Relationships.* Online: dfat.gov.au/about-us/publications/Documents/womens-centre-survey-womens-lives.pdf (accessed 8 December 2015).

———. 'About: What the Vanuatu Women's Centre does'. *Vanuatu Women's Centre.* Online: vanuatuwomenscentre.org/about/ (accessed 5 December 2015).

Voice of ToRot. 2014. 'Madang police fight domestic sexual violence', 1 July. Online www.voiceoftorot.com/news/madang-police-fight-domestic-sexual-violence/ (accessed 13 December 2015).

White, Geoffrey M. and Lamont Lindstrom (eds). 1997. *Chiefs Today: Traditional Pacific Leadership and the Postcolonial State.* Stanford: Stanford University Press.

Wilson, Richard A. 2006. 'Afterword to "Anthropology and human rights in a new key": The social life of human rights', ed. Mark Goodale, *American Anthropologist* 108(1): 77–83.

Wilson, Richard Ashby and Jon P. Mitchell. 2003. 'Introduction: The social life of rights'. In *Human Rights in Global Perspective*, ed. Richard Ashby Wilson and Jon P. Mitchell, pp. 1–15. London: Routledge.

Wilson, Richard Ashby and Jon P. Mitchell (eds). 2003. *Human Rights in Global Perspective*. London: Routledge.

'Women should protest, not celebrate'. 2014. *Vanuatu Daily Post*, 16 May.

Zimmer-Tamakoshi, Laura. 2001 [1997]. '"Wild pigs and dog men": Rape and domestic violence as "women's issues" in Papua New Guinea'. In *Gender in Cross-Cultural Perspective*, ed. Caroline B. Brettel and Carolyn F. Sargent, pp. 538–53. Englewood Cliffs, NJ: Prentice-Hall.

United Nations Documents

Committee on the Elimination of Discrimination against Women (CEDAW Committee). 2000. 'Initial report of States parties: Fiji Islands'. CEDAW/c/FJI/1. Online: www.un.org/womenwatch/daw/cedaw/cedaw26/fji1.pdf (accessed 14 December 2015).

——. 2004. 'Consideration of reports submitted by States parties under Article 18 of the Convention on the Elimination of All Forms of Discrimination against Women. Combined initial, second and third periodic reports of States parties, Vanuatu'. CEDAW/C/VUT/1-3. Online: www.capwip.org/readingroom/CEDAWCR/CEDAW%20Country%20Report%20Vanuatu%201st,2nd%20&%203rd%2030Nov2005.pdf (accessed 3 December 2015).

——. 2008. 'Consideration of reports submitted by States parties under article 18 of the Convention on the Elimination of All Forms of Discrimination against Women. Combined second, third and fourth periodic reports of States parties: Fiji'. CEDAW/C/FJI/2-4. Online: www.bayefsky.com//reports/fiji_cedaw_c_fiji_2_4_2008.pdf (accessed 14 December 2015).

——. 2009. 'Consideration of reports submitted by States parties under article 18 of the Convention on the Elimination of All Forms of Discrimination against Women: Combined initial, second and third periodic report of States parties: Papua New Guinea'. CEDAW/C/PNG/3, p. 28, item 2.2. Online: www.bayefsky.com//reports/papua_cedaw_c_png_3_2008.pdf (accessed 27 November 2015).

Committee on the Rights of the Child. 2003. 'Consideration of reports submitted by State parties under article 44 of the Convention: Initial reports of State parties due in 2000: Papua New Guinea'. CRC/C/28/Add.20. Online: www.refworld.org/docid/3f8d18e74.html (accessed 10 June 2016).

Convention on the Elimination of All Forms of Discrimination against Women (CEDAW). 1979. *UN Women*. Online: www.un.org/womenwatch/daw/cedaw/text/econvention.htm (accessed 11 December 2014).

UN Population Fund (UNFPA). 2008. 'An assessment of the state of violence against women in Fiji'. Suva: UNFPA Pacific Sub Regional Office. Online: www.un.org/womenwatch/ianwge/taskforces/vaw/Fiji_VAW_Assessment_2008.pdf (accessed 14 December 2015).

UNGA. 2014. 'Report of the working group on the Universal Periodic Review: Vanuatu', 4 April, A/HRC/26/9. Online: www.ohchr.org/EN/HRBodies/HRC/RegularSessions/Session26/Pages/ListReports.aspx (accessed 9 June 2016).

8

'When She Cries Oceans': Navigating Gender Violence in the Western Pacific

Margaret Jolly

The Australian National University

Now there's something in her eyes something constant and persistent
Even lying 'tween her thighs she is somewhere in the distance
Friend you say you won the war but I'm telling you that depends
For her it never ends, cause it seems to me that
When she cries oceans
She finds ways to hide
When she bleeds roses
She bleeds all inside.[1]

These are the poignant words of Fred Smith, an Australian folk singer and a diplomat intimately involved in the peace monitoring operations which ultimately helped to end the war in Bougainville.[2] They are

---

1   The lyrics are from a verse of 'When She Cries', the fourth song on the CD *Bagarap Empires* by Iain 'Fred' Smith, 2012, 10th Anniversary edition. CD and line notes in author's collection.
2   I say ultimately since there had been years of attempts to make peace at different scales. As Ruth Saovana-Spriggs (2008), John Braithwaite, Hilary Charlesworth, Peter Reddy and Leah Dunn (2010) and Anna-Karina Hermkens (2012) and others have documented so powerfully, women were critical to these efforts, and as Saovana-Spriggs argues used their particular position as 'mothers of the land', not just as mothers of individual soldiers but as nurturers of people and place, by deploying their powers, especially in matrilineal parts of Bougainville to intervene between combatants and make peace. But as several authors have demonstrated, as the peace-

written from the perspective of a young Bougainville Revolutionary Army soldier whose wife had been raped by men of the Papua New Guinea Defence Force. This is one song on a superb CD, *Bagarap Empires*, rereleased in 2012 to celebrate the tenth anniversary of the end of that horrific war—between Bougainville and PNG, and between Bougainvilleans. The congregation of songs consummately conveys diverse perspectives: of male soldiers fighting in such Pacific conflicts; of women widowed by wars stretching from World War II to the twenty-first century; of women like 'Sweet Anne Marie' working tirelessly in Christian groups to foster peace in both Bougainville and Solomons conflicts; of young men, *'rasta mangkes'* trying to find a road beyond violence; and of an Australian man like Fred, enraptured by the beauty of the Pacific, entranced by the grace of its people, troubled by its colonial past and present predicaments, longing for a more hopeful future where peace and love might prevail. But although these wars and other violent conflicts have ended in much of the western Pacific, the war on women, the primary manifestation of gender violence in the region, has not.[3] Rape in war may have diminished but women and girls are still often raped, bashed and brutally tortured not so much by enemy soldiers but by male intimates in their familial lives: their husbands, their lovers, their fathers, their brothers, their uncles, their cousins. This war on women is so constant that the NGO Médecins Sans Frontières (MSF), usually engaged in humanitarian intervention

---

making process scaled up from local to national and regional levels, women were progressively excluded from the peace-making talks and acts of conciliation. See Ruth Vatoa Saovana-Spriggs, 2007, 'Gender and peace: Bougainvillean women, matriliny, and the peace process', PhD thesis, The Australian National University; John Braithwaite, Hilary Charlesworth, Peter Reddy and Leah Dunn, 2010, *Reconciliation and Architectures of Commitment: Sequencing Peace in Bougainville*, Canberra: ANU E Press; and Anna-Karina Hermkens, 2012, 'Becoming Mary: Marian devotion as a solution to gender-based violence in urban PNG', in *Engendering Violence in Papua New Guinea*, ed. Margaret Jolly, Christine Stewart and Carolyn Brewer, pp. 137–62, Canberra: ANU E Press.

3   For a detailed discussion of terms and the use of Merry's definition of gender violence, see Margaret Jolly, 2012, 'Introduction—engendering violence in Papua New Guinea: Persons, power and perilous transformations', in *Engendering Violence in Papua New Guinea*, ed. Margaret Jolly, Christine Stewart and Carolyn Brewer, pp. 1–45, Canberra: ANU E Press; Sally Engle Merry, 2009, *Gender Violence: A Cultural Perspective*, Chichester: Wiley-Blackwell, p. 3. Merry defines it as an act of violence in which the gender of the parties is relevant. It can thus include women, men and transgendered persons as either perpetrators or victims; although the predominant form in the western Pacific is of male perpetrators and female victims, there is a tendency to occlude rarer forms. See Holly Wardlow, 2012, 'Treating gender violence: MSF's project in Tari, Papua New Guinea', paper presented at Anthropology Seminar Series, The Australian National University, Canberra, 15 August.

in violent wars, ethnic conflicts and emergencies, has been working in parts of Papua New Guinea where, it is said, the incidence of acts of violence against women approximates a war or an emergency.[4]

How can scholars like ourselves, writing from the distance of Australia or the United States, deal with such gruesome daily horrors of gender violence in the region without compounding the hurt by engaging in a sort of 'pornography' in representation[5]—which reports these horrors in graphic detail and thus shocks foreign funders and feminists into action, which thereby risks reducing the women so hurt to further victimhood and which contributes to a broader popular portrait of the western Pacific, especially prevalent in Australia, as dystopia.[6] There are several things we can do to vitiate such risks. First, as Aletta Biersack and Martha Macintyre do in the introduction to this volume, we can stress the universality of gender violence and its pervasive and perduring presence in countries like Australia and the United States. That does not necessarily negate the high prevalence nor the continuing legitimacy of gender violence in the western Pacific, nor its particularities, like the frequency of gang rape in Papua New Guinea, and the links to patterns of witchcraft and sorcery and HIV infection in the region. Second, we can dwell not on the horrific injuries and the most egregious cases of torture of female victims, but on the agency of those women and men who are struggling to redress gender violence, who are working through state agencies and NGOs to change those beliefs and practices which catalyse and legitimate it, as Biersack does.[7] When Christine Stewart, Carolyn Brewer and I edited a collection on gender violence in Papua New Guinea we decided not to reproduce images of battered and assaulted women, such as those used in anti-violence poster campaigns in that country, but rather selected Christine's photographs of a large street march in Port Moresby where

---

4   Médecins Sans Frontières (MSF) (Doctors Without Borders), 2011, *Hidden and Neglected: The Medical and Emotional Needs of Survivors of Family and Sexual Violence in Papua New Guinea*, Boroko: MSF; See also Wardlow, 'Treating gender violence'.

5   On rape cases in PNG, see Jean Zorn, 2012, 'Engendering violence in the Papua New Guinea Courts: Sentencing in rape trials', in *Engendering Violence in Papua New Guinea*, ed. Margaret Jolly, Christine Stewart and Carolyn Brewer, pp. 163–96, Canberra: ANU E Press, pp. 170–71.

6   See Greg Fry, 1997, 'Framing the Islands: Knowledge and power in changing Australian images of "the South Pacific"', *The Contemporary Pacific* 9(2): 305–44; Margaret Jolly, Helen Lee, Katherine Lepani, Anna Naupa and Michelle Rooney, 2015, *Falling Through the Net? Gender and Social Protection in the Pacific*, Discussion Paper for UN Women for Progress of the World's Women 2015–2016, Report in association with G20 meetings.

7   Aletta Biersack, 'Human rights work in Papua New Guinea, Fiji and Vanuatu', this volume.

women and men joined together to protest gender violence and hear the inspiring words of Dame Carol Kidu.[8] Finally, we can link our scholarly analyses with practical political action by joining with local agents and allies in transnational coalitions of state and NGO actors to offer modest support and culturally sensitive advice rather than presuming an imperial maternalism that we are 'saving our sisters'.[9]

But how helpful is the discourse of human rights in such efforts? Here I focus on three questions which have haunted me in reading this fine collection. First, I turn to the question of whether the notions and values of the *person* which pervade the discourse of human rights and the cultures of the region are incommensurable, often conceived in scholarly lore as the stark difference between the autonomous individual of egalitarian liberal democracies and the 'dividual' or relational person of hierarchical 'traditional' cultures. Second, I ponder how we best conceptualise the process of *translation* of human rights not as the 'hypodermic insertion' or infiltration of the global into the local,[10] of the foreign into the indigenous, but as a process of mediation, a reciprocal flow of meanings, values and powers which some have termed 'indigenisation' and others 'vernacularization'.[11] Third, I ponder the limits of human rights promoted through the instruments of international and national legal regimes given broader economic and political shifts in an era marked not just by political instabilities, coups and wars, but by heightened capitalist development, neoliberal aid conditionalities and the burgeoning influence of NGOs, including those dedicated to stopping gender violence.

8   Margaret Jolly, Christine Stewart and Carolyn Brewer (eds), 2012, *Engendering Violence in Papua New Guinea*, Canberra: ANU E Press.
9   See Lila Abu-Lughod, 2013, *Do Muslim Women Need Saving?* Cambridge, MA: Harvard University Press.
10   See Biersack, 'Human rights work in Papua New Guinea, Fiji and Vanuatu', this volume; Jean Zorn, 'Translating and internalising international human rights law: The courts of Melanesia confront gendered violence', this volume.
11   Sally Engle Merry, 2006, *Human Rights and Gender Violence: Translating International Law into Local Justice*, Chicago and London: University of Chicago Press.

Incommensurable persons? From founding fathers and mothers to porous subjects

Aletta Biersack quotes Sally Engle Merry's suggestion that '"Human rights promote ideas of individual autonomy, equality, choice and secularism" which are foreign to cultural zones which are "less individualistic and more focused on communities and responsibilities"'.[12] This opposition engages longstanding polarities between autonomous, free individuals situated in a secular, progressive West and sociocentric persons located in a non-West characterised by constraining collectivities: cultures, ethnic groups, religious communities. Some go so far as to see these divergent notions and values of the person as incommensurable. But are they?

I would argue that Western human rights discourse, even in its earliest manifestations, also accommodated more collective visions of the rights of workers, of women, of people of colour and that this has been accentuated in recent decades, especially in the contexts of global women's movements.[13] Moreover, I would argue that in non-Western contexts, contending notions of personal autonomy and equality can be present.[14] A contemporary vision of the autonomous individual endowed with choice travelling from New York through the global ideoscape to places shrouded in tradition reproduces a stark binary

---

12   See Merry, *Human Rights and Gender Violence*, p. 4; Biersack, 'Human rights work in Papua New Guinea, Fiji and Vanuatu', this volume.
13   See Anne-Marie Hilsdon, Martha Macintyre, Vera Mackie and Maila Stivens (eds), 2000, *Human Rights and Gender Politics: Asia-Pacific Perspectives*, London and New York: Routledge; Margaret Jolly, 2000, '*Woman Ikat Raet Long Human Raet O No?* Women's rights, human rights and domestic violence in Vanuatu', in *Human Rights and Gender Politics: Asia-Pacific Perspectives*, ed. Anne-Marie Hilsdon, Martha Macintyre, Vera Mackie and Maila Stivens, pp. 124–46. Updated and expanded version of prior publication in *Feminist Review* 52: 169–90 (1996); Jolly, Lee, Lepani, Naupa and Rooney, *Falling Through the Net?*
14   See Bronwen Douglas, 1998, 'Traditional individuals? Gendered negotiations of identity, Christianity and citizenship in Vanuatu', State, Society and Governance in Melanesia, Research School of Pacific and Asian Studies'. Discussion papers 98/6, Canberra: The Australian National University; Martha Macintyre, 2000, '"Hear us, women of Papua New Guinea": Melanesian women and human rights', in *Human Rights and Gender Politics: Perspectives in the Asia Pacific Region*, ed. Anne-Marie Hilsdon, Martha Macintyre, Vera Mackie and Maila Stivens, pp. 141–71; Martha Macintyre, 2011, 'Money changes everything: Papua New Guinean women in a modern economy', in *Managing Modernity in the Western Pacific*, ed. Mary Patterson and Martha Macintyre, pp. 90–120, St Lucia: University of Queensland Press; and Katherine Lepani, 2012, *Islands of Love, Islands of Risk: Culture and HIV in the Trobriands*, Nashville: Vanderbilt University Press.

with a long, if contested, genealogy in scholarly writing.[15] Karl Smith suggests that the terms of this old debate have been exhausted, but still suggests a contrast, after Charles Taylor, between buffered and porous subjects.[16] I suggest that we witness a co-presence and a dialectical relation between these two models of persons or selves rather than an either/or binary.[17]

Many founding fathers of Western scholarship plotted such stark differences between notions of the person in non-Western and Western contexts, between those persons more embedded in collectivities and cultures and the more individuated and autonomous persons of 'civilised' European societies. Moreover, they often envisaged a progress from one to the other in the march of modernity. The details of such plots differered, for instance between Karl Marx, Max Weber and Emile Durkheim, that holy trinity of seminal 'founding fathers'. More relevant here is how the early anthropology of Oceania was brought into such global discussions through the writings of Marcel Mauss, influential scholar of the College de France, and Maurice Leenhardt, missionary ethnographer long resident in New Caledonia. The work of both authors has been reanimated and reassessed in both French and English scholarship in recent decades.[18]

In his last essay Marcel Mauss addressed the challenging question of the universality of the idea of the person, of the self as a 'category of the human mind'.[19] He acknowledged that his daring comparisons

15   Karl Smith, 2012, 'From dividual and individual selves to porous subjects', *The Australian Journal of Anthropology* 23: 5–64.

16   Smith, 'From dividual and individual selves to porous subjects'; Charles Taylor, 1985, 'The person', in *The Category of the Person: Anthropology, Philosophy, History*, ed. Michael Carrithers, Steven Collins, Steven Lukes, pp. 257–81, Cambridge: Cambridge University Press; Charles Taylor, 1989, *Sources of the Self: The Making of the Modern Identity*, Cambridge: Cambridge University Press; Charles Taylor, 1991, *The Ethics of Authenticity*, Cambridge: Harvard University Press.

17   See Holly Wardlow, 2006, *Wayward Women: Sexuality and Agency in a New Guinea Society*, Berkeley: University of California Press; Margaret Jolly, 2015, '*Braed praes* in Vanuatu: Both gifts and commodities', in *Gender and Person in Oceania*, Special Issue of *Oceania*, ed. Anna-Karina Hermkens, Rachel Morgain and John Taylor, 85(1): 63–78.

18   Michel Naepels and Christine Salomon (eds), 2007, *Terrains et destins de Maurice Leenhardt*, Paris: École des Hautes Études en Sciences Sociales, Cahiers de l'Homme; James Clifford, 1982, *Person and Myth: Maurice Leenhardt in the Melanesian World*, Berkeley: University of California Press.

19   Marcel Mauss, 1985 [1938], 'A category of the human mind: The notion of person; the notion of self', trans. W.D. Halls, in *The Category of the Person: Anthropology, Philosophy, History*, ed. Michael Carrithers, Steven Collins and Steven Lukes, pp. 1–25. Cambridge: Cambridge University Press.

were 'at inordinate speed' across space and time but posited a human universal in that no language lacks an 'I/me' (though some suppress it through positional emphasis) and in that 'there is always a human being aware of his [sic] spiritual/physical individuality'. Yet his central plot traces the historical movement from an emphasis on *personnage* (personage) to *personne* (person) and self. Leenhardt retained Mauss's notion of *personnage* as pertaining to what he saw as the archaic participatory mode of Kanak engagement with the world.[20] As Clifford's lucid interpretation suggests, Kanak viewed the person not as separated by the skin of individuated bodies but as relational and plural.[21] Leenhardt acknowledges the potential for individuation in the Kanak world, in acts of nonconformity and rebellion (for example, a woman refusing an arranged marriage or a nephew disobeying an uncle) but suggests that such acts render such persons adrift and vulnerable to death by sorcery. But for him it is modernity, detachment from the world of the *tribu*, education in rational thought and Christianity which catalyses an ineluctable movement towards a new kind of person, an *individu* (an individual) and a 'new view of the world'.

A founding mother in this lineage emerged later in the 20th century. In conversation with Mauss more than Leenhardt, in her hugely influential book *The Gender of the Gift* (1988), Marilyn Strathern invited us to conceive the difference between the western 'individual' and the Melanesian 'dividual'.[22] She sees the Melanesian person as relationally constituted, 'the plural and composite site of the relationships that produced them',[23] continuously composed and decomposed through transactions of bodily substances (blood, semen, milk) and other things (pigs, shells, crops). Both corporeal substances and valuables circulate as parts of persons, detached and attached, as aspects of a composite self are externalised and objectified in transactions with others. Persons only emerge fleetingly as unitary actors; though in this evanescence men seem more often able to suppress the parts of their persons owed to women in performances of same-sex unity. Although she proposed

---

20   Maurice Leenhardt, 1979, *Do Kamo: Person and Myth in the Melanesian World*, English trans. Basia Miller Galati, Preface by Vincent Crapanzano, Chicago: University of Chicago Press.
21   Clifford, *Person and Myth*, pp. 173–74.
22   Marilyn Strathern, 1988, *The Gender of the Gift: Problems with Women and Problems with Society in Melanesia*, Studies in Melanesian Anthropology, No. 6, Berkeley and Los Angeles: University of California Press.
23   Strathern, *The Gender of the Gift*, p. 13.

this as a heuristic play of ideal figures, a 'thought experiment', the power of this binary so long entrenched in Western thinking about the other was amplified in decades of scholarly debates between enthusiastic acolytes of Strathern and congeries of critics who refused the binary as either an ideal typical or a real world description of the differences between persons in the West and Melanesia.[24]

Many critics have highlighted the diverse notions of the 'individual' in the West: the possessive individual of capitalist ownership, in which private property extends to the self; the individuated and typically masculine citizen of the liberal democratic state, who exercises choice in the public sphere; the isolated corporeal subject of biomedicine whose illness and health is explained through aetiologies stopping at the boundaries of the skin rather than adducing the collective condition of the body of the group or notions of divine causation; and the solitary soul of Christian and especially Protestant theology, confronting God alone in the quest for salvation in the afterlife. All of these figures are ideal types rather than real world depictions of 'selves' in the West. Others argued that Strathern's model of the Melanesian 'dividual' was equally apt for characterising the 'porous subjects' of secular modernity.[25] There is the competing figure of the sedimented self as analysed in psychoanalytic theory (id/ego/superego), often associated with the claim that the non-Western other is dominated by the id.[26] And finally there is the figure of the fragmented, dispersed non-unitary Western person and the death of the author so beloved of poststructuralists.[27]

24   For example, Edward Li Puma, 1998, 'Modernity and forms of personhood in Melanesia', in *Bodies and Persons: Comparative Perspectives from Africa and Melanesia*, ed. Michael Lambek and Andrew Strathern, pp. 53–79, Cambridge: Cambridge University Press, Edward Li Puma, 2001, *Encompassing Others. The Magic of Modernity in Melanesia*, Ann Arbor: University of Michigan Press; Lisette Josephides, 1991, 'Metaphors, metathemes and the construction of sociality: A critique of the New Melanesian ethnography', *Man* 26(1): 145–61; see also Sabine Hess, 2006, 'Strathern's "dividual" and the Christian "individual": A perspective from Vanua Lava, Vanuatu', *Oceania* 76(3): 285–96.
25   Smith, 'From dividual and individual selves to porous subjects'; Taylor, 'The person'; Taylor, *Sources of the Self*; Taylor, *The Ethics of Authenticity*.
26   Warwick Anderson, Deborah Jenson and Richard C. Keller (eds), 2011, *Unconscious Dominions: Psychoanalysis, Colonial Trauma, and Global Sovereignties*, Durham: Duke University Press.
27   Judith Butler, 1990, *Gender Trouble: Feminism and the Subversion of Identity*, New York: Routledge; Judith Butler, 1993, *Bodies that Matter: On the Discursive Limits of Sex*, New York: Routledge.

Other critics argued that Strathern had wrongly compared theoretical ideals in the West with ethnographic realities in Melanesia.[28] Moreover, a series of ethnographers of Papua New Guinea discerned what Holly Wardlow called 'incipient individualism' in that country: catalysed by capitalist economics which was creating new subject positions as producers/workers and consumers; by state politics which was interpellating people as individuated voting citizens of the nation and not just members of particular clans, language or ethnic groups; by biomedicine which was dealing with the isolated body of the patient severed from the relational aetiologies of indigenous medicines; and by evangelical Christianities which summoned converts as individual souls to be saved, not as inherently connected by kinship or affinal ties.[29] The role of Christianity and especially evangelical and Pentecostal Christianities in transforming notions of the person was fiercely debated between two eminent scholars of PNG, Joel Robbins and Mark Mosko, and several other prominent anthropologists in the pages of the *JRAI* in 2010.[30]

Strangely, given its origins in Strathern's book, this latter debate was rather detached from considerations of gender, of how for instance 'incipient individualism' might differ for men and women given their different situation vis-a-vis commodity economics, the state, Christian churches, and the sphere of biomedicine, especially in the context of the HIV epidemic. The writings of Holly Wardlow, Lisette Josephides and Martha Macintyre were unusual in this regard. Holly Wardlow suggested for the Huli and PNG more broadly that, rather than *either* a relational *or* an individuated mode of personhood, both are co-present:

> If one accepts that these dual modes of personhood [relational and individual] can coexist, if in highly contested ways, then a variety of questions emerge. For one, might a transformation be occurring, with more individualistic expressions of agency coming to the fore ... or, conceptualized somewhat differently, are the contexts that elicit more autonomous modes of agency becoming more predominant in the contemporary context? And if 'modernity' has something to do with

---

28   Li Puma, 'Modernity and forms of personhood in Melanesia'; Li Puma, *Encompassing Others*.

29   Wardlow, *Wayward Women*.

30   Mark Mosko, 2010, 'Partible penitents: Dividual personhood and Christian practice in Melanesia and the West', *Journal of the Royal Anthropological Institute* 16(2): 215–40. See responses by several authors in same volume; see Joel Robbins, 2004, *Becoming Sinners: Christianity and Moral Torment in a Papua New Guinea Society*, Berkeley: University of California Press.

an increase in individualism, what is it about modernity that has this effect? Further, how might the expression of a more individualized sensibility be gendered?[31]

These questions are consummately explored in her book *Wayward Women* which focuses on those *pasinjia meri* among the Huli who are articulating a novel autonomous agency by resisting the practices of 'bride price' controlled by men (often used to justify forced conjugal sex and gender violence) and selling their own bodies in a way they see as akin to selling things in a store. Also in the Highlands context, Lisette Josephides has compared how men and women author themselves in life history narratives.[32] And Martha Macintyre in a compelling comparison of poor women working for the mine in Lihir and educated urban women in PNG has suggested that there is a novel individualism emergent among both groups as women find autonomy in paid work. Some resist the pressure that bride price be paid for them in marriage since that confers control on husbands and affines; some even refuse to marry at all to avoid the violent control of a husband and thus bear and nurture children alone or with the support of natal female kin.[33]

These recent debates about the gendered character of 'incipient individualism' are relevant to several chapters in this volume: most notably Lynda Newland on Fiji and Philip Gibbs and Katherine Lepani on Papua New Guinea.

Lynda Newland's persuasive paper discerns a fundamental contradiction between the notions of the individual advanced in human rights discourse and the prevailing models of personhood in Fiji. Although she does not reference the anthropological debate alluded to above, she sees a stark contradiction between these divergent models of the person rather than, as Wardlow suggests, their tense co-presence.[34] There is clearly a gendered dimension insofar as the ideals of relational persons embedded in and controlling Fijian collectivity are predominantly embodied by men and especially male chiefs, while women are portrayed as disembedded and marginalised from a masculinist collectivity by both gender hierarchy and gender

---

31   Wardlow, *Wayward Women*, p. 20.
32   Lisette Josephides, 2008, *Melanesian Odysseys: Negotiating the Self, Narrative and Modernity*, New York and Oxford: Berghahn.
33   Macintyre, 'Money changes everything'.
34   Wardlow, *Wayward Women*.

violence. Newland focuses on the practice of *bulubulu/i soro*,[35] a ritual of atonement practised by *iTaukei* (indigenous Fijians) in many contexts but particularly to resolve cases of domestic violence between husbands and wives, rape and child sexual abuse. On the basis of extensive research done with local research assistants in several parts of urban and rural Fiji, she challenges Merry's earlier optimism that the *bulubulu* was becoming rarer, that it was being transformed so that the interests of the female victim were better recognised, and that reparation and gender justice were thus increasingly possible.[36] Both Newland and Nicole George in their chapters in this volume confidently assert that *bulubulu* continues to be widely practised to resolve cases of gender and sexual violence in Fiji and that the emphasis continues to be on restoring communal harmony and male authority (the chief, the husband) rather than acknowledging the suffering of the victim and her right to reparation.

In his compelling case study of 'Men's Matters' in the Catholic diocese of Western Province, PNG, Philip Gibbs charts how Caritas, the church-based agency, has been important in 'interpreting rights language and values into cultural frameworks meaningful to people in a given local context'. Through the accumulation of insights in workshops over several years, these men explored multiple masculinities through the discussion of figures such as the chief, the warrior, the wise man and the lover. They discussed the differences between past patterns of gender hierarchy and future visions of gender equality, starkly represented in the plotting of triangles and circles in Figure 5 in his chapter.[37]

But, as Gibbs and his interlocutors perceive, isolating male and female subjects in this way occludes how these contrastive figures are embedded in a wider collective life and indeed a broader terrain of relationality. Ultimately Gibbs is hopeful that, despite the fact that empowering women necessarily entails wresting power from men, men will find fulfilment not just in better, less violent relations with women but in a broader communal vision. He sees Christian theology

35   The Fijian words differ by region: *bulubulu* is used in Bau or 'standard' Fijian; *i soro* elsewhere.
36   Sally Engle Merry, 2004, 'Tensions between global law and local social justice: CEDAW and the problem of rape in Fiji', paper delivered at the Justice Across Cultures Conference, Brandeis, March; Merry, *Human Rights and Gender Violence*.
37   Philip Gibbs, 'Men's Matters: Changing masculine identities in Papua New Guinea', this volume.

as providing a space for framing a discourse on equality within a discourse on difference, since men and women though different are 'one in Christ'. Following Merry's notion of 'layering' of frameworks[38] he suggests that the dissimilar models of hierarchical and egalitarian gender relations are layered rather than mutually exclusive, and are alike grounded in a Christian community. Apropos gender violence he suggests 'there would be values and safeguards to prevent such violence, based not on a modern liberal philosophy but more on human solidarity and the common good within the community'.[39]

In her chapter, Katherine Lepani avows the continuing importance of notions of relational personhood in the Trobriands in the context of the twin national epidemics of gender violence and HIV.[40] Starting with a tragic vignette of the death of a young Trobriand woman detached from her family in Alotau and married to a violent husband from the Highlands, she offers a 'moral narrative of modernity' (after Webb Keane).[41] She observes not just the diversity of patterns of gender and gender violence in PNG but also how they are locally typified by stereotypic images of the Trobriands and the Highlands. Yet the popular portrait of the Trobriands as a site of gender equality, female autonomy, and a sex-positive culture is, she suggests, relatively faithful to reality, even if this is sensationalised in monikers such as *Islands of Love*.[42] She sees sex as integral to the flows between persons which constitute the relational Trobriand person, woman or man. Moreover, the Trobriands is a space relatively free of gender violence compared to the Highlands and other parts of the country.

Yet, in the conventional cartography of the HIV epidemic, the Trobriands is located as a 'hot spot', because of the 'high risk' behaviour associated with sexual expression in adolescence, the preference for multiple partners before settling into the pleasures of monogamous marriage and the high rates of divorce and remarriage. This notion of risk not only reveals a negative, moralistic view of human sexuality but conceives those exposed to such risks as isolated individuals. Lepani emphasises how the discourse of human rights entered PNG primarily

---

38   Merry, *Human Rights and Gender Violence*, p. 194.
39   Gibbs, 'Men's Matters'.
40   Katherine Lepani, 'Proclivity and prevalence: Accounting for the dynamics of sexual violence in the response to HIV in Papua New Guinea', this volume.
41   Webb Keane, 2007, *Christian Moderns: Freedom and Fetish in the Mission Encounter*, Berkeley, Los Angeles and London: University of California Press, p. 4.
42   See Lepani, *Islands of Love, Islands of Risk*.

in the context of the HIV epidemic and the associated 'epidemic' of gender violence, and how the person imaged in human rights discourse was confluent with the isolated subject or patient of biomedicine.[43] The policy response in PNG powerfully conjugates the epidemics and prioritises large quantitative surveys like the stalled IBBS survey funded by the World Bank in evaluations of 'evidence-based practice'.[44] The language of individual rights resurfaces in the context of voluntary testing, treatment and counselling with the added rhetorical claim in the PNG context that this is confidential (a claim hard to realise in practice). The Tok Pisin phrase promises: *testim na tritim, em raet bilong yu* (test and treat, it's your right). But, as Lepani concludes, this can be a hollow promise given the unequal power relations between clients and service providers and the incapacity of the health system to follow up or deliver ART services for all positive people.

Translating and vernacularising human rights in the Pacific: *Tok ples* and *talanoa*

There are many words and underlying metaphors which have been used to describe the way in which the notions and values of human rights move around the world, from the meeting rooms of the United Nations in New York and Geneva to the modest environs of Pacific universities, government and NGO offices, to rural workshops in thatch and bamboo huts or in the open air. This volume as a whole rejects the notion of a unidirectional flow from global to local, of seeing globalisation as akin to 'hypodermic insertion' or even 'infiltration' (two words saturated with organic corporeal metaphors in their conception of local cultures and contexts).[45] Rather the authors and editors of this volume prefer to deploy the linguistic concepts of translation and vernacularisation

---

43   Ibid.

44   On indicator culture compare Sally Engle Merry, 2011, 'Measuring the world: Indicators, human rights, and global governance', in *Corporate Lives: New Perspectives on the Social Life of the Corporate Form*, ed. Damana Partridge, Marina Welker and Rebecca Hardin, Wenner Gren Symposium Series, *Current Anthropology*, 52 Supplementary Issue 3: S83–S95; Peggy Levitt and Sally Engle Merry, 2011, 'Making human rights in the vernacular: Navigating the culture/ rights divide', in *Gender and Culture at the Limit of Rights*, ed. Dorothy Hodgson, pp. 81–100, Philadelphia: University of Pennsylvania Press.

45   See Biersack, 'Human rights work in Papua New Guinea, Fiji and Vanuatu'; and Zorn, 'Translating and internalising international human rights law', this volume.

which have been focal to the influential writings of Sally Engle Merry on gender violence and human rights.[46] They equally witness the problems and limits of this focus.

These linguistic concepts can be used in a way which gives primacy to the original utterance or text and sees the process of localisation as one in which that text or utterance is translated into a local or vernacular language, *tok ples* to use the word in Melanesia pidgin. Yet, in accord with many recent theorists of translation,[47] Merry stresses not a unidirectional flow but a *reciprocal* flow of meanings and values in which particular languages and cultural contexts not only localise and modify the global text or utterance, but can also radically transform, distort or even subvert the meanings and values of human rights, and thus impinge on the character of the global discourse itself.

Merry has witnessed the 'vernacularization' of human rights pre-eminently in global debates about gender violence. In 2006, she described a process whereby local agents made international human rights laws and ideas applicable or resonant in local contexts, initially in campaigns against gender violence in Fiji, India and Hong Kong.[48] She suggested that although 'human rights ideas are repackaged in culturally resonant wrappings, the interior remains a radical challenge to patriarchy'.[49] That interior was filled with ideas of 'autonomy, choice, bodily integrity, and equality, ideas embedded in the legal documents that constitute human rights law' which 'endure even as the ideas are translated'.[50] She highlights how those who experience human rights violations, like women who are victims of gender violence, come to see their experience through the 'mediation of middle level and elite activists who reframe their everyday problems in human rights terms'.[51]

---

46   Merry, *Human Rights and Gender Violence*; Merry, *Gender Violence*.
47   For example, Ronit Ricci, 2011, *Islam Translated: Literature, Conversion and the Arabic Cosmopolis of South and Southeast Asia*, Chicago: Chicago University Press; Linda Jaivin, 2013, *Found in Translation: In Praise of a Plural World. Quarterly Essay* 52, Collingwood: Griffen Press.
48   Merry, *Human Rights and Gender Violence*; Sally Engle Merry, 2006, 'Transnational human rights and local activism: Mapping the middle', in *Anthropology and Human Rights in a New Key*, ed. Mark Goodale, *American Anthropologist* 108(1): 38–51.
49   Merry, *Human Rights and Gender Violence*, p. 221.
50   Ibid., p. 221.
51   Ibid., p. 219.

For Merry this is *not just* a top down flow from global universal meanings to local parochial understandings through the practices of such activists engaged in translation. It is rather a reciprocal process, 'from the global arenas down and from local arenas up'.[52] She sees such intermediaries as Janus-faced, looking both ways between the worlds of 'transnational human rights and local cultural practices', as empowered in their capacity to broker knowledge, to mediate meanings and hopefully to deliver results to both local communities and states and transnational actors including donors. But she also witnesses their vulnerability since their commitments are ambiguous and they are subject to 'charges of disloyalty and double-dealing'.[53] She plots different examples on a continuum: from processes of vernacularisation which replicate international messages of women's human rights against gender violence with only a thin cultural repackaging (like battered women's centres in Hong Kong offering Western-style group therapy), to those which offer a thicker repackaging in cultural contexts (like Native Hawaiian Christian anger management programs), to those which are effectively hybridised such as *nari adalats* or women's courts which emerged in India from the mid-1990s to promote women's rights.[54] She highlights the difficulties of all such work in maintaining the trust of the women who suffer violence, the communities and states within which they are embedded and the international agencies and donors which are supporting or funding their work. That work is limited both by active resistance to human rights and superficial compliance, but also by the discursive limits of the rights regime, which 'focuses on individual injury and cultural oppression rather than structural violence',[55] those global and national inequalities of class, race and gender.

Ultimately then, despite her stress on the reciprocal potential of translation in vernacularisation, Merry suggests that the dominant flow is a 'top-down process from the transnational to the local and the powerful to the less powerful' and thus 'human rights ideas are not fully indigenised',[56] since their foreign, EuroAmerican origins are visible and palpable. They are 'embedded in a distinctive vision

---

52   Merry, 'Transnational human rights and local activism', p. 38.
53   Ibid., p. 40.
54   Ibid., pp. 44–46.
55   Ibid., p. 48.
56   Ibid., p. 49.

of the good society that envisions the state as the provider of social justice and the individual as responsible for making rights claims on the state'.[57] She sees this as a modernist, emancipatory, homogenising vision, which promotes human rights along with 'democracy, the rule of law, capitalism and the free market'.[58] So, for her, to be part of the human rights system advocates must emphasise 'individualism, autonomy, choice, bodily integrity and equality'.[59] Thus, Merry was early alert to some of the questions posed by critics of the transnational translations of human rights, as a novel cultural imperialism. She was also alert to how inequities in global political economy and the unidirectional flows of aid and development limited the 'bottom up' flow of meanings and values.

Merry's writing helps us to situate the western Pacific in this transnational context. We can witness how the original articles of the Convention on the Elimination of All Forms of Discrimination against Women[60] have been translated into Pacific languages and used not just in legal judgements,[61] but in government and NGO campaigns against gender violence.[62] But vernacularisation is not just translating

---

57 Ibid.

58 Ibid.

59 Ibid.

60 Convention on the Elimination of All Forms of Discrimination against Women, G.A. Res. 34/180, U.N. GAOR, 34th Sess. Suppl. No. 46, at 193, U.N. Doc. A/34/46 (1979).

61 Zorn, 'Translating and internalising international human rights law', this volume.

62 On Grace Mera Molisa, see Margaret Jolly, 1991, 'The politics of difference: Feminism, colonialism and decolonization in Vanuatu', in *Intersexions: Gender/Class/Culture/Ethnicity*, ed. Gill Bottomley, Marie de Lepervanché and Jeannie Martin, pp. 52–74, St. Leonards, NSW: Allen & Unwin; Margaret Jolly, 1996, '*Woman Ikat Raet Long Human Raet O No*? Women's rights, human rights and domestic violence in Vanuatu', *Feminist Review* 52: 169–90; Jolly, Lee, Lepani, Naupa and Rooney, *Falling Through the Net?*; Nicole George, 2012, *Situating Women: Gender Politics and Circumstance in Fiji*, Canberra: ANU E Press; on Fiji, Lynda Newland, 'Villages, violence and atonement in Fiji', this volume; and Nicole George, '"Lost in translation": Gender violence, human rights and women's capabilities in Fiji', this volume.

In 2014, I reflected on how Grace Mera Molisa was a fine exemplar of what Merry calls 'mapping the middle', Janus-faced between the global and the local and thus in a perilous position. I compare the appropriation of rights discourse in the struggle for land rights and indigenous citizenship in the independence movement of the 1970s in which both men and women were involved and where rights language was rarely critiqued as not indigenous. By contrast when human rights discourse was deployed in the 1990s in relation to gender discrimination and gender violence it was characterised as foreign by opponents. See Margaret Jolly, 2014, 'Vernacularization in Vanuatu: Human rights and *raet* in engendering persons and collectivities', paper presented in panel Anthropological Approaches to Law, Gender and Human Rights: Papers in honour of Sally Engle Merry at the American Anthropological Association Meetings, Omni Shoreham Hotel, Washington, D.C., 5 December. See also the recent paper Selina Tusitala Marsh, 2014, 'Black Stone Poetry: Vanuatu's Grace Mera Molisa', *Cordite Poetry Review*, 1 February.

between languages but between broader epistemologies and histories, engaging rival notions of the person and of gender, and situated in terrains of power and property framed by colonialism, Christianity and contemporary globalisation.

Resistance is equally patent in how many Pacific states long failed to ratify CEDAW (Tonga and Palau until the time of writing and Tuvalu till 1999, although then without reservations). Others refused to accept certain foundational articles such as Article 5a which urges the modification of customary practices which are based on the idea of 'inferiority or the superiority of either of the sexes' and are thus seen to discriminate against women (for example, bride price in PNG or *bulubulu* in Fiji). Some Pacific states which have ratified CEDAW have been very slow to file the mandatory annual reports on progress in implementation; for example, PNG ratified CEDAW in 1995, but filed the first, second, third and fourth periodic reports only in 2008 at the instigation of Dame Carol Kidu.[63] Rejection is also there in the judgements by local courts which negate the salience of CEDAW or the Convention of the Rights of the Child in favour of national state laws or community values.[64]

But the flow from the local to the global is not just the negative agency of refusal or resistance. This is patent in the very inclusion of gender violence as a form of discrimination against women, which was not included in the original articles of CEDAW but rather through the auspices of the General Assembly's Resolutions of 1985 and 1990 which declared 'freedom from gender violence a human right' and by a General Recommendation of the CEDAW Committee in 1992 which added gender-based violence as part of the definition of discrimination. These, like the original convention, were the result of a diverse array

Taylor observes, however, that the translation of 'right' into Bislama as *raet* can signal not so much the right embodied in a person, but the right of one person over another. This was the sense deployed by that male movement on the island of Espiritu Santo, called Violence Against Men, which saw the proposed change in family laws (passed in modified form in 2008) and the funding given by foreign donors to women's equality as an attack on the *raet* of men to assume authority over women. See John P. Taylor, 2008, 'The social life of rights: "Gender antagonism", modernity and *raet* in Vanuatu', in *Changing Pacific Masculinities*, ed. John P. Taylor, special Issue of *The Australian Journal of Anthropology* 19(2): 165–78.

63   See Zorn, 'Translating and internalising international human rights law', this volume.
64   Ibid.

of women's movements and feminist NGOs coalescing to effect change through the UN. Increasingly through the 1980s, 1990s and 2000s Pacific women's movements were vitally involved in this process.[65]

In Merry's understanding, this process of 'vernacularization' is inherently political as much as linguistic or cultural.[66] This is clear in how she critically deploys the cognate concept of 'culture', which she argues can be used to describe not just the particularistic local cultures of the Global South but those very congregations which form at the United Nations, constituted by representatives of states and NGOs, lawyers and gender experts, policymakers and activists. In labelling this a 'culture' with its own particular practices and discourses she echoes Dipesh Chakrabarty's *Provincializing Europe*,[67] challenging the presumptions of imperial universals by showing how these concepts and values emerge from a particular time and place. In this vision, United Nations fora in New York and Geneva are not imperial centres hovering above the globe, but emplaced, even provincial or parochial. It may be that the notion of the human in human rights has a distinctively European and Enlightenment genealogy, and emerged as a compelling moral value in the aftermath of the horrors of World War II and the Holocaust. But, like many other feminist scholars,[68] Merry stresses how non-Western women and particularly women from the Global South have been centrally involved in talking about and promoting human rights for decades, and have thus expanded and transformed its core meanings and values. It is difficult then to dismiss human rights values as quintessentially Western imperial or even 'foreign' to the Pacific. I also doubt the characterisation of human rights regimes as 'authoritarian' since, although they may embed doctrinal values, it is clear that conventions like CEDAW often fail to be truly legitimated by states or carry authority, let alone authoritarian power, in practice. Rather we witness a *talanoa*, the Fijian word for 'extended discussion' or 'dialogue' between Pacific women about human rights.

---

65   See Annelise Riles, 2000, *The Network Inside Out*, Ann Arbor: University of Michigan Press; George, *Situating Women*.
66   Merry, *Human Rights and Gender Violence*; Merry, *Gender Violence*.
67   Dipesh Chakrabarty, 2008 [2000], *Provincializing Europe: Postcolonial Thought and Historical Difference*, second edition, with preface by author in response to critics, Princeton and Oxford: Princeton University Press.
68   Hilsdon, Macintyre, Mackie and Stivens (eds), *Human Rights and Gender Politics*.

Merry also critiques the culture concept as it is used by some activists and experts who are promoting CEDAW and struggling to redress gender violence.[69] 'Culture' here becomes a monolithic obstacle, a roadblock in the free circulation of the notion of human rights.[70] Although anthropologists have thoroughly critiqued the concept of culture as something bounded, consensual and eternal, it is still being used in that way by some involved in gender and development and in struggles against gender violence. Crucially this criticism equally pertains to those local Pacific conservatives who deploy a reified concept of 'culture' to defend the values of gender hierarchy as cherished traditions, unable to be transformed by the novel values of women's equality with men and freedom from discrimination and gender violence.[71] This is why Merry asks: 'Who speaks for culture?'[72] In her view we cannot concede that only senior, high-ranking or powerful men can so speak. Women and young people must be able to speak for culture too, and this entails seeing culture not as a 'Frankenstein's corpse' revived to intimidate women and the powerless,[73] but as created and contested, open and changing.

It is interesting to compare the debates about the 'vernacularization' of human rights in recent decades in the Pacific with the discussion of the indigenisation of Christianity in the region. Of all the foreign agents associated with the longue durée of European colonialism, missionaries were the most successful in transforming local beliefs and practices through processes of Christian conversion. In this process the crucial role of Pacific Islander missionaries as translators and agents of transformation is slowly being acknowledged. They were involved in 'mapping the middle'[74] in ways similar to Pacific human rights activists today and were similarly often in perilous and vulnerable positions, like those early Samoan missionaries, men

69   Merry, 'Tensions between global law and local social justice'; Merry, 'Transnational human rights and local activism'.
70   See also Jane K. Cowan, Marie-Bénédicte Dembour and Richard A. Wilson, 2001, 'Introduction', in *Culture and Rights: Anthropological Perspectives*, ed. Jane K. Cowan, Marie-Bénédicte Dembour and Richard A. Wilson, pp. 1–26, Cambridge and New York: Cambridge University Press; Jane K. Cowan, 2006, 'Culture and rights after *Culture and Rights*', in *Anthropology and Human Rights in a New Key*, ed. Mark Goodale, *American Anthropologist* 108(1): 9–24; and Levitt and Merry, 'Making human rights in the vernacular'.
71   See Newland, 'Villages, violence and atonement in Fiji', this volume.
72   Merry, *Human Rights and Gender Violence*, p. 19.
73   Grace Mera Molisa's words; see Jolly, 'The politics of difference'.
74   Merry, 'Transnational human rights and local activism'.

and women, who were martyrs in southern and central Vanuatu.[75] Throughout the Pacific today Christianity is avowed as indigenous, as crucial to quotidian ways of life in villages and towns and the nationalist foundations of independent states such as Papua New Guinea, Vanuatu and Fiji which are the focus of this volume. Despite earlier anthropological critiques of Christianity as a foreign colonial force,[76] along with the occupation of lands by settlers, the extraction of commodities and people, and the formation of colonial states, *lotu* is today regularly avowed as 'of the place' in a way *bisnis* and *gavman* are often not. Recently anthropologists have been eager to acknowledge and analyse this process of indigenisation.[77] And yet, in an historical irony, present moves to vernacularise human rights are sometimes impeded by the results of that successful earlier project of vernacularisation, namely Christian conversion. This historical process has produced the predicament whereby introduced Christian forms of gender hierarchy have creolised with indigenous gender hierarchies to produce recalcitrant and militant forms of male domination which are staunchly defended as traditional: *iTaukei* or *kastom*. God's divine ordination of male authority is thereby powerfully proclaimed as indigenous.[78]

This process is palpable both in Fiji and Vanuatu, as revealed in the chapters by Newland and by John Taylor and Natalie Araújo in this volume. Newland connects the gender violence amongst *iTaukei* in Fiji, and especially the endemic problems of domestic violence, rape and child sexual abuse, to pervasive patterns of gender hierarchy. She argues that the under-reporting of such violent acts to police is motivated by a 'focus on maintaining village harmony between men,

---

75   Latu Latai, 2014, 'From open *fales* to mission houses: Negotiating the boundaries of "Domesticity" in Samoa', in *Divine Domesticities: Paradoxes of Christian Modernities in Asia and the Pacific*, ed. Hyaeweol Choi and Margaret Jolly, pp. 299–324, Canberra: ANU Press; Latu Latai, 2016, 'Covenant keepers: A history of Samoan (LMS) missionary wives in the western Pacific from 1839 to 1979', PhD thesis, The Australian National University.

76   For example, Roger M. Keesing, 1992, *Custom and Confrontation: The Kwaio Struggle for Cultural Autonomy*, Chicago: Chicago University Press; Margaret Jolly and Martha Macintyre (eds), 1989, *Family and Gender in the Pacific: Domestic Contradictions and the Colonial Impact*, Cambridge: Cambridge University Press, digital reprint 2009.

77   For example, Robbins, *Becoming Sinners*; and Mosko, 'Partible penitents', for PNG; Christina Toren, 2003, 'Becoming a Christian in Fiji: An ethnographic study of ontogeny', *Journal of the Royal Anthropological Institute* 9(4): 709–27; and Matt Tomlinson, 2009, *In God's Image: The Metaculture of Fijian Christianity*, Berkeley: University of California Press, for Fiji.

78   See Taylor, 'The social life of rights'.

not on reparations for the victim'.[79] The value of *vakaturaga*, literally 'in the way of the chief', is not just a reinscription of the indigenous cultural authority of male chiefs, revealed in the hierarchical patterns of drinking kava (*yagona*), but enshrines these chiefs as God's representatives in a divine order to which both women and subordinate men must submit. Similarly husbands are seen not just as secular heads of households but as having divine authority over their wives; as one interlocutor remarked, 'Man represents God in the family'.[80]

As Newland observes, Fijian domesticity radically changed with Christian conversion: from polygyny to monogamy, from men's houses to nuclear family households and from a focus on sibling to conjugal bonds. Women's land rights and mobility were curtailed in the early colonial period. New marriages are often marked by high levels of violence inflicted by husbands on wives, especially if she is a cross-cousin where a relation of gender parity has to be transformed into hierarchy.[81] Virilocal residence means wives have little support from natal kin. A husband's violence is often legitimated by blaming the wife for lack of respect, and local efforts by chiefs and lay preachers are directed towards reconciliation of the couple rather than justice for the victim. Newland argues that *bulubulu* practices of atonement, although Christianised in some respects, persist relatively untransformed, perpetuate gender hierarchy and legitimate male violence. Yet, she also acknowledges that many Christian churches have been vitally involved in the provision of places of refuge for victims in urban areas, even though both distance and stigma make these places unappealing for most rural women and girls who are victims of gender violence.

In their chapter John P. Taylor and Natalie Araújo discern rather different processes at work in the creolisation of indigenous and introduced Christian gender hierarchies in Vanuatu. They focus on the pervasive beliefs, practices and narratives concerning *nakaemas* (sorcery). In comparison to Fiji, indigenous patterns of rank in Vanuatu were diverse and complex, with achieved titles in public 'graded societies' (both male and female) and male 'secret societies' in

---

79   Newland, 'Villages, violence and atonement in Fiji', this volume.
80   Ibid.
81   Christina Toren, 1995, 'Cosmogonic aspects of desire and compassion in Fiji', in *Cosmos and Society in Oceania*, ed. Daniel de Coppet and André Itéanu, pp. pp. 57–82, Oxford and Herndon: Berg.

the north and more ascribed chiefly powers in central and southern parts of the archipelago.[82] They observe how, in the past, high-ranking men and chiefs were thought able to exert positive powers to make things grow and heal and negative powers to destroy and harm. Today there is a widespread perception that with Christian conversion and the erosion of such customary hierarchies, such power has become unleashed and democratised and is now too often in the hands of young men who use awesome methods such as *su* to steal property and to seduce and sexually assault women. Taylor and Araújo document two chilling cases of *nakaemas* being used in gang rapes and, in the second case, the murder of a young ni-Vanuatu woman. Sorcery is thus a form of gender violence, and one chronically neglected by aid agencies involved in development until very recently. Yet a report by the Vanuatu Women's Centre in 2011 documented that 49 per cent of ni-Vanuatu women considered that of all forms of violence 'violence due to sorcery' was their greatest concern.[83]

The gendering and sexualisation of *nakaemas* is grounded in the profound inequalities of men and women not just in Vanuatu *kastom* but in the dynamics of a 'rapidly transforming capitalist political economy', especially in the port towns of Vila and Luganville. The autonomy and mobility of young urban women and girls is threatened by a punitive form of male surveillance, which reinforces homosocial and hierarchical bonds between men. They are not, as the mobile phone company Digicel promises, 'free to roam'; indeed, young women often turn their mobile phones off at night to avoid *nakaemas* infiltrating through the network. Christian leaders, like police and judges, are not immune from accusations of using *nakaemas* themselves. Indeed, as Taylor graphically shows elsewhere,[84] the *taviu* of the Anglican Melanesian Brotherhood are credited with ambivalent divine power, both to combat and to effect sorcery.[85]

---

82   See Margaret Jolly, 1994, *Women of the Place:* Kastom, *Colonialism and Gender in Vanuatu*, Amsteldijk: Harwood Academic Publishers.

83   John P. Taylor and Natalie Araújo, 'Sorcery talk, gender violence and the law in Vanuatu', this volume.

84   John P. Taylor, 2010, 'The troubled histories of a stranger god: Religious crossing, sacred power, and Anglican colonialism in Vanuatu', *Comparative Studies in Society and History* 52(2): 418–46; John P. Taylor, 2016, 'Two baskets worn at once: Christianity, sorcery and sacred power in Vanuatu', in *Christianity, Conflict, and Renewal in Australia and the Pacific*, ed. Fiona Magowan and Carolyn Schwarz, pp. 139–60, Leiden: Brill Publishers.

85   See also Sabine Hess, 2009, *Person and Place: Ideas, Ideals and Practice of Sociality on Vanua Lava, Vanuatu*, Volume 2 in Series *Person, Space and Memory in the Contemporary Pacific*, Oxford: Berghahn; Thorgeir Kolsus, 2007, '"We are the Anglicans": An ethnography of empowering

Those who seek to oppose gender violence in such Pacific contexts are thus often in a perilous position, vulnerable to being accused of being traitors to their 'culture' and subject to violent forms of repression and male backlash, through physical coercion, persuasive threats and even nefarious forces.[86] Nicole George shows how activists working at the Fiji Women's Crisis Centre and the Fiji Women's Rights Movement have been subject to forms of state violence sanctioned by current and past military regimes.[87] Feminist leaders and activists have been arrested, interrogated and sometimes silenced.[88] Even as military regimes in Fiji have endorsed what seemed to be progressive principles such as the 'no drop' policy (whereby once gender violence is reported to police the charges cannot be dropped), or the more recent announcement of 'zero tolerance' of gender violence, the very authoritarian forms of implementing such policies can generate perverse effects. Reporting to the police is even further discouraged as communities close ranks to protect male perpetrators and their collective reputation while women continue to suffer not just the original violence but forms of justice which favour a male-dominated harmony rather than the rights of the victim to reparation.

As Merry attests in her books and elsewhere, those who struggle against gender violence and promote women's human rights are often in a fraught and precarious situation. It is not just a case of benign interpretation or mediation between local and global cultures.[89] The very tensions and political contests between competing values can leave such activists perilously alienated from both their domestic environment and the transnational networks and circuits on which they move. This is obvious in high profile cases such as the young Pakistani woman Malala Yousafzai targeted by the Taliban for going to school and promoting the cause of women's education.[90] It is also clear for those women who have used the language of human rights not just

---

conversions in a Melanesian island society', Dr. polit thesis, Oslo: University of Oslo.
86   John P. Taylor, 2008, 'The social life of rights: "Gender antagonism", modernity and *raet* in Vanuatu', in *Changing Pacific Masculinities*, ed. John P. Taylor, Special Issue of *The Australian Journal of Anthropology* 19(2): 165–78; Biersack, 'Human rights work in Papua New Guinea, Fiji and Vanuatu', this volume.
87   George, *Situating Women*.
88   See Newland, 'Villages, violence and atonement in Fiji'; and George, '"Lost in translation"', this volume.
89   Merry, 'Transnational human rights and local activism'.
90   See Aletta Biersack and Martha Macintyre, 'Introduction: Gender violence and human rights in the western Pacific', this volume.

to oppose the Burmese army's 'license to rape' but the very nationalist, secessionist armies of which they were a part.[91] Women involved in peace-making processes in both Bougainville and Solomons conflicts were often themselves at risk of injury or death in mediating conflicts,[92] especially when they raised confronting issues of gender violence in war, of rape and sexual torture, used by all militarised male protagonists, including their own kin or men on their side of the conflict.

Lost in translation? Women's capabilities and prospects of economic and political empowerment

Translation is the invisible skein that binds our world.[93]

In her compelling chapter Nicole George argues that an undue emphasis on culture, translation and vernacularisation, evinced in the work of Sally Engle Merry and others, has meant that broader questions of women's capabilities for economic and political empowerment have been occluded. She is inspired by the capabilities approach of Sen, Nussbaum and Macintyre. As suggested above, I consider Merry's approach as 'cultural' only insofar as she critically deploys that concept to highlight the political stakes at play in contests about culture. As we saw above, Merry is keenly aware how reciprocal acts of translation are constrained or even negated by the inequities of global political economy and the flow of aid and development from the rich and powerful to the relatively poor and weak. But I absolutely agree with George that the emphasis on the power of the law and especially of international law to combat gender violence has not only been unduly optimistic but has sometimes failed to acknowledge

91   Jane M. Ferguson, 2013, 'Is the pen mightier than the AK-47? Tracking Shan women's militancy within and beyond the ongoing internal conflict in Burma', *Intersections: Gender and Sexuality in Asia and the Pacific* 33.
92   See Rebecca Monson, 2013, 'Vernacularising political participation: Strategies of women peace-builders in Solomon Islands', *Intersections: Gender and Sexuality in Asia and the Pacific* 33; and Anna-Karina Hermkens, 2013, '"*Raits blong mere*?" Framing human rights and gender relations in Solomon Islands', *Intersections: Gender and Sexuality in Asia and the Pacific* 33.
93   Jaivin, *Found in Translation*, p. 2.

how changes in the broader economic and political situation in which Pacific women are situated powerfully moulds and often constrains their capabilities to redress gender violence.

Jean Zorn's excellent chapter shows what *has* been achieved legally by reviewing the way in which CEDAW has been used (or not) in legal cases heard in Pacific jurisdictions. She stresses that CEDAW, as a convention ratified (or not) by states, is technically non-enforceable, since it lacks direct sanctions. Its ratification requires due diligence by states and is limited to their behaviour, since it does not extend to the behaviour of individual citizens.[94] It generates effective action primarily by persuasion and the powers of international shaming of those who fail to sign or comply. Yet, as Biersack points out, the lack of coercive sanctions does not totally negate forcible persuasion given that most of the Pacific states considered here, although sovereign, are relatively poor and weak and thus subject to the conditionalities of foreign aid, especially as exercised by states like Australia and the United States (China has its conditionalities too, though these are often less public and transparent).[95] Signing onto CEDAW by Pacific states was clearly not merely a sign of passionate commitment to gender equality by predominantly male politicians.[96]

Still, as is clear from Zorn's analysis of case law across several jurisdictions in the Anglophone Pacific, CEDAW has had a definite impact and indeed a 'salutary effect' on island nations across the Pacific, including PNG. She weighs up the relative merits of Sally Engle Merry and Bonita Meyersfeld's assessments of CEDAW's impact in terms of their respective models of 'vernacularization' and 'infiltration' and adjudges it a qualified success, insofar as an international convention can only aspire to shape the behaviour of states rather than of individuals within those states. Clearly there is a difference between a non-enforceable international convention and a national law as enshrined in statute. But courts can translate the provisions of CEDAW into their decisions even if the national parliament has not enacted a statute binding on its citizens.

---

94   Zorn, 'Translating and internalising international human rights law', this volume.
95   See Biersack, 'Human rights work in Papua New Guinea, Fiji and Vanuatu', this volume.
96   Biersack and Macintyre, 'Introduction: Gender violence and human rights in the western Pacific', this volume; Biersack, 'Human rights work in Papua New Guinea, Fiji and Vanuatu', this volume.

This is precisely what has happened in several states of the Pacific, including PNG, Vanuatu, Fiji and Samoa. CEDAW has been invoked in court cases primarily to assert its relevance and more rarely to deny it. It has been used variously as a precedent, as an authority for change, as a way of invalidating the currency of local statutes or customs and even in ways that presumes its powers are parallel to a domestic statute.[97] It has been used in a wide variety of cases apropos gender issues in customary land law, in arranged marriages and most frequently in sexual violence or rape. The most empowering use of CEDAW has perhaps been by the Australian feminist barrister and judge Jocelynne Scutt, even in the dark days of Bainimarama's military regime in Fiji. Acting as a judge of the High Court of Fiji, Family Division, she voided five cases of arranged marriages within Fiji's Indian community in 2008–09 on the grounds that arranged marriage was itself coercive (and that no proof of physical injury or threat was needed). Annulment was granted since such marriages were seen to violate CEDAW; section 26 of the Family Law Act of Fiji requests courts to take CEDAW into account when reaching decisions. Given Justice Scutt's history as scholar and feminist on questions of gender violence, Zorn is inclined to adjudge that this reference to CEDAW was her own initiative and that her judgements inspired other young men and women in similar situations to turn to the courts.

Dame Carol Kidu was equally central in promoting the crucial significance of CEDAW in combatting gender violence and promoting human rights both in PNG and the region more generally. She was a prime mover behind the PNG CEDAW report of 2008 which covered several reporting periods and which, says Zorn, was 'not shy' in finding women's subordination in the patriarchal patterns of customary norms and institutions, Christianity and introduced patterns of politics. At the national level this is symbolised by the *Haus Tambaran*, modelled on a Sepik men's house where only men congregate, in a fashion similar to the national parliament of that period, where Dame Carol was the sole female member. Dame Carol Kidu's promotion of CEDAW extended beyond PNG; she clearly not only 'mapped the middle' between the local and the global but created a novel cartography for empowering women in the region.

---

97   Zorn, 'Translating and internalising international human rights law', this volume.

Even though Kidu has now retired as a member of parliament and a minister in PNG she is still vitally engaged in promoting women's empowerment, nationally, regionally and globally.

But, as the chapters by Aletta Biersack and Nicole George show, it is important not to be unduly optimistic about the gains made nor the power of CEDAW and the discourse of human rights to redress gender violence in the region. Biersack recounts a trio of rather sobering histories from Papua New Guinea, Fiji and Vanuatu. These evince the faltering progress of efforts to reduce gender violence in these three countries despite decades of efforts by state agencies like the Department of Community Development in PNG and a range of NGOs, including the Fiji Women's Crisis Centre and the Fiji Women's Rights Movement, the Vanuatu Women's Centre, Women Arise, and Family and Sexual Violence Action Committees in PNG (which link government agencies, private sector and civil society partners). Like Zorn,[98] she highlights the delays in the ratification of CEDAW, the initial reservations and caveats (usually on the basis of preserving indigenous culture) and the long delays in filing reports for all these three states. Like Zorn, she acknowledges how international conventions signed by sovereign states require only that they exercise 'due diligence'; these are non-enforceable laws. But Biersack cogently observes that, although sovereign, these three states are poor and aid dependent, and thus vulnerable to pressures from aid donors to sign on to such conventions and to promote the values of gender equality and human rights.

Much effort to redress gender violence has been expended on legal reforms, through acts of legislation like the Crimes Decree passed by Fiji's Parliament in 2009, the Family Protection Act passed by the Vanuatu Parliament in 2008 or the new Criminal Code passed by the National Parliament of PNG in 2002. These variously updated notions of gender violence and sexual penetration, legislated penalties for offenders and offered protection for women and children who were victims. But resistance to such legal reform was widespread. For example, the Family Protection Bill in Vanuatu was first drafted in 1997 but not passed till over a decade later, because of virulent opposition including from the all-male Malvatumauri Council of Chiefs, the Vanuatu Christian Council and a short-lived but powerful male backlash movement based in Luganville, sardonically called the

---

98   Zorn, 'Translating and internalising international human rights law', this volume.

Violence Against Men and Family Protection Centre.[99] Opponents mounted conservative arguments to respect the male authority inherent in *kastom*, in resistance to what is portrayed as the neo-colonial regime of the international human rights agenda. Given such resistance it is not surprising that these three histories are frustratingly non-linear. Still, we must acknowledge that feminist gains have hardly been linear in the United States and Australia either. Struggles for reproductive rights, affordable child care and equal pay have been waged and resisted, in a strenuous choreography of moves for and against gender equality.

In the Pacific, resistance to gender equality often entails an insistence on customary modes of justice rather than those of the introduced law. Restorative justice in Fiji, Vanuatu and PNG can be portrayed as win-win in that it seeks harmony and reconciliation rather than the win-lose of the state legal system. But it is focused on restoring relations between men rather than pursuing justice for the female victim. Echoing Newland on Fiji, Biersack shows similar processes at work elsewhere which dissuade women from reporting gender or sexual violence to the police: an undue sense of shame and heavy familial, communal and church pressures, even threats of being ostracised from communities. As earlier observed, sometimes progressive legal reforms can have perverse effects: the 'no drop' policy in Fiji meant women were even less likely to report gender violence since charges could not be withdrawn and the current zero-tolerance campaign may, through the introduction of gatekeeper committees in communities, rather be reinforcing a desire for communal resolution before gender or sexual violence is reported to police. Biersack stresses that not all men are united in their resistance to the novel values of gender equality and human rights; indeed male advocacy has been important in all three countries.[100] The Pacific, like Australia, has its 'male champions for change'.[101] Yet, overall, this sequence of legal solutions has had little effect in actually reducing levels of gender violence and there is even some evidence of increasing severity, especially in urban areas. Biersack refuses to be totally pessimistic about future possibilities and envisages a more reciprocal process of influence between global

---

99 Taylor, 'The social life of rights'.
100 See Gibbs, 'Men's Matters', this volume.
101 See Elizabeth Broderick, 2014, 'Progressing gender equity and the role of male champions for change', Address by Australia's Sex Discrimination Commissioner to third anniversary of Gender Institute, Australian National University, 21 March 2014.

and local forces which will dislodge the 'hypodermic' model of UN influence and precipitate the emergence of many worlds of human rights regimes rather than one world of universal, imperial visions.[102]

Nicole George similarly stresses the importance of connecting the processes of translation and vernacularisation of human rights with the questions of women's 'capabilities' to claim their rights and to redress gender violence. Echoing arguments made in her book *Situating Women* she shows how the space of women's agency is constrained by the broader political economy of a country, the region and the world.[103] That book showed how the relatively expansive agenda of women's groups like the YWCA in Fiji in the 1970s and 1980s gave way to a far more confined and issue-specific feminist agenda with the resurgence of ethno-nationalism in Fiji, the growth of militarism through a cycle of coups and the simultaneous emergence of neoliberal policies and audit cultures of aid.

In this volume she stresses how the military regime in Fiji has not only silenced and coralled the women's movement there but has created an economic and political climate in which women are poorer, more vulnerable and more dependent on men both for economic survival and physical protection. Gender violence has been exacerbated both by uneven capitalist development[104] and by the militarism of Fiji's political culture. The juridical success of the human rights agenda in redressing gender violence has not been matched by an actual decrease in the incidence of gender violence. Indeed, though it ostensibly opposed gender violence, the Bainimarama military regime daily performed a paradox whereby it attacked the values of human rights by silencing critics (including Fij's feminist activists) and by its authoritarian enactment of a zero-tolerance approach to gender violence.[105]

---

102 See Biersack, 'Human rights work in Papua New Guinea, Fiji and Vanuatu', this volume.

103 George, *Situating Women*.

104 On Vanuatu, see also Taylor and Araújo, 'Sorcery talk, gender violence and the law in Vanuatu', this volume.

105 Bainimarama stood down in early 2014 as head of the military to contest the elections in Fiji (17 September 2014) and his Fiji First party attained a large majority in the new parliament. His election was no doubt aided by the efficacy of the military state to effect practical changes like building bridges and roads and the way in which he supported ordinary Fijians rather than the chiefly hierarchy, and opposed ethnonationalism against Indo-Fijians. Of course his control of the media also enabled his victory, and the lack of media freedom and the dominance of military personnel in civilian roles in the government continues. It will be interesting to see what the new

The chapters in this volume thus offer a sobering and realistic evaluation of how Pacific women (and some men) are navigating turbulent waters to redress if not end gender violence. There are reasons to despair, there are also reasons to hope. The work of governments, aid donors and NGOs is ongoing alongside the efforts of ordinary Pacific people, women and men to try to redress the scourge of gender violence in this region, through persisting and innovative efforts. In ending I can only offer a few final words from another poignant song by Fred Smith from his CD *Bagarap Empires*: 'The Infinite Ocean'.

The infinite Ocean collects all the tears that we cry.[106]

Acknowledgements

Margaret Jolly especially thanks the Australian Research Council for support of this volume and this chapter in particular as part of her ARC Laureate Fellowship Project, *Engendering Persons, Transforming Things: Christianities, Commodities and Individualism in Oceania* (FL100100196). She also thanks The Australian National University for long term support of her research and of the very successful Gender Institute, where colleagues have created an empowering and mutually supportive environment. She thanks the many colleagues including the Laureate team and her co-editors who gave incisive comments on various iterations of this chapter. She offers heartfelt thanks to Carolyn Brewer for her meticulous, patient work in copyediting of the volume, for her creative attention to the images and for the final preparation for publication to ANU Press style. Finally, many thanks to the editors of final proofs at ANU Press.

References

Abu-Lughod, Lila. 2013. *Do Muslim Women Need Saving?* Cambridge, MA: Harvard University Press.

---

political environment and the election of several women to parliament means for Fijian women in the future. See Stewart Firth, 2014, 'Rights, representation and legitimacy in Fiji Politics', paper presented at East-West Centre Honolulu, 10 December.

106 These are the final words of the song 'The Infinite Ocean', song 14 on the CD *Bagarap Empires* by Iain 'Fred' Smith, 2012, 10th Anniversary edition. CD and line notes in author's collection.

Anderson, Warwick, Deborah Jenson, Richard C. Keller (eds). 2011. *Unconscious Dominions: Psychoanalysis, Colonial Trauma, and Global Sovereignties*. Durham: Duke University Press.

Bottomley, Gill, Marie de Lepervanche and Jeannie Martin (eds). 1991. *Intersexions: Gender/Class/Culture/Ethnicity*. St. Leonards: Allen & Unwin.

Braithwaite, John, Hilary Charlesworth, Peter Reddy and Leah Dunn. 2010. *Reconciliation and Architectures of Commitment: Sequencing Peace in Bougainville*. Canberra: ANU E Press. Online: press.anu.edu. au/publications/series/peacebuilding-compared/reconciliation-and-architectures-commitment (accessed 22 December 2014).

Broderick, Elizabeth. 2014. 'Progressing gender equity and the role of male champions for change'. Address by Australia's Sex Discrimination Commissioner to third anniversary of Gender Institute, Australian National University, 21 March. Online: genderinstitute.anu.edu.au/gender-institute-third-anniversary (accessed 22 December 2014).

Butler, Judith. 1990. *Gender Trouble: Feminism and the Subversion of Identity*. New York: Routledge.

———. *Bodies that Matter: On the Discursive Limits of Sex*. New York: Routledge.

Carrithers, Michael, Steven Collins and Steven Lukes (eds). 1985. *The Category of the Person: Anthropology, Philosophy, History*. Cambridge: Cambridge University Press.

Chakrabarty, Dipesh. 2008 [2000]. *Provincializing Europe: Postcolonial Thought and Historical Difference*. Second edition, with preface by author in response to critics. Princeton and Oxford: Princeton University Press.

Clifford, James. 1982. *Person and Myth: Maurice Leenhardt in the Melanesian World*. Berkeley: University of California Press.

Convention on the Elimination of All Forms of Discrimination against Women, G.A. Res. 34/180, U.N. GAOR, 34th Sess. Suppl. No. 46, at 193, U.N. Doc. A/34/46 (1979). Online: www.un.org/womenwatch/daw/cedaw/text/econvention.htm (accessed 11 December 2014).

Coppet, Daniel de and André Itéanu (eds). 1995. *Cosmos and Society in Oceania*. Oxford and Herndon: Berg.

Cowan, Jane K. 2006. 'Culture and rights after *Culture and Rights*'. In *Anthropology and Human Rights in a New Key*, ed. Mark Goodale. *American Anthropologist* 108(1): 9–24.

Cowan, Jane K., Marie-Bénédicte Dembour and Richard A. Wilson. 2001. 'Introduction'. In *Culture and Rights: Anthropological Perspectives*, ed. Cowan, Dembour and Wilson, pp. 1–26. Cambridge and New York: Cambridge University Press.

Cowan, Jane K., Marie-Bénédicte Dembour and Richard A. Wilson (eds). 2001. *Culture and Rights: Anthropological Perspectives*. Cambridge and New York: Cambridge University Press.

Douglas, Bronwen. 1998. 'Traditional individuals? Gendered negotiations of identity, Christianity and citizenship in Vanuatu'. State, Society and Governance in Melanesia, Research School of Pacific and Asian Studies. Discussion papers 98/6. Canberra: The Australian National University. Online: hdl.handle.net/1885/41815 (accessed 12 December 2014).

Ferguson, Jane M. 2013. 'Is the pen mightier than the AK-47? Tracking Shan women's militancy within and beyond the ongoing internal conflict in Burma'. *Intersections: Gender and Sexuality in Asia and the Pacific* 33. Online: intersections.anu.edu.au/issue33/ferguson.htm (accessed 8 February 2016).

Firth, Stewart. 2014. 'Rights, representation and legitimacy in Fiji Politics'. Paper presented at East-West Centre Honolulu, 10 December.

Forsyth, Miranda. 2009. *A Bird that Flies with Two Wings: Kastom and State Justice Systems in Vanuatu*. Canberra, ACT: ANU E Press.

Fry, Greg. 1997. 'Framing the Islands: Knowledge and power in changing Australian images of "the South Pacific"'. *The Contemporary Pacific* 9(2): 305–44.

George, Nicole. 2012. *Situating Women: Gender Politics and Circumstance in Fiji*. Canberra: ANU E Press. Online: press.anu.edu.au/publications/situating-women (accessed 17 November 2014).

Gibbs, Philip. 2012. 'Engendered violence and witch-killing in Simbu'. In *Engendering Violence in Papua New Guinea*, ed. Margaret Jolly, Christine Stewart, and Carolyn Brewer, pp. 107–35. Canberra: ANU E Press. Online: press.anu.edu.au/publications/engendering-violence-papua-new-guinea (accessed 28 October 2014).

Hermkens, Anna-Karina. 2012. 'Becoming Mary: Marian devotion as a solution to gender-based violence in urban PNG'. In *Engendering Violence in Papua New Guinea*, ed. Margaret Jolly, Christine Stewart and Carolyn Brewer, pp. 137–62. Canberra: ANU E Press. Online: press.anu.edu.au/publications/engendering-violence-papua-new-guinea (accessed 28 October 2014).

——. 2012. 'Journeys of resistance: Marian pilgrimages during the Bougainville conflict'. In *Pilgrimage in the Age of Globalization. Constructions of the Sacred and the Secular in Late Modernity*, ed. Nelia Hyndman-Rizk, pp. 58–78. Newcastle upon Tyne UK, Cambridge Scholars Publishing.

——. 2013. '"*Raits blong mere*?" Framing human rights and gender relations in Solomon Islands'. *Intersections: Gender and Sexuality in Asia and the Pacific* 33. Online: intersections.anu.edu.au/issue33/hermkens.htm (accessed 22 December 2014).

Hess, Sabine. 2006. 'Strathern's "dividual" and the Christian "individual": A perspective from Vanua Lava, Vanuatu'. *Oceania* 76(3): 285–96.

——. 2009. *Person and Place. Ideas, Ideals and Practice of Sociality on Vanua Lava, Vanuatu*. Volume 2 in Series *Person, Space and Memory in the Contemporary Pacific*. Oxford: Berghahn.

Hilsdon, Anne-Marie, Martha Macintyre, Vera Mackie and Maila Stivens (eds). 2000. *Human Rights and Gender Politics: Asia-Pacific Perspectives*. Routledge, London and New York.

Hodgson, Dorothy (ed.). 2011. *Gender and Culture at the Limit of Rights*. Philadelphia: University of Pennsylvania Press.

Hyndman-Rizk, Nelia. 2012. *Pilgrimage in the Age of Globalization. Constructions of the Sacred and the Secular in Late Modernity*. Newcastle upon Tyne UK, Cambridge Scholars Publishing.

Jaivin, Linda. 2013. *Found in Translation: In Praise of a Plural World. Quarterly Essay* 52. Collingwood: Griffen Press. Online: www.quarterlyessay.com.au/essay/2013/11/found-in-translation (accessed 16 November 2016).

Jolly, Margaret. 1991. 'The politics of difference: Feminism, colonialism and decolonization in Vanuatu'. In *Intersexions: Gender/Class/Culture/Ethnicity*, ed. Gill Bottomley, Marie de Lepervanche and Jeannie Martin, pp. 52–74. St. Leonards, NSW: Allen & Unwin.

——. 1994. *Women of the Place:* Kastom, *Colonialism and Gender in Vanuatu*. Amsteldijk: Harwood Academic Publishers.

——. 1996. '*Woman Ikat Raet Long Human Raet O No*? Women's rights, human rights and domestic violence in Vanuatu'. *Feminist Review* 52: 169–90.

——. 2000. '*Woman Ikat Raet Long Human Raet O No?* Women's rights, human rights and domestic violence in Vanuatu'. In *Human Rights and Gender Politics: Asia-Pacific Perspectives*, ed. Anne-Marie Hilsdon, Martha Macintyre, Vera Mackie and Maila Stivens, pp. 124–46. London and New York: Routledge. Updated and expanded version of prior publication in *Feminist Review* 52: 169–90 (1996).

——. 2012. 'Introduction—engendering violence in Papua New Guinea: Persons, power and perilous transformations'. In *Engendering Violence in Papua New Guinea*, ed. Margaret Jolly, Christine Stewart and Carolyn Brewer, pp. 1–45. Canberra: ANU E Press. Online: press.anu.edu.au?p=182671 (accessed 29 October 2014).

——. 2012. 'Prologue: The place of Papua New Guinea in contours of gender violence'. In *Engendering Violence in Papua New Guinea*, ed. Margaret Jolly, Christine Stewart and Carolyn Brewer, pp. xvii–xxvii. Canberra: ANU E Press. Online: press.anu.edu.au?p=182671 (accessed 29 October 2014).

——. 2014. 'Vernacularization in Vanuatu: Human rights and *raet* in engendering persons and collectivities'. Paper presented in panel Anthropological Approaches to Law, Gender and Human Rights: Papers in honour of Sally Engle Merry at the American Anthropological Association Meetings, Omni Shoreham Hotel, Washington, DC, 5 December.

———. 2015. '*Braed praes* in Vanuatu: Both gifts and commodities'. In *Gender and Person in Oceania*, Special Issue of *Oceania*, ed. Anna-Karina Hermkens, Rachel Morgain and John Taylor, 85(1): 63–78.

Jolly, Margaret and Martha Macintyre (eds). 1989. *Family and Gender in the Pacific: Domestic Contradictions and the Colonial Impact*. Cambridge: Cambridge University Press. Digital reprint 2009.

Jolly, Margaret, Christine Stewart and Carolyn Brewer (eds). 2012. *Engendering Violence in Papua New Guinea*. Canberra: ANU E Press. Online: press.anu.edu.au/publications/engendering-violence-papua-new-guinea (accessed 29 October 2014).

Jolly, Margaret, Helen Lee, Katherine Lepani, Anna Naupa and Michelle Rooney. 2015. *Falling Through the Net? Gender and Social Protection in the Pacific*. Discussion Paper for UN Women for Progress of the World's Women 2015–16, Report in association with G20 meetings. No. 6, September. Online: www.unwomen.org/en/digital-library/publications/2015/9/dps-gender-and-social-protection-in-the-pacific (accessed 23 March 2016).

Josephides, Lisette. 1991. 'Metaphors, metathemes and the construction of sociality: A critique of the New Melanesian ethnography'. *Man* 26(1): 145–61.

———. 2008. *Melanesian Odysseys: Negotiating the Self, Narrative and Modernity*. New York and Oxford: Berghahn.

Keesing, Roger M. 1992. *Custom and Confrontation: The Kwaio Struggle for Cultural Autonomy*. Chicago: Chicago University Press.

Kolsus, Thorgeir. 2007. '"We are the Anglicans": An ethnography of empowering conversions in a Melanesian island society'. Dr polit thesis. Oslo: University of Oslo.

Lambek, Michael and Andrew Strathern. 1998. *Bodies and Persons: Comparative Perspectives from Africa and Melanesia*. Cambridge: Cambridge University Press.

Latai, Latu. 2014. 'From open *fales* to mission houses: Negotiating the boundaries of "Domesticity" in Samoa'. In *Divine Domesticities: Paradoxes of Christian Modernities in Asia and the Pacific*, ed. Hyaeweol Choi and Margaret Jolly, pp. 299–324. Canberra: ANU Press. Online: press.anu.edu.au/publications/divine-domesticities (accessed 22 December 2014).

——. 2016. 'Covenant keepers: A history of Samoan (LMS) missionary wives in the western Pacific from 1839 to 1979'. PhD thesis, The Australian National University, under examination.

Leenhardt, Maurice. 1979. *Do Kamo: Person and Myth in the Melanesian World*. English trans. Basia Miller Galati. Preface by Vincent Crapanzano. Chicago: University of Chicago Press.

Lepani, Katherine. 2012. *Islands of Love, Islands of Risk*: *Culture and HIV in the Trobriands*. Nashville: Vanderbilt University Press.

Levitt, Peggy and Sally Engle Merry. 2011. 'Making human rights in the vernacular: Navigating the culture/rights divide'. In *Gender and Culture at the Limit of Rights*, ed. Dorothy Hodgson, pp. 81–100. Philadelphia: University of Pennsylvania Press.

Li Puma, Edward. 1998. 'Modernity and forms of personhood in Melanesia'. In *Bodies and Persons: Comparative Perspectives from Africa and Melanesia*, ed. Michael Lambek and Andrew Strathern, pp. 53–79. Cambridge: Cambridge University Press.

——. 2001. *Encompassing Others: The Magic of Modernity in Melanesia*. Ann Arbor: University of Michigan Press.

Macintyre, Martha. 2000. '"Hear us, women of Papua New Guinea": Melanesian women and human rights'. In *Human Rights and Gender Politics: Perspectives in the Asia Pacific Region*, ed. Anne-Marie Hilsdon, Martha Macintyre, Vera Mackie and Maila Stivens, pp. 141–71. London and New York: Routledge.

——. 2011. 'Money changes everything: Papua New Guinean women in a modern economy'. In *Managing Modernity in the Western Pacific*, ed. Mary Patterson and Martha Macintyre, pp. 90–120. St Lucia: University of Queensland Press.

———. 2012. 'Gender violence in Melanesia and the problem of Millennium Development Goal No. 3'. In *Engendering Violence in Papua New Guinea*, ed. Margaret Jolly, Christine Stewart and Carolyn Brewer, pp. 239–66. Canberra: ANU E Press. Online: press. anu.edu.au/publications/engendering-violence-papua-new-guinea (accessed 29 October 2014).

Mauss, Marcel. 1985 [1938]. 'A category of the human mind: The notion of person; the notion of self', trans. W.D. Halls. In *The Category of the Person: Anthropology, Philosophy, History*, ed. Michael Carrithers, Steven Collins and Steven Lukes, pp. 1–25. Cambridge: Cambridge University Press.

Médecins Sans Frontières (MSF) (Doctors Without Borders). 2011. *Hidden and Neglected: The Medical and Emotional Needs of Survivors of Family and Sexual Violence in Papua New Guinea*. Boroko: MSF. Online: www.msf.org.uk/article/papua-new-guinea-hidden-and-neglected (accessed 17 November 2014).

Merry, Sally Engle. 2004. 'Tensions between global law and local social justice: CEDAW and the problem of rape in Fiji'. Paper delivered at the Justice Across Cultures Conference, Brandeis, March. Online: www.brandeis.edu/ethics/pdfs/internationaljustice/other activities/JAC_Merry.pdf (accessed 29 October 2014).

———. 2006. 'Transnational human rights and local activism: Mapping the middle'. In *Anthropology and Human Rights in a New Key*, ed. Mark Goodale. *American Anthropologist* 108(1): 38–51.

———. 2006. *Human Rights and Gender Violence: Translating International Law into Local Justice*. Chicago and London: University of Chicago Press.

———. 2009. *Gender Violence: A Cultural Perspective*. Chichester: Wiley-Blackwell

———. 2011. 'Measuring the world: Indicators, human rights, and global governance'. In *Corporate Lives: New Perspectives on the Social Life of the Corporate Form*, ed. Damana Partridge, Marina Welker and Rebecca Hardin, Wenner Gren Symposium Series, *Current Anthropology*, 52 Supplementary Issue 3: S83–S95.

Monson, Rebecca. 2013. 'Vernacularising political participation: Strategies of women peace-builders in Solomon Islands'. *Intersections: Gender and Sexuality in Asia and the Pacific* 33. Online: intersections.anu.edu.au/issue33/monson.htm (accessed 22 December 2014).

Mosko, Mark. 2010. 'Partible penitents: Dividual personhood and Christian practice in Melanesia and the West'. *Journal of the Royal Anthropological Institute* 16(2): 215–40. See responses by several authors in same volume.

Naepels, Michel and Christine Salomon (eds). 2007. *Terrains et destins de Maurice Leenhardt*. Paris: École des Hautes Études en Sciences Sociales, Cahiers de l'Homme.

Patterson, Mary and Martha Macintyre (eds). 2011. *Managing Modernity in the Western Pacific*. St Lucia: University of Queensland Press.

Ricci, Ronit. 2011. *Islam Translated: Literature, Conversion and the Arabic Cosmopolis of South and Southeast Asia*. Chicago: Chicago University Press.

Riles, Annelise. 2000. *The Network Inside Out*. Ann Arbor: University of Michigan Press.

Robbins, Joel. 2004. *Becoming Sinners: Christianity and Moral Torment in a Papua New Guinea Society*. Berkeley: University of California Press.

Saovana-Spriggs, Ruth Vatoa. 2007. 'Gender and peace: Bougainvillean women, matriliny, and the peace process'. PhD thesis. The Australian National University.

Smith, Iain ('Fred'). 2012. *Bagarap Empires*. CD, 10th Anniversary edition, Canberra.

Smith, Karl. 2012. 'From dividual and individual selves to porous subjects'. *The Australian Journal of Anthropology* 23: 5–64.

Strathern, Marilyn. 1988. *The Gender of the Gift: Problems with Women and Problems with Society in Melanesia*. Studies in Melanesian Anthropology, No. 6. Berkeley and Los Angeles: University of California Press.

Taylor, Charles. 1985. 'The person'. In *The Category of the Person: Anthropology, Philosophy, History*, ed. Michael Carrithers, Steven Collins and Steven Lukes, pp. 257–81. Cambridge: Cambridge University Press.

——. 1989. *Sources of the Self: The Making of the Modern Identity*. Cambridge: Cambridge University Press.

——. 1991. *The Ethics of Authenticity*. Cambridge: Harvard University Press.

Taylor, John P. 2008. 'The social life of rights: "Gender antagonism", modernity and *raet* in Vanuatu'. In *Changing Pacific Masculinities*, ed. John P. Taylor. Special Issue of *The Australian Journal of Anthropology* 19(2): 165–78.

——. 2010. 'The troubled histories of a stranger god: Religious crossing, sacred power, and Anglican colonialism in Vanuatu'. *Comparative Studies in Society and History* 52(2): 418–46.

——. 2016. 'Two baskets worn at once: Christianity, sorcery and sacred power in Vanuatu'. In *Christianity, Conflict, and Renewal in Australia and the Pacific*, ed. Fiona Magowan and Carolyn Schwarz, pp. 139–60. Leiden: Brill Publishers.

Tomlinson, Matt. 2009. *In God's Image: The Metaculture of Fijian Christianity*. Berkeley: University of California Press.

Toren, Christina. 1995. 'Cosmogonic aspects of desire and compassion in Fiji'. In *Cosmos and Society in Oceania*, ed. Daniel de Coppet and André Itéanu, pp. 57–82. Oxford and Herndon: Berg.

——. 2003. 'Becoming a Christian in Fiji: An ethnographic study of ontogeny'. *Journal of the Royal Anthropological Institute* 9(4): 709–27.

Tusitala Marsh, Selina. 2014. 'Black Stone Poetry: Vanuatu's Grace Mera Molisa'. *Cordite Poetry Review*, 1 February.

Wardlow, Holly. 2006. *Wayward Women: Sexuality and Agency in a New Guinea Society*. Berkeley: University of California Press.

———. 2012. 'Treating gender violence: MSF's project in Tari, Papua New Guinea'. Paper presented at Anthropology Seminar Series, The Australian National University, 15 August.

Zorn, Jean. 2012. 'Engendering violence in the Papua New Guinea Courts: Sentencing in rape trials'. In *Engendering Violence in Papua New Guinea*, ed. Margaret Jolly, Christine Stewart and Carolyn Brewer, pp. 163–96. Canberra: ANU E Press. Online: press.anu. edu.au/publications/engendering-violence-papua-new-guinea (accessed 3 November 2014).

Contributors

Aletta Biersack's Papua New Guinea research has been among the Ipili speakers of the Porgera and Paiela valleys, Enga Province. The research topics upon which she has published include gender; ritual, mythology and cosmology; kinship, marriage and social networks; gold mining in Porgera and at Mt Kare; and the history of Ipili speakers in the twentieth and early twenty-first centuries. She is also the editor of *Clio in Oceania*, *Papuan Borderlands*, and *Ecologies for Tomorrow*, and co-editor of *Reimagining Political Ecology* and *Emergent Masculinities in the Pacific*. She is professor of cultural anthropology at the University of Oregon.

Martha Macintyre is an Honorary Principal Fellow at the University of Melbourne and until 2015 was editor of *The Australian Journal of Anthropology*. She has undertaken research in Milne Bay and New Ireland Provinces in Papua New Guinea over a 30-year period and has co-edited several volumes on gender, economic and social change in Papua New Guinea. Her most recent volumes are *Managing Modernity in the Western Pacific*, co-edited with Mary Patterson, and *Emergent Masculinities in the Pacific*, co-edited with Aletta Biersack.

Lynda Newland lectured in Social Anthropology at the University of the South Pacific in Fiji for a total of nine years. During this time, she conducted research on gender-based violence as well as researching and writing about Christianity and politics in Fiji. She then became an Honorary Fellow at the University of Western Australia, before moving to the UK to lecture at the University of St Andrews. Since writing this paper, she has conducted further research on gender-based violence as part of a larger report on gender inequity in the Pacific for the European Union.

Nicole George is an ARC DECRA Fellow and Senior Lecturer in Peace and Conflict Studies in the School of Political Science and International Studies at the University of Queensland. Her research is presently focused on gender, violence, peacebuilding, conflict transition and environmental security in the Pacific Islands. She is author of *Situating Women: Gender Politics and Circumstance in Fiji* (ANU Press) and has articles on aspects of her research appearing in *International Political Science Review, Australian Journal of International Affairs, The Contemporary Pacific, The Australian Feminist Law Journal*, and *Oceania*.

Philip Gibbs from New Zealand is a Catholic priest with the Society of the Divine Word. He first came to Papua New Guinea in 1973 and since then has worked in pastoral ministry and research in various parts of the country. He has a postgraduate Diploma in Anthropology from Sydney University, and a Doctorate in Theology from the Gregorian University, Rome. Currently he is head of the Department of Governance and Leadership at Divine Word University, Madang. His publications include 'Engendered Violence and Witch-killing in Simbu' in *Engendering Violence in Papua New Guinea*, ANU Press, 'Hardly Fair: Gender equity during the 2012 Papua New Guinea National Elections in the Wabag Open electorate', *Catalyst* 45(1): 43–60; and 'Practical Church Interventions on Sorcery and Witchcraft Violence in the PNG Highlands', in *Talking it Through: The Problems and Victims of Sorcery and Witchcraft Practices and Beliefs in Melanesia*, ANU Press.

Katherine Lepani is an anthropologist with a public health focus and many years of experience working in Papua New Guinea on gender, health and development issues. She is currently a Visiting Fellow in the College of Asia and the Pacific at The Australian National University. Her book *Islands of Love, Islands of Risk: Culture and HIV in the Trobriands* (Vanderbilt University Press, 2012) is the first full-length ethnography that examines the interface between biomedical and cultural understandings of gender, sexuality and HIV in a Melanesian context.

John Taylor is a Senior Lecturer in Anthropology at La Trobe University. He is the author of two books, *Consuming Identity: Modernity and Tourism in New Zealand*, and *The Other Side: Ways of Being and Place* *in Vanuatu*, and co-editor of *Working Together in Vanuatu: Research Histories, Collaborations and Reflections* (with Nicholas Thieberger) and the forthcoming *Touring Pacific Cultures* (with Kalissa Alexeyeff).

Natalie Araújo is a lecturer in Anthropology of Sustainability and Development at La Trobe University. She holds a Masters in Latin American Cultural Studies and PhD in Social Anthropology from the University of Manchester and Juris Doctor from the University of Melbourne. She has conducted fieldwork in Europe, Latin America, Asia, and Australia and has researched and written on a range of topics including cultural citizenship, gender-based violence, educational inclusion and cosmopolitan identities.

Jean Zorn is currently the Senior Associate Dean for Administrative and Financial Services at the City University of New York School of Law (CUNY Law School), where she was on the faculty for many years. As a faculty member at CUNY, she taught Lawyering Skills, Contracts and Real Property Law, as well as Law and Custom, Law and Anthropology, and Native American Law. She has also been a member of the law faculties at Florida International University College of Law, the University of the South Pacific (Port Vila), and the University of Papua New Guinea. Her longstanding interest in customary land law, gender and law, and in the relations of custom, customary law and state law in the Pacific has led to numerous writings on these topics. Her publications include '"Women's Rights are Human Rights": International Law and the Culture of Domestic Violence', in *To Have and To Hit: Cultural Perspectives on Wife Beating* (ed. Dorothy Ayers Counts, Judith K. Brown and Jacquelyn C. Campbell), University of Illinois Press, Urbana, 1999; 'Women, Custom and International Law in the Pacific', Occasional Paper No. 5, University of South Pacific, Port Vila, 2000; 'Women and Witchcraft: Positivist, Prelapsarian, and Post-Modern Judicial Interpretations in PNG', in *Mixed Blessings: Laws, Religions, and Women's Rights in the Asia-Pacific Region* (ed. Amanda Whiting and Carolyn Evans), Martinus Nijhoff, Leiden, 2006; and 'The Paradoxes of Sexism: Proving Rape in the Papua New Guinea Courts', in *LAWASIA*, 2010.

Margaret Jolly (FASSA) was an Australian Research Council Laureate Fellow 2010–2015. She is a Professor in the School of Culture, History and Language in the College of Asia and the Pacific at The Australian National University. She has taught at Macquarie University in

Sydney, the University of Hawai'i and the University of California, Santa Cruz, and has been a visiting scholar in Anthropology at Cambridge University and at Centre de recherche et documentation sur l'Océanie (CREDO) in Marseille. In 2009 she held a Poste Rouge with the Centre national de la recherche scientifique (CNRS) in France. She is an historical anthropologist who has written extensively on gender in the Pacific, on exploratory voyages and travel writing, missions and contemporary Christianity, maternity and sexuality, cinema and art. Her most recent book is *Divine Domesticities: Christian Paradoxes in Asia and the Pacific* (ed. with Hyaeweol Choi), ANU Press, 2014.